Mohammad Mosaddeq and the 1953 Coup in Iran

Modern Intellectual and Political History of the Middle East
Mehrzad Boroujerdi, *Series Editor*

Mosaddeq being carried away by his supporters outside the parliament building after an address on oil nationalization, September 27, 1951. Copyright © 2003 AP/Wide World Photos.

MOHAMMAD MOSADDEQ

and the 1953 Coup in Iran

• • •

Edited by Mark J. Gasiorowski
and Malcolm Byrne

 SYRACUSE UNIVERSITY PRESS

First Edition 2004
12   13   14   15   6   5   4   3

∞ The paper used in this publication meets the minimum requirements
of the American National Standard for Information Sciences—Permanence
of Paper for Printed Library Materials, ANSI Z39.48-1992.

For a listing of books published and distributed by Syracuse University Press,
visit our website at SyracuseUniversityPress.syr.edu.

ISBN: 978-0-8156-3018-0

Library of Congress Cataloging-in-Publication Data

Mohammad Mosaddeq and the 1953 coup in Iran / edited by Mark J. Gasiorowski
and Malcolm Byrne. — 1st ed.
p. cm. — (Modern intellectual and political history of the Middle East)
Includes bibliographical references and index.
ISBN 0–8156–3018–2 (cl. : alk. paper)
1. Iran—Politics and government, 1941–1979. 2. Mosaddeq, Mohammad, 1880–1967
I. Gasiorowski, Mark J., 1954– II. Byrne, Malcolm. III. Series.
DS316.6.M64 2004
955.05'3—dc22
2004001922

Manufactured in the United States of America

◆　◆　◆

We dedicate this book to all Iranians
who have struggled to make their country
independent and democratic.

Contents

Illustrations

Tables

Contributors

Fakhreddin Azimi is a professor of history at the University of Connecticut. He has written widely in both English and Persian. His publications in English include *The Quest for Democracy in Iran: A Century of Struggle Against Authoritarian Rule*—winner of the Mossadegh Prize, Mossadegh Foundation and the Saidi-Sirjani Award, International Society for Iranian Studies—and *Iran: The Crisis of Democracy, 1941–53*.

Maziar Behrooz is an assistant professor in the Department of History at San Francisco State University. He is the author of *Rebels with a Cause: The Failure of the Left in Iran* (1999) and several articles on modern Iranian history.

Malcolm Byrne is deputy director and research director of the George Washington University-based National Security Archive, where he directs the U.S.-Iran Relations Project. He is the author of a forthcoming study of the Iran-Contra affair, as well as coeditor of *The Iran-Contra Scandal: The Declassified History* (1993) and *The Chronology: The Documented Day-by-Day Account of the Secret Military Assistance to Iran and the Contras* (1987) as well as other publications.

Mark J. Gasiorowski is a professor in the Department of Political Science at Louisiana State University. He has also been a visiting professor at the Faculty of Law and Political Science of the University of Tehran and a visiting fellow at St. Antony's College, Oxford University. He is the author of *U.S. Foreign Policy and the Shah* (1991), coeditor (with Nikki Keddie) of *Neither East Nor West: Iran, the Soviet Union, and the United States* (1990), and the author of many articles on Iranian politics and democracy in the Third World.

Mary Ann Heiss is an associate professor in the Department of History at Kent State University. She is the author of *Empire and Nationhood: The United States, Great Britain, and Iranian Oil, 1950–1954* (1996) and coeditor of *NATO in the Post-Cold War Era: Does It Have a Future?* (1995) and *Empire and Revolution: The United States and the Third World since 1945* (2001).

Homa Katouzian is Iran Heritage Research Fellow, St. Antony's College, Oxford University; a member of the Faculty of Oriental Studies, Oxford University; and an honorary research fellow in the Department of Politics at the University of Exeter. He is the author of *Musaddiq and the Struggle for Power in Iran* (1990) and *The Political Economy of Modern Iran* (1981), editor of *Musaddiq's Memoirs* (1988), and author of many other books and articles on Iranian politics, economics, and culture.

Wm. Roger Louis is the Kent Professor of English History and Culture and Distinguished Teaching Professor in the Department of History at the University of Texas. An Honorary Fellow of St. Antony's College, Oxford University, he is past president of the American Historical Association. He is editor in chief of the Oxford History of the British Empire and chairman of the Historical Advisory Committee of the U.S. Department of State. His books include *Imperialism at Bay* (1976) and *The British Empire in the Middle East* (1984). He is coeditor (with James Bill) of *Musaddiq, Iranian Nationalism, and Oil* (1988).

Introduction

Malcolm Byrne

In a major address on U.S.-Iran relations in March 2000, timed to coincide with the traditional Persian New Year (1378/1379), U.S. secretary of state Madeleine Albright made the following statement: "In 1953, the United States played a significant role in orchestrating the overthrow of Iran's popular prime minister, Mohammad Mosaddeq. . . . The Eisenhower administration believed its actions were justified for strategic reasons, but the coup was clearly a setback for Iran's political development. And it is easy to see now why many Iranians continue to resent this intervention by America in their internal affairs."[1]

Albright's remarks were the first public acknowledgment by a senior American official of Washington's part in the coup. Yet, Iran's reaction was mostly negative. The secretary of the influential Expediency Council called the speech "a new chapter" in U.S.-Iran relations. But Ayatollah Ali Khamenei, the country's supreme leader, ripped the admission on 1953 as "deceitful" and complained that it "did not even include an apology."[2] Both sides' comments reflected the perpetuation of deep sensitivities toward the event almost half a century later.

In fact, the "28 Mordad 1332" coup, as it is known by its Persian date, was a watershed for all of the countries concerned. The joint U.S.-British operation marked the denouement of what began as a popular drive to assert Iran's sovereign control over its own resources by nationalizing the Anglo-Iranian Oil Company (AIOC), Britain's largest overseas concern, which had dominated Iran's petroleum industry for years. Mohammad Mosaddeq, a charismatic politician from a wealthy landowning family, had long championed national independence and constitutional rule. For his opposition to the self-styled Pahlavi dynasty, whose regime, established in 1925, he considered corrupt and unconstitutional, he spent several years in political exile, including brief periods in jail. After the 1941 ouster of Reza Shah Pahlavi, ironically at the hands of the Soviet Union and Great Britain, he was freed from prison and staged a speedy political comeback. In late April 1951, Iran's new monarch, Shah Mohammad Reza Pahlavi (Reza Shah's son), acquiesced to public pressure and appointed Mosaddeq prime minister at the head of a coalition of reform-oriented forces called the National Front. Three days later, the shah signed into law Iran's nationalization of the AIOC.

But this was just the beginning of the struggle. The AIOC immediately staged an economic boycott, with backing from the other major international oil companies, while the British government started an aggressive, semicovert campaign to destabilize the Mosaddeq regime. With the expansion of the cold war, the United States also stepped into the dispute. Although ostensibly neutral, the Truman administration quietly abided by the boycott. As U.S. worries over Iran's political and economic deterioration increased, patience with Mosaddeq wore thin. When President Dwight D. Eisenhower took office in January 1953, the United States launched a more aggressive assault against world communism, and within two months the new administration had approved the concept of a joint U.S.-British operation to remove Mosaddeq from office. The coup, code-named TPAJAX, finally got underway in mid-August 1953. After a disastrous beginning, followed by several days of mass confusion, the coup plotters managed to turn their fortunes around. By noon on August 19 pro-shah crowds had control of the streets, and retired army major general Fazlollah Zahedi, handpicked to replace Mosaddeq by the coup plotters, had declared himself the new prime minister.

The effects of the coup resonated on many levels. Domestically, it brought to an end a vibrant chapter in the history of Iran's nationalist and democratic movements. For all of the troubles that arose during his premiership, Mosaddeq came to symbolize for many the principle of opposition to Great Power intrusions on Iranian independence. Despite his uncompromising drive to expand his powers during his final months in office, he was also admired by certain sectors for continuing the tradition of the Constitutional Revolution and for advocating the political rights of Iranian citizens against the authority of the shah. His removal signaled the beginning of the end of the country's brief experience with democracy. In the years following the coup, the shah reasserted his position with respect to the Majlis and the government and cracked down on dissidents, and over the course of the next decade he steadily expanded his authority to the point of establishing a virtual dictatorship. One of the consequences of the shah's accretion of power was the elimination of any opportunity for the development of even a moderate political opposition inside Iran. With no outlet for dissent, animosities grew, and radicalism built to the point of explosion during the 1978 revolution.

Aside from influencing the direction of Iran's internal politics, the coup and its aftermath affected U.S. policies and standing in Iran as well. The United States replaced Britain as the predominant outside power shaping events inside Iran. But this was a two-edged sword. Because of its role in the coup, many Iranians came to identify Washington as the shah's all-powerful patron, and it was assumed that Washington implicitly supported his repressive actions, regardless of U.S. attempts in subsequent years to curb the regime's excesses. This virtually guaranteed that burgeoning hostility toward the shah would also be directed against the United States when the revolutionary Islamic regime came to power in 1979.

Similarly, Washington's role in the coup tarnished America's reputation with other moderate forces in the Middle East. For example, Egyptian president Gamal Abdel Nasser, who once had been willing to discuss common security goals with John Foster Dulles, undoubtedly drew the clear lesson from Iran's experience that he could not act passively over the Suez issue in the face of Anglo–U.S. imperialism. The hopes of the Truman administration and even President Eisenhower that the United States would be seen as the defender of regional aspirations for independence began to seem especially hollow after August 1953. Such hopes were genuinely held, but ultimately they paled next to perceived threats to U.S. security. American officials at first rejoiced over the coup's success—albeit behind closed doors—seeing it as a vindication of the concept of covert intervention. With a remarkably modest investment, the United States had kept a vital cold war asset from falling into the communist camp. Surely the same tactic would work elsewhere. Without full regard for Iran's unique circumstances in 1953, U.S. planners treated TPAJAX as a model for future clandestine operations, including operations in Guatemala in 1954, in Syria in 1958, and at the Bay of Pigs in 1961. The coup's legacy thus reached far beyond the borders of Iran and lasted as long as—even longer than—the cold war itself.

This book presents a series of essays on the Mosaddeq regime and the coup by leading experts who prepared them originally for an extraordinary conference that took place in Tehran in June 2000. Hosted by the Institute of Political and International Studies, a research arm of the Iranian Foreign Ministry, the conference brought together scholars from Iran, the United States, and the former Soviet Union (participation by the visiting foreign scholars was supported by the George Washington University-based National Security Archive) to discuss the controversial oil nationalization period of 1951–53, including the coup d'état. Because of the historical sensitivity of the Mosaddeq era in Iran, the conference took on special significance as the first-ever multinational airing of the subject in an Iranian public setting. As one indication of its favorable reception, government-run television broadcast major portions of the conference repeatedly to nationwide audiences throughout the remainder of the year.

The contributors later had the opportunity to refine and present their most recent findings at another conference in June 2002 hosted by the Middle East Centre at St. Antony's College, Oxford, and cosponsored by the National Security Archive. That event, "Mohammad Mosaddeq and the 1953 Coup in Iran," also featured a roundtable discussion with former Central Intelligence Agency (CIA) official John Waller, who coordinated U.S. participation in the coup from Washington; Sir Sam Falle of the British Foreign Office, who played a part in elaborating British plans to overthrow Mosaddeq; and Sir Denis Wright, also of the Foreign Office, who served as counsellor in Iran shortly after the coup.

Although all of the authors have written previously about their topics,[3] this volume contains a wealth of new information that adds meaningfully to our understanding of the coup and its complex sociopolitical setting. The most important new source is a recently published CIA history of TPAJAX, written in March 1954 by Donald N. Wilber, one of the operation's chief architects.[4] The *New York Times* published the still-classified 200-page document, *Overthrow of Premier Mosaddeq of Iran: November 1952–August 1953,* in two installments on its Web site in 2000.[5] That publication helped break a logjam on secrets that the CIA, along with British intelligence, have maintained for many years. In 1989, the agency refused to allow key documents describing U.S. participation in the overthrow to appear in the State Department's *Foreign Relations of the United States: Diplomatic Papers* series, billed as "the official record of the foreign policy of the United States."[6] A decade later, nothing had changed. The CIA rebuffed a 1999 National Security Archive lawsuit seeking the Wilber document and another internal agency history, declassifying only a single sentence, on the grounds that further "disclosure could reasonably be expected to damage the national security" or "lead to unauthorized disclosure of intelligence sources and methods."[7] The U.S. and British intelligence communities, by steadfastly refusing to declassify important, but no longer sensitive, historical information on the coup have consequently made it much more difficult to come to closure historically—and arguably politically—on the overthrow. Fortunately for history, and with no discernible harm to America's security, perhaps the most significant missing piece of the puzzle has now become available, and each chapter in this volume makes rich use of its many new details.

But it should also be noted that the authors go significantly beyond the CIA history to include other newly uncovered American and British records, Iranian sources, and even Soviet-era archival materials from Russian and Azerbaijani archives. In addition, the contributors conducted interviews with former U.S. and British intelligence officials and Iranians who participated in the events studied here. Drawing on these fresh sources, the book features chapters that discuss the historical context of the Mosaddeq regime, focus on the political and social background to the coup, and evaluate the numerous underlying factors as well as domestic and foreign actors that contributed to Mosaddeq's downfall.

Homa Katouzian opens the volume by providing historical context for the Mosaddeq period. He places the 1953 coup d'état within "a long cycle of arbitrary rule–chaos–arbitrary rule in Iranian history," where dictatorships have been overturned by revolts that "invariably" produce periods of turmoil until a new absolute ruler steps in. By modern times, "chaos" had become more or less synonymous with the search for democracy—of which the Mosaddeq-led oil nationalization and the domestic reform movement were the latest chapter. Popular support for the coup and restoration of the shah, where it existed, was therefore partly the predictable expression of a need for stability after the social and political unraveling that characterized Mosaddeq's second government (formed after the July 1952 uprising [30 Tir 1331]). However, a critical point, Katouzian writes, is that much of the chaos of that period was the direct result of the "politics of elimination"—attempts not only by the British and Americans but also by a growing number of domestic opponents to topple the Mosaddeq government. As for the domestic legacy of the coup, many Iranians clung to the idea, however simplistic, that the United States bore responsibility for Iran's return to dictatorship, a belief that helps to explain the heavily anti-American character of the revolution in 1978.

Surveying Iran's political environment in the early 1950s, Fakhreddin Azimi provides an intricate account of the domestic forces on either side of the Mosaddeq divide. Although he points out the "inseparability of domestic and foreign anti-Mosaddeq opposition," he emphasizes the key role of the Iranians who increasingly lined up against the prime minister. His analysis begins with a nuanced look at the social bases of support and opposition to Mosaddeq. After analyzing each of the main opposition groups—the royalists, Anglophiles and "defectors," and Tudeh—and their leading representatives, he traces their actions and interactions through the crises of July 1952 and February 1953 to the "final showdown." He ends with a consideration of whether Mosaddeq and the National Front could have put up a more effective fight or whether they faced too many constraints, structural or personal, against success.

Maziar Behrooz takes on one of the most significant domestic actors, the Tudeh Party. Noting that the CIA history emphasizes the Tudeh, and by extension Soviet, threat as a justification for the coup, Behrooz uses internal party sources and interviews to present a more realistic picture of the organization, its characteristics, and its role during the coup period. Even though U.S. intelligence did not foresee an imminent Tudeh takeover in Iran, there was virtually unanimous agreement within U.S. official circles that the communists were growing in strength, cohesion, and political momentum. But Behrooz disputes those perceptions, showing that a number of legal and other obstacles, including serious political differences and personal rivalries, had split the leadership and fundamentally weakened the organization's effectiveness. Furthermore, according to the party's own theoretical precepts, Iran was not yet ripe for a communist-led takeover. Therefore, in hindsight, the Tudeh seems to have had neither the intention nor the capability of seizing power in the near term, as its inept handling of the coup confirms.

The next several chapters deal with the international aspects of the coup. First, Wm. Roger Louis thoroughly explores Britain's unceasing campaign to destabilize and depose Mosaddeq, providing new details about the often forgotten but pivotal British role throughout the crisis. London's larger strategic concern over Iran was that Mosaddeq's virulent anti-British "obsession" would cause him to lean too far in the direction of the communists, who would eventually overwhelm him and take control of the country. Most British officials had reacted immediately and negatively to Mosaddeq's election as premier; only a few were receptive to his impulses for independent control over Iran's national resources. There were also splits, under both Labour and Conservative governments, over whether to favor AIOC interests over broader foreign policy concerns. But the various differences melted away in the wake of the July 21, 1952/30 Tir 1331 riots and other events, which convinced even Mosaddeq's sympathizers that he had become irrational and had to be removed. It took a bit longer, but the Americans finally came to the same conclusion, a process Louis traces in some detail and attributes mainly to shared conceptions of the larger stakes of the cold war.

Mary Ann Heiss looks at an often neglected factor behind Mosaddeq's downfall: the British-led oil boycott beginning in 1951. She focuses on the roles of the British and U.S. governments and the major international oil companies in promoting the boycott. At first, the U.S. petroleum giants criticized the AIOC for its refusal to be more accommodating toward the Iranians; they believed that good relations with host governments were vital to the success of their operations. But once Iran nationalized the AIOC, the U.S. majors did an abrupt about-face and unanimously sided with the British out of fear for their own contractual arrangements with foreign governments. Top U.S. officials, Heiss writes, also changed their views, making it official State Department policy to back the U.S. companies' decision to join the boycott. Thus, Heiss argues, the Truman administration, despite claims to be a neutral broker in the dispute, actually sided with Britain early on. The powerful combination of governments and petroleum interests never managed to bring Iran's economy to its knees, but it did further the boycott's larger purpose of unseating Mohammad Mosaddeq.

Malcolm Byrne's chapter presents the political and geostrategic factors that underlay U.S. policy toward Iran during the early post–World War II period. A central question he addresses is how to explain the evolution from Truman's relatively even-handed approach to Eisenhower's advocacy of direct, covert intervention. A variety of factors came into play, but the fundamental explanation lies in the unfolding cold war rivalry between the United States and the Soviet Union. A string of events, primarily in the region, helped convince the White House that the Kremlin posed a fundamental threat to expanded postwar U.S. interests. In fact, Truman and Eisenhower's philosophies were much closer than was commonly understood at the time. Eisenhower's 1952 election victory raised expectations for a global rollback of communism, but he did not come into office convinced that Mosaddeq had to be overthrown. Only after events persuaded him that time had run out on the previous administration's approach of sticking by Mosaddeq and pressing for a negotiated settlement did he, in July, finally authorize the covert plan to proceed.

Mark Gasiorowski follows with the most authoritative account available of the coup from the U.S. perspective. In November 1952, the British proposed a joint covert operation to unseat Mosaddeq. Truman administration officials, then in their final months in office, agreed that Iran's increasing instability presented a "serious risk" to U.S. national security, but it was not until the advent of the Eisenhower administration in January 1953 that official American cooperation was forthcoming. Weaving in a wealth of new detail from the CIA history of the coup and updated interviews with former CIA operatives,

Gasiorowski gives a thorough description of every stage of the planning and execution of the operation, which built on existing destabilization activities by both U.S. and British intelligence and depended heavily on Iranian agents and collaborators already in place. Ultimately, the initial plan failed, for reasons Gasiorowski explains. But with a combination of resourcefulness and determination by the American and Iranian operatives, mistakes by the Mosaddeq forces, and pure luck, the anti–Mosaddeqists managed to turn disaster into improbable victory.

Finally, in Mark Gasiorowski's conclusion to the volume, he pulls together the main themes raised in each chapter and assesses the relative impact of the forces responsible for Mosaddeq's ouster. Clearly, the foreign powers—through the CIA and British intelligence—played a direct role, first by helping to destabilize Mosaddeq, then by coming up with a plan, money, and networks of agents, and finally by a simple unwillingness to give up. But a wide array of Iranians also made crucial contributions, either by steadily undermining the prime minister's position or by bringing about the overthrow itself. General Zahedi and his supporters, the shah, the growing crowd of "defectors" and other opponents to Mosaddeq, the Tudeh Party, and even the National Front loyalists and Mosaddeq himself, through their mistakes, were essential to the coup's success. Of particular note was the participation of Ali Jalali and Faruq Kayvani, the CIA's main agents in the country, and Britain's principal agents, the Rashidian brothers, as well as their subagents. In turn the actions of all of these groups played out against a background of broader domestic and international conditions that helped determine the general course of events in Iran.

This volume appears under the auspices of the Iran-United States Relations Project at the National Security Archive. Begun in early 1998 following the appeal by Iranian president Mohammad Khatemi for a "dialogue of civilizations" between Iran and the West, the National Security Archive sought out opportunities in Iran to work with scholars who had similar interests in exploring the controversial history of Iran-U.S. ties from a nonpolitical, multinational, scholarly perspective. Thanks to the cooperation of several institutions and individuals in Iran and the generous assistance of numerous American scholars, the project has enabled Americans, Russians, Britons, Azeris, and others to participate in two international conferences and a range of other scholarly activities, of which this volume is a part. The National Security Archive and the editors acknowledge with gratitude the following Iranian organizations: the Institute for Political and International Studies (IPIS) of the Iranian Foreign Ministry, the Centre for Documents and Diplomatic History, and the Institute of Iranian Contemporary Historical Studies. Special thanks go to Seyyed Ali Moujani, director of the Centre for Documents and Diplomatic History, Kazem Sajjadpour, director general of IPIS, Sadeq Kharrazi, then deputy foreign minister for research and education, and many other friends and colleagues in Iran.

Grateful thanks from the National Security Archive also go to all of the contributors to this volume. We are indebted, as always, to fellow pathbreakers Thomas S. Blanton, James G. Hershberg, Leila J. Afzal, and Kian Byrne, as well as to Mary Clark and Elena Gasiorowski. At the National Security Archive, we are obliged to Catherine Nielsen, Gregory F. Domber, Eddie Meadows, and Barbara Elias for their efforts.

We are also extremely appreciative of the generous cooperation and support we received from Eugene Rogan, director, and Elizabeth Anderson, secretary, of the Middle East Centre at St. Antony's College, Oxford University. We also thank Stephen Langlie and Farhad Diba for allowing the use of their photographs, and to Homa Katouzian and Hedayat Matin-Daftari for helping with identification of certain photos.

We would like to make clear that the views expressed in each of the chapters are solely those of the authors.

The National Security Archive and the editors are also grateful for the generous patronage of the Winston Foundation for World Peace, the Open Society Institute (New York), the Open Society Archives at Central European University, the Ford Foundation, and the W. Alton Jones Foundation. Special appreciation for their support is due to Gary Sick (for his early encouragement of the National Security Archive while at the Ford Foundation, and more recently at Columbia University), John Tirman, Wade Greene, Anthony Richter, István Rév, Mahnaz Ispahani, and George Perkovich. The U.S. Institute of Peace in Washington kindly supported a portion of Mark Gasiorowski's time on the project.

Finally, we are grateful to Syracuse University Press, particularly to Mary Selden Evans and Mehrzad Boroujerdi (as well as to the anonymous outside reviewer), for their interest and cooperation in this volume.

Washington, D.C.   Malcolm Byrne

Mohammad Mosaddeq and the 1953 Coup in Iran

1

Mosaddeq's Government in Iranian History

Arbitrary Rule, Democracy, and the 1953 Coup

Homa Katouzian

The campaign for the nationalization of Iranian oil, and the resulting Popular Movement (Nehzat-e Melli), was a political experience, at once national and international, with momentous consequences for the country's political development. It still affects and influences political ideas, attitudes, and events in Iran. At the time of writing, the legacy of Mosaddeq and the Popular Movement is probably most symbolic for the many Iranians of both religious and secular persuasions who favor political development toward a democratic society. In its broader sense the Popular Movement began before 1951. It was not just about improving Iran's oil revenues, and it did not vanish after the 1953 coup, as witnessed by the current state of politics in Iran. The establishment of parliamentary democracy is at present so popular that conflicting political parties and movements claim to believe in it, even though they differ on its meaning and implications and the pace at which it may be pursued. This chapter explains the background of the Popular Movement, describes its proponents and opponents and its achievements and mistakes, and assesses the consequences of its failure in 1953 for later developments in Iranian politics, state, and society.

The Historical Background

The 1953 coup marks the first important watershed in postwar Iranian history. The twelve years separating the abdication of Reza Shah and the overthrow of

Mosaddeq was a period of interregnum or dual sovereignty.[1] The principal objective of oil nationalization as declared by Mosaddeq and his colleagues was to attain complete oil independence in order to establish a lasting democratic government in Iran. This was frustrated by the coup d'état of 1953, which was carried out by a combination of domestic and foreign forces. But the event and the subsequent developments were consistent with the long cycle of arbitrary rule–chaos–arbitrary rule in Iranian history.

It is characteristic of Iranian history that the fall—often even the mere death—of an absolute and arbitrary ruler has resulted in rebellion and chaos, and persisting chaos has ended up in the return of absolute and arbitrary government (*estebdad*). This pattern was also observed in the twentieth century, although in a modern form. Traditional Iranian revolts involved the active or passive support of all the social classes to bring down an "unjust" arbitrary ruler and replace him with a just one. Invariably, the result was chaos, until one of the contestants for power eliminated the rest and restored absolute and arbitrary government, much to the relief of the common people, who by then were desperately longing for basic peace and security. This explains the long cycles of arbitrary rule–chaos–arbitrary rule in Iranian history, chaos and arbitrary rule being two sides of the same coin, each one justifying the other. Until very recent times what most educated Iranians—both conservative and radical—understood by "dictatorship" was arbitrary rule, and by "democracy" the traditional Iranian chaos.

Fifty years before oil nationalization, the Constitutional Revolution was fought, for the first time in Iranian history, not just to overthrow an unjust arbitrary ruler but ultimately to replace the ancient arbitrary rule by the rule of law. And by establishing a constitution along democratic lines, it succeeded in achieving considerably more. Yet the country's age-old habit of reverting to chaos after the collapse of an arbitrary state was still very strong, and the growing interference of imperial powers during the First World War helped the process. But it must be emphasized that the postconstitutional chaos did not just occur in the provinces, and was not just due to nomadic rebellion and brigandry, as is normally believed. It also occurred right at the center, in the center of politics, in Parliament, among journalists, and within the ranks of political grandees and magnates. Indeed, it is unlikely that regional chaos would have continued without the persistence of destructive conflict in the center of politics itself. For it is characteristic of the country's history that whoever has the center also has the periphery. The growing chaos and threat of disintegration ended up in the coup d'état of 1921.[2]

Reza Khan/Reza Shah's rule in the 1920s was at first welcomed as an antidote to chaos. It was increasingly *dictatorial* but not yet *arbitrary*. That is when he accomplished most of his achievements and had a significant, though declining, amount of support among the politically aware public. But in the 1930s his rule became increasingly harsh and arbitrary. Even those who worked for him began to resent and fear him, and he was persuaded to abdicate in 1941 when the Allies came to Iran. Yet, his abdication would not have been necessary—perhaps not even possible—if the public had been sympathetic to him rather than angry, especially as after the cease-fire he was prepared to cooperate with the Allies.[3]

Then began another period of chaos—the period 1941–51—corresponding to the postrevolutionary period of 1909–21, although the more recent chaos was not as destructive as that of the earlier period, largely because of the physical presence, later influence, of the Great Powers. And just like the earlier chaos, it was at work not only in the provinces but also at the center and in the very center of politics, among the political parties, the press, the notables, the Majles, the very frequently changing cabinets (it would be misleading to call them governments), and the royal court.[4]

Between 1941 and 1951, when Mosaddeq became prime minister, cabinets generally did not last more than a few months, and there were revolts in the provinces and destructive conflict within the Majles itself. Government lacked authority to deal with most ordinary affairs, unable to reach an agreement even on an annual budget. Revolts in Azerbaijan and Kurdistan and rebellions perpetrated by the southern tribes during that time are well-known examples of the politics of chaos in the provinces.[5] To give but two examples of chaos in the center, in 1942 bread riots in the capital were organized, with the shah's involvement, with the express purpose of bringing down Ahmad Qavam's government. In 1946, when Qavam was prime minister once again, the antiroyalist and sensationalist weekly *Mard-e Emruz* offered—on its front page—a large bounty to anyone who would assassinate Qavam.[6]

Naturally, both the state and society had undergone certain changes after the Constitutional Revolution. For example, the Majles was retained (although purely in form) even under Reza Shah; modern education was expanded, as were urbanization and the modern middle class; political parties of sorts came into being; and so on. But the traditional state-society conflicts and strong tendencies toward arbitrary rule and chaos were still manifest, sometimes in new forms.

Mosaddeq and the Nationalization of Oil

Mosaddeq was born in 1882 into a rich and upper-class family. He studied law and public finance in Neuchâtel and Paris, obtaining his doctorate in law from the University of Neuchâtel in 1914. He had campaigned in the Constitutional Revolution before that, and later became a professor of law in the Tehran School of Law and Political Science (1915). He served as deputy minister of finance (1917), governor of the province of Fars (1920), minister of finance (1921), governor of the province of Azerbaijan (1922), foreign minister (1923), and Majles deputy (1924–28). He lived in self-imposed banishment from 1928 to 1940, was imprisoned, for unexplained reasons, between 1940 and 1941, and again served as a Majles deputy from 1943 to 1945. He joined the campaign against the Gass-Golsha'iyan or Supplemental Oil Agreement in 1949.

Mosaddeq had good relations with Reza Khan in the early 1920s. But he opposed Reza Khan's successful bid to become shah in 1925, saying that he would still support him as a strong constitutional prime minister but would not agree to his being both shah and ruler, describing such a situation as "sheer reaction, sheer arbitrary government." Thus Mosaddeq had to withdraw from politics in 1928 and was arrested and banished to a prison-citadel in Khorasan and later, in 1940–41, to his own estate, until some time after the Allied invasion of Iran and the consequent abdication of Reza Shah. As noted, he was elected Tehran's first deputy in 1943 but withdrew from politics in anger in 1947, when, in the Fifteenth Majles elections, his campaigns against ballot rigging failed. Throughout his life he suffered from a chronic nervous disease that, in moments of high tension, led to his getting a lump in his throat and/or fainting.[7]

Two years later, he was persuaded by the very few opposition deputies of that Majles to return to politics and lead the campaign against the Gass-Golsha'iyan or Supplemental Oil Agreement. The first step was a campaign against ballot rigging in the Sixteenth Majles elections, resulting in the return of eight deputies from the National (Popular) Front. Enjoying immense popular support, Mosaddeq became chairman of the Majles's ad hoc Oil Committee, managed to carry a resolution through the House against the Supplemental Agreement, and proposed the nationalization of Iranian oil, which was voted by the Majles and Senate in March 1951, in the wake of the assassination of Gen. Ali Razmara, the prime minister. Two months later he was voted prime minister by the Parliament immediately after it had passed his private members' bill for the implementation of oil nationalization, that is, the Law of Repossession (*khal'-e yad*).

The Movement's Objectives and Its Opposition

Mosaddeq and the Popular Movement's declared aim was to establish and extend constitutional and democratic government. Under Mosaddeq's govern-

ment, political parties and groups were free; this included the Tudeh Party, although not in name, because it had been banned by an act of the Majles in
1949. The press was so free that, in part, it may be described as licentious. The
government did not rig elections, although various power centers did use
power and influence to have their own candidates elected. Government ministers, although not necessarily models of efficiency, were nevertheless honest as
well as responsible to the Majles and public. The courts were entirely independent, and all the military and other special courts were abolished. Yet, the
politics of chaos and elimination did not cease; the other main political forces
did not believe in democracy and were not prepared to observe its rules of the
game. In fact the chaos became more intense, because both the internal and external stakes were considerably higher.

There was a fierce struggle by the Left as well as the Right, each wanting to
bring down Mosaddeq's government and eliminate the other as a political
force. Eventually, the Right succeeded in achieving this goal with the crucial—
in fact, indispensable—aid of America and Britain. That help was needed, in
part, because Mosaddeq's government was stronger and longer-lived than all
the 1940s cabinets. He carried much greater authority because he had public
support and because the country was involved in a grave international conflict.
He was prime minister for almost two and a half years and was overthrown by
unlawful means, whereas the average life of governments between 1941 and
1951 was about six months, and none of those governments was brought down
by a coup. The only other relatively strong and enduring government had been
that of Ahmad Qavam in 1945–47, and it was toppled by the shah through his
influence among the Fifteenth Majles deputies. The experiment of 1951–53
might have led either to a stable democracy or to a dictatorship. For reasons explained below, dictatorship was more likely and ultimately won the day.

While the shah and conservatives saw themselves as natural clients or allies
of Britain and (later) America, and the Tudeh of the Soviet Union, the attain-
ment of sovereign control and real independence were powerful as well as popular objectives. But Mosaddeq and his colleagues emphasized that sovereign
control and independence were necessary steps toward the establishment of a
genuine democratic regime. The strongest motive behind oil nationalization
was thus political rather than economic, although the priority given to political
development did not mean that the economic importance of the oil industry
was underrated.

Mosaddeq and other Popular Movement leaders argued that so long as a
large and powerful foreign company owned the country's most important
modern industry, effectively controlled one of its provinces, and interfered in

its politics to defend and promote its own interest, it would not be possible to establish either sovereign or democratic government. Therefore they agreed to compensate the Anglo-Iranian Oil Company on similar terms to the nationalization of private industries in Europe, for example, the British coal industry, which had recently been nationalized. But they would not consider settlements involving a new concession, in an open or disguised form, which, they thought, would have meant the return of the company in a different form, even if that would bring significantly higher revenues. The company and the British government, on the other hand, were intent on obtaining another concession.

Britain was unhappy with a Mosaddeq government from the start. As early as May 1951, when Mosaddeq became prime minister, Britain was actively canvassing the shah and Mosaddeq's conservative opponents to bring him down by a vote of no confidence in the Majles. British documents show that the shah and other Mosaddeq opponents were very receptive to British suggestions, putting forward proposals for weakening his government. They kept emphasizing to British diplomats in Tehran to try and make sure that a settlement with Mosaddeq would not be reached, since a settlement would contribute to the persistence and endurance of his government. They even said that oil exports should be suspended forthwith so that there would be no prospect of revenues. Mosaddeq must not be made to look as if he had won, they insisted.[8]

The prime candidate to replace Mosaddeq was Sayyed Zia, a veteran Anglophile politician, although he was by no means a paid agent of British imperialism as was almost universally believed. The alternative was Ahmad Qavam, a strong politician, whom neither British diplomats nor the shah liked, but who was seen as a fall-back option.[9] At first replacing Mosaddeq looked like an easy task because the shah and the conservatives held a large majority in the Sixteenth Majles. But it proved almost impossible, mainly because of Mosaddeq's great popularity—especially as the issue at stake had a strong anti-imperialist tone, shaking the resolve of many conservative Majles deputies to vote against Mosaddeq. Besides, the absence of organized parliamentary parties made the control of factions extremely difficult.

Early Developments of the Oil Dispute

Busy though British diplomats in Tehran were in trying to bring down Mosaddeq's government by a Majles vote of no confidence, Britain nevertheless sent Richard Stokes, Lord Privy Seal in Clement Attlee's Labour government, to negotiate a settlement. At the same time, President Truman sent Averell Harriman as his goodwill ambassador to help smooth the Stokes–Mosaddeq negotiations. Stokes's proposals to Mosaddeq on behalf of the company and the British government in the summer of 1951 might have resulted in something similar to but considerably better than the Consortium Agreement of 1954, which was signed shortly after the coup. But by then oil had been nationalized, amid great excitement, and the thought of giving another concession to the company was exceedingly difficult to entertain and unlikely to succeed. There followed Iran's repossession of the oil operations in September 1951, leading to the boycott of Iranian oil by all the main international oil companies, backed up by the Royal Navy in the Persian Gulf and beyond. Thus, Iran's principal source of public revenue and foreign exchange was cut off, while it had to pay the labor and maintenance costs of a virtually idle oil industry.[10]

Britain had obtained a World Court injunction to stop Iran from repossessing the oil industry. This was ignored by Iran on the argument that, since the 1933 agreement had been signed between Iran and a private company (APOC, later AIOC), only Iranian courts had jurisdiction in the matter, a position the World Court eventually upheld in July 1952. Britain then took the matter to the UN Security Council but did not gain its support. While Mosaddeq was in the United States in October at the head of the Iranian delegation to the Security Council, George McGhee, the U.S. assistant secretary of state, came up with a brilliant formula to resolve the dispute. Dean Acheson, the secretary of state, supported McGhee's proposed solution. And in their meetings with Mosaddeq (in New York and Washington), the two American politicians persuaded him to accept it. But when Acheson personally put the proposal to Anthony Eden, the British foreign secretary, Eden dismissed it out of hand.

At the same time, the World Bank offered to mediate by restoring the production and export of Iranian oil for two years. This would have considerably reduced the scale of confrontation between Britain and Iran and might well have led to a permanent settlement of the dispute. Mosaddeq was receptive at first, but some of his advisers insisted that the letter of agreement should include a statement that the bank was acting on behalf of the Iranian government, so as to refute the charge by their opponents that the government was selling out to Western powers. On the other hand, Britain would obviously not have agreed to the mediation of the bank if it were acting as the agent of Iran.

This was the best available solution at the time to restore Iran's foreign exchange earnings and provide a suitable atmosphere for looking for a permanent settlement. The Tudeh Party was already declaring the World Bank mission as clear evidence supporting their view that Mosaddeq was an "agent of American imperialism" and that his mission was to deliver Iran's oil industry to the United States. Even Mosaddeq's right-wing opponents were spreading rumors that the whole nationalization policy had been set in motion by the United States in order to get a share of Iran's oil. On the other hand, the bank's proposal was the best guarantee for the survival of Mosaddeq's government, especially as at that time—winter of 1951—it was at the peak of its unity and strength and carried a great deal of authority both inside and outside the country. Furthermore, accepting the solution would have maintained American goodwill.

The bank's attempt having failed, the government embarked upon a temporary policy of "non-oil economics," which, in the circumstances, it managed well by adopting realistic, albeit unpopular, measures. Clearly, non-oil economics could not, and was not expected to, promote social welfare and economic development. On the contrary, it was regarded as a relatively short-term measure to enable the country to resist the pressure to enter into an unacceptable deal.[11]

Nevertheless, right until the coup of August 1953, Mosaddeq was keen to reach an agreement via direct negotiations. But Britain's Conservative government, which had been elected in October 1951, was opposed to direct negotiations. In fact, it preferred not to reach a settlement with Mosaddeq and continued to look for a suitable successor to him. Thus the embassy continued its campaign even in summer 1951, when Stokes's mission was busy negotiating with Mosaddeq for a settlement.[12] Later, the British government, through the embassy, decided to try and replace Mosaddeq with Ahmad Qavam, having reached the conclusion that Sayyed Zia was too unpopular for the task. On the other hand, the fact that Britain preferred not to settle the oil dispute with Mosaddeq does not mean that it would or could have refused to settle under any and all conditions. More specifically, if a solution had been found in 1952 that looked fair and acceptable in the U.S. government's eyes, Britain would have had to accept it; after the coup, it settled for only 40 percent of Iran's oil, instead of the AIOC's total concession. And such a solution would have been possible earlier if the Iranians had been prepared to settle for less than what they regarded as absolutely fair. Many of the British officials then involved in the matter later came to the view that the British government had made a mistake in not controlling the AIOC and its hawkish attitude toward Mosaddeq and the oil dispute, which had been determined by the haughty AIOC chairman, Sir William Fraser.[13] Meanwhile, the Sixteenth Majles having finished its term, parliamentary elections were held for the Seventeenth Majles. The number of government deputies rose from five to about thirty, which made them the strongest minority faction in the new Majles, while Mosaddeq continued to obtain votes of confidence from other parliamentary factions as well for continuing in office. But the shah, Britain, and Iranian conservatives were still looking for an opportunity to bring down his government by peaceful means.

They got their first real opportunity in July 1952 when Mosaddeq resigned in a conflict with the shah over which of the two had the constitutional right to appoint the minister of war (later changed to "minister of defense" by Mosaddeq). The shah appointed Ahmad Qavam to the premiership.[14] There was a popular uprising and Mosaddeq was triumphantly restored to office. At exactly the same time, the World Court rejected the British case, confirming that only Iranian courts had jurisdiction in the AIOC's dispute with Iran. These events were followed by the Truman-Churchill proposal, which still stopped short of direct negotiations. Its fundamental point was that Iran should consent to World Court arbitration against certain concessions. Iran's fundamental counterproposal was that it would consent, so long as the AIOC's compensation was to be determined on the basis of the market value of Iran's property at the time of nationalization. Britain rejected this on the grounds that the company should be compensated for its profit losses until 1990, when the period of the 1933 concession would have come to an end.

To put the British position simply and briefly, Britain demanded one of the two following terms of settlement: Either Iran should grant another concession along the lines suggested by Richard Stokes, or it should compensate the company for all the oil that the company would have extracted until 1990 if Iranian oil had not been nationalized. This would have been analogous to a demand by owners of British coal mines, after the British government nationalized their property a few years earlier, that they should be compensated not on the basis of the current value of their property, but for all the coal that would have been extracted from the mines until their total depletion.

The final Anglo-American proposal—presented by the American ambassador to Iran and so named as the Henderson proposal—did not succeed, basically on the same issue. It was an improvement on the Truman-Churchill offer, but it still demanded compensation for operations until 1990. Mosaddeq went one step forward and agreed to World Court arbitration on that basis, on the condition that Britain declare its maximum compensation demand from the outset. He argued that any litigant claiming compensation from a court would normally name the amount of compensation sought. This was a significant retreat from his previous position that the AIOC should be compensated purely for the market value of its property. Yet, Britain turned this down, and the proposal failed.

Neither of the two alternative British demands—another concession or compensation for operations until 1990—would have been made, let alone succeeded, if Britain's dispute had been with Holland, Sweden, or any other small European country. It was clear that Iran's position was weak, not on legal grounds, but in terms of the country's relative world power. But precisely for that reason, the Popular Movement would not have succeeded without a settlement of the oil dispute that would have been tolerable to Britain and America. That is why some of Mosaddeq's less idealistic advisers believed that he should settle for something less than the ideal so as to save the movement and his own government. On the other hand, many more of his advisers were afraid of cries of "sell-out" the minute he began to entertain such a settlement. Their fear of the fickleness of the Iranian public might have been exaggerated, but they were not unrealistic.

July 21, 1952

The initial attempts at rallying Majles conservatives to bring down the government having failed, Ahmad Qavam began to emerge as the candidate with whom Britain preferred to negotiate a settlement. The opportunity arose shortly after the opening of the Seventeenth Majles, when Mosaddeq began to form a new cabinet. He had just returned from The Hague, where the World Court was hearing the British case against Iran. Being convinced that the court would rule in favor of Britain, he had decided to resign and spend the rest of his life abroad.[15] It was in such a pessimistic mood that he went to see the shah to discuss the list of cabinet members he was going to present to the Parliament and to tell the shah that he himself would "supervise" the Ministry of Defense. It had become a convention for the shah to appoint a general to that ministry, although this was not the constitutional position. The popular view that the dispute was over who was commander in chief of the armed forces is incorrect, although even that would have been constitutionally valid. Mosaddeq believed that all departments of state should be answerable to the cabinet and Parliament, not to the shah. His most famous motto was "The shah should reign, not rule." Apart from that, he did not intend to run the Ministry of Defense directly. Eventually, he appointed three generals nominated by the shah as his advisers in that ministry, and they effectively ran its affairs. But this did not happen without a full-scale Iranian drama.

When the shah insisted on making the appointment himself, Mosaddeq resigned without a fuss and disappeared from public view. The shah appointed Qavam prime minister, and—quite uncharacteristically—Qavam made a tactical blunder by making a speech threatening repression. There was a popular uprising on July 21, 1952, led by Ayatollah Abolqasem Kashani, the Popular Movement faction of the Majles, and pro-Mosaddeq parties. Mosaddeq returned to office just at the time that the World Court ruled in Iran's favor.[16] This was the Popular Movement's finest moment, and it was shortly afterward that the unsuccessful Truman-Churchill proposal was made.

Cracks and Schisms in the Movement

The July uprising was also a turning point against the Popular Movement's fortunes. Soon afterward, Ayatollah Kashani as well as Mozaffar Baqa'i, Hossein Makki, and Abolhasan Ha'erizadeh—three leading figures in the Popular Movement's parliamentary faction—began to fall out with Mosaddeq and the rest of the movement. Many of the differences had their roots in personality conflicts and rivalries, and they went back to earlier times, although they had not surfaced in public before.[17] A late public warning of the schism was the split in the Zahmatkeshan (Toilers) Party in October 1952, which occurred when the majority faction led by Khalil Maleki did not accept Baqa'i's proposal for a policy of confrontation with Mosaddeq.[18] A few days later, General Zahedi and Gen. Abdolhossein Hejazi were suspected of secret activity against the government, helped by the British embassy in Tehran. Hejazi was arrested but released shortly afterward. Zahedi could not be arrested because, as a senator, he enjoyed parliamentary immunity. He had been contacted as the British candidate to replace Mosaddeq by Monty Woodhouse, the MI6 chief in Tehran, and Sam Falle, the Oriental secretary at the British embassy, shortly after the uprising of July 21 and Mosaddeq's return to power.[19] Iran broke off diplomatic relations with Britain on the argument that it was interfering in Iran's internal affairs.

When he formed his second government after the July revolt, Mosaddeq asked for and obtained some delegated powers (*ekhtiyarati*) from the Parliament, that is, the Senate as well as the Majles, to which the shah had duly assented. This would enable him to enact a number of bills, notably for financial, judicial, and social reform. These bills would then be put into operation for six months before submitting them to Parliament. Without these powers Mosaddeq would not have been able to run the country in the circumstances, and, as he made plain, he would have resigned. The reasons were that the country was confronting a world power, the government had powerful domestic enemies of both the Right and the Left often engaged in extraparliamentary campaigns against it, and there was a serious economic problem due to the international

Crowds raising portraits of Mosaddeq on the parliament gate, March 2, 1953.
Copyright © 2002 by AP/Wide World Photos.

boycott of Iranian oil and the resulting non–oil economics. Besides, the Parliament was so strong that the government had to submit a bill to it each time it
wished to increase the money supply, yet at the same time it was divided and
lacked proper parties and factions to help process new legislation at a tolerable
speed. Often, the government even had to haggle with individual deputies to
gain their support for government legislation.

Later, Mosaddeq's opponents described the delegated powers as evidence
that he was a dictator. But this is contrary to the facts. The powers were delegated to him by the Parliament for a short period to enable him to implement
financial, judicial, and other reforms. The Parliament remained open and there
were daily debates about all matters of political interest. In times like that, even
democratic countries (such as Britain in the Second World War) have suspended the constitution in part or as a whole, whereas the power that the shah
and Parliament delegated to Mosaddeq was for taking decisions, some of

which—such as changing the money supply—do not require an act of Parliament in Western democracies, even in normal times. Rather than being a dictatorship, Mosaddeq's government was so open and tolerant that it did not even stop the activities of such well-known conspirators as the Rashidian brothers against it. Nor did the government take measures against its opposition among the Right or the Left for serious violations of the law.

The delegated powers bill had had the support of Baqa'i, Kashani, and others, and had passed through both houses of Parliament unopposed. The Majles continued its increasingly lively existence, not least when cracks began to show within the leadership of the Popular Movement and its parliamentary faction. From January 1953 onward, Baqa'i was the most outspoken opponent of the government in the Majles. Mosaddeq, on the other hand, used the device of periodically asking for and obtaining a vote of confidence to demonstrate the constitutional legitimacy of his government. The delegated powers became a serious bone of contention when, in January 1953, the act fell due for renewal for another year. Ayatollah Kashani, who was Majles Speaker, and Baqa'i, Makki, and Ha'erizadeh energetically campaigned against its renewal. But they did not in the end vote against it, because it had been tied to a vote of confidence for the government.

From the outset, there had been three distinct approaches toward the Popular Movement among religious leaders and activists. The conservatives, who dominated the religious establishment in Qom, Tehran, and elsewhere, did not display much enthusiasm for oil nationalization, and even less for the Popular Movement and Mosaddeq's premiership. They are often described as "quietists," although this may be misleading: if they looked apolitical, it was because, at the time, their politics led them to support the shah and the conservative political establishment. And, like the latter, they saw on matters of foreign policy the choice being simply between the Soviet Union and Britain, and they preferred the latter. Therefore, as relations between the shah and Mosaddeq deteriorated, and at the same time the Anglo-Iranian oil dispute reached a deadlock, their lack of enthusiasm for Mosaddeq and the movement turned into more active opposition, although this was often communicated through informal channels. Ayatollah Sayyed Mohammad Behbahani represented them most in the capital. And he in turn was represented most by Mohammad Taqi Falsafi among the leading preachers.

The second tendency among the religious leadership and community was proconstitutional and anti-imperialist. Ayatollah Kashani, who strongly supported oil nationalization and Mosaddeq's premiership, was the supreme leader of that approach until the time—especially after the events of February 28, 1953—when he openly joined Mosaddeq's opposition. But there were others both inside and outside the Majles, although not of his rank, who remained loyal to the Popular Movement until the end. They included two Tehran *moj-taheds* (and brothers) Sayyed Abolfazl and Haj Aqa Reza (later Ayatollahs) Zanjani, Sayyed Mahmud (later Ayatollah) Taleqani, Sayyed Ja'far (later Ayatollah) Gharavi, Shaikh Bah'al-Din (later Ayatollah) Mahallati, and most of the (lower) ulama among the Majles deputies, such as Haj Sayyed-Javadi, Angaji, Shabestari, Musavi Jalali, Milani, and so on, some of whom later became ayatollahs.

The militant group of Feda'iyan-e Islam represented the third distinct tendency, although the group did not compare either in rank, number, or popular base with the first two tendencies, its fame being due to the emotional activism of its adherents, which included political assassination as a means to their ends. They were a group of young men who campaigned for the creation of an Islamic state and supported the Popular Movement until Mosaddeq became prime minister. But, almost immediately, they fell out with both Mosaddeq and Kashani and with the entire movement because they had hoped for an Islamic revolution, which neither of the two leaders had promised or even desired. Within a short period, the Feda'iyan-e Islam became mortal enemies of the movement and its leaders, and so shot and permanently wounded Hossein Fatemi, a leading journalist and Majles deputy who later became foreign minister. They supported the coup but eventually fell out with the postcoup regime, until their unsuccessful attempt on Premier Hossein Ala's life in 1955 led to the arrest and execution of four of their leaders.[20]

The events of February 28, 1953, brought all three religious groups together for the first time, not in any open or tacit coalition, but insofar as all of them demonstrated explicit and active hostility toward Mosaddeq and his government. A few days earlier, the shah had sent word to Mosaddeq that he and Queen Soraya wished to go to Europe for treatments for suspected infertility, emphasizing that the matter must be kept secret until he had left the country, lest it create public concern. Mosaddeq had counseled against it, but agreed to cooperate. He was therefore puzzled to discover on the day of the shah's departure—February 28, 1953—that the matter had become public knowledge despite the shah's initial insistence on secrecy. Ayatollah Behbahani was first to make this known to him. Later, the ayatollah visited the shah to dissuade him from leaving, and addressed an anti-Mosaddeq crowd outside the palace. Kashani appealed to the public to stop the move, saying that "if the shah goes, everything we have will go with him." Whether the ayatollas were just pretending, or had been misled by others, they gave the impression that Mosaddeq was pushing the shah out of the country for his own ends. Mosaddeq, on the other hand, was certain that the whole thing had been designed to start the riots to bring him down and/or kill him in the process. Thus the mob went on to attack Mosaddeq's home after he miraculously escaped from the royal palace through a back door. This time, too, he was lucky to escape over the wall and make it to the Majles, which was in an emergency session.[21]

The Coup

The next episode was the kidnapping and murder of the country's police chief, Gen. Mahmud Afshartus, the following April. The intention was to force Mosaddeq's resignation by kidnapping a number of important officials and dignitaries. Afshartus was first on the list because he headed the entire civilian police and security apparatus. In the event, police inquiries quickly pointed to the likely perpetrators, who immediately killed Afshartus in the cave where he was being held. Four generals and a couple of junior officers confessed to having been involved in the plot, and they implicated Baqa'i and his close friend, Hossein Khazibi, in the plot.[22]

By then it had become clear that the government's right-wing opposition—the shah, the recently retired army officers who still had links to the army, landlords and conservative politicians, and all the three tendencies among religious leaders and groups—were now prepared to resort to violent as well as peaceful methods to bring down the government. They had been receiving increasing encouragement, at different levels and with growing firmness and intensity, from the American and British governments via their diplomatic and intelligence staff and agents in Iran.

The CIA history written by Donald Wilber, *Overthrow of Premier Mosaddeq of Iran: November 1952-August 1953,* refers obscurely to a Qashqa'i/Amini alternative plan, and even mentions Abolqasem Amini, the acting minister of the royal court, whom the shah did not trust at all, as one of the Iranians involved in the coup.[23] This is misleading. In fact, to forestall or counteract potential Qashqa i resistance to the coup, the planners eventually decided to contact them, and it is in that context that the CIA history mentions "the alternative Qashqa'i/Amini plan" without further explanation. According to Naser Qashqa'i's diaries of the time, after the failure of the August 16 coup, the

Qashqa'is turned down the American offer of $5 million to use their resources in helping Zahedi to take power (see further below).

The absence of such important details is largely due to the fact that the CIA account, even from the viewpoint of American and British operations alone, is not a complete history of the coup. The largest omission, from the Iranian viewpoint, is its silence on the murder of Afshartus, probably because some of the Iranians involved in the August coup were also implicated in that plot. The largest omission from the American viewpoint is the history's complete silence about the decisions and activities of the State Department and the U.S. embassy in Tehran, except in its occasional references to the full cooperation of Loy Henderson, the American ambassador.

According to State Department documents, in a joint meeting with Abolqasem Amini and Naser Qashqa'i, Amini told Henderson that either America should give economic aid to Mosaddeq or it should suggest that he step down to become Iran's senior statesman and choose his own successor, who should then be given American support. Qashqa'i agreed with Amini that if either Mosaddeq or his chosen successor were given American support, then it would be possible to take much of the radical wind out of the sails of current Iranian politics. Amini also stressed that any coup against Mosaddeq would be "bloody," that it would destroy all the achievements of the Popular Movement, that, in any case, it would not be acceptable, and that it would have a very small chance of success.[24]

It is clear from various dispatches by Henderson that Amini was in fact in favor of an open and peaceful settlement with Mosaddeq and that Henderson and other American embassy staff did not trust Amini.[25] Later, in a message to the embassy, the shah firmly rejected Amini's suggestion that his brother, Gen. Mahmud Amini (commander of the gendarmerie), should replace General Riahi as the chief of staff.[26] This is in fact what the pro-Mosaddeq army officers had proposed to Mosaddeq, but he had chosen Riahi on strong recommendations from the latter's Iran Party friends.[27] The pro-Mosaddeq officers believed that General Amini was a better combat officer. Apart from that, he and his two brothers, Ali and Abolqasem, were distrusted and disliked by the shah.[28]

The coup d'état of August 1953 is studied in detail in another chapter of this volume.[29] It is important to emphasize, however, that the coup was a product of the close collaboration of Mosaddeq's domestic and foreign opponents, even though the role of the two foreign powers, especially the United States, in organizing and financing it was all but indispensable. Mosaddeq's Iranian opponents were too divided and too unsure of themselves as well as each other to or-

ganize and act in unison. Some of them, notably the shah himself, even suspected that the British were secretly behind Mosaddeq and so they were hesitant to commit themselves. On the other hand, the foreign powers could not
possibly have brought down Mosaddeq by a coup without the cooperation of
his domestic opponents. Between the time of Afshartus's murder in April and
the coup in August, there were widespread rumors of an impending coup. Indeed, on August 13, the daily *Niruy-e Sevvom* openly declared on its front page
that "the suspicious activities of foreign agents in the past two weeks . . . show
that a secret organization is hopelessly working against Dr. Mosaddeq's government, and that the American and British imperialists have not yet lost faith in
the use of their trump card [i.e., Zahedi]." On the same day, *Behsu-ye Ayandeh,*
the Tudeh Party's leading open daily, also reported strong rumors about an imminent coup.

In July, Mosaddeq, fearing that he was about to be given a vote of no confidence in the Majles, decided to dissolve the Seventeenth Majles by referendum
and hold fresh elections. He suspected that Britain and America were at work
among the Majles deputies to create a majority against him. After all, Britain
had been trying to turn the Majles against him since the beginning of his first
government in May 1951. The recent CIA evidence now shows that in June
1953 they had been planning to buy off some Majles deputies to topple the government, although there are doubts as to whether in fact money was paid.[30] If
Mosaddeq had any specific knowledge of this effort, he did not make it public in
his trials and in his posthumously published memoirs. But, in more general
terms, he did make it clear on several occasions that he suspected that efforts
were being made to obtain a vote of no confidence in him from the Majles.

At this point a relatively insignificant Majles decision aroused Mosaddeq's
suspicion that the Majles was about to vote against his government. A supervi-
sory board that included a Majles deputy acted as the watchdog committee for
the issuing of new notes at Bank Melli of Iran (then the central bank). In June
1953 the Majles deputy's position became vacant, and Hossein Makki was
voted into the post. Mosaddeq was alarmed that Makki might make a big issue
of the 3.1 billion rials that had been issued over a period of nine months, a legal
and necessary measure for managing the policy of non-oil economics. Shortly
afterward, Ali Zohari tabled a motion of censure against the government.
Mosaddeq was convinced that that was the opposition's moment and a concocted majority was ready to vote for the motion, thus forcing him to resign.

On the other hand, the dissolution of the Majles via a controversial referendum would have made it much easier to bring down the government by force,

backed up by the notice of Mosaddeq's dismissal. The Americans eventually obtained such a notice from the shah, after the referendum. Most of Mosaddeq's close colleagues and supporters, including Gholam Hossein Sadiqi, Khalil Maleki, Karim Sanjabi, Mahmud Nariman, Ali Shayegan, Daryush Foruhar, and others, opposed the referendum on political grounds. Abdollah Mo'azzami, the pro-Mosaddeq Majles speaker, resigned in protest and left town. The unintended consequence of the referendum was to make it easier for the coup makers, by encouraging the shah to agree to sign the notice of Mosaddeq's dismissal and eliminating the possibility of resistance against the notice by the Majles.

This is exactly what Mosaddeq's advisers had feared. The first CIA plan—laid out in "The London Draft," which had been outlined before the decision to hold the referendum—had envisaged that the shah would appoint Zahedi as chief of the army, who would then proceed to complete the coup with the help of religious groups and some Majles deputies. In the plan that was actually implemented after the referendum and in the absence of the Majles, the CIA planners simply obtained a notice from the shah for Mosaddeq's dismissal and a notice for Zahedi's appointment to the premiership, because now the Majles had been dissolved. There followed the coups of August 16 and 19, which overthrew Mosaddeq's government.[31]

Gen. Fazlollah Zahedi *(seated)* on August 19, 1953, shortly after the coup. Copyright © 2003 AP/Wide World Photos.

But the CIA did not succeed in buying off a Majles majority to vote against Mosaddeq, since almost two-thirds of the Majles deputies voluntarily resigned their seats to facilitate the dissolution of the Majles as soon as Mosaddeq announced his decision to hold a referendum for that purpose. Clearly, they would not have voted for Zohari's motion of censure if it had come to a vote.

If the Coup Had Not Succeeded

Would the Popular Movement have survived in the long run without the coup? This is not an easy question to answer. There is little doubt that the Anglo-American powers would not have ceased their efforts to bring the government down, either through the Majles or by other means. Apart from that, both real economic difficulties and, more likely, the exaggerated predictions of imminent economic doom by the government's opponents would have played a role in weakening its position. But there were some fundamental long-term problems stemming from the very nature of Iranian politics that would have made the creation of modern democratic government difficult at the time. Mosaddeq and his colleagues believed in the system of parliamentary democracy, whereas their opposition, both of the Right and of the Left, were in the tradition of what I have described elsewhere as "the politics of elimination." [32]

It went further than that. The government's response to secret, underhanded, or openly illegal campaigns against it was extremely lenient. The Rashidians were known to be constantly at work conducting a campaign to overthrow the government. The government's response to organized riots against it was very inadequate, a good example being the case of the organizers and mobsters who ran riot on February 28 and twice almost killed the prime minister. Zahedi, accused of being involved in the kidnapping and murder of General Afshartus, was allowed to take *bast* (political sanctuary) in the Majles, thus escaping judicial investigation. Moreover, when he broke *bast* and left the Majles about a month before the coup, he was not arrested and was allowed to go into hiding. He left the Majles on the eve of the anniversary of the July 21 uprising, fearing that, during the next day's demonstrations, a mob might break into the House and attack him. Zahedi's fears might have been reasonable, although the Majles had a military guard. But it is unclear why he was not arrested on the standing charge after he broke *bast,* and was allowed to leave the Majles openly and with the government's knowledge.

The government did not ban the Tudeh newspapers that published highly libelous statements against the government and Mosaddeq himself until February 1953 when Mosaddeq refused to renew the Soviet Union's fishing concession in the Caspian Sea, although they became more circumspect after February 28. Nor did they stop the chorus of mushrooming newspapers, subsidized or paid for by the Rashidians, and, later, directly from the CIA funds specifically allocated for the campaign to bring down the government. Without exaggeration, these newspapers conducted the vilest, most vitriolic, and patently illegal campaign against the person of Mosaddeq as well as his government.[33] The government thus practiced (if this be an adequate description) extreme liberal democracy where their powerful opponents would not even observe the law. In fact many of the government's opponents had little respect for law and constitutional government, whether democratic or otherwise.

It is therefore difficult to think how Mosaddeq's government would have survived in the long run, except perhaps if the oil dispute was settled, the oil boycott was lifted, and America decided to work with Mosaddeq rather than against him. The shah and conservatives wished not just to defeat the Popular Movement and the Tudeh Party in a constitutional process but to eliminate them as active political forces. The Tudeh Party likewise wished to eliminate the other two forces and monopolize political power. But Mosaddeq and the Popular Movement—whatever their shortcomings, of which quite a few have been mentioned here and elsewhere[34]—believed in a plural as well constitutional society and did not wish to eliminate anyone else. Hence they were unlikely to have survived in the long run unless they too became eliminationist, which was against their very nature and raison d'être; or the other two forces ceased to be eliminationists, which was against theirs. But if the West had helped rather than worked against their efforts to build up a democratic system, then they would have been in a much stronger position to survive and continue their program for political development.

From the Coup to the Revolution

The coup did not result in total loss of legitimacy for the shah and his domestic allies. They certainly lost their legitimacy with the Popular Movement's social base, that is, the modern middle class, including professionals and intellectuals, as well as much of the bazaar. But they themselves had a considerable base—backed by landed property and influence—that included many of the religious leaders and preachers and their followers, as well as landlords and provincial magnates. As a result, the postcoup regime, in its early years, did not lead to arbitrary rule but resembled a modern dictatorship, comparable to—although clearly not quite the same as—the early to late 1920s when Reza Khan was prime minister and shah.

Like his father, Mohammad Reza Shah was not prepared to share power with his coup and postcoup allies. The sacking of Zahedi in 1955 was the first clear move toward the concentration of power, a trend that was speeded up with the appointment of Manuchehr Eqbal to the premiership (after Hossein Ala's caretaker government). Ali Amini was respectfully removed from the cabinet on becoming ambassador to Washington, and, not long afterward, Abdolhasan Ebtehaj, the country's able and financially honest technocrat, felt impelled to resign his post as head of the Plan Organization, the body in charge of planning economic development.

The growing tendency toward the concentration of power was disrupted for a couple of years by serious economic difficulties as well as by changes in the attitudes of the two superpowers toward the regime. The Soviet Union, which had established good relations with the regime after the coup, became angry when Iran concluded a mutual defense pact with the United States instead of the nonaggression treaty it was about to sign with the USSR. On the other hand, the regime's misuse of generous American foreign aid and rapidly increasing oil revenues found powerful critics in the United States. The troubles peaked in 1960 when John F. Kennedy, who was a critic of the shah's regime, became president, and at the same time the country plunged into high inflation, growing unemployment, and a runaway balance of payments deficit. In the next three years, there was a power struggle that determined the fate of the country's politics for the next fourteen years, that is, until 1977 when the revolutionary movement began and led to the regime's demise in February 1979.

After the shah defeated Amini's reformist but loyal government in the summer of 1963, he took over Amini's land reform policy, although in a different style and, later, with an increasingly different agenda.[35] By then, the religious leadership and community had begun to be alienated from the regime. Even Ayatollah Behbahani, who had been a major supporter of the shah, went over to the opposition. Landlords were angry at the threat of being eliminated as a class, both in economic and in political terms. With the launching of the White Revolution and the opening of the Twenty-first Majles, which was virtually appointed by the state, even the conservative politicians, including such loyal men as Hossein Ala and Sardar Fakher Hekmat, were excluded from politics. Thus the process of "the politics of elimination," which had begun with the 1953 coup, was completed with the suppression of the riots of June 1963.[36]

There is neither scope nor space to analyze these momentous and far-reaching events, especially as this has been done already in various other studies. The important point is that, after these events, the state began to lose its legitimacy and social base, much as had happened under Reza Shah from the late 1920s until 1941. If, after the land reform, the state had allowed the middle classes—modern as well as traditional—to play a role in the country's politics, even to the limited extent that landlords and conservative politicians were allowed political participation after the coup, then political and economic development would have taken a radically different form. In such a case, there might even have been developments comparable to those in Spain under Franco, or in South Korea and Southeast Asia in the 1960s and 1970s—countries whose natural resources and foreign exchange earnings were much more limited and whose international position was likewise considerably less favorable than that of Iran.

Much of the above is attested to by a brilliant American diplomat's long dispatch to Washington in 1964 (endorsed by the American ambassador in Tehran), assessing the political situation in a document called "Some Intangible Factors in Iranian Politics," factors that, unbeknownst to him, arose from the nature of the arbitrary state and society. He pointed out that while the shah had been thoroughly successful in the recent power struggles with the National Front, the Amini group, and the religious leadership, he lacked a social base, and his rule lacked a firm base even among its beneficiaries. Here is a passage from the long dispatch that is particularly relevant to our present analysis:

> Since the opposition is weak, divided and dispirited, the regime ought to be feeling happy and secure, particularly as it has important political assets to its favor. But one of the remarkable factors is that the regime has so few supporters. Evidence of this is to be found at every turn: prominent members of the New Iran Party who express the belief, quietly and privately, that their party is a sham and a fraud and that no political party can be expected to do useful work as long as the Shah's heavy hand rests on the decision-making process; hand-picked Majles members who deplore "American support" for a regime which they call a travesty of democracy; civil adjutants of the Shah who belong to his most devoted supporters, yet who express the belief that Iran will never be able to solve its problems as long as there is no freedom of expression, no delegation of authority, and so little selection of personnel for merit; prominent judges who declare, with surprising lack of circumspection, that the anti-corruption campaign cannot get anywhere as long as it is known that certain people are immune from prosecution; military officers who tip off the National Front regarding actions planned against its demonstrators; Foreign Ministry officials who privately advise against courses of action they are officially urging on the U.S. with respect to the treatment of opposition spokesmen in the United States. These are not members of the opposition. They are

members of the Establishment who, even while loyal to the Shah, are suffering from a profound malaise, from lack of conviction in what they are doing, from doubts about whether the regime deserves to endure.[37]

This was June 1964, when absolute and arbitrary rule was just beginning. By the mid-1970s it had climbed to its peak, and that is how it began to come down. The rapid, then explosive, growth of oil revenues in the 1960s and 1970s led to sustained and cumulative growth of GNP and increased levels of consumption even by the lower strata of the society, who could not have hoped for such growth. On the other hand, their expectations were daily increasing, and real and imagined tales of official corruption and "the plunder of the country's wealth by American imperialism"—as they firmly believed—continuously added fuel to the anger and frustration even of the state's clientele. It was the ancient logic of the society versus the state, such that an absolute and arbitrary state can in no way purchase the society's sustained loyalty and legitimacy merely by handing out goods to it.[38]

Twenty-four years ago I argued that the consequences of arbitrary rule would have been quite different if the growing and then exploding oil revenues in the 1950s and especially the 1970s had not weakened U.S. influence in Iranian politics and strengthened the state vis-à-vis the domestic social classes.[39] America was thus in the contradictory position of being regarded, largely by virtue of the 1953 coup, as the chief architect and instructor of the regime, while, at least as regarded domestic Iranian politics and policies, its real influence had considerably declined since the mid-sixties.

But the matter was perceived very differently by almost all the social classes, not least the educated, well-to-do, privileged modern middle classes, most of whom were clients and dependent beneficiaries of the arbitrary oil state, that is, of what I then described as "petrolic despotism."[40] The reason was that the real imperialism mattered much less than its perceived image and effect. What mattered most was the very strong emotional conviction—for which the starkest and most deprecated evidence was the 1953 coup—that Western imperialism was behind virtually every decision of the modern arbitrary state. If the Soviet Union had had a similarly close relationship with the regime, it would have been viewed in the same vein and held responsible for all the anger that essentially arose from the alienation of society from the state. Indeed, Russia was also disparaged to the extent that it had good relations with the regime, just as was China the minute it changed its attitude toward it.

The reality of the deep anger against the United States in particular can hardly be underrated. And there were many reasons for it. But the central reason was that it was known as the power that overthrew Mosaddeq's government in 1953, and it was wrongly perceived to be the real power behind, and the daily instructor of, the absolute and arbitrary state. The slogans against arbitrary government were some of the most prominent during the revolution of 1977–79. But they did not appear to be as unique and central as they had been during the Constitutional Revolution. This was partly because some of the anti-arbitrary objectives had indirectly found expression in anti-imperialist slogans. It is also true that various ideologies and programs such as different concepts of Islamist state, communist society, and democratic government were represented, just as radical, moderate, and conservative agendas had been represented within the general framework of the Constitutional Movement at the turn of the twentieth century.[41] What bound all of them together, nonetheless, was the determination to remove one man at all costs. The most widespread slogan uniting all the revolutionaries and their supporters and sympathizers regardless of party and program was "Let *him* [the shah] go and let there be flood afterward" (In beravad, har cheh mikhahad beshavad).

It is not just that the leading political organizations and movements were united behind this slogan. The sociology of the slogan is more instructive even than its politics. That is, the fact that almost every class and rank in the society—rich and poor, modern and traditional, educated and uneducated, religious and nonreligious—were either united behind, or would not be prepared to raise their voice against, it. Apart from that, there was not a single social class as such that took one step against the revolution, whatever the misgivings of some of their members about a swift and disorderly change of regime.

Those who lost their lives in various cities throughout the revolution certainly played an important part in the process. But the outcome would have been significantly different if the commercial and financial classes, which had benefited from the oil bonanza certainly no less than any other single social class, had not financed the movement. And, more especially, if the oil company employees, civil servants, judges, lawyers, university and schoolteachers, students, and so on had not declared an indefinite general strike. Or, if the armed forces had united and resolved to crush the movement.[42]

Thus the pattern reveals itself to be very similar to the Constitutional Revolution, although, instead of constitutionalism and modernism, now authoritarian and anti-Western agendas of different brands had much the upper hand. This may look curious, but it has its own logic from Iranian history: when Iranian society rises against the state, it rejects everything that is identified with the state. Around the turn of the twentieth century, this was traditionalism; seventy years later, it was modernism and Americanism.[43] Many changed their minds afterward and at various stages, but they did not and would not have changed their minds so long as the objective of removing the shah had not been achieved. Indeed, doubts and conflicts resulting from the intrarevolutionary clashes shortly after the triumph of February 1979 quickly disappeared for a crucial period following the occupation of the American embassy and hostage taking in November 1979. The reason was that—certainly in the minds of those masses of people who frenetically supported it—the hatred for the fallen ruler and the fear that America would somehow restore him to power was still very great. That too was a legacy of the 1953 coup.

Iran's long-term historical dynamics have displayed continuing cycles of arbitrary rule-chaos-arbitrary rule. The Constitutional Revolution of the turn of the twentieth century did not result in the disappearance of this cycle despite the fact that it was the first Iranian revolt for the establishment of lawful, as opposed to arbitrary, rule. But it did create a basis for constitutional, even democratic, government. It was this that Mosaddeq and his colleagues wished to extend and establish when they decided to nationalize Iranian oil. That, they believed, was incompatible with the existence, or return in another form, of the Anglo-Iranian Oil Company, and this was the real reason behind the deadlock over a settlement of the dispute with Britain. It led to stiffening domestic opposition by Right and Left, although the Tudeh Party softened its opposition somewhat toward the end of Mosaddeq's government. America at first tried to act as a neutral intermediary but later decided to play Britain's senior partner in organizing a coup against Mosaddeq. However, this would not have been possible without the collaboration of various royal, military, conservative, and religious opponents of the Popular Movement.

The 1953 coup marked a watershed in modern Iranian history in several ways. It was the first military coup that was planned and executed by foreign governments (British officers and diplomats on the ground had had a hand in the 1921 coup, but the British government had been kept completely in the dark, despite the Iranians' near-universal belief to the contrary).[44] It quickly led to large-scale American involvement in Iranian politics, which the Iranian public increasingly regarded in a very negative light. Sections of the army, landlords, conservative politicians, and the bulk of the religious establishment directly or indirectly helped the coup and provided the new regime's social base. This did not last long, and by the time those classes too were eliminated from politics, the regime was left with no real social base or legitimacy and increasingly had to rely on instruments of coercion and the support of foreign powers, especially the United States. And, although this was far from the truth, the regime eventually came to be perceived as no more than the domestic instrument of American imperialism, which was believed to be exploiting the country's riches and trying to destroy its religious and other cultural traditions. There can be no justification for the hostage taking of American diplomats in November 1979.[45] But the above analysis may be considered as an explanation of that unfortunate incident.

2

Unseating Mosaddeq

The Configuration and Role of Domestic Forces

Fakhreddin Azimi

"I did that," says my memory. "I can't have done that," says my pride.
In the end, memory gives way.
> —Nietzsche, *Beyond Good and Evil*

Defeat goes deeper into the human soul than victory.
> —Albert Hourani, *A History of the Arab Peoples*

The coup of August 1953 occupies an immensely significant place in the modern Iranian historical and political consciousness. The coup is widely seen as a rupture, a watershed, a turning point when imperialist domination, overcoming a defiant challenge, reestablished itself, not only by restoring an enfeebled monarch but also by ensuring that the monarchy would assume an authoritarian and antidemocratic posture. It continues to be seen as having

I would like to record my indebtedness to three outstanding individuals who were exemplary representatives of the Mosaddeqist civic nationalist tradition: late Gholam Hossein Sadiqi, Mehdi Ha'eri-Yazdi, and Ali Ardalan. I would also like to express my gratitude to Nosratollah Khazeni, a senior member of the prime minister's office throughout Mosaddeq's premiership; I have benefited from his intimate knowledge of that era and his prodigious memory and generosity. Over the years, Iraj Afshar has been a supportive friend and a constant source of inspiration. Finally, I must thank Sir Denis Wright for his help in clearing up a number of points for me, and Mark Gasiorowski for his helpful suggestions.

marked a major setback for and indeed a clear subversion of the democratic aspirations and struggles of the Iranian people. The role of foreign powers, and
the contrast between what happened and what should have happened, have a
deep resonance in the Iranian historical imagination and have continued to in-
fuse the Iranian collective memory and political culture. Although the general
tendency has primarily been to blame the foreign perpetrators of the coup, the
role not only of Iranian collaborators but also of the active domestic opposition
to Mosaddeq should not be ignored; indeed it has not been, and it continues to
cause controversy.[1]

During the turbulent interval between the forced abdication of Reza Shah
in September 1941 and the coup of August 1953, no prime minister faced as
much protracted domestic and foreign opposition as Mohammad Mosaddeq,
and none lasted as long (twenty-eight months). Ahmad Qavam, the second
longest serving prime minister in this period, remained in office for twenty-
two and a half months primarily because of his indispensible role in resolving
the crisis arising from the Soviet promotion of an autonomy movement in the
province of Azerbaijan and the Soviets' refusal to evacuate Iranian territory.
Qavam was tolerated by the royal court as long as the crisis and its immediate
aftermath continued. But when the crisis was resolved, he was ousted at the
royal behest with relative ease, despite having formed a seemingly powerful political party that, through electoral manipulation, had achieved an absolute majority in the Majles. His parliamentary majority evaporated rapidly, and he
ended up facing charges of embezzlement and corruption.

In the case of Mosaddeq, his rise to leadership of the movement for the nationalization of the oil industry and his premiership were anathema to the
shah's aspirations for uncontested hegemony over the governmental process,
relentlessly pursued since the beginning of his reign and partially upheld by the
Constituent Assembly of 1949/1328, which formally increased his prerogatives. The shah, however, felt ill equipped and unable to confront or oppose
Mosaddeq publicly. Unlike his predecessors, Mosaddeq had assumed office at
the head of a movement that contested British imperial hegemony and advocated democratic and civic nationalist values. Dislodging him would thus require extensive, combined, and mutually reinforcing domestic and foreign
efforts. Mosaddeq also parted company with his predecessors by defying the
narrow confines and ethos of elitist and clientelist politics to cultivate and resort
to a civic populist reliance on public support. A corollary to this was the promotion of a nascent public sphere characterized by a multiplicity of associa-
tional and ideological activities.

Determined to defeat Mosaddeq and the movement he led, Britain resorted to a panoply of extensive measures. Such measures would not, however, have proved effective without concerted Iranian collaboration. Conversely, Mosaddeq's domestic opponents would have been crippled without substantial British and, later, U.S. support. Exhausted by the cumulative effects of relentless and corrosive foreign-backed destabilizing campaigns and the limiting constraints of the existing institutional and administrative arrangements, as well as by the activities of the Tudeh Party and traditionalist forces, Mosaddeq's vulnerability was further increased when a number of his supporters actually sided with his vocal opponents. The primary aim of this essay is to chart the course of the destabilization of Mosaddeq's government and to investigate the role and configuration of its domestic opponents, which also inevitably requires highlighting the intricate and crucial involvement of his foreign antagonists.

Social Bases of Support and Opposition

Support of and opposition to Mosaddeq cannot be easily explained along clearly delineated class lines or in terms of distinct social categories. Both support and opposition, as well as indifference, had a cross-class, hybrid, and syncretic character. Civic nationalism, a consequence of Iran's prolonged exposure to imperialist intrusions and its encounter with modernity, sought to promote national dignity and freedom from foreign domination, as well as political and civil rights and liberties, participatory politics, and meaningful citizenship. It generally appealed to the urban middle-class strata, particularly the intelligentsia. The modern or politically literate middle-income or underprivileged segments of the urban population constituted the core of the movement that brought about the nationalization of oil and Mosaddeq's premiership, but the movement also enjoyed considerable support among forces conventionally regarded as traditional. Certain guilds were distinctly and actively pro-Mosaddeq: restaurateurs (*chelo-kababis*), led by the tireless philanthropist and civic patriot Hasan Shamshiri, and coffee- and teahouse owners, led by the capable Ebrahim Karimabadi, were prominent in this category. Other guilds—according to a British embassy minute of February 1952, the guilds of bakers, butchers, and confectioners—were opposed to the government or could be used against it. Their resentments were attributable to factors such as the government's taxation and pricing policies.[2] They were also provoked by political opponents of the government who targeted such groups and tried, through various means, including bribery, to win over their leaders.

Many leading bazaar merchants, as well as several prominent clerics, actively supported Mosaddeq and were at the core of the National Resistance Movement that was formed following his overthrow.

The bazaar's political orientations and behavior could, however, vary, as they were situationally specific and affected by shifting alliances and changing exigencies and by the relative success or failure of Mosaddeq's supporters and opponents in swaying them, as well as by socioeconomic interests. For instance, small manufacturers as well as exporters were favorable to the government, while importers tended to oppose it. Pro-Mosaddeq sentiments in the bazaar could be undermined by invoking the threat of the Tudeh Party. Agents of both Britain and the royal court concentrated much of their efforts on stimulating discontent and mobilizing fear in the bazaar, relying heavily on formal or informal guild activists as well as mob leaders, petty political brokers, and rumor-mongers. The anti-Mosaddeq clerics also expended much energy molding opinion in the bazaar. With growing pessimism concerning an early resolution of the oil dispute, unpromising economic prospects, and tangible financial difficulties, the larger segments of the propertied, mercantile, and entrepreneurial strata were to become impatient with or turn against Mosaddeq. In this process efforts to manufacture pessimism and discontent played an important role. The Chamber of Commerce, dominated by anti-Mosaddeq notables such as Sen. Abdulhossein Nikpur, its president, prepared a gloomy economic report that was submitted to the shah by Mohammad Reza Kharrazi, the chamber's vice president, in April 1952. The report was meant not only to highlight the disaffection of leading merchants and the existing economic difficulties but also to draw public attention to and augment them to Mosaddeq's clear detriment.[3]

Workers were also divided along various lines. Pro-Tudeh workers followed the party strictures; they, along with other Tudeh elements, constituted a constant source of irritation to Mosaddeq's government through their relentlessly unruly behavior and numerous street demonstrations. Anti-Tudeh parties and groups such as Baqa'i's Toilers Party also attempted to win workers' support or purported to represent them. In addition to self-appointed workers' leaders who claimed to enjoy influence among workers, there were also officially sponsored trade unionists who often supported the court or the British. Regardless of external stimulation, workers' discontent had tangible causes. Severe financial constraints and insufficient revenues prevented the government from adequately attending to welfare measures or job creation. In this context, the unchecked, if not growing, lower-class poverty, unemployment, and underemployment were helping to create a reservoir of discontent. An apathetic, opportunistic, or cynical urban underclass was easy prey for mob leaders and could be manipulated by opponents of Mosaddeq.

The general tendency in the countryside and smaller towns was for the inhabitants to follow the lead of their own long-standing notable representatives in the capital, that is, those leading figures of the area's prominent families who could be relied upon as well-connected patrons and protectors, those who interceded with the central government on behalf of the local population. Nevertheless, pro-Mosaddeq sentiments were in evidence even in areas where the notables were opposed to him. Pastoral nomadic people too followed their leaders. Many of these leaders, particularly in the south, had traditionally maintained close ties with the British, and the British contemplated provoking unrest among the nomadic population.[4] The anti-Mosaddeq opposition schemes invariably anticipated the support of such elements. Owing to kinship ties to Queen Soraya, the shah's second wife, at least some Bakhtiaris tended openly to support the royal court. The short-lived rebellion of Abolqasem Bakhtiari in February 1953 was seen by Mosaddeq as an indication of a court-sponsored campaign to bring down his government.[5] Qashqa'i magnates and politicians were, on the other hand, generally pro-Mosaddeq; they were also anticommunist, and this appealed to the Americans, who tried to enlist their support for Gen. Fazlollah Zahedi or for other anti-Mosaddeq moves. The Qashqa'is had cooperated with Zahedi in a pro-German organization during World War II and later during the Azerbaijan crisis of 1946.[6] They were, however, unprepared to move against Mosaddeq.[7]

Urban notables, particularly absentee landowners, constituted the bulk of actual or potential, although not necessarily active, opponents of Mosaddeq. Mosaddeq's agrarian reforms, which reduced their share of agricultural profits, deepened their opposition. Included among the notables were professional politicians, senior administrators, and high-ranking military or police officers linked to each other and to big merchants through kin or convivial ties, and connected to the court or to embassies such as Britain's. They also relied on their own individual clientele, whose interests they furthered in exchange for support when needed. Such clienteles sometimes included mob leaders, who were capable of mobilizing underclass elements. Even though some may have been of undistinguished family backgrounds, the urban notables had achieved elite status through patronage and/or marriage into more established families. Their aim was to perpetuate the conditions that would preserve their privileges and influence; this involved endeavoring to sustain an oligarchic predominance of notables or clusters of notables in the context of a mildly constitutional and circumscribed monarchy. They did not welcome an unfettered autocracy. Politics, in their eyes, was essentially an elite pursuit, a cultivated mode of brokerage and exchange involving mutual material or symbolic rewards, an activity readily disposed to barely disguised manipulation of the masses but unencumbered by any serious attention to the public or public opinion. They tended to dismiss politics of conviction or any political conduct actively responsive to public opinion as dangerous demagogy.

An entrenched clause in the political subculture of the notables was a belief in the ubiquity of British influence in Iran. Even if they regretted such influence, they viewed challenging it as dangerous, and as beneficial only to communism or radical politics. There was also an underlying consensus that the existing political clans or clusters of notables needed to maintain an equilibrium, preventing any single force from outmaneuvering and crippling others. They feared that drastic constriction of royal power would either result in an autocratic backlash or would destroy the monarchy altogether. They wanted to ensure that the Parliament retained sufficient credibility and capability to resist royal whims and contest the shah's quest for undue control over the political process. They found Mosaddeq's populist approach abhorrent and his civic nationalism and democratic constitutionalism unrealistic. Mosaddeq rejected the very perceptual basis of their political conduct and tried to undermine its foundations by cultivating public participation and insisting on the necessity of a strong, court-independent executive branch, which would oblige the shah to abide by the democratic spirit of the Constitution.

The majority of urban notables, however, tended largely to confine themselves to passive opposition to Mosaddeq. Active domestic opposition to him involved a relatively small but influential number of notables. Their opposition, irrespective of merely opportunistic and hired-collaborator components, was rooted in endangered vested interests and animated by fear that the success of civic nationalism in its interrelated objectives of undermining British influence and restraining the monarchy would mean an end to a host of entrenched and long-enjoyed privileges. Such opponents rationalized or justified their opposition by invoking the lofty objectives of saving the country from economic ruin, chaos, territorial disintegration, or communism. They also insisted on the necessity of preserving and protecting an interventionist monarchy not only as a culturally sanctioned institution but also as virtually the only conceivable and viable form of governance in Iran.

The Shah, the Court and the Royalists

In the post-1941 era, the young and inexperienced Mohammad Reza Shah, who had acceded to the throne with grudging British acquiescence, shaken by the fate of his exiled father and having avowedly undertaken to abide by the Constitution, was not in a position to act as an autocrat; yet he was, though, irresistibly inclined and able to cripple strong prime ministers. He not only undermined Qavam but also succeeded in turning the capable and energetic general Hajji Ali Razmara into an ineffectual politician and a politically incapacitated prime minister. This attitude was partly due to the shah's character and mentality but was largely a result of exigencies arising from the monarchy's institutional salience and its capacity to control the flow of patronage. The shah was the incumbent of an office that was institutionally and structurally empowered to manipulate, ignore, or defy fragile constitutional provisions and play a crucial role in the Iranian body politic. The shah's capacity to dominate or influence the political process led the opponents of Mosaddeq, both domestic and foreign, to expend immense efforts to persuade, cajole, or coerce the monarch to abandon his hesitant and passive opposition to Mosaddeq in favor of active confrontation. Almost until the very end of Mosaddeq's premiership, however, the shah remained reluctant to confront him openly and actively.

The British opponents of Mosaddeq invariably tended to explain the shah's position in terms of his indecision, lack of courage, and moods of resignation and gloom when facing crisis. They were also cognizant of the shah's lurking distrust and dislike of the British. The shah did indeed, during the greater part of Mosaddeq's premiership, succumb to a mood of melancholy and resignation; he lamented the erosion of his prerogatives and prestige[8] and was overcome by a deep pessimism about the future of monarchy in Iran. Moreover, readily susceptible to prevailing conspiratorial delusions, he was deeply suspicious of the British and their real objectives. Clearly the shah had more reason to oppose Mosaddeq than any other prime minister. Indeed, no prime minister had ever been as systematically insistent on and determined to revitalize the authority of the prime minister and to force the monarch to abide by the spirit of the Constitution by acting as a constitutional, that is, ceremonial sovereign. Earlier, in his capacity as a deputy in the Sixteenth Majles, Mosaddeq had not only strongly opposed the setting up of the Constituent Assembly, which extended royal prerogatives, but also thwarted the shah's desire to acquire the right of suspensory veto over parliamentary bills. And yet the shah found it immensely difficult and politically costly to oppose Mosaddeq publicly or vehemently.

Mosaddeq differed markedly from those prime ministers whose position the shah had undermined with relative ease. He was the chief protagonist of an anti-imperialist civic nationalist movement the aim of which was to revitalize democratic aspirations and principles as well as procedures embedded in the

Iranian Constitution, and to link this aim strategically with the more immediate objective of asserting Iranian national sovereignty as symbolized by the nationalization of the AIOC. The Mosaddeq-led National Front's primary objective had been to promote political and civic rights embodied in the Constitution, particularly electoral and press freedom, in order to ensure that a parliament would emerge that would not succumb to domestic and foreign pressures and would resist an unsatisfactory oil settlement with Britain. It was the successful linking of democratic aspirations with a civic nationalist, anti-imperialist struggle that enabled Mosaddeq to assume the prominence that he did, rendering the shah effectively incapable of opposing him publicly.

The shah had feared the consequences of the nationalization of the oil industry, as it not only was certain to antagonize Britain but was also likely to jeopardize his own designs for enhancing his power. He had, in fact, against the advice of his ministers—who wanted to avoid a repetition of Reza Shah's involvement in the 1933 oil agreement—intervened in the oil negotiations and supported the ill-fated Supplemental Oil Agreement.[9] And yet, he was unable to oppose Mosaddeq on the oil issue. No matter how bitterly resentful he was, the shah, as sovereign, felt incapable of openly opposing a prime minister who was publicly acclaimed as an unwavering patriot and dedicated defender of Iranian sovereign rights vis-à-vis British imperialism. In late September 1951, he confided to the new U.S. ambassador, the seasoned cold warrior Loy Henderson, that he knew that Mosaddeq's policies were "leading Iran towards ruin" and that British "friendship and support" were needed for Iran's independence. However, considering that Iranian national feelings were against Britain, if he were to act against Mosaddeq, the Crown would be accused of having "degenerated" into a mere British tool, and the prestige of the monarchy would thus suffer gravely. He had no choice but to remain patient.[10]

While under immense pressure to oppose Mosaddeq publicly, the shah was also pressed by Mosaddeq and his supporters to refrain from any move likely to damage the country's anti-imperialist struggle. Mosaddeq had long admonished the shah that if he wished to retain his throne he should overcome autocratic temptations. He had not failed to criticize, oppose, and try to thwart royal moves that, in his eyes, contravened the spirit of the Constitution.[11] Much of the advice Mosaddeq proffered to the shah, the concerns he expressed and criticisms he made of the monarch's political conduct, were shared to varying degrees by many prominent nonservile politicians. Qavam, for instance, had publicly warned the shah, rebuking him for tampering with the Constitution,[12] and Hossein Ala, the veteran politician and court minister, privately regretted and criticized the conduct of the royal family.[13] The shah's adoption of a passive stance was not, however, in any way an indication of his willingness to embrace the role of a constitutional monarch. Although appearing to be entirely eclipsed by Mosaddeq, the shah, assisted by variously motivated supporters, not only indirectly endorsed anti-Mosaddeq moves but was also in a position, even through inaction, to add significantly to Mosaddeq's problems; nor was he fully willing to restrain the royal court.

The court-based anti-Mosaddeq opposition had its own dynamics: the court was the focal point of considerable anti-Mosaddeq activity, under the auspices of the shah's mother, Taj al-Moluk, Reza Shah's second and most influential wife, who found it intolerable that her crowned son should be merely a shadow of his powerful father.[14] There was also the flamboyant and scheming Princess Ashraf, the shah's twin sister, who seemed indefatigable in the unfailing pursuit of her own ambitions and desires whether political, material, or carnal. She was the patroness of a host of aspiring younger politicians who looked upon her patronage as a sure guarantee of political success. Mosaddeq had publicly rebuked her, in contrast to her older sister, Princess Shams, whom he considered as commendably restrained from political involvement.[15] The extent of the involvement of the shah's mother and Princess Ashraf in encouraging and sustaining opposition activities led Mosaddeq frequently to complain about them, particularly Princess Ashraf, whom he threatened to denounce in public unless she refrained from political activity.[16] Following the bloody street clashes of mid-July 1951/23 Tir 1330, Ashraf left the country, returning some eight months later to play an important role in Qavam's assumption of the premiership. The queen mother, however, remained in the country and continued tirelessly to encourage and assist the opposition. In December 1951, in a message to Ala, Mosaddeq threatened to resign unless she too went abroad, while the shah pleaded with him not to proceed with his threat.[17] Eventually, after the July 1952 uprising (30 Tir), not only Ashraf but also the queen mother departed from the country. In addition, other members of the extended Pahlavi clan, including the shah's several brothers, with various political and business interests, were committed to protecting their privileges, which were threatened by Mosaddeq.

There was also a host of courtiers regularly liaising with the British embassy, some of whom were particularly active in stirring up opposition to Mosaddeq. Ernest Perron, the shah's Swiss private secretary and confidant, headed the list. He had befriended the shah in Switzerland, where, as crown prince, the monarch attended a private school. The friendship continued when

Perron moved to Iran, despite Reza Shah's deep suspicion of him. Enigmatic and oblique, Perron exercised considerable influence over the shah.[18] He believed that the shah's direct intervention against Mosaddeq could be "fatal."[19] His "favorite thesis" was that a "wise course of action" for the shah "was to do nothing" and act through the Majles.[20] Perron tirelessly met with British embassy personnel, particularly the equally elusive Robin Zaehner, a man of Swiss origin who had served as assistant press attaché and then press attaché at the embassy from 1943 to 1947. Zaehner was lecturer in Persian at Oxford and one of several British scholars of Iran who came from a diplomatic background, a man who seemed to relish exotic adventures and the thrill of espionage, and readily mixed scrupulous scholarly pursuits with inevitably unscrupulous meddling in the shady underworld of covert operations. He had been called upon to return to Tehran as acting counsellor, on the advice of his predecessor and fellow academic A. K. S. (Nancy) Lambton,[21] to help intensify the embassy's anti-Mosaddeq campaign.

Another courtier involved in anti-Mosaddeq machinations was the deputy court minister Ahmad Human [Basiji], a French-educated lawyer who had, as a member of the Edalat Party, cooperated with, among others, future senators Ali Dashti and Ebrahim Khajehnuri, as well as deputy Jamal Emami, who were all now at the forefront of Mosaddeq's staunchest opposition. Along with Perron, Human was embroiled with anti-Mosaddeq forces, acting, in the words of Zaehner, like a "beaver among the deputies."[22] Human blamed the court minister, Ala, for advising the shah to remain passive.[23] Perron, whose relations with Ala were strained, concurred. Earlier he had advocated Ala's replacement.[24] Soleiman Behbudi, a veteran senior court official identified by the CIA as a British agent,[25] appeared less active than Human. He did, however, play an important role in the crucial few weeks prior to the coup when the shah's unequivocal cooperation was being aggressively sought. Amir Asadollah Alam, the scion of a highly influential provincial family of magnates, had also established himself as an active royalist. He had assumed ministerial position when barely thirty years old, owing his political rise to his kin ties and to court patronage. In early July 1952/Tir 1331, Alam was appointed to manage the Pahlavi lands and properties, but his tasks involved a variety of other activities on behalf of the shah and other members of the royal family, including involvement in schemes to undermine Mosaddeq. He advocated and tried to promote a nonconciliatory policy toward Mosaddeq in coordination with his pro-British opponents.

In his zeal to advocate confrontation with Mosaddeq, Alam was too junior to override the shah's senior advisers: Court Minister Ala, the veteran royalist and devoted companion of both Reza Shah and his son, Gen. Mortaza Yazdanpanah, and Abolfath Diba [Heshmat al-Dawleh], Mosaddeq's half brother. Such men were, in Alam's view, responsible through "sheer incompetence" for the failure of Qavam and the return of Mosaddeq to power following the July uprising.[26] Alam's own court-sponsored anti-Mosaddeq activities eventually led to his effective exile to his native Birjand.[27] Following the coup he would resume his previous position; as a devoted servant of the shah he seemed happy even to play the role of an "errand boy,"[28] but he actively groomed himself for grander positions. For some time after the coup, impressed by the dogged British campaign to defeat Mosaddeq, he relentlessly sought British advice or support on numerous occasions.[29]

Despite tacitly approving or condoning covert court-based anti-Mosaddeq activities, the shah, almost until the very end of Mosaddeq's tenure as premier, seemed unsure that any statesman other than Mosaddeq would be able to negotiate a publicly acceptable oil settlement and extricate the country from crisis.[30] Nor was he willing, despite the immense pressures on him, to modify his passive stand. He could not have failed to realize that persistent passivity would also be deeply damaging to his standing and lingering desire to become the country's undisputed leader. He would, therefore, try on various occasions not only to persuade his supporters that his inaction was expedient but, particularly after the February 28, 1953/9 Esfand 1331 episode (see below), cautiously to reassure them that at the propitious moment he would not hesitate to act.

To the chagrin and frustration of his supporters, the shah continued, however, assiduously to pursue a strategy of avoidance and evasion. He wanted to defer any blatant opposition to Mosaddeq until the latter's public support and appeal had been clearly undermined, his failures demonstrated, and, ideally, at least some of those who had helped to bring him to power had actively joined the opposition against him.[31] The crucial February 1953 episode led the shah and others to conclude that at least to some extent this had already happened. Prior to the February episode the shah's predominant position was to adhere to a nonconfrontational strategy and encourage the opposition tacitly and discreetly, while acting in such a way as to be able plausibly to claim noninvolvement.

Heartened by the February episode, the shah began more discernibly, but still indirectly, to support anti-Mosaddeq activities. In justifying his refusal directly to support the plan of the CIA and the British Secret Intelligence Service (SIS) to overthrow Mosaddeq, he maintained, among other things, that he was not "an adventurer and hence could not take the chances of one." [32] Clearly the shah faced a deeply unsettling dilemma: to continue to bide his time, face an uncertain future, even jeopardize his retention of the throne, or to try to secure his position through collaboration with an Anglo-American plan. He could not but fear that such a collaboration, in case of failure, would disgrace the monarchy and terminate his reign and even the dynasty; even if successful, it would, upon disclosure, inevitably mar his credibility and legitimacy. In view of such disturbing considerations, the shah still clearly preferred Mosaddeq to be unseated by domestic forces and quasi-legal means. Finally, he hesitatingly agreed to collaborate with the plan; enlisting his seemingly unequivocal collaboration, however, required various assurances, enormous pressure, even barely disguised threats, and a host of intermediaries dispatched as part of the joint CIA-SIS operations. Such intermediaries included Princess Ashraf. She initially showed "no enthusiasm at all," [33] but upon being furnished with a substantial amount of money by the SIS officer Norman Darbyshire, she pledged full cooperation. [34] On July 25, 1953, Ashraf returned to Iran for a brief stay, to plead with and encourage her brother and reassure him that proposals put to him by the Rashidian brothers carried Anglo-American approval. She paved the way for the intercession of others such as General Norman Schwarzkopf and Kermit Roosevelt, reinforcing the efforts of the relentlessly persistent Asadollah Rashidian. [35]

The shah's lingering dilemmas had not been readily understood or appreciated by most royalists or by other domestic and foreign opponents of Mosaddeq. Some of the shah's senior confidants were, however, for some time inclined to share his anxieties and apprehensions. Ala, previously described by Mosaddeq as an old friend, "well-meaning, humble, temperamentally democratic and sincere," [36] was for many months of the opinion that Mosaddeq "must go honorably." [37] Before actively turning against Mosaddeq, particularly after July 1952, he represented the more prudent royalists who had been unwilling to press the shah prematurely for precipitous action. General Yazdanpanah, Mosaddeq's war minister from December 1952 to July 1953, had also seemed apprehensive of the consequences of drastic open and premature confrontation with Mosaddeq, as was the other court confidant, Abolfath Diba, who also counseled caution.

Ala in particular, although entirely pro-Western, had in fact not been unsympathetic to certain aspects of Mosaddeq's ideas. Nor would he disagree with the substance of Mosaddeq's objections to the conduct of the royal family. As a veteran court minister, Ala had long resented and disapproved of the activities of members of the royal family; in October 1947, in a letter to Sayyed Hasan Taqizadeh, then Iranian ambassador to Britain, while complaining of the mutual frictions and jealousies of the two sisters Ashraf and Shams, he wrote, "The queen mother interferes in all the affairs of the court and has tremendous influence, which she abuses; her retinue are all corrupt . . . ; it would be very expedient if the shah would send his mother to Mashhad or Switzerland."[38] Following the coup and the resumption of his duties as court minister, Ala made explicit recommendations to the shah concerning the conduct of the monarch and the royal family that in substance and spirit resembled what Mosaddeq had advocated.[39] Specifically, Ala was critical of the shah's mother and more so of Princess Ashraf, with whom he had never had cordial relations.[40] Members of the royal family gradually returned to Iran after August 1953, but Ashraf's return was considerably delayed. A few days after the coup, Ala wrote to the shah, "It has been heard that Her Royal Highness, the Queen Mother, and Princess Ashraf intend to return to Iran shortly. As they will not abandon their previous behavior and will certainly resume their customary interference in political affairs, and will surround themselves with notorious elements such as [Abbas] Shahandeh, Boyuk Saber, [Mohammad Ali] Nosratian, Jamal Emami, [Mehdi] Pirasteh, and others, it is in His Majesty's interest not to permit them to return, and if they do, they should not remain in Tehran."[41]

Ala's attitude to Mosaddeq, however, shifted gradually but drastically; even well before the July uprising, Ala had perceptibly turned against Mosaddeq. He particularly concentrated on enlisting the support of the willing Henderson to put pressure on the shah to act. Concerned that the shah's passivity was damaging to his prestige,[42] Ala persuaded Henderson to encourage the shah to act more decisively. Henderson reminded the shah that if Mosaddeq stayed on and continued with his oil policies, Iran would continue to "drift towards ruin."[43] The strategy of involving Henderson would have entailed not only a sharing of responsibility for the consequences of action against Mosaddeq but also greater commitment from Henderson to support a successor to Mosaddeq. Thanks to Ala and for some time unknown to Mosaddeq, Henderson was fully informed of all developments in the relationship between the shah and Mosaddeq, developments that, in Mosaddeq's view, did not concern a foreign ambassador. In the course of events leading to the February 1953 episode in particular, Ala not only sought to embroil Henderson in the conflict between Mosaddeq and the shah but increasingly encouraged him to put pressure on the shah to act against Mosaddeq. Actively siding with Zahedi as Mosaddeq's successor, Ala tried to enlist the Grand Ayatollah Mohammad Hossein Borujerdi's support for Zahedi.[44] He increasingly reminded the shah that failure to act decisively against Mosaddeq would be detrimental to the monarch. Unwavering in his strategy of avoiding direct confrontation with Mosaddeq, the shah continued to await and only indirectly encourage action by the Majles. Ala had not himself given up hope that the Majles could be used to unseat Mosaddeq. In mid–April 1953, in collusion with Henderson, he devised a scheme to prevent a parliamentary quorum, with the aim of aggravating further the intense conflict between the Majles opposition and Mosaddeq's government.[45] Such activities on Ala's part, which could no longer be easily disguised, resulted in his resignation on April 21, 1953/1 Ordibehesht 1332, and his replacement by Abolqasem Amini, who served as acting court minister.

The judicious former prime minister Mohammad Ali Foroughi had described Ala as "simple minded and unreflective, but hard working and sincere."[46] Qasem Ghani, the sharply judgmental, learned politician and diplomat, concurred with this assessment in his more generous moments. He had, however, feared that Ala's "stupidity" could result in his manipulation by agents of foreign embassies.[47] Ala's political conduct vis-à-vis Mosaddeq cannot, however, be satisfactorily explained in terms of his manipulation by Henderson; indeed it appears that it was Ala who was trying to do the manipulating. On the other hand, such contextually complicated relations, affected by a variety of unexpressed interests and considerations, invariably involved various degrees of mutual manipulation.

Clearly the royalists, both civil and military, resented, disliked, or were baffled by the royal attitude. Whether owing their position of prominence to royal patronage or viewing a strong monarchy as a symbol and guarantor of stability, their idée fixe was that Mosaddeq's continuation in office would seriously endanger the foundations of the monarchy. The attitudes of many royalists overlapped with those of the Anglophiles; they both castigated Mosaddeq for deviating from the Constitution and harming national interests. In the absence of a clear royal lead, many royalists were, however, unwilling openly to oppose Mosaddeq or they invoked the absence of such leadership to justify their own inaction. The position of the Anglophiles was, however, different.

The Anglophiles

The Anglophiles were the product and promoters of a milieu in which belief in the pervasiveness of British influence saturated the political culture. They consisted of an assortment of politicians, journalists, and other public figures who

had close links with the British embassy or the AIOC, both effectively functioning as institutional components of Iranian politics. The Anglophiles genuinely or tactically favored active British influence, which they appeared to
consider not only ineradicable but altogether beneficial for the country. Some
of them maintained that the interests of Britain and Iran converged intimately.
Virtually all of them benefited from actual or putative links with Britain. They
were often influence peddlers, and their primary mode of public activity was
political brokerage.

Many Anglophiles feared the decline of British influence more than they
did the weakening of the shah. They and many other opponents of Mosaddeq
basically concurred on a common conventional wisdom concerning the political possibilities of Iranian society. They shared an overlapping consensus, albeit
implicit, that an oligarchy of notables and clusters of high-ranking influence
peddlers should be politically predominant, under the auspices of a monarchical regime strong enough to ensure the perpetuation of the existing order and
weak enough to be incapable of undermining it. They were not favorable to
royal autocracy and wished to remain capable of manipulating or influencing
the shah. Many of them were hampered by the realization that in the context of
the prevailing nationalism, openly supporting Britain was ill advised and unpa-
triotic, and could even be construed as treason. On the other hand, they believed that complacency vis-à-vis Mosaddeq was tantamount to abandoning
much of their influence and interests. Convinced that in its confrontation with
Mosaddeq Britain would ultimately emerge victorious, they could reassure
themselves that they were siding with the winner. Although they varied in their
actual pro-British commitment as well as their motives and assumptions, they
generally tended to consider measures such as the nationalization of the oil
industry as impractical and dangerous. Some were concerned that the decline
of British influence would pave the way for communism, and many of them
justified their anti-Mosaddeq stance by invoking the threat of communism,
the dangers for Iranian national interests of antagonizing Britain, or the need
for countering U.S. influence.[48] Mosaddeq rejected the Anglophiles' contention that if the British did not derive any tangible benefits from Iran, the
British government would have no reason to defend Iran's independence; in
his view historically, the British government had never believed in Iranian
independence.[49]

The most influential and consistent Anglophile was Sayyed Zia al-Din
Tabataba'i, collaborator of Reza Khan in the coup of 1921, who had reentered
the Iranian political scene after an exile of twenty-two years. Toward the end of

World War II, through activities such as the organization of a right-wing political party (the National Will Party), he played an important role in anticommunist activities, enjoying the assistance of Zaehner and a number of other
British embassy personnel and agents. Widely regarded as dedicated to promoting British influence in Iran, he was reviled by leftists and civic nationalists.
Aided by the wealthy, who feared the growth of the Tudeh Party, he was
elected as a deputy to the Fourteenth Majles. Although he subsequently did
not serve in any parliamentary or governmental capacity, he maintained close
links with the shah and remained informally capable of exerting considerable
influence in Iranian politics. He also consistently provided the British embassy
with detailed advice and was invariably regarded by British officials as the most
desirable and suitable prime ministerial candidate. In fact, he had been expecting to be appointed prime minister by the shah when, due to the apparent
blunder of another, albeit more discreet and realistic, Anglophile, Jamal
Emami, Mosaddeq was invited to accept the premiership. It would appear that
Emami had not believed that Mosaddeq would accept the office; more significantly, he did not seem convinced that Sayyed Zia, in view of his notoriety as a
dedicated Anglophile, stood a real chance of becoming or succeeding as a viable prime minister when the nationalist movement was at its peak and Mosaddeq's popularity uncontested.

Emami's assumption was not shared by the British Foreign Office, the embassy, or AIOC officials, who had been actively promoting Sayyed Zia's premiership for some time. Undeterred by their setback or the misgivings of some
of their more prudent Iranian supporters, the British continued for some time
to promote him actively as Mosaddeq's successor. This contextually inexplicable insistence was rooted in the British tendency either to dismiss nationalism as
a pernicious phenomenon to be countered,[50] or to view Iranian nationalism as
represented by Mosaddeq as spurious and artificial, an incoherent and transi-
tory outburst of superficial emotions and irrational xenophobia.[51] The British,
clearly unwilling to countenance the anti-imperialist thrust and resonance of
Iranian nationalism, and unrelenting in their deep-seated belief concerning the
intrinsic flaws of the "Persian character," which they had long derided as infused not only with emotionalism and irrationality but also with duplicity and
cowardice, believed that a show of force, resolution, and firmness would produce the desired results.

The result sought by the British was either to force Mosaddeq to accept an
oil arrangement that in effect did not significantly differ from a fifty-fifty split
of profits, or to engineer his downfall and reach a settlement with his successor.

Perceptually ill-equipped and politically unwilling to comprehend or recognize the extensive public support for the movement that had resulted in the nationalization of the oil industry and the premiership of Mosaddeq, they began, as soon as Mosaddeq assumed office, actively to undermine him with the aim of forcing him to capitulate or quit.[52] They encouraged and supported the Anglophiles and were, in turn, aided and abetted by them.

The Anglophiles maintained that the overriding British strategy in countering Mosaddeq had to be emphatic refusal to negotiate with him seriously or to concede to him. Fearing that any breakthrough in negotiations would mean that they would lose their raison d'être, they not only encouraged the British not to compromise but also endeavored to push Mosaddeq toward intransigence. Following the failure of early and perfunctory attempts to reach an oil settlement, and much encouraged by their Iranian supporters, the British began increasingly to propagate, through the BBC, the idea of the futility of negotiations with Mosaddeq and the impossibility of reaching a settlement with him.[53] This, in effect, became a self-fulfilling prophesy. Eventually, either Mosaddeq had to be toppled or there had to be a radical modification in British and AIOC policies.

The primary Iranian component of the operational core of anti-Mosaddeq activities consisted of the Rashidian brothers (Asadollah, Saifollah, and Qodratollah), dedicated SIS agents and well-to-do businessmen whose father, Habibollah, had also served the British. They collaborated extensively with the British embassy's intelligence-gathering and operational networks, and in particular with Zaehner. Zaehner's brief was "to rely on the SIS to provide him with any amount of money he needed to secure the overthrow of Mosaddeq through legal or quasi-legal means." Many British officials in Tehran and London were not "officially" informed of Zaehner's activities. He distributed large sums of money, often hidden in empty biscuit tins, to promote and sustain opposition to Mosaddeq. Altogether he spent "well over a million and a half pounds," distributed via the Rashidians.[54] The recipients of these sums, enormous by local standards, and the precise ways in which they were used are not as yet known, but they were spent on activities likely to subvert and bring down Mosaddeq's government, including supporting certain opposition groups and organizations, payments to actual or would-be effective opponents, subsidizing the opposition press, promoting propaganda damaging to Mosaddeq's image and credibility, provoking antigovernment discontent and its vocal expression, mobilizing mob leaders, leaders of the guilds, and other influence peddlers in the bazaar and among the traditional strata, providing protection for prominent opponents, and helping to sustain and strengthen the organizational and infra-structural bases of support for viable contenders for succeeding Mosaddeq, such as Sayyed Zia, Qavam, and later Zahedi.

Whether the Rashidians provided any account of how they spent the money, and the extent to which they themselves benefited, is also unknown. They seemed willing to resort to any action likely to contribute to the defeat of Mosaddeq. The flamboyance of the Rashidians could not, however, over-shadow their inadequacies and failings. The CIA was concerned about their "weaknesses"; the SIS was also "aware" but maintained that "one of the strongest points in their favour was their avowed willingness to risk their pos-sessions and their lives in an attempt against Mossadeq [*sic*]." The CIA con-curred, noting that "in the critical days of August 1953 the Rashidians did display such a willingness."[55] The Rashidians maintained an extensive network of contacts among Tehran's political circles, including members of the royal family, in particular Princess Ashraf, and had access to the shah. Asadollah would remain close to the shah, acting in various capacities on his behalf.[56] As entrepreneurs, their collaboration with Britain enabled them to enrich them-selves further. After the coup, when the virtually all-new British embassy staff in Tehran wished to distance themselves from the less savory aspects of past British policies, the Rashidians would be politically shunned or encouraged not to invoke their links with Britain for material advantage. The Foreign Of-fice would, of course, be constantly reminded of their indispensable services during the Mosaddeq era by their erstwhile patrons and loyal friends, particu-larly Sam Falle, the former Oriental counsellor in Tehran.[57]

Besides Zaehner, the British personnel involved in various aspects of the anti-Mosaddeq campaign of destabilization included Oriental counsellors Lancelot Pyman and Sam Falle. Col. Geoffrey Wheeler, a former Oriental counsellor who had served in Iran from 1946 to 1950 and headed the MI6 (the external arm of the SIS) station in the country, also returned for some time to help with the anti-Mosaddeq moves. His successor was C. M. "Monty" Wood-house, who arrived in Tehran in mid-August 1951 and "took up a nominal post" in the embassy.[58] Woodhouse was assisted by Norman Darbyshire, an-other MI6 officer. Darbyshire had been able to acquire an intimate knowledge of Iranian politics, having served in Tehran from late 1943 until mid-1947, when for three and a half years he shared a house with Zaehner. He returned to the country in late 1949 and again served in Iran, from 1963 to 1967.[59]

Encouraged and assisted by a host of embassy personnel and SIS agents, the Anglophiles and their hangers-on engaged in a protracted, bitter, and multifaceted war of attrition against Mosaddeq. The locus of the opposition to Mosaddeq was a vociferous minority of deputies in the Sixteenth Majles. Virtually all of these deputies and gradually a sizeable number of senators, as well as many journalists, were directly or indirectly, financially or otherwise, supported by the British embassy. The Majles opposition, consisting of some sixteen deputies, was led by Jamal Emami.

Born in 1901 into an Azeri family of religious and political notables, the Belgian-educated Emami became active in the post-Reza Shah era as a member of Ali Dashti's Edalat Party. He served as a deputy in the Fourteenth Majles, was among the pro-Western politicians detained by Qavam in 1946 to conciliate the Soviet government, served as a minister without portfolio, and was elected to the Sixteenth Majles. He maintained an extensive network of social and political contacts and had close links with the court, most notably with Princess Ashraf, as well as with many other opponents of Mosaddeq, among them Zahedi. He cultivated a clientele that included well-known mob leaders. As a right-wing anticommunist, he was opposed to Mosaddeq's advocacy of neutralism and viewed him as reckless in his antagonism to Britain and complacent in his attitude toward the Tudeh Party.

The enormity of the problems that Mosaddeq faced, particularly the oil issue and determined British hostility, led many Anglophiles, including Jamal Emami and particularly Sayyed Zia, to believe that Mosaddeq's premiership would be short-lived.[60] And yet the Anglophiles, backed by the British embassy and the court, impatiently sought to hasten his downfall. Their strategy included full utilization and manipulation of parliamentary procedures and loopholes. Relying on the core of deputies openly opposed to Mosaddeq, they orchestrated quasi-parliamentary maneuvers, spearheaded by deputies such as Emami and Mohammad Ali Shushtari, who increasingly subjected the premier to acrimonious and abusive speeches. They tried to utilize various opportunities and pretexts to break the quorum in the Majles; they packed the Majles spectators' gallery with ruffians whose task was to shower the prime minister with invective with the aim of undermining his aura and public image. They relentlessly chastised Mosaddeq, accusing him both of failing to compromise with the British and of being in collusion with them; they accused him both of resorting to heavy-handed suppression and of tolerating and encouraging disorder. They encouraged seeking sanctuary in the Majles or mosques as a publicly visible, symbolically evocative protest against an unjust and intolerant government. Through the press, on the floor of the Majles, or by other means and venues, they disseminated malicious rumors as part of a war of nerves and psychological campaign of attrition. Their disorientation-enhancing harassment paved the way for and foreshadowed those activities later resorted to more intensively by the combined operations of the CIA and SIS. The parliamentary opponents continued unfailingly to insist that the British should not negotiate with Mosaddeq or make any significant concessions to him. Mosaddeq's success would have meant the negation of the very conditions that had sustained them. The prospect of a real breakthrough in negotiations would have ended the distribution of large sums of money by the Rashidians. The opposition strongly disapproved of and regretted the internationalization of the oil dispute, such as the British appeal to the United Nations, which, they maintained, offered Mosaddeq the opportunity to present himself as Iran's national champion and render opposition to him exceedingly difficult.[61]

Besides Sayyed Zia and the hard core of activist Anglophiles, the British embassy benefited from the cooperation of other more discreet supporters of Britain, who provided the embassy with detailed advice on how to handle Mosaddeq. Hadi Taheri, a veteran deputy and influential political patron who covertly opposed Mosaddeq, advised the embassy to deny Mosaddeq any chance of success regarding the settlement of the oil dispute and to designate his successor, preferably Sayyed Zia, who would then organize and protect his own supporters and vigorously campaign to unseat Mosaddeq. Everything should be done, he argued, to encourage the shah to oppose Mosaddeq.[62] Other Anglophiles, including Hossein Farhudi, Azizollah Nikpay, Hasan Mokarram, Ahmad E'tebar, and Ali Sohaili, provided similar advice. Anglophiles who were confidants of the court, such as Senators Ali Dashti and Javad Emami (Zahir al-Islam), as well as Hasan Emami (Emam-e Jom'eh) and Alam, insisted that the British embassy should give the shah decisive advice and press him for action.[63] Reza Hekmat, Speaker of the Majles, while publicly feigning neutrality, claimed credit for initiating the tactic of sit-ins or sanctuary seeking. Insisting on the necessity of a certain amount of bloodshed in the process of unseating Mosaddeq, he advocated recruiting a few hundred "assassins" to bring this about.[64] Others, such as former minister Abbasqoli Golsha'iyan, maintained that nothing other than a "direct American approach" would affect the shah.[65]

Despite the expressed reservations of many Anglophiles, Sayyed Zia remained Britain's favored candidate to succeed Mosaddeq. Encouraged by the shah and with the help of the Rashidians, Sayyed Zia revived his National Will Party in September 1951,[66] with the aim of lending substance to his claim to be a credible successor to Mosaddeq and detaching the traditional middle-class strata from the pro-Mosaddeq movement. Scarcely any of his notable Iranian supporters, including his brother, believed, however, that he would be palatable as prime minister immediately after Mosaddeq, given his incontrovertible Anglophile reputation.[67] The British embassy, nevertheless, insisted on him.[68] Incessantly, albeit indirectly, pressed by the British to support Sayyed Zia, the shah, unable to comprehend the wisdom of such a move, was only likely to become more suspicious of the real British aims. Although he saw Sayyed Zia on a weekly basis,[69] he was certain that siding with him would be to defy Iranian nationalism openly and dangerously.[70]

Eventually, in the face of royal as well as American opposition, Sayyed Zia and his British supporters reluctantly resigned themselves to seeking an alternative. Ahmad Qavam, the senior patrician and veteran statesman, had seemed a far more viable contender to replace Mosaddeq than Sayyed Zia. Encouraged by many of Mosaddeq's opponents, he was aided by a host of active supporters, including the influential senator Nikpur, politicians Abbas Eskandari and Ahmad Ali Sepehr, and the talented journalist Hasan Arsanjani, as well as by less prominent henchmen and go-betweens such as Daliri, Ali Arianpour, Moqtader Shaf'ia, and Ahadpur. Undeterred by his age and the enormity of the challenge, the octogenarian Qavam had for some time come to view himself as the only credible alternative to Mosaddeq. He enjoyed the active backing of the shah's mother but faced the unenviable task of enlisting the unequivocal favor of the shah, who seemed at best noncommittal. Relations between the two had never been cordial. In 1947 the shah had engineered the disintegration of Qavam's Democratic Party of Iran and his ouster as prime minister. Qavam had later retaliated by publicly rebuking the shah's encroachments against the Constitution, provoking a bitterly reproachful response from the court minister, Ebrahim Hakimi.[71]

Qavam also faced the far easier task of overcoming the opposition of the British, who had harbored a deep-seated grudge against him since his sudden anti-British stance of 1947. They and Sayyed Zia feared that there was a possibility that as premier he could be tempted to become intransigent. In the wake of the extensive activities of his clientele and promises of goodwill that he and his supporters provided, prompted by Sayyed Zia the British demanded certain assurances from Qavam, who complied by submitting a signed pledge to be cooperative on the oil issue.[72] This helped remove any obstacle to active British support for him. Royal misgivings, however, proved more resilient; nor had he as yet succeeded in enlisting the support of Henderson. Pessimistic about his prospects, Qavam left for Europe in late December 1951. Once again, and with no more tangible success, Sayyed Zia stepped in to test his chances as a serious contender for the premiership.

The types of politicians at the forefront of anti-Mosaddeq opposition, including Jamal Emami and Sayyed Zia, and the nature of the activities they resorted to, worried others who disagreed with Mosaddeq on certain issues but were in principle sympathetic to his campaign to promote Iranian national sovereignty. The latter, including Senate president Sayyed Hasan Taqizadeh and a number of other senators affiliated with the small but influential Amiyun group, were averse to entanglement in foreign-backed activities against Mosaddeq. Taqizadeh dismissed the justifiability and morality of such entanglements and rejected the legitimacy and propriety of British pressure on Iranian politicians to oppose Mosaddeq. He told Henry Grady, Henderson's predecessor, that Mosaddeq "was the only man who can present a program to the Majles that has any chance of acceptance."[73] Taqizadeh favored the continuation of efforts to reach a settlement with Mosaddeq. In fact, one factor that helped to reduce the effectiveness of British-backed opposition to Mosaddeq was Taqizadeh's refusal to cooperate in mobilizing senators to act in concert with the Majles opposition against Mosaddeq.

Viewed as strongly pro-British not only by left-wingers and nationalists but also by certain royalists such as Alam,[74] Taqizadeh had often acted with greater patriotic dignity than many of his detractors. He had long deplored and condemned the ways in which some of his compatriots had, in the post-1941 era, tried to ingratiate themselves with the British embassy.[75] He regretted the exaggerated manner in which his compatriots attributed enormous power to Britain.[76] As a deputy in the Fifteenth Majles, seemingly prompted by Abbas Eskandari—the vociferous supporter of Qavam who had found it politically opportune to champion Iran's sovereign rights over its sources of oil as well as over Bahrain's—Taqizadeh made a seminal speech in which he revealed the circumstances surrounding the signing of the despised oil agreement of 1933.[77] He asserted that as finance minister he had indeed signed the agreement, but he had merely acted as an unwilling and hapless accomplice of the dictatorial Reza Shah. Through this speech, which considerably strengthened the case of the critics and opponents of the AIOC, Taqizadeh hoped to atone for what he had done in 1933.[78]

Taqizadeh refused to bow to pressure from the British ambassador, Sir Francis Shepherd, to follow the example of Reza Hekmat, the Speaker of the Majles. He bluntly chastised Shepherd for his inappropriate meddling in Iranian domestic politics, leading the ambassador to commend him for his "statesmanship."[79] Taqizadeh's relations with Sayyed Zia and Qavam were not cordial, and he disapproved of them as contenders for succeeding Mosaddeq; his refusal to cooperate with the British-sponsored anti–Mosaddeq opposition was, however, more discernibly informed by patriotic sensibilities than other considerations. In the summer of 1952, when more senators turned openly against Mosaddeq. Mosaddeq's supporters began to look upon the Senate as a bastion of royalist and pro-British opposition. As moves to neutralize the Senate gained momentum, Taqizadeh would also join the opponents of Mosaddeq. Although disapproving of "extremism" and of certain of Mosaddeq's tactics and conduct, he continued to lend qualified support to many of the premier's objectives.[80]

Unable to enlist the support of senators such as Taqizadeh, the anti-Mosaddeq opposition nevertheless included several senators, among them Dashti, Khajehnuri, Abbas Mas'udi, and Nikpur, who were not as vocal and open in their opposition as some of the deputies but were no less interested in precipitating Mosaddeq's downfall. In their destabilization efforts, the government's opponents continued to utilize both the Majles and the Senate. Taking advantage of Mosaddeq's almost seven-week absence from the country, in the course of which he defended Iran's case before the UN Security Council, they unsuccessfully tried to postpone the elections for the Seventeenth Majles. Their failure was partly due to Taqizadeh's refusal to allow the Majles bill for electoral postponement to be approved by the Senate. Upon Mosaddeq's return (November 23, 1951) and his call for a vote of confidence, his Majles opponents were only able to cast sixteen votes of abstention, while the Senate voted unanimously for Mosaddeq.

As the Sixteenth Majles was approaching the end of its term, the increasingly desperate opposition intensified its efforts. In December 1951, street clashes between left-wing and right-wing opponents of the government and its supporters provided the dejected parliamentary opposition with new pretext and ammunition. Fifteen deputies took sanctuary in the Majles, joined by more than twenty journalists.[81] Some forty-five clerics also took sanctuary in a nearby mosque. On December 11, upon attending the Majles, Mosaddeq was subjected to relentless invective from both opposition deputies and preinstalled spectators in the public gallery.[82] The National Front reacted by organizing pro-Mosaddeq demonstrations. The prime minister threatened to resign, primarily attributing responsibility for the intensification of antigovernment activities to the queen mother, while the shah and Ala urged him not to resign.[83]

The very prospect of the government entering into negotiations with the World Bank in late 1951 further frustrated Mosaddeq's opponents, who had long advocated a strict policy of nonnegotiation with the Mosaddeq government. The news that Mosaddeq would personally attend The Hague to represent the Iranian case before the International Court of Justice was an added blow to the opposition. As elections for the Seventeenth Majles were approaching, some opposition deputies began to seek reconciliation with the Mosaddeqists. The contention that Mosaddeq's prime ministerial tenure would be short-lived had proved clearly unwarranted. The British could not console themselves that their efforts and expenditure in sustaining Mosaddeq's parliamentary and other opponents had paid commensurate dividends. Conversely, frustrated opposition leaders such as Jamal Emami and Abolhasan Amidi-Nuri blamed the British embassy for the opposition's failure.[84] In desperation, Emami led the tabling of an abortive motion of interpellation against the government, but the impending elections meant that there would be no quorum to debate the motion. Emami and his acolytes appealed to the court but to no avail.

The opponents now began assiduously to pursue a two-pronged strategy: to use any means possible to deny Mosaddeq a reliable majority in the Seventeenth Majles, and also to concentrate on the Senate as a focus of growing anti-Mosaddeq opposition. As Taheri noted, the absence of a quorum rule made the Senate more effective in undermining Mosaddeq; the British continued, through Hekmat among others, to persuade senators more openly to oppose Mosaddeq.[85] Measures were also adopted to enhance the Senate's public profile. With the aim of making the Senate an authoritative locus for hearing and redressing antigovernment complaints, arrangements were made, for instance, for anti-Mosaddeq representations by guilds to be made to the Senate.

Mosaddeq's policy of refraining from improper governmental interference in the elections considerably benefited his opponents; the court, army commanders, and local notables ensured that opponents of the government were elected in many provincial and rural areas. With the support of the court, for instance, the notorious Mehdi Mir-Ashrafi was elected deputy for Meshkinshahr in Azerbaijan,[86] while the royalist Shi'ite cleric Hasan Emami won the seat for the Kurdish-Sunni city of Mahabad, which he had never visited.[87] Mosaddeq's realization that his opponents, particularly the shah, were determined to deny him a cooperative Majles, together with actual or threatened violence and disorder in a number of areas, led Mosaddeq to suspend the elections after only seventy-nine deputies had been elected.

In a sternly worded letter to the Majles, Mosaddeq raised the issue of undeniable electoral abuses and irregularities, appealing to the deputies to address and rectify them.[88] However, despite his expressed desire that the credentials of those who had been fraudulently elected, that is, the likes of Mir-Ashrafi and Emami, be rejected, Hasan Emami was elected Speaker of the Majles. The composition of the Majles and its likely political leanings were deeply encouraging to many Mosaddeq opponents. So certain was Perron of the impending collapse of the government by the parliamentary machinations of the new Majles that he asked Zaehner not to press for the return of Princess Ashraf, who had left Iran as a result of government pressure. Were she to return, Perron maintained, she would claim for herself the entire credit for Mosaddeq's fall.[89] The speakership of Emami, indicating an unmistakable defiance of Mosaddeq, was the result not only of the support that Emami enjoyed from the British and the Anglophiles, but also more crucially of the shah's willingness to endorse and favor him. Sayyed Zia, cooperating closely with Mir-Ashrafi and other opponents, appealed to the shah not only to help in this regard but also to support the credentials of the known anti-Mosaddeq deputies.[90] Hekmat, Khajehnuri, Taheri, Alam, and Gen. Abbas Garzan, the army's chief of staff, among others, joined with Sayyed Zia in support of Emami as Speaker.

Hasan Emami, a forty-eight-year-old lawyer and cleric, had studied Islamic theology in Iraq and law in Switzerland. During Reza Shah's reign he became a judge and discarded his religious attire, which he resumed in 1947 upon assuming the royally sanctioned position of Tehran's congregational prayer leader *(enam-e jom'eh),* long held in his family. In August 1950, he narrowly escaped an assassination attempt on his life. He was closely associated with the court and, although related to Mosaddeq, was staunchly hostile to him. As a committed Anglophile he regretted and criticized what he considered to be inadequate British attention to Iran, leaving the country, a "three-year-old child," to its own devices and allowing the Americans to gain the upper hand.[91] He was one of those who demanded money from the British in order to engage in propaganda and to form "gangs" to counter Mosaddeq.[92]

Setback: The July 21, 1952/30 Tir 1331 Uprising

One of Hasan Emami's chief tasks as Speaker of the Majles was to restart and invigorate the Parliament-based campaign to unseat Mosaddeq, focusing on Qavam as the leading viable candidate for replacing the premier. In view of the shah's attitude, the question of a successor to Mosaddeq had remained unresolved. Qavam's return to Iran in the second week of April after an absence of three and a half months had rekindled the hopes of his supporters. The court, particularly the shah's mother, Princess Ashraf, and Prince Abd al-Reza, actively favored him, as did Hassan Emami. Not only did Middleton, the British chargé d'affaires, avidly work to support him, but Henderson, who had met Qavam twice, also proved favorable. Privy to the details of shah-Mosaddeq relations through Ala and assisted by him, Henderson had been encouraging the shah to act against Mosaddeq and to assert his authority.[93] The adverse consequences of open British support for Qavam were not ignored. "I think," Zaehner noted, "it would be a tactical mistake to do any overt campaign on behalf of Qavam; we did this with Sayyed Zia and this did him no good."[94] Qavam was nevertheless perceived as enjoying not only active British support but also American backing. Even Sayyed Zia apparently recommended him to the shah. The shah continued, however, to remain noncommittal. Although the shah was encouraged to act by Ala, Yazdanpanah, and Dashti, who maintained that Mosaddeq did not enjoy the support of a parliamentary majority,[95] and reassured by the presence of a sizeable number of anti-Mosaddeq deputies in the Majles, he wanted the Majles to take the initiative in expressing its preference for Qavam; without a clear royal lead not enough deputies could, however, be prevailed upon to do so.

Aware of the ongoing and intensified maneuvers against him, Mosaddeq astutely opted to act assertively and from a position of strength. Despite moves to unseat him, fifty-two out of sixty-three deputies voted to support his renewed premiership, and despite intensive efforts among senators by British agents and embassy staff, particularly Sam Falle,[96] out of thirty-six senators, fourteen voted in Mosaddeq's favor, while nineteen abstained. Mosaddeq realized, however, that he could only meaningfully continue in office with enhanced authority. His desire to acquire extra powers, expressed in a private session of the Majles, provoked hostility, while his demand to extend civilian control over the army was rejected by the shah, leading the premier to tender his resignation on July 16, 1952, thus paving the way for the seemingly unproblematic appointment of Qavam.

With Mosaddeq's resignation on his own initiative, the painstaking efforts expended on Qavam's behalf resulted in an anticlimax and ended in a fiasco. The triumphalism of the rejoicing opposition soon gave way to confusion and despair. Despite Henderson's and Middleton's pressure on the shah to support Qavam actively and their own efforts to help him,[97] Qavam's position was doomed from the outset. He was perceptually ill equipped to navigate the new Iranian political landscape or comprehend the elite-transcending activism of an intrusive public infused with civic nationalism. He was as organizationally and practically unprepared as were his boastful supporters; his stern and ill-advised inaugural proclamation helped to aggravate his tenuous position and further provoke Kashani and the Mosaddeqists alike. He could hardly have expected or hoped to be able to consolidate his position merely on the basis of Anglo-American support and without dissolution of the Majles; such a course of action would not, however, readily commend itself to the shah. Qavam's ignominious fall following the violent uprising of July 21, 1952/30 Tir 1331 was a major setback for opponents of Mosaddeq, whether royalist or Anglophile. The disconcerted Anglophiles lost the support of Zaehner, a convivial participant in endless sessions of scheming and plotting, in which drinking and smoking opium had often seemed to constitute the main preoccupation. He returned to Oxford a disillusioned man, unsure about the prospects of the subversive anti-Mosaddeq campaign he had diligently worked to sustain.[98] The large sums of money he had spent had scarcely produced tangible results.

Previously, the British insistence on Sayyed Zia as successor to Mosaddeq had helped to justify the shah's strategy of avoidance and evasion. Courtiers such as Yazdanpanah and Diba had reminded the shah of the dangerous implications of supporting Sayyed Zia. The shah had perceived his own political survival as being more safely assured through adherence to constitutional formalities, an appearance of neutrality, and refusal to defy nationalist sensibilities. He had proved ready to condone any course of action against Mosaddeq as long as it did not directly involve or implicate him. The shah's position had, in turn, been invoked by those deputies who were under pressure from the British embassy in order to justify their own limited success in countering Mosaddeq. The shah seemed to have a more accurate appreciation of Mosaddeq's popularity and of the strength of the prevailing nationalism than did many of his advisers.[99] He appeared to view Mosaddeq as more trustworthy than Sayyed Zia or Qavam, and to understand the advantages and popular acceptability of any oil settlement worked out by Mosaddeq, in contrast to a settlement reached by an unpopular successor. He was, moreover, not only pressured by the royalists, as well as the Anglophiles and their foreign backers, but also by the Mosaddeqists.

Nevertheless, the shah's support for Hasan Emami's election to the speakership of the Seventeenth Majles was crucial and a turning point. It was fully consistent with his strategy, as his emissaries told the sardonically dismissive Zaehner that Mosaddeq should be removed by the Majles, the elections for which the premier had himself conducted, and by the very forces that had helped him to assume power.[100] The Anglophiles had regretted the shah's "complete collapse" or "virtual impotence,"[101] but his clear support for Emami's speakership, in defiance of Mosaddeq's expressed disapproval, could not be interpreted as anything other than a clear shift in the royal position. Of course, fearing the consequences, the shah failed to bolster Qavam actively and thus dealt a lethal blow to his chances. Qavam's defeat, in turn, damaged and humiliated the shah. Henderson had earlier reported, "I am becoming more and more convinced that he [the shah] is lacking in courage and in resolution; that he is conscious of his weaknesses and that he is inclined to endeavor to conceal his true character by finding excuses for inaction and even by laying blame for past mistakes on those around him." [102] The British, having long regarded the shah as hopelessly irresolute, came also to view him as decidedly anti-British. [103]

Mosaddeq had been adamant in not gratuitously providing the shah with any valid reason to fear the fate of the monarchy. [104] However, the shah's surrender of formal control over the army to Mosaddeq, and the latter's injunction barring deputy defense ministers from directly reporting to the shah, weakened the shah's position considerably. The closure of the private offices of the shah's brothers and sisters, the departure of the queen mother, Princess Ashraf, and several other members of the royal family from Iran, together with the suspension of Hasan Human and the resignation of Emami from the speakership and effectively from membership of the Majles, unmistakably indicated the shah's diminished stature, prestige, and authority. The shah could, ironically, feel vindicated in his misgivings about premature moves against Mosaddeq. Portraying himself as a hapless victim of a premier bent on defying constitutional procedures and practices could also help to win him sympathy and support.

The pro-British forces were soon to regroup and reconsider their tactics, awaiting new opportunities, which would soon arise. Mosaddeq's renewed popular mandate, his enhanced authority, and the extra powers he acquired from the Parliament, including formal control over the army, strengthened his position in the short run. His very success aggravated not only the deep-seated hostility of his old opponents but also the latent resentments of some of his prominent supporters. Such simmering resentments had, of course, long been stimulated by the British and royal agents. Perron credited the shah's "astute policy" for detaching Kashani, Makki, and Baqa'i from Mosaddeq, adding that "thanks to the shah, the National Front had practically ceased to exist." Zaehner attributed this development to factors "created and directed" by the Rashidians, adding that neither the shah nor Ashraf "deserved the slightest credit for anything." [105] The defection of disgruntled elements of the National Front cannot, however, in any sense be reduced to the mere consequences of the divisive techniques and ploys of such agents.

The Defectors

The main defectors from the ranks of Mosaddeq supporters were Ayatollah Abolqasem Kashani, Hossein Makki, Mozaffar Baqa'i, and Abolhasan Ha'erizadeh. They played an important role in the formation of the civic nationalist movement and a far more significant role in its destruction. They became "the most dangerous, the most harmful and the most callous enemies of Mosaddeq"[106] Their hostility greatly facilitated the task of Mosaddeq's other enemies. Their defection could be portrayed or seen by the British and the Americans as indicating that the civic nationalist movement had disintegrated and was vulnerable to Tudeh Party challenge. In their increasingly hostile criticism of Mosaddeq, the defectors had very few constructive or reflective suggestions to offer. Concerning the vexed issues of oil, economic difficulties, law and order, or the requirements of a viable constitutional polity, apart from indulging in generalities and slogans, they had no positive contribution to make.

The political cosmology of the defectors and many like-minded politicians, including Anglophiles such as Jamal Emami, seemed entirely devoid of probing reflections concerning the requirements of meaningful governance and the prerequisites of a functioning constitutional-parliamentary polity. They seemed unable to comprehend the necessity of an executive independent of the court and not vulnerable to royal intrigues, which enjoyed parliamentary support and was preferably sustained by party-political backing, and was thereby able effectively to execute its duties. They proved incapable of imagining the dangerous implications of inevitable political stalemate, which their preferred version of parliamentary politics entailed. If Makki, Baqa'i, or Kashani could have predicted what the coup of 1953 would involve in terms of enabling the foreign-backed monarchy to overshadow and undermine all constitutional provisions and institutions, it is highly unlikely that they would have readily helped to make it happen. They could not have imagined that the post-Mosaddeq era would foster and complete their own marginalization and exclusion. And yet their very failure to reflect on the possible consequences of their actions was itself symptomatic of the severe limitation of their political vision and perceptual capabilities. Such a failure was perhaps rooted more in their political mentality than in the constraints of character or purely opportunistic concerns. Yet their wholehearted support for anti-Mosaddeq forces seems inexplicable and incomprehensible purely in such benign terms as an absence of foresight. In the eyes of their Mosaddeqist ex-comrades, disagreements with Mosaddeq and dissatisfaction with their share of the transient political spoils were not sufficient grounds for actively helping to undermine a movement that they themselves had helped to create and whose seminal ideals they claimed unfailingly to support.

Save in their opposition to Mosaddeq the defectors' aims were not identical. Kashani primarily wished to reestablish himself in his populist role of commanding public support and attention, to reassert his claim to national leadership, and to influence the course of Iranian politics. Ha'erizadeh would have settled for more tangible gains. Baqa'i and Makki wanted to continue to enjoy the opportunity of liaising with the court as influential brokers. They also considered a real measure of royal authority as necessary to counterbalance Mosaddeq. Fearing Mosaddeq's marginalization of the shah as detrimental to their own interests, they increasingly sided with and bolstered the shah. They displayed a selective and utilitarian attitude to principles and ideals, and their conception of politics and constitutionalism, despite their populist postures, was essentially traditional, elitist, and manipulatory. In deserting the Mosaddeqists they could not join their pro-British counterparts, as they were fiercely anti-British. Their alliance with the royalists, however, entailed indirect cooperation with the Anglophiles. The defectors appeared to fear Mosaddeq's enhanced authority but not, it seems, the strong likelihood of royal autocracy sustained by the West as its alternative. They appeared myopically unconcerned with the consequences of siding with Mosaddeq's royalist and pro-Western opponents in seriously jeopardizing the very survival of a movement whose aims they still claimed to cherish.

Kashani

In his long political career Ayatollah Abolqasem Kashani skillfully utilized his religious credentials and his gifts both for tenacity and flexibility to advance his political ends. He fought British imperialism in Iraq and served as a member of the Constituent Assembly that formalized Reza Shah Pahlavi's assumption of the throne. Interned during World War II on grounds of pro-German sympathies and exiled by Qavam and later by the shah following the failed assassination attempt on the shah's life, Kashani returned to active politics by lending his support to the oil nationalization movement. The anti-imperialist character of the movement attracted him; it also afforded him an opportunity to assume national prominence.

Kashani considered his role in the movement as no less, if not more, crucial than that of Mosaddeq. He acted to protect or maintain his claim to being a leader at least of equal national stature as Mosaddeq, considering his support for Mosaddeq as vital for the latter's survival. At the same time, as a patron he remained responsive to the demands and expectations of his extensive clientele, including kinsmen. His efforts to satisfy this clientele included readily interceding on their behalf with governmental departments, tirelessly writing recommendations (*towsiyeh-nameh)* to this effect, and trying to influence the appointment of governmental personnel or the elections for the Seventeenth Majles. Such activities, and particularly the issue of the elections in which Kashani and his sons wished to play an active role, caused Mosaddeq and his supporters considerable consternation.[107]

During the first year of Mosaddeq's premiership, Kashani supported the Mosaddeqists in defeating concerted antigovernment moves; among other things, he helped to deter the shah from siding with contenders like Qavam. Relations between Kashani and Mosaddeq were, however, bound to deteriorate, as they differed in political values as well as approach and priorities but resembled each other in dismissing the justifiability of each other's claim to be indispensable to the movement's survival. Kashani had not refrained from expressing dissatisfaction with Mosaddeq even before the July uprising and favored candidates such as Javad Bushehri as Mosaddeq's successor.[108] Nevertheless, deeply averse to Qavam, Kashani played an important role in helping to unseat him in Mosaddeq's favor.

In the aftermath of the July uprising, aiming to intensify and looking forward to benefiting from the barely disguised rivalry between Kashani and Mosaddeq, the prime minister's opponents arranged for the election of Kashani as parliamentary Speaker. Baqa'i and Ha'erizadeh also played key roles in making this happen. Those very deputies who had previously rallied around Hasan Emami now extended their full support to Kashani. With Kashani as head of the legislature when Mosaddeq intended to enhance the authority of the executive, they had the added assurance that discord between the two men would be much augmented by conflict between the two offices. As predicted, personal differences between Kashani and Mosaddeq were aggravated by disagreements between the two in their official capacities. As Speaker of the Majles, Kashani was bound sanctimoniously to uphold the cause of "the Constitution" when Mosaddeq appeared to be deviating from it by rejecting its prevalent stalemate-generating interpretation.[109] The prevailing interpretation was shared by a host of Anglophiles such as Jamal Emami, Reza Hekmat, Hadi Taheri, and Sayyed Zia, and also by Kashani, Makki, Baqa'i, and Ha'erizadeh.

Following the July uprising, Kashani openly disapproved of a number of

Mosaddeq's appointees, including the deputy defense minister, but failed to sway Mosaddeq, who resented such interference in the administrative affairs of the country and viewed some of Kashani's moves as irresponsible.[110] Mosaddeq's policy was generally to ignore Kashani's ubiquitous recommendations on behalf of individuals. The dangers of open friction between the two leaders provoked mediation efforts and a much-publicized meeting in mid-September 1952. Real cooperation, however, proved increasingly unlikely. Reluctant to oppose Mosaddeq openly, for a considerable time Kashani continued to deny that there was any friction between them, and confined himself to the tactic of criticizing Mosaddeq's retinue while claiming to support the premier himself.[111] In December 1952, aggravated frictions came to the fore as Mosaddeq demanded that the extra powers granted to him by the Parliament be extended for a further twelve months. In his capacity not only as a leading national figure but also as Speaker of the Majles, Kashani publicly and sternly disapproved of such a move and tried to block it.[112]

The extra powers bill was, nevertheless, approved by an overwhelming vote; the humiliated Kashani retreated, claiming that his pronouncements had been misunderstood. The alarming deterioration in relations between the two leaders resulted in protracted efforts to work out a rapprochement, but to little avail. In late January 1953, for instance, mediation efforts resulted in a meeting between the two and a declaration of continued cooperation, but there was no doubt that the two leaders' paths had unbridgeably diverged.[113] Kashani increasingly insisted on the necessity of the proper observance of the Constitution and encouraged moves likely to aggravate Mosaddeq's difficulties, while Mosaddeq pointedly ignored him, believing that the prerequisites of a sustained mutual understanding and consensus over critical issues facing the government were lacking. Mosaddeq realized that Kashani was determined to resort to any measure, particularly in his capacity as Speaker, to paralyze the prime minister and strengthen the shah. He did not, however, appear to appreciate fully the implications of Kashani's irretrievable alienation and may have underrated the extent of Kashani's readiness to side actively with the royalists and the Anglophiles to engineer his collapse.

On the eve of the February 28, 1953/9 Esfand 1331 episode, some Mosaddeqists, embittered by Kashani's hostility and his closeness to the shah, favored first attenuating Kashani's residual influence and then similarly dealing with the shah.[114] No move was, however, made against Kashani, while the February episode provided him with an opportunity to avenge his recent setbacks. As a CIA report observed, he used the shah in the course of this episode to further

Majlis Speaker Ayatollah Kashani and Prime Minister Mosaddeq
conferring on January 28, 1953, during the battle with Parliament
over Mosaddeq's demand for extended emergency powers.
Copyright © 2003 AP/Wide World Photos.

his own aims in countering Mosaddeq.[115] Kashani not only publicly and unmistakably sided with and bolstered the shah and other opponents of Mosaddeq, he also played a crucial role in convincing them that Mosaddeq was
seriously vulnerable. As the shaken Mosaddeq reasserted his authority, Kashani
felt obliged once again and even less convincingly to express his formal support
for him.[116] Kashani, however, assumed a greater role in controlling the Majles,
which, largely as a result of open friction between the Mosaddeqists and
Kashani's tactical supporters, had succumbed to open factionalism and relentless acrimonious confrontations.[117]

In April 1953, the chief of police, Gen. Mahmud Afshartus, was murdered
as a result of a plot involving British agents and pro-Zahedi forces. Zahedi,
flanked by Mir-Ashrafi, who had become a fervent supporter of Kashani, escaped arrest by taking refuge in the Majles with Kashani's express blessing.
Kashani had become the opposition's major source of inspiration to such an extent that the Americans and the British did not discount the possibility of his
own assumption of the premiership.[118] The Americans considered Kashani op-

portunistic and feared that were he to assume office, his power base would be much narrower than Mosaddeq's.[119] Mosaddeq's royalist, Anglophile, and other conservative opponents, having long concentrated on using Kashani against Mosaddeq, continued to insist that the prime minister would not be able to retain his position without Kashani's support. Their tactic of exaggerated emphasis on the indispensability of Kashani appealed to his vanity and helped to invigorate him; it also contributed to Mosaddeq's determination to reassert his authority, thereby further deepening Kashani's animosity.[120] In early July the Mosaddeqists won what appeared to be a major victory by thwarting Kashani's reelection as Speaker. With the disruptive tactics of the opposition, however, the very functioning of the Majles became increasingly problematic, while its exploitability by opposition forces to bring down the government increased. Mosaddeq's move to dissolve the Majles through a referendum removed all restraints on Kashani's acrimonious hostility toward him,[121] Kashani's home becoming a major locus of anti-Mosaddeq activity.

Mosaddeq's tactic of ignoring or cold-shouldering Kashani was prompted by his belief that Kashani had, unforgivably, shown willingness to side with forces dedicated to retrieving foreign influence.[122] Kashani felt that his role in supporting and sustaining Mosaddeq's premiership had neither received due recognition nor resulted in a commensurate share of the political and symbolic dividends. However, the single most crucial factor accounting for Kashani's increasing enmity toward Mosaddeq—and the lingering hostility of other Islamists—was the fact that a secular leader riding the tide of civic nationalism had succeeded in overshadowing, outmaneuvering, and marginalizing a high-ranking, activist, political ayatollah.

Makki

Hossein Makki owed his effective entry into politics to Qavam: it was through membership in Qavam's Democratic Party that he was elected as deputy to the Fifteenth Majles. In this capacity he abandoned his patron to embrace the nationalist cause; he befriended Mosaddeq, who had been prevented by Qavam from election to the Majles, and played an important role in thwarting parliamentary approval of the Supplemental Oil Agreement (the Gass-Golsha'iyan agreement). This enabled Makki to acquire national prominence. In October 1949/Mehr 1328, out of a large crowd called upon by Mosaddeq to protest against election rigging, Makki was among the twenty public figures selected to take sanctuary in the Marble Palace. These protesters proceeded to form the

National Front, a loose coalition dedicated to civic nationalist and democratic objectives. Along with Mosaddeq, Makki was one of a handful of individuals elected to the Sixteenth Majles despite the concerted efforts of the government. Capable of exercising tremendous moral authority, this parliamentary group steered the course of Iranian politics in a direction that resulted in the nationalization of the oil industry and the premiership of Mosaddeq.

As a pro-Mosaddeq parliamentarian, Makki helped to counter the vociferous anti-Mosaddeq opposition. He considered himself a pioneering champion of the oil nationalization movement[123] but was embittered by not being included in the delegation that accompanied Mosaddeq to New York to address the UN. His frequent expressions of resentment led the opposition to view him as a potential ally. Encouraged by Middleton, supporters of Qavam tried to co-opt him.[124] He was elected to the Seventeenth Majles by an unprecedented number of votes. He did not discount the possibility of becoming prime minister. Following the July 1952 uprising, his differences with Mosaddeq, clearly discernible much earlier, gradually came to the surface. Makki's inflated self-image had begun to verge on disconcerting arrogance: believing that he had played the most crucial role in the developments that had resulted in Mosaddeq's premiership,[125] he saw himself as eclipsed by newcomers around Mosaddeq. He joined other disgruntled National Front members in resenting Mosaddeq's acquisition of extra powers from the Parliament and openly opposed the renewal of these powers, but in the face of Mosaddeq's victory resorted to a tactical retreat. Increasingly embittered, he unmistakably sided with the shah in the February episode.

Although more restrained than Baqa'i and Ha'erizadeh, Makki likewise did not confine himself to withdrawing his support for Mosaddeq but actively joined his opponents, particularly Zahedi.[126] His abusive onslaught of June 7, 1953, against Ahmad Razavi, the pro-Mosaddeq deputy speaker of the Majles,[127] served as a public display of the extent of his hostility. His election by the Majles to the highly sensitive position of monitoring the government's note issue contributed to Mosaddeq's determination to resort to a referendum to dissolve the Majles.

In 1951, when the oil industry was nationalized, Makki was a dashing forty-year-old parliamentarian. From a mercantile background but with no university education, he felt ill at ease in the company of the mostly French-educated academics, lawyers, and other intellectuals and professionals who had gathered around Mosaddeq. This led Makki to exhibit a cultivated snobbery and to endeavor to gain intellectual credentials by trying to establish himself as a historian.[128] Though lugubrious and occasionally uncouth, he was neverthe-less an effective speaker, a skillful mediator who proved successful in countering those opponents of Mosaddeq who were unresponsive to intellectual finesse. Prior to his desertion Mosaddeq treated him with warm affection, and his words carried much weight with the premier.[129] In terms of political disposi-tions, however, Makki fully shared the prevailing assumptions that parliamen-tary politics required countering not only a powerful monarch but also, and more significantly, a powerful prime minister. He, along with Baqa'i and Ha'erizadeh, had been a member of the eight-man committee that upheld Mosaddeq's reading of the Constitution that the monarch should reign and not rule, but also like them he helped to prevent the parliamentary approval of the committee's report. His desirable polity was one in which individuals such as himself would continue to act as influential power brokers needed by the shah as well as by the prime minister, while enjoying the opportunity to pose as un-compromising advocates of the Constitution, as well as champions of opposi-tional causes. Makki's anti-British posture did not prevent Middleton, upon his return to London, from placing him among the Young Turks of Mosaddeq's entourage, who hoped to see a "genuine national revival" in their country. [130] Other Foreign Office officials were less generous. A. K. Rothnie, describing Makki as an ex-sergeant in the Iranian air force expelled "on charges of stealing equipment," added, "It has frequently been reported that he was willing to abandon the National Front if we would pay him. . . . He probably has the am-bition to succeed Mosaddeq as a young dictator, but his vanity and quarrelsome nature will make his cooperation with other elements difficult. His complete lack of principle and scruples would make him a most unwelcome leader of Persia." [131]

Baqa'i

Mozaffar Baqa'i too used Qavam's patronage to acquire a seat in the Fifteenth Majles and abandoned him when he felt he was a liability. He came from a prominent provincial family, the son of Mirza Shahab, and took pride in his father's constitutionalist credentials and good name; he acquired higher educa-tion in France and was able to pursue an academic career at Tehran University that was, however, overshadowed by his preferred vocation of politics. His service as head of the Education Department in his native Kerman enabled him to acquire a considerable local following, and he was one of those politicians who commanded extensive support and loyalty in their place of birth, which could serve as a reliable power base. It was, however, as a Majles deputy that Baqa'i gained national prominence, becoming, at the age of forty, one of the founders of the National Front. His vociferous opposition to the premiership of Razmara added to his fame. Elected to the Sixteenth and the Seventeenth Majles, he proved to be both an effective supporter and an effective opponent of Mosaddeq, turning against him in the aftermath of the July uprising and strongly objecting to several of the prime minister's policies, particularly the renewal of the extra powers extended to him by the Majles. Some Mosaddeqists regretted Baqa'i's defection,[132] viewing him not only as a capable supporter but also as a dangerous enemy.

Unlike Makki, Baqa'i had his own political party, the Toilers Party, to which he had co-opted the talented Tudeh defector Khalil Maleki, a sharp critic of Soviet communism. Following the appearance of rifts between Baqa'i and Mosaddeq and dissension over issues such as the contacts between Issa Sepahbodi,[133] Baqa'i's lieutenant, and Qavam on the eve of the July uprising, the pro-Mosaddeq Maleki and his followers were deviously discarded.[134] Baqa'i's party become more narrowly a coterie of his clients and cronies, if not a cabal of henchmen. He was a political boss who had sought to find other leaders, including Mosaddeq, to follow,[135] abandoning them all in favor of a single-minded pursuit of his own oblique ambitions. Baqa'i ostentatiously befriended secular and anticlerical intellectuals such as Sadeq Hedayat, but he also flirted with the clerics and opportunistically ingratiated himself with them. He was a professor of ethics, capable of considerable charm, refinement, convivial urbanity, and civil dialogue but also of a surprising degree of roughness, even malice, and of calculated thuggery and callousness. He demanded unswerving loyalty from his followers, while he himself made a habit of disloyalty. Following the July uprising he was at the forefront of relentless pressure for the punishment of Qavam, his former patron, with whom he had earlier covertly tried to reach an understanding, and whom Mosaddeq, on grounds of civility, was trying to protect.

Maintaining close links with a number of mob leaders, Baqa'i was able to rely on and mobilize elements from the urban underclass of south Tehran.[136] He had shady links with an array of people, among them members of army intelligence, officers associated with General Hasan Arfa' (Razmara's arch enemy), American diplomatic or intelligence personnel, and functionaries of the court. Dismissing Baqa'i as "an alcoholic and no great personality in his own right," Middleton maintained that "his party and his newspaper have been kept going by support from the Government, the Americans and the Court, and owe little to their own efforts."[137] Baqa'i's mutually beneficial relations with the shah were more than casual.[138] His tactic was to portray himself as a monarchist dedicated to protecting the shah's best interests, while at the same time denouncing most of the putative royalists for manipulating the shah and leading him to deviate from the Constitution. In the post-1953 era, with the declared aim of countering such deviations, he engaged in an intermittent, sometimes quixotic campaign to promote "truth and liberty," but he merely succeeded in placing himself more firmly in the political wilderness.[139]

Baqa'i was an ardent political adventurer, a restless and fearless intriguer, an elusive ally susceptible to real or feigned conspiratorial delusions, a loner with an inflated, almost narcissistic, self-image—a veritable enfant terrible of Iranian politics. One of his close aides took part in the murder of Mosaddeq's chief of police, General Afshartus. Baqa'i emphatically denied any involvement,[140] but the Mosaddeqists believed it unlikely that his aide would have acted on a matter of such gravity without his knowledge and approval. The government's demand that Baqa'i be stripped of his parliamentary immunity to stand trial significantly added to the issues crippling the Majles. The depth of his growing enmity toward Mosaddeq led him to resort to whatever measures he thought necessary to unseat him. He superseded many royalists and Anglophiles in defying Mosaddeq, increasingly denouncing him in his party newspaper, *Shahed,* for acting in league with the Tudeh Party and assiduously paving the way for communism.[141]

Like Makki, Baqa'i's political mentality had been shaped by a facile oppositional stand that befitted the mood of frustration characteristic of the post-Reza Shah era. Nor did he, despite his better education, differ from Makki in his meager appreciation of the prerequisites of a functioning parliamentary polity, and neither of them had any senior administrative experience at the national level. For Makki, Baqa'i, and their ally Ha'erizadeh, attachment to principles seemed to function less as a restraining guide for political action than as a convenient ploy, often skillfully deployed, for the acquisition of political fortune and fame. Aspiring to sustain their fame, their political maneuvers and invocation of lofty principles were carefully choreographed and driven by unhindered self-regard and self-righteous belief in their entitlement to public recognition and leadership. They wished to be perceived as having broken ranks with the Mosaddeqists purely due to the latter's unacceptable deviation from the nationalist movement's original objectives. In the eyes of their detractors, however, they were inexcusably guilty not only of using every opportunity, idea, or person to further their own political ends, but also of lending themselves, unwittingly or otherwise, to manifest co-optation by others for the furthering of ends that they publicly disclaimed.

Ha'erizadeh

The political career of the former cleric Abolhasan Ha'erizadeh started in 1921; he represented Yazd, his birthplace, in the fourth, fifth, and sixth terms of the Majles. His later prominence rested, however, on his membership in Qavam's party, which enabled him, along with Makki and Baqa'i, to win a seat in the Fifteenth Majles. He too abandoned Qavam soon thereafter in favor of more politically fruitful causes and would not hesitate to change his political affiliations in the light of changing circumstances. As a founding member of the National Front, he was elected to the Sixteenth Majles but was one of the first supporters of Mosaddeq openly to question his judgment and leadership and subsequently break ranks. He did not hide his opposition to Mosaddeq's acquisition of extra powers, and vociferously opposed its renewal. Ha'erizadeh unhesitatingly and fiercely attacked Mosaddeq when, in the course of the February episode, the premier went to the Majles, having been forced to abandon his residence.[142] Playing a key role in undermining Mosaddeq's hold over the Majles and having formed the relentlessly anti-Mosaddeq Freedom faction, Ha'erizadeh continued to cripple the Majles to the government's detriment. Single-mindedly pursuing the goal of using the Seventeenth Majles as a platform to abuse and undermine the government, he played a role very similar to that played by Jamal Emami in the Sixteenth Majles. The similarities did not end there; he was as politically unrefined, acrimonious, and reckless as Emami, and perhaps more ill tempered.[143] In line with Zahedi and many other opponents of Mosaddeq, he insisted that Iran owed no compensation to the AIOC and castigated Mosaddeq for willingness to pay compensation.[144] He was apparently willing to be dispatched abroad as inspector of Iran's diplomatic missions, but Kashani, needing his presence in Tehran, prevailed upon him not to accept the position.[145] Maintaining close ties with Zahedi, he supported him diligently, collaborated with him in the process leading to the coup, and was one of the deputies who maintained contact with him following the failure of the coup's military stage.[146]

The Feda'iyan and the Religious Right

From the outset of his premiership Mosaddeq faced the vociferous enmity and threats of the Feda'iyan-e Islam, a small, shadowy group of lower-class zealous religious activists who had attracted attention through their assassinations of the controversial historian and essayist Ahmad Kasravi, as well as the former premier and court minister Abdolhossein Hazhir and Premier Razmara. Deeply averse to the secular tenor of civic nationalism, the Feda'iyan emphasized a narrowly conceived version of Islam as the authentic locus of Iranian identity and a sufficient source of guidance and inspiration for activism and popular mobilization. They deeply feared and denigrated political, civic, and social liberties and rights envisaged and aspired to by civic nationalists, and wished to reverse what they viewed as the decadent modernity and secular ethos of the prevailing social arrangements.

The Feda'iyan's views were reflected in the demands they made of Mosaddeq, which included the imposition of the veil, the expulsion of female employees from government positions, a ban on the sale and consumption of alcoholic beverages, and obligatory public prayer for all government employees.[147] Mosaddeq's not unexpected refusal to entertain such demands provided the Feda'iyan with the requisite justification to unleash their hostility against him. The threat from the Feda'iyan was one of the primary factors accounting for Mosaddeq's decision to move the prime minister's office to his own residence. The detention in early June 1951 of Sayyed Mojtaba Mir-Louhi (Navvab Safavi), leader of the Feda'iyan, further antagonized the group. They continued through various means, including their main newspaper, *Nabard-e Millat,* public statements, or private messages sent to Mosaddeq and his colleagues, to threaten them with assassination.[148] Their statements were given wide and sympathetic coverage in anti–Mosaddeq newspapers such as *Dad* and *Tolu'.* An assassination attempt, planned by Abdolhossein Vahedi, the group's second in command, and executed by a teenage member of the group, on the life of Hossein Fatemi, Mosaddeq's dynamic and capable aide, on February 15, 1952/25 Bahman 1330 left Fatemi badly wounded and effectively disabled for almost eight months.[149]

Resenting Kashani's public support for Mosaddeq, the Feda'iyan also expressed enmity toward Kashani, threatening him with assassination,[150] but the emergence of rifts between the two leaders helped to improve the group's relations with Kashani. Kashani and his supporters sponsored parliamentary clemency for Khalil Tahmasebi, Razmara's assassin, which boosted the group's morale. This was followed by the release in early February 1953 of Navvab Safavi, while Vahedi, who had masterminded Fatemi's assassination, was not arrested. Nevertheless, the group continued to be not only a major irritant but a source of demoralizing harassment for the government.[151] In terms of the deep-seated anticommunist and traditionalist proclivities, as well as the traditional lower–class or underclass origins of the group, it had much in common with the followers of Sayyed Zia or those groups he targeted to further his own agenda. Sayyed Zia's agents tried to influence and may indeed have infiltrated the group. Mehdi Eraqi, a one-time Feda'iyan member, is cited as attributing his own defection and that of a number of others from the group to close contacts between an associate of Sayyed Zia and Navvab Safavi.[152]

Religious right-wing or traditionalist forces not only generally tended to disapprove of or oppose Mosaddeqists but were often willing to treat them with active hostility. This was clearly reflected in the fact that virtually all anti-Mosaddeq opposition schemes, including the CIA-SIS operations, anticipated or included considerable reliance on the actual or potential support of such forces.[153] Some clerics suggested that clerical opposition to Mosaddeq be procured through financial largesse.[154] Ayatollah Mohammad Behbahani and his extended family were involved in a variety of activities against Mosaddeq and collaborated in various schemes to stir religious and traditionalist anxieties and opposition to the prime minister. Mohammad Reza Behbahani, for instance, reportedly received money from the shah's mother to arrange for a group to take sanctuary in opposition to Mosaddeq.[155] The role of Ayatollah Behbahani himself was more crucial; in the February episode, for instance, he played a key role in terms of helping both to mobilize and to stir public agitation in favor of the shah, and in recruiting mob leaders such as Tayyeb Haj Reza'i to help assemble and lead the rampaging crowds.[156] Behbahani also significantly contributed to the eventual success of the operations of August 1953.

Closely associated with Behbahani and also enjoying the support of Hassan Emami,[157] the preacher Mohammad Taqi Falsafi, whose captivating oratory carried weight with the traditional classes, unequivocally used the pulpit to undermine Mosaddeq's popular support, provoking countermeasures from the Mosaddeqists. Contrary to the expressed wishes of Kashani, Falsafi refused to speak in support of the nationalization of the oil industry.[158] Although contending that he only began to oppose Mosaddeq after the July uprising and the considerable rise in power and freedom of the Tudeh Party, he had, in fact, denounced Mosaddeq and even Kashani long before the July uprising.[159] In May 1952, the Mosaddeqists prevented him from public preaching, but he was able to resume his public sermons some six months later, on Kashani's initiative. Kashani's conflict with Mosaddeq helped to place Kashani, Falsafi, and other traditionalist right-wing clerics on the same platform.

Falsafi generally had a reputation for willingness to adjust his fluctuating political allegiances for tangible gains. According to British embassy sources, Falsafi's opposition to Mosaddeq's government was rooted in less than lofty considerations. From Razmara's government Falsafi had received a large sum of foreign currency at the favorable government-controlled exchange rate for the purchase of a printing press. His demand for a further sum at the controlled rate was summarily refused by Mosaddeq, "implying that he had improperly utilized the previous grant, which was in some measure true."[160] For his part, Falsafi invoked the threat of communism in order to justify his anti-Mosaddeq stand; he later contended that faced with the stark choice between monarchy and communism, he could not but side with the "lesser evil," that is, the monarchy.[161] By emphasizing nationalism, Mosaddeq was, in Falsafi's view, guilty of underestimating the religiosity of the Iranian people.[162] According to Falsafi, the premier had angered the clerics by granting freedom to communist newspapers to publish whatever they wished, disregarding the complaints of the faithful and their leaders.[163] In Falsafi's assessment, in the last few months of Mosaddeq's premiership "the religious people thought that Mosaddeq was paving the way for the assumption of power by the Tudehists."[164]

The rift between Kashani and Mosaddeq was likely to make the latter more vulnerable to religiously inspired opposition; it aided those who had long wished to place the Mosaddeqists and the Tudeh Party on the same platform. More and more, traditional ulama conspicuously sided with the shah and showed less hesitation in castigating Mosaddeqists or confronting them. Behbahani's counterparts elsewhere, such as Sayyed Nureddin in Shiraz, would resort to strong-arm tactics against the Mosaddeqists.[165] The Mosaddeqist front did not, of course, lack clerics of high rank or stature.[166] Moreover, despite incessant pressure on Grand Ayatollah Borujerdi to side with the shah, as long as Borujerdi was pursuing a politically balanced course, Mosaddeq was not easily vulnerable. Mosaddeq had maintained good and respectful working relations with Borujerdi;[167] he indicated his gratitude and appreciation of Borujerdi's position by signing a bill in late April 1953, making it a punishable offense to insult or defame the foremost religious authority in the country (namely, Borujerdi). No other member of the ulama would, of course, enjoy such protection or privilege.[168] This greatly aggravated the enmity of the likes of Behbahani and Kashani, sardonically referred to by Mosaddeq as "the ulama of the 9 Esfand episode."

Undeterred by the discernible erosion of public respect caused by open enmity toward Mosaddeq,[169] Kashani and Behbahani, despite their own differences, lent full support to active moves to unseat Mosaddeq, who was increasingly portrayed as seriously endangering not only the monarchy but also Islam.[170] The combined efforts of Mosaddeq's domestic and foreign enemies in mobilizing and exploiting religious sentiments reached their peak during the final weeks of the Mosaddeq government and rested on manufacturing a credible threat of an impending communist takeover. In the context of the ongoing CIA-SIS war of nerves, every effort would be made to enlist Borujerdi's support, including the planned dispatch of Behbahani to Qom to extract an anticommunist fatwa from Borujerdi.[171] There was even a plan to pledge to Borujerdi the revival of the effectively defunct clause of the Constitution ensuring formal religious scrutiny of legislation.[172] Failure to enlist Borujerdi's active support helped to thwart several preplanned actions, including large-scale orchestrated sit-ins. Allegations of collusion between Mosaddeqists and communists, together with manufactured rumors of Borujerdi's opposition to Mosaddeq and the likelihood of his imminent intervention on the shah's behalf, continued, however, to be widely disseminated and used to sway popular opinion.[173] The aim was to convince more and more people that the safest road to avoiding communism, chaos, and irreligion was to side with the shah and against Mosaddeq.

The Tudeh Party

Having been outlawed in 1949, the Tudeh Party, operating through a number of front organizations, was less constrained than it previously was to subscribe to any recognizable notion of public responsibility. The party was by no means homogeneous; its leadership was fractious and divided by rivalries and differences of personality as well as political sensibilities and principle. And yet, irrespective of such divisions and the occasional differences between the leadership and the rank and file, the party was ideologically predisposed to contest civic nationalism, and its overall policy was active opposition to Mosaddeq. Its Leninist-Stalinist ideology, in one of its many glaring antinomies, perceived or portrayed Mosaddeq's actions and dispositions as determined by his class origins and interests, and yet demanded that he act differently. The party not only considered the National Front as a rival but attacked its professed principles as well; it denounced civic nationalism as dedicated to maintaining the existing socioeconomic order as well as the perpetuation of Western hegemony. The party also dismissed Mosaddeq's anti-imperialism, which did not involve embracing the Soviet Union and was not as openly anti-American as it was anti-British.[174] Mosaddeq, the party propaganda maintained, only intended to replace British with American imperialism.[175] Having played an important role in heightening the public consciousness of and opposition to the preponderant British influence in Iran, the party did not want to eliminate all foreign influence but wished to replace British with Soviet influence. Disguising its sub-servience to the Soviets under the veneer of internationalism, the party was committed to Soviet foreign policy objectives and dismissed Mosaddeq's advo-cacy of a neutralist stand. It had in the past favored counterbalancing the British oil concession in Iran by granting an oil concession to the Soviets. Its policy re-garding the oil nationalization movement had been at best dubious. Subse-quently, the party concentrated its efforts on radicalizing public opinion and promoting an attitude of defiance and intransigence regarding any oil settle-ment with Britain. It depicted flexibility as surrender.[176] It advocated termina-tion of the oil negotiations, expulsion of the Americans as well as the British, negotiations with the Soviet Union, and implementation of the Tudeh agenda in domestic politics.[177]

The party's explanation and indictment of the existing inequities and ills of Iranian society and its proffered remedies were appealing; concomitantly, its repertoire of radical rhetoric and slogans helped to alarm and frighten large segments of the population. The party endeavored to radicalize and alienate the younger segments of the intelligentsia, particularly students, from the National Front and civic nationalism, and used its inexhaustible ideological parapherna-lia as well as well-tried techniques of propaganda and disinformation to sow disaffection among Mosaddeq's supporters. It worked to undermine Mosad-deq's image, spread doubts about the sincerity of his claims, and demeaned the significance of his undertakings and achievements. Unresponsive not only to publicly valued adherence to patriotic sensibilities and culturally sanctioned civic virtues but often to conventional tenets of ethical conduct as well, most party leaders and activists adhered to a Machiavellian-Stalinist view that noble ends justified ignoble means. Committed ultimately to the overthrow of the existing order, the party's attitude toward parliamentary procedures, constitu-tionalism, and political and civic rights was inherently instrumentalist and cyn-ical; it invoked and utilized them to further its own aims.

Unconcerned with the government's severe economic difficulties and its inability adequately to address the demands and expectations of the lower classes, the party concentrated on stimulating worker and other lower-class dis-content and on stirring labor unrest.[178] It relentlessly organized provocative demonstrations and deployed a variety of maneuvers and propaganda tactics aimed at challenging or weakening Mosaddeq and corroding his public sup-port.[179] Not only did the party newspapers normally not spare Mosaddeq any abuse, but much to the delight of his right-wing enemies, the party indefatiga-bly worked to undermine Mosaddeq's authority and claims to be fully in control and capable of maintaining law and order. It readily branded any measures to maintain order as fascist repression. In July 1951, large demonstrations organized by the party to commemorate the Abadan oil workers' strike of five years earlier and also to coincide with the arrival of the prominent American envoy W. Averell Harriman, resulted in considerable violence and bloodshed, thereby damaging Mosaddeq's foreign and domestic standing and causing tension in the cabinet.[180] Other demonstrations and clashes involving Tudeh supporters and opponents in December 1951 gave both the party and its right-wing opponents further ammunition to intensify their antigovernment war of attrition. The Tudeh tactics of harassment and street demonstrations enabled Mosaddeq's opponents, including the anticommunist Anglophiles such as Jamal Emami, increasingly to denounce him not only for his failure to maintain public order but also for deliberately promoting the party through lenience or inaction.[131]

In April 1951 Shepherd had estimated the Tudeh Party's nationwide membership to be twenty-five hundred, of which two thousand members were in Tehran.[182] Publicly, however, Mosaddeq's foreign as well as right-wing or traditionalist domestic opponents sought to exaggerate the size and organizational scale of the party. Not surprisingly, the Tudeh Party did not eschew any opportunity to lend substance to such assumptions and to demonstrate its capabilities. Mosaddeq was generally inclined to tolerate the party on democratic grounds; his attitude enabled the party to expand and to extend its activities to the government's detriment, but not to the extent that Mosaddeq's opponents claimed. The ongoing military and police monitoring of the party were not abandoned, and Mosaddeq did not hesitate to use legal means to control and confront the party's disorderly and disruptive demonstrations. Short of systematically suppressive measures, the party's activities, particularly street demonstrations, could not, however, be fully contained. These demonstrations often provoked countermeasures by anticommunist activists such as members of Baqa'i's party and other small anticommunist, ultranationalist, or right-wing groups. The resulting confrontations, also often involving British and American agents or other elements that benefited from Mosaddeqist-Tudeh conflicts, invariably had regrettable consequences.

Paradoxically, having contributed much to undermining Mosaddeq, the party, or segments of it, appeared willing to support him whenever his government was seriously challenged by the combined efforts of the Anglophiles and the royalists. Perhaps portions of the party's rank and file were genuinely willing to support Mosaddeq whenever his overthrow seemed a real possibility.

The party leaders, too, could not have failed to realize that in all likelihood Mosaddeq's successor would be far less tolerant of the party than he. It would have been difficult, however, to imagine that the party's persistent enmity could give way to anything other than tactical nonopposition or temporary suspension of hostility. In any case and not surprisingly, the party's tactical and half-hearted support was as damaging to Mosaddeq as its persistent opposition.

Like the right-wingers, the party used the elections for the Seventeenth Majles to expose "the hollowness" that, according to party papers, had always characterized Mosaddeq's democratic claims.[183] Following the renewal of his extra powers, a party newspaper, *Shahbaz,* branded Mosaddeq's government as the most scandalous fascist dictatorship.[184] Mosaddeq refused, however, to bow to pressure from the Right and also from some of his leftist supporters to curb the party's activities more vigorously; he strove to avoid any course of action that could be construed as suppressive or would contravene his avowed policy of tolerating right- and left-wing groups and organizations as well as the press.

The Tudeh Party's ideological configuration and the party's unmistakable pro-Soviet allegiance left Mosaddeq with no illusion about the party's policies and aims. Contrary to the propaganda of Mosaddeq's domestic and foreign opponents, no meaningful and sustainable cooperation between Mosaddeqists and the Tudeh Party was conceivable or possible.[185] Mosaddeq dismissed the Tudeh Party as wittingly or unwittingly advancing British policy and interests.[186] He also argued plausibly that the Western powers operated through the elite and state institutions while the Soviet government attempted to exert its influence through the Tudeh Party.[187] Mosaddeq did not fear the Tudeh Party or an attempted communist takeover. In his dealing with the Americans he did, however, sometimes invoke the party as a likely alternative should his government continue to be debilitated by British policies and American failure to support Iran. This tactic was altogether counterproductive, as the British and later the Americans envisaged and sought to foster an alternative both to his government and to the Tudeh. Even if Mosaddeq had not resorted to such a tactic, it would have made little difference to the British and the Americans, who were fully prepared to invoke the communist threat to justify their campaign to engineer his downfall.

While the Tudeh Party denounced Mosaddeq for his "fascist" policies in restraining the party, Mosaddeq's other opponents, particularly right-wingers and traditionalists, blamed him for allowing the party free rein. According to such groups, Mosaddeq's "biggest mistake, which resulted in the toppling of his government, was the unlimited freedom granted to the 'detested and xenophiliac Tudeh party.' "[188] In its often single-minded defiance of existing patriotic sensibilities and its myopic adventurism and relentless self-aggrandizing maneuvers, the party caused Mosaddeq's government immense problems and enabled its opponents to invoke the threat of communist takeover with increasing plausibility. The Tudeh's rhetoric and tactics rendered credible the activities of CIA and SIS agents provocateurs purporting to be Tudeh supporters. Intending to alarm religious leaders, CIA agents resorted to "black propaganda" in the party's name, "threatening these leaders with savage punishment if they opposed Mossadeq [sic]. Threatening phone calls were also made to them, in the name of the Tudeh, and one of several planned sham bombings of the houses of these leaders was carried out."[189]

In the context of the extensive agitation and anxieties provoked primarily by the CIA's and SIS's intense propaganda campaign, not only to emphasize Mosaddeqist-Tudeh commonalities but also to manufacture evidence of their covert collusion, the Mosaddeqists were increasingly hesitant to appear to reiterate or condone ideas or slogans associated with the Tudeh Party. For instance, the Tudeh Party's increasing advocacy of a "democratic republic" following the events of August 16, 1953, barred most Mosaddeqists from seriously considering a republican alternative to the monarchy. In the same vein, any possibility of even tactical Mosaddeqist-Tudeh cooperation to thwart the coup was not meaningfully conceivable. The CIA-SIS campaign of propaganda and disinformation had to a large extent contributed to this situation, but in fact the essential prerequisites for such an unlikely cooperation had always been manifestly nonexistent.[190]

Retrenchment

In the aftermath of the July uprising, the Anglophiles and, increasingly, many royalists continued with their strategy of utilizing quasi-legal means, as well as covert subversive measures, to destabilize the government. An array of possible successors to Mosaddeq, whether from the ranks of the National Front or its opponents, would continue to be considered by the shah or pressed upon him. Resort to a coup was also increasingly contemplated. More immediately, efforts were concentrated on stimulating and utilizing splits in the National Front and trying to steer Mosaddeq away from any flexibility that might result in fruitful negotiations leading to a possible oil settlement. Sayyed Zia, echoing the sentiments of other Anglophiles, continued to emphasize that there was no possibility of a satisfactory oil agreement with Mosaddeq and that "if we [the

British] cooperated with him it would be tantamount to complete surrender and would entail, at any rate for some time, the collapse of our influence in Persia."[191] Realizing that Mosaddeq might not be easily toppled and believing that his successor might not deviate radically from his stance, the Americans, mostly in coordination with British officials, initiated a series of fresh efforts to negotiate with him. Neither the British nor the Americans were, however, prepared to allow Iran to benefit from the nationalization of its oil in a manner likely to jeopardize oil arrangements elsewhere.[192] Following the failure of Zaehner, many British officials, particularly the Conservative foreign secretary, Anthony Eden, who had been the staunchest supporter of Zaehner's mission, came increasingly to advocate the need for full American cooperation in anti-Mosaddeq moves. In order to enlist such cooperation the British needed to show that they were willing to negotiate with Mosaddeq, albeit with the ultimate aim of convincing the Americans that such negotiations were futile, and that there was no feasible alternative to toppling Mosaddeq's government.

American efforts to find provisional solutions or to assist Iran in overcoming its fiscal and economic problems were invariably undermined by British insistence on extracting unequivocal concessions from Mosaddeq and linking any U.S. assistance to Iran to a convincing Iranian commitment and readiness to reach an expeditious settlement. Despite some American reservations about the extent and advisability of acting in full concert with Britain vis-à-vis Iran,[193] the British succeeded in enlisting formal American cooperation, as symbolized by the Truman-Churchill joint communiqué of August 1952. In the words of Churchill's private secretary, John Colville, "W. [Winston] has persuaded Truman to join with him in sending a message, signed by them both, to Mossadeq [*sic*] in Tehran about the Persian oil question. W. himself did it and the F. O. and oil people agreed. It is the first time since 1945 that the Americans have joined with us in taking overt action against a third power."[194] Churchill's success in overcoming Truman's misgivings about "ganging up" against Mosaddeq and formally siding with Britain against Iran, which in Churchill's view was an "effective assertion of right over wrong,"[195] proved deeply damaging to Mosaddeq. The Americans could no longer claim to be neutral, and Mosaddeq could no longer claim to be able to use them against the British.

The joint Anglo-American stance immensely encouraged Mosaddeq's opponents. It disappointed Mosaddeq but did not surprise him, as he had long been aware of close Anglo-American cooperation. In the context of relentless British-backed efforts to unseat him, Mosaddeq tended to view with deep suspicion British overtures to negotiate, including offers made through the Americans. In any event, he could not agree to any arrangement that might be portrayed as surrender to foreign pressure or deviation from his publicly stated principles, particularly regarding Iranian sovereignty. Many of his opponents, whether pro-British or former supporters, increasingly adopted the tactic of denouncing him as being ready to surrender by agreeing to negotiate on the issue of compensation. Their tactical advocacy of a position far more inflexible than that taken by Mosaddeq further restricted his room for maneuver.

The failure of Qavam had demonstrated the limitations of quasi-parliamentary maneuvers that were not supplemented by other coordinated measures. Without in any way abandoning efforts to utilize quasi-legal means, including the Parliament, decisive measures such as a coup d'état proved more appealing averting communism would serve as the main justification. As early as June 1951, the pro-British Amir Amir-Keyvan, an officially sponsored trade unionist, described among other things as "worker member of the Higher Labour Council and secretary of the textile workers union in Isfahan," was perhaps the first Iranian to provide the British with a detailed scheme for the overthrow of Mosaddeq through a coup led by General Zahedi, a wealthy seventy-year-old politician and soldier and then Mosaddeq's minister of the interior.[196] In September 1951 Shepherd concluded that the "Iranian political character" might make a coup d'état inevitable.[197] By January 1952, Sayyed Zia and Falle had also come to the conclusion that there might be no alternative to a coup.[198] Zahedi's relations with Mosaddeq had sharply deteriorated as a result of Zahedi's failure as interior minister both to contain and to account satisfactorily for the street clashes of mid-July 1951 involving the Tudeh Party. Following his resignation from the cabinet on August 2, 1951, Zahedi covertly but decidedly joined Mosaddeq's opponents and was viewed favorably by the British as an alternative to Qavam. Even before the July uprising, he had maintained close links with Makki, Baqa'i, Ha'erizadeh, and Kashani; following Qavam's fall he increased such links and offered Kashani a say in the appointment of his ministers in exchange for supporting his assumption of power.[199] He increasingly emerged as the most likely alternative to Mosaddeq, and concentrated on cultivating British support by claiming to be wholeheartedly pro-British. His virtues were compellingly underlined by A. H. Hamzavi, the Iranian pro-British former Iranian press attaché in London.[200]

Following the July uprising, George Middleton, the British chargé d'affaires, although a man of much greater sense and subtlety than Shepherd, concluded that Mosaddeq's "megalomania is now verging on mental instability" and that communism could only be averted through a coup.[201] Henderson concurred: the Mosaddeq government could not be replaced other than through a coup.[202] An unnamed former member of Mosaddeq's cabinet spoke to Henderson along these lines.[203] Similarly, several other Iranians underlined the necessity of a coup, among them the right-wing deputy Mir-Ashrafi, who wanted to lead a coup himself. Falle commented that "it would be better to enlist his help and get him to cooperate with Zahedi," adding that Mir-Ashrafi was ready "to follow our advice even at great risk to his own life as he has done in the past."[204] More significantly, the British War Office asked the military attaché at the Tehran embassy to assess the capability of the Iranian armed forces for a successful coup.[205] The military attaché was optimistic that most officers would support a coup, adding that it should be carried out in the shah's name. The attaché described Zahedi as "probably more willing to assume" the leadership of a coup than most other candidates, but "unlikely to have much support in the army."[206] For his part, Mosaddeq had long realized that efforts to unseat him would only intensify. In late August 1952 he told Henderson that the British pursued a "leisurely" attitude to the resolution of the oil issue because they were hoping for some kind of a coup and were preoccupied with making it happen.[207]

In contrast to quasi-legal and parliamentary means, a coup d'état was evidently a risky and deeply problematic course of action. On the other hand, it could mark a sharp and clean break with the past. Any successor to Mosaddeq, assuming power through seemingly normal parliamentary processes, could not radically deviate from the course of action and policies pursued by Mosaddeq. His successor was bound to have a far easier task in reversing Mosaddeq's policies if such policies could be demonstrably discredited as having led the country to an impasse and if Mosaddeq were personally disgraced through removal from power by drastic measures such as a coup, portrayed as necessary for saving the country. Foreign-inspired efforts to mobilize hostility to Mosaddeq, and discrediting him by equating his term of office with failure and chaos, also significantly and unmistakably entailed discrediting and discarding his approach to the oil issue in favor of an approach acceptable to his British antagonists.

Considering the adverse reactions caused by Sayyed Zia's candidacy, Zahedi's nonidentification with the British and his war-time arrest by them was an asset. Falle was adamant that Zahedi's links with Britain should remain undisclosed,[208] and the Rashidians were hopeful about his prospects and about launching a coup with the help of the army and the clerics in his support.[209] Moreover, Zahedi enjoyed not only the support of disgruntled National Front leaders but also of a number of deputies and fellow senators such as Khajehnuri, who had introduced him to the Americans.[210] He counted on extensive backing in the army, and the association of retired officers was firmly behind him. Ala too strongly favored Zahedi and reassured Henderson that in addition to disaffected National Front supporters, particularly Kashani and Ha'erizadeh, he was backed by many clerics, merchants, officers, and politicians.[211]

The position of the shah was still a problem; according to Middleton, in his own "indirect" way the monarch was "encouraging the Senate to oppose the Government,"[212] but he neither fully trusted Zahedi nor was he readily prepared to support him.[213] Hoping to allay the shah's misgivings, Zahedi later offered to submit to him his undated signed resignation.[214] In the meantime, he continued cautiously but more discernibly to act and rally support as the only viable successor to Mosaddeq. He followed the well-tried tactic of impressing upon the British and the Americans that any negotiations with Mosaddeq would undermine his plans.[215] Enjoying parliamentary immunity as a senator enabled Zahedi to act and speak with considerable impunity. By October 1952, in Middleton's assessment, Zahedi was "feeling much encouraged." He was the center of anti-Mosaddeq opposition; his optimism was particularly rooted in encouragement he received from Ha'erizadeh, "who violently attacked Mosaddeq on all counts and expressed himself willing to support Zahedi."[216] Zahedi's activities did not escape government attention. On October 13, 1952/21 Mehr 1331, Hossein Fatemi, the government spokesman, announced the arrest of Gen. Abdolhossein Hejazi and the Rashidians (Habibollah and his two sons Qodratollah and Asadollah), for plotting against the government in association with a foreign (that is, the British) embassy; he similarly accused Zahedi, who could not be arrested due to parliamentary immunity.[217] Contributing to the severance of Anglo-Iranian diplomatic relations, this development was a disconcerting blow to the opposition as well as to the British. Various other government opponents, including Alam and Khajehnuri, were implicated, but the arrest of the Rashidians was particularly alarming. The British embassy unpersuasively denied any improper links with Mosaddeq's opponents, and Zahedi went on the offensive, publicly defending himself while rebuking the premier.[218] In the event, the government's stand vis-à-vis active opponents proved less than firm. Zahedi and other opponents were not deterred; the Rashidians were released six weeks later at the end of November, and the pace and momentum of anti-Mosaddeq activities accelerated.

On October 23, 1952, the variously motivated consternation of both Mosaddeqists and supporters of Kashani resulted in the Majles reducing the Senate's term to two years and thus effecting its dissolution. Coinciding with the rupture of diplomatic relations with Britain,[219] this constituted a major set-back for Zahedi. The breakdown in Anglo-Iranian relations did not, however, severely affect the capabilities of the Anglophiles, and in a crucial respect bene-fited Zahedi, as it reaffirmed the long-standing British position that negotia-tion with Mosaddeq was impossible or fruitless. Having been enormously encouraged by the increasing defiance of Mosaddeq by his former supporters, Zahedi and other opponents of Mosaddeq received a considerable boost from the November 1952 Republican victory in the U.S. presidential elections. Fearing that there could be a breakthrough over the vexed issue of compensa-tion, Zahedi had joined others in publicly chastising Mosaddeq for willingness to pay compensation.[220]

A Proto-coup: February 28, 1953/9 Esfand 1331

In the course of protracted negotiations with Henderson to find a solution to the oil issue, particularly settlement of the question of compensation, Mosad-deq continued to resist committing Iran to paying compensation for the AIOC's loss of "enterprise."[221] He had not denied the necessity of paying com-pensation to the AIOC and was willing to consider a lump sum; any compen-sation had, however, to be publicly justifiable in circumstances in which Mosaddeq's opponents all strongly denounced flexibility. Henderson acknowl-edged that Mosaddeq had been repeatedly accused of "having 'sold out' to the US."[222] It was of course not only sensitivity to such charges but deep distrust of the British that led Mosaddeq to proceed cautiously. The British, he told Hen-derson, pretended to be interested in solving the oil question but used their nu-merous contacts in Iran to unseat him, through an alliance of forces, including Bakhtiaris and other tribal elements, "fanatical religious groups, led by irre-sponsible mullahs, disgruntled politicians, reactionary elements in [the] army and bureaucracy, discarded politicians and communist front organizations."[223]

Believing that the British would not settle for anything less than punishing Iran by, among other things, imposing an unbearable compensation, by the middle of February 1953 Mosaddeq and his advisers had come to feel that there was no choice but to reject the latest Anglo-American oil proposal. There was no doubt that the eventual failure of recent negotiations, when disclosed, would embolden Mosaddeq's opponents further, and the court, now enjoying the support of National Front defectors, would be enabled to play a greater and more justifiable role in opposing him. Before publicly rejecting the latest pro-posals, while expectations had been raised that there could be a breakthrough,

Mosaddeq wanted to resort to a preemptive move against the court in order to restrain it and diminish its exploitability by his opponents. It had not escaped his attention that his opponents, particularly former supporters, increasingly and more successfully sought to encourage the shah to act against the government. Forestalling the shah's possible action against the government and undermining the court's capacity to do so would have meant strengthening his own position as prime minister. This, in turn, could perhaps result in a more favorable Anglo-American proposal. In Mosaddeq's view, a possible breakthrough in the oil negotiations could only ensue from an Iranian position of strength and as large a display of national unity as possible. National unity and strength had, however, continued irretrievably to erode, due to the efforts of old and new enemies.

Mosaddeq demanded that the shah confine himself to a government-designated budget, give up the revenue from the Mashhad shrine, and transfer the Crown lands to the State.[224] Mosaddeq's supporters urged the shah to impress upon the army that it should obey Mosaddeq; they also asked him to refrain from receiving government opponents, and to use the revenues from Crown lands for the public welfare.[225] The shah seemed amenable; he also offered to take a vacation abroad, which Mosaddeq initially rejected but later approved. The shah's apparent willingness to continue to conciliate Mosaddeq and the news of his imminent departure galvanized Mosaddeq's enemies. Ala lost no time in seeking to involve Henderson; he described the shah as in an "almost hysterical state" and feared that he might succumb to a "complete nervous breakdown."[226] Heartened by the possibility of a confrontation between Mosaddeq and the shah, Kashani, who seemed "pleased," informed Ala that if Mosaddeq were to attack the shah in the Majles, the Majles would give "overwhelming support to the shah."[227] Similarly, Makki contacted Ala asking him to encourage the shah not to seek reconciliation with Mosaddeq. Makki "insisted" that if Mosaddeq attacked the shah, the majority of deputies and people would be "outraged" and would support the monarch.[228]

Clearly the open rift between the shah and Mosaddeq provided a major opportunity for the latter's enemies. Kashani, taking advantage of a "heaven-sent" opportunity to recover lost ground,[229] joined Ayatollah Behbahani not only in publicly supporting the shah and mobilizing a clamorous pro-shah crowd but also in testing and confirming Mosaddeq's vulnerability to manufactured popular agitation. Many of those who would act so effectively in the coup of August were at work in the February episode. Mob leader Tayyeb Haj Reza'i was recruited by Behbahani and retired chief of staff Gen. Abbas

Garzan, a pro-Zahedi royalist.[230] Other well-known thugs, such as Sha'ban Ja'fari—who had maintained links with Makki, Baqa'i, and more closely with Kashani—would be at the forefront of antigovernment demonstrations, along with his followers.[231] They were joined by the pro-shah, court-financed Arya Party, the small fascist party SOMKA, and gangs of underclass elements brought in by army trucks and harangued by senior retired officers. Subsequently, Haj Reza'i, Ja'fari, and several of their acolytes were imprisoned but released in time to take part in the August coup.[232] The February episode revealed the feasibility of a tactical alliance of virtually all anti-Mosaddeq forces, relying on hired crowds and benefiting from aroused royalist sentiments and popular fears. Such sentiments and fears could be stimulated by portraying the shah as maligned and victimized and by forewarning of the imminent abolition of the monarchy and a communist takeover. Immensely emboldening Mosaddeq's domestic and foreign opponents, this episode severely weakened the Mosaddeqists and paved the way for the intensified final campaign under the joint auspices of the CIA and SIS; it set the scene and served as a dress rehearsal for the events of August 19, 1953. Mosaddeq's opponents, having ensured that his challenge to the shah's residual influence would backfire, appeared to have learned far more from this crucially instructive episode than did his supporters.

In the face of violent mob attacks against his residence, Mosaddeq went to the Majles, where he encountered the intractable hostility of deputies such as Ha'erizadeh, who acted with Kashani's blessing.[233] Eventually, public order was restored. Mosaddeq had earlier appointed General Afshartus as chief of police, and he now replaced the chief of staff, General Mahmud Baharmast, with the reliable general Taqi Riahi. He also appointed Gen. Mahmud Amini as deputy defense minister.[234] The latter three officers were senior members of the pro-government Association of Nationalist Officers.[235] In Mosaddeq's view, Baharmast was guilty of dereliction of duty; throughout the critical hours of February 28, rather than attending to his duties, the chief of staff had remained at the court.[236] He had told the U.S. air attaché that he was going to the court to tell the shah that the entire general staff had decided to resign should the shah proceed with his plan to leave the country.[237]

In circumstances where some of Mosaddeq's former allies pledged their unequivocal support for the shah, the latter found an opportunity to test his chances, being psychologically in need of an uplifting expression of public support. Public clamor, albeit organized, for abandoning his trip not only boosted his morale but reaffirmed the monarchy's institutional weight and place in the popular imagination. In a report to the U.S. president, the CIA observed that the institution of the Crown "may have more popular backing than was expected." [238] The February episode also destroyed the last vestige of trust Mosaddeq may have had in the shah. Blaming the shah and the court for deceiving him and even intending to eliminate him through an unleashed mob, he subsequently refused any audience with the shah. [239] Henderson concluded that reconciliation between the shah and Mosaddeq was not possible other than through the shah's capitulation. [240] This was, however, an outcome that Mosaddeq's domestic and foreign opponents, including Henderson, were determined to prevent.

The February episode also deeply and adversely affected relations between Mosaddeq and Henderson. In his approach to Iran and to Mosaddeq in particular, Henderson shared many of the assumptions of his British counterpart. In early January 1952 he had described Iran as a "sick country" and Mosaddeq as "one of its most sick leaders." [241] By late May he had concluded that there would be no oil solution as long as Mosaddeq remained in power. [242] Believing that Mosaddeq was leading Iran to ruin, he acted against the prime minister in the course of the developments resulting in the July uprising. With Mosaddeq's return to power, however, and realizing that his removal might prove difficult, the ambassador modified his stance. On the eve of the February episode, Henderson, prompted by Ala, unhesitatingly sided with the shah against Mosaddeq; this once again revealed the inseparability of domestic and foreign anti-Mosaddeq opposition. Mosaddeq reminded Henderson of the adverse effects of his intervention. [243] He even implicitly considered Henderson to have been involved in schemes to eliminate him. According to Mosaddeq, while he was in the palace bidding the shah farewell, Henderson went to the prime minister's residence and urgently requested to speak to him without, in fact, having any pressing matter to discuss. This would have required Mosaddeq to leave the palace and thus expose himself to mob violence, which, if not resulting in his physical elimination, could have irretrievably and adversely affected his dignity, pride, and public image, leaving him no choice but to resign. [244]

Following the February episode and the rejection of the Anglo–American oil proposal, Henderson became more discernibly anti-Mosaddeq. While admitting that there was no evidence that Mosaddeq had made arrangements with the Tudeh Party, he contended that Mosaddeq was capable of doing so to maintain his hold on power. [245] In his highly tendentious dispatch of March 10, 1953, which echoed many themes laboriously reiterated by Shepherd, Henderson reported, "Mosaddeq [is] so much [a] creature [of] his own emotion[s], prejudices and suspicions, that attempts to analyze motives [of] his various actions in [the] light [of] ordinary rules [of] logic or [on the] basis of reason might well lead one astray." [246] Clearly intending to provide further justification for toppling Mosaddeq, he blamed him for searching out "some new opponents to blame and destroy." Portraying Mosaddeq's opponents as virtually blameless victims of his irrational phobias, Henderson warned that Mosaddeq might do to the Americans what he had done to the British, namely, break off diplomatic relations. [247]

The Final Showdown

Following the February episode, Mosaddeq's opponents in the Majles, who had became increasingly vocal since late 1952, became more adamant on using the Majles against the government. Led by Ha'erizadeh and Baqa'i, a number of deputies deserted the pro-Mosaddeq bloc to form new factions irreconcilably opposed to the government. Invariably invoking the Constitution and Mosaddeq's deviation from it, the parliamentary opponents, encouraged and led by his former supporters, resorted to various tactics and onslaughts to cripple him. Mosaddeq had in the past deftly succeeded in discomfiting such opponents, forcing them to retreat. They were now bent on resorting to every conceivable means to frustrate and discomfit him. He could not now disregard the looming possibility of defeat through quasi-legal means masterminded by his embittered former supporters, acting in full concert with his other enemies. The whole array of Mosaddeq's opponents, including Ala and Henderson, looked to the Majles with reassuring anticipation and worked to encourage it and help it succeed. What had proved impossible to bring about through the Sixteenth Majles could now feasibly be accomplished by its successor. Increasingly the Majles ceased to function meaningfully; it became an arena of acrimonious confrontations, punctuated by doomed mediation efforts.

Subversive efforts assumed a new dimension with the kidnapping and murder of General Afshartus in April 1953, which was the outcome of a convoluted plot mainly involving British agents and pro-Zahedi retired officers and activists. According to Darbyshire, there had been no intention to murder Afshartus, but his abusive remarks about the shah drove one officer to shoot him. [248] Iranian government investigations concurred that there had been no premeditated plan to murder Afshartus but maintained that he had been strangulated, on the orders of retired general Ali Asghar Mozayyani. [249] It is difficult to imagine, however, that murder would not have been the inevitable outcome of Afshartus's abduction and severe torture. The investigations quickly resulted in the arrest of seventeen suspects, including six retired officers. The government asserted that the plotters had also planned to kidnap Riahi, Fatemi, and other senior government officials with the ultimate aim of creating an atmosphere of terror and bringing down Mosaddeq.[250] Summoned for questioning, Zahedi went to the Majles and, with Kashani's express approval, took sanctuary; through his supporters among the deputies he continued to communicate with his followers. Baqa'i, also implicated, escaped arrest because he enjoyed parliamentary immunity;[251] he accused the government of torturing those under arrest and castigated Mosaddeq for collusion with the Tudeh Party to abolish the monarchy.[252]

No direct links, with the Rashidians or others, were uncovered. Afshartus certainly knew more than any other pro-Mosaddeq senior police officer about the activities of the Rashidians, Zahedi, and others, which may have proved the decisive factor in his elimination. At the same time, his abduction and murder served the objective of destabilizing the government; his fate not only warned and demoralized other officers but also helped to cripple the government's capability to maintain public order and curb subversive activities. It further exposed and enhanced the vulnerability of the government, while sluggish legal proceedings against the suspects emboldened its opponents.[253]

The government's declared intention to punish the perpetrators of Afshartus's murder further aggravated animosities in the Majles. By preventing the required quorum, Mosaddeq's opponents ensured that the Majles would not be able to approve a committee report reaffirming Mosaddeq's control over the army and his constitutional contention that the shah's tasks were essentially ceremonial. Mosaddeq's supporters succeeded, however, in unseating Kashani as Majles Speaker and replaced him with the pro-Mosaddeq Abdollah Mo'azzami. Opposition deputies did not remain passive; Baqa'i's protégé Ali Zohari promptly tabled a motion of interpellation against the government alleging that it tortured those accused of Afshartus's murder.[254] They also succeeded in arranging Makki's election to oversee the government's note issue. This move deepened Mosaddeq's conviction that the primary strategy of his opponents was to utilize the Majles to give a semblance of legality to his overthrow. In fact, as early as May 20 CIA and SIS operatives had been "specifically authorized" to spend one million rials ($12,000) a week, an inordinate sum by local standards, "in purchasing the cooperation" of the deputies.[255] They had calculated that for a quorum of fifty-three deputies, of whom forty-one would vote against Mosaddeq, they needed to purchase twenty deputies in addition to those they already controlled.[256] When Mosaddeq's supporters began to resign, the CIA and SIS agents tried to prevent others from following suit, encouraging them to "take up *bast*" (political sanctuary) in the Majles and to act as the "legitimate parliamentary body."[257]

Mosaddeq was aware of his opponents' moves and did not hesitate to proceed with the referendum to dissolve the Majles. Some deputies, including supporters such as Mo'azzami, unsuccessfully tried to dissuade him, arguing that the continued resignation of deputies made a referendum unnecessary. Mosaddeq, however, maintained that the behavior of the Majles minority endangered the nationalist movement.[258] Resorting to a referendum, which as an idea had preoccupied Mosaddeq at least since early 1953, was, despite the understandable reservations of some of his supporters, a shrewd move designed to deny his opponents the quasi-legal camouflage for his engineered overthrow, pursued through a variety of covert and overt measures. Mosaddeq was determined to deny his opponents, including the shah, the satisfaction of ousting him with the help of a Majles the elections for which he himself had conducted. The dissolution of the Majles, and the reluctance of prominent religious dignitaries, most notably Ayatollah Borujerdi, to support active opposition to Mosaddeq, thwarted the implementation of a significant component of the CIA-SIS plan, which was to organize religiously sanctioned mass sit-ins in the compound of the Majles, thereby paving the way for the deputies to unseat Mosaddeq by giving him a vote of no confidence.[259]

Following the February episode the shah, although considerably encouraged and emboldened, persisted in his strategy of awaiting Mosaddeq's removal through the Majles. He reassured the deputies and the civilian and military officials supporting him that his present silence was expedient.[260] In response to increasing pressure from Ala and others, he remained adamant that he would not dismiss Mosaddeq unless the Majles gave the premier a vote of no confidence.[261] Even at the end of May the shah still seemed reluctant to support Zahedi. In conjunction with the CIA-SIS plan, Henderson had a crucial meeting with the shah in which the shah continued to maintain that he would support Zahedi if Zahedi were to assume office "through legal parliamentary means," if he enjoyed a "wide measure of political support," and if he was acceptable to the United States and Britain, which should be ready to help the new government financially and through "massive economic aid."[262] Persistent in his suspicions of the British, the shah had earlier, through an emissary, given vent to his lingering complaints against Britain, stating that if they "wished him to go he should be told immediately so that he could leave quietly."[263] Henderson did his best to reassure the monarch of American and British backing and conveyed to him a personal message of support from Churchill. The shah appeared to be reassured;[264] his anxieties, however, would not easily evaporate.

Pessimistic about the shah and without initially sharing British optimism about Zahedi, Henderson believed that the only way to unseat Mosaddeq was a coup in the shah's name but without the shah's knowledge.[265] He continued to maintain that "the premise that the shah would cooperate actively was fallacious."[266] In view of the Crown's demonstrated utility in mobilizing popular sentiments, and in the absence of the Majles, the idea of a coup without active royal support, however, did not seem viable. Without the Majles to lend an appearance of legitimacy to Mosaddeq's removal, royal support or acquiescence was crucial to the success of a monarchist coup. It was the only available mechanism of legitimation, and would help to sway the army and appeal to royalist sentiments. Mosaddeq's opponents had long considered the cooperation of the shah as essential; it was now more so than ever. The CIA operative Kermit Roosevelt considered it "hopeless to attempt to proceed without the shah."[267] Hence the CIA and the SIS undertook immense efforts to enlist the shah's cooperation.

In the aftermath of the February episode, the murder of Afshartus, and the effective elimination of the Majles, the government could not discount the possibility of imminent drastic action by its opponents. Lacking the requisite organizational, infrastructural, military, and intelligence capabilities, the Mosaddeqists were, however, ill prepared. Mosaddeq was informed about the impending coup through various sources, including a senior finance ministry retiree and government supporter,[268] before General Riahi, the army chief of staff, learned of it. Riahi resorted to countermeasures that were inadequate. His leadership capabilities have often been questioned, and it has been alleged that he acted complacently.[269] Nevertheless, even if he had possessed the requisite will and presence of mind, Riahi did not have the necessary resources and opportunity to accomplish much more than he did. Finding reliable and capable officers to command the key units of the army and the police had not proved an easy task. Riahi's contingency and precautionary measures were no more inadequate than measures resorted to by the government itself. In the event of having to face a stark choice, the army's traditional structure and organizational interests would in all likelihood have led the majority of its rank and file to favor the shah. In extending civilian control over the army, Mosaddeq had proceeded with tact, delegating most tasks such as determining retirements, promotions, or transfers to committees of reputable officers. The disgruntled retirees and other officers who were adversely affected had, however, come to blame

Mosaddeq, actively working for his downfall. And yet the shah no longer controlled the army; the army could not be relied upon to disobey its Mosaddeqist commanders and was divided along various lines. In the CIA's assessment, "Officers were generally 'pro-Shah,' 'pro-Mossadeq [*sic*],' or 'fence-sitters.' The intensity of individual *political* motivations was different in each case, and was often less important than *personal* motivations such as ambition, jealousy, young officers' resentments of old officers and vice versa." [270]

For the first time in Iranian history and despite numerous obstacles, a civilian government had succeeded in exerting such a degree of control over the army that not only Zahedi but even the shah could not count on tangible military support.[271] The army's chief of staff as well as a number of other senior officers, such as General Amini, commander of the rural police (gendarmerie), were progovernment; the commanders of the five brigades stationed in Tehran had also sworn loyalty to Mosaddeq.[272] The army did not appear willing to act against Mosaddeq on its own initiative. The local plotters of the coup had primarily counted on the support of the royal guards and on the collaboration of officers lured through various inducements. Despite prolonged encouragement and the opportunity to perceive of and portray himself as the main contender for succeeding Mosaddeq, and in spite of the presumption that he was relying heavily on his military laurels, Zahedi had placed his hopes primarily on his foreign backers. The CIA's assessment of him was damning: he lacked "drive, energy and [a] concrete plan";[273] he had virtually "no military assets" [274] and had designated no "military secretariat." The CIA had to furnish him with a military plan and forces.[275] His redeeming features were not his military or political capabilities but his readiness to be "the only man openly bidding for the prime ministership" and the fact that he was "known to be pro-American." [276] Zahedi's various failings were replicated at the level of the entire opposition to Mosaddeq, which was heterogeneous and discordant and had no clear plan other than to bring about his downfall with foreign backing. It lacked genuine public support and was devoid of statesmen of real national standing and prestige. Without cumulative and effective foreign backing, such opposition could not have achieved its objectives; the majority of those who came out in its support did so with the realization or in anticipation of being on the winning side.

Insufficiently aware of the scale and nature of foreign support for the coup, the Mosaddeqists believed that the plotters, having suffered a setback, would be too demoralized and disoriented to regroup and react promptly. The cumulative impact of the prolonged and enervating war of attrition to which the

Mosaddeqists had been subjected ensured that they themselves were more disoriented than their opponents. In those crucial few days scarcely a member of Mosaddeq's entourage appeared to be mentally prepared to face such a situation or capable of thinking and acting imaginatively in search of a viable way out of the crisis. Virtually none of Mosaddeq's colleagues showed any real initiative, and the cabinet succumbed to a state of disarray.[277] Many of them were at best dedicated administrators; they were not imaginative statesmen. The account provided of those days by Gholam Hossein Sadiqi, Mosaddeq's loyal, respected, and learned interior minister, reveals a narrowly bureaucratic and inappropriately routine and complacent approach to the crisis.[278] More crucially, the fragility of the Mosaddeqists' hold on power severely narrowed their options. In the meantime, Riahi and other military and police chiefs remained reassuring; the plot appeared to have been foiled and, as it was later admitted, the plotters themselves had succumbed to "pangs of despair."[279] The turn of events did not therefore seem unduly alarming to the Mosaddeqists.

In the context of ongoing CIA-SIS operations and the activities of agents provocateurs to promote panic and chaos, outbreaks of disorder, whether by or in the name of the Tudeh Party, had to be controlled.[280] The "Tudeh" demonstrations organized by the CIA and the SIS on August 17 and 18 considerably alarmed the general populace and gave a sense of urgency to efforts to maintain calm and restore order. This also meant restraining progovernment forces. The speed and nature of developments also prevented the Mosaddeqists from carefully considering their options and acting accordingly. Foreign Minister Hossein Fatemi's vehement public attacks against the shah,[281] considered by a number of other Mosaddeqists as ill advised and counterproductive, indicated that at least for some Mosaddeqists the shah's reign, if not his dynasty or the monarchy itself, had come to an end. Some Mosaddeqists, notably Ahmad Zirakzadeh, Fatemi, and Razavi, favored radical measures such as establishing a republic, a move strongly advocated by the Tudeh Party. Shouldering a tremendous burden of responsibility and despite pressure from various quarters, Mosaddeq wanted to steer a more cautious course.[282] On August 18, Henderson, who had returned to Tehran the day before, called upon Mosaddeq not only to ascertain his intentions but also to add to his disorientation and weaken his resolve, and perhaps neutralize his intended countermeasures,[283] all the while feigning ignorance of what was taking place, as Mosaddeq later noted.[284] Ironically, later that day, when the CIA and the SIS, after another day "featured by depression and despair," were ready to call off the operation,[285] Mosaddeq was moving toward adopting strong measures such as asking the shah to abdicate or even putting an end to the Pahlavi dynasty.[286] On the next and very day that his government was toppled (August 19, 1953/28 Mordad 1332), Mosaddeq intended to prepare for a referendum to determine the political future of the country.[287] In the face of growing turmoil in the streets, on that fateful day it took the government, which was accustomed to street unrest, some time to awaken to the gravity of the situation. Of course, had Mosaddeq appealed to the public, he would in all likelihood have been able to turn the tide of events in his favor. Despite the insistence of several of his loyal followers, he was, however, averse to doing so,[288] as he had been in the course of the July 1952 crisis. He was apprehensive of the consequences and unwilling to countenance violence. Mosaddeq's refusal to call upon his supporters crucially benefited the plotters.

Having with deep trepidation given his support to the coup, the shah fled in haste as the plans backfired.[289] Even with constant bolstering by domestic and foreign supporters, the shah had not seemed optimistic that he could retain the throne.[290] The Pahlavi clan was not popular; the shah's flight damaged his prestige and perhaps his self-respect further, and yet, in the context of the campaign of propaganda and war of nerves coordinated by the CIA and the SIS, his flight, increasingly portrayed as eviction by Mosaddeq, benefited the plotters and added to existing apprehension and anxieties about the consequences of

Tanks in Ferdowsi Square, August 19, 1953. Stephen Langlie Collection, GB165–0351–2.1.19, Middle East Centre Archive, St. Antony's College, Oxford. Courtesy Stephen Langlie USAF/MAAG.

the monarchy's collapse. It helped to galvanize sectors of the Tehran lower and underclasses, who felt a sense of attachment to the Crown, as it provided an assurance of continuity, or they perceived in its glamour a sublimation of their unfulfilled desires. Clamorous, actively pro-shah crowds were, however, instigated, organized, and stage managed by the coup operatives who had paved the way through propaganda, relying on financial largesse and the help of professional mob leaders.[291]

The Mosaddeqists' reaction to the coup was characterized by a remarkable lack of agility and decisiveness, but the performance of the coup's perpetrators was no more impressive. Despite extensive foreign support and rigorous planning, the initial or military stage of the coup was executed ineptly; several officers were arrested, many faltered, and leading figures were saved only through American protection. The coup's subsequent course and success were haphazard and contingent. The coup must, of course, not be understood narrowly; it was in many respects a concentrated final blow delivered against a cumulatively incapacitated, fragile government. The Mosaddeqists might have succeeded in averting collapse in August, but in the face of overwhelming odds, they could only hope to maintain their hold on power by adopting a revolutionary cast of mind and course of action, for which they were fundamentally ill equipped. The singular purpose of the relentlessly bitter hostility to Mosaddeq had been to render his position ultimately untenable. The coup was the culmination of a prolonged process to unseat a government that had seriously threatened an array of vested interests: it neither conceded to resolve the oil issue to the satisfaction of the West nor condoned competing clusters of notables vying for spoils and influence under the auspices of a patronage-dispensing monarchy. Determined to retrieve their endangered interests and influence, and unconcerned with the lasting damage to Iranian patriotic sensibilities and democratic aspirations, the British and later the U.S. governments inspired, shaped, sustained, and manipulated the domestic opponents wishing to undermine Mosaddeq, while such opponents helped to encourage, rationalize, and camouflage the extensive activities of Mosaddeq's foreign enemies.

Mosaddeq in Context:
Possibilities and Structural Constraints

Mosaddeq's aristocratic family background and kinship ties to Qajar royalty do not shed much light on his political conduct or orientations. He should be viewed in the context of a distinct tradition of political conduct associated with a number of publicly acclaimed, reputable statesmen who emerged on the eve of or following the Constitutional Revolution. This tradition was anchored in socially valued and culturally sanctioned notions of personal integrity (*pak-damani*) and honor (*sharaf*), as well as patriotism. It was geared to the pursuit of an ethical politics or a politics strongly informed by principle-centered moral considerations and shaped by public expectations and responses. Premised on a sharp contrast between the state (*daulat*) and the nation (*mellat*), this tradition more congenially lent itself either to a morally hygienic oppositional politics or to readiness to abandon governmental service in politically adverse circumstances where integrity could be compromised or reputation tarnished. Notwithstanding, Mosaddeq's long record of service did not merely comprise his career as a parliamentarian; he had served as minister, deputy minister, and provincial governor and had the requisite practical knowledge of administration. The task of assuming the premiership at one of the most critical junctures in Iranian history was, however, a venture requiring not only experience, mental preparedness, courage, and patriotic commitment but also a certain degree of willful optimism. Such optimism rested on the belief that his goal of promoting Iranian national sovereignty would continue to have extensive and unopposable public resonance, assuring him of widespread popular support. He also believed that regardless of his own success or failure, the intensified struggle that had culminated in the nationalization of the oil industry was bound to continue if Iran were eventually to enjoy the fruits of national sovereignty and democracy.

Mosaddeq accepted the premiership not as the head of an established political party well prepared to assume power but as the leader of a heterogeneous, almost spontaneous movement intrinsically geared to an oppositional stance, and ill suited as a basis for government. He lacked an effective organizational base of support and had to rely primarily on public support and confidence, sustained mainly through his own carefully cultivated, untarnished image of personal integrity and patriotic dedication. This, although a great source of strength, was bound to limit his room for maneuver; he often had to avoid politically expedient courses of action that were likely to harm or erode his public image. To speak of Mosaddeq as a leader is, of course, to underline his power and agency in defiance of unqualified structural determinism and to maintain that it was within his power to act differently. Nevertheless, a facile rational-choice or decisionist approach should be abandoned in favor of greater attention to structural determinants of action. The context as well as the constraints within which Mosaddeq operated, including the absence of a sustained organizational base of support and relentless destabilization maneuvers, severely debilitated him and deprived him of a whole range of options.

Mosaddeq was the incumbent of the office of prime minister, which was formally in charge of the executive but was structurally and institutionally incapable of effective and sustained exercise of authority. The prevailing perception of the Constitution severely limited the authority of the prime minister. Such authority had to be negotiated through a complex and exhausting process involving the court and a host of political brokers both inside and outside Parliament; it remained intrinsically tenuous. The prevalent assumptions and practices, shared even by some of his own supporters, were, in Mosaddeq's eyes, contrary to the spirit of the Constitution and the prerequisites of democracy. He refused to countenance or indefinitely tolerate a situation in which the prime minister, who formally headed the executive, was systematically enfeebled, while the politically unaccountable monarch was the chief player and the focal point in the political process as well as the primary dispenser of patronage. Mosaddeq had also realized the extent to which the Parliament could be manipulated to undermine the government. His demand for extra powers to draft and provisionally implement bills was a response, albeit an ad hoc and temporary one, to this untenable situation with which he had coped for over a year. He hoped that such powers would reduce occasions for friction between the government and the Parliament and would diminish the opportunity of his foreign-backed opponents to manipulate the Parliament against the government.[292] Without such powers, he did not believe he could meaningfully continue in office.[293] Similarly, Mosaddeq's efforts to extend civilian control over the army was a crucial step toward a meaningful constitutional government. No prime minister to date had, of course, succeeded in acting with any real measure of authority without antagonizing both the Parliament and the court.

Mosaddeq had always insisted on free elections and had argued that if "real" representatives of the people were elected, they would not deviate from dedication to the greater good of the country. His main strategy for ensuring free elections was, however, to advocate better laws and procedures, and even in this he proved unsuccessful. There are no indications that he had adequately addressed the issues of how and on the basis of what viable strategy or practical plan, a supportive Majles, which his cabinet desperately needed, could come about. His almost literal noninterventionist approach to electoral freedom was highly counterproductive and in no way conducive to the emergence of a Parliament in which a majority of deputies consistently supported the government. In his idiosyncratic understanding of noninterference in the electoral process, he seemed deeply troubled by the idea of promoting pro-National Front candidates, nor was he confident that such a policy was fully legitimate or compatible with democratic principles of fair and free elections. He was, therefore, inexcusably bereft of any clear approach to ensuring electoral freedom and thwarting the customary electoral manipulation in the provinces, other than insisting that there should be no inappropriate governmental interference.[294] Nor did his successive interior ministers have the ability or the opportunity and administrative means to ensure that nonintervention would not readily benefit vocal opponents of the government, who were in a position to manipulate the procedures to their advantage. The illiterate rural and nomadic populations were easily manipulated by provincial notables, and the majority of would-be voters in the provinces, accustomed to believing that their votes made no difference, abstained or voted as instructed by local leaders or officials. Mosaddeq's various opponents remained determined to deny him a secure majority in the Majles. The army commanders did not follow his instructions, and certain army chiefs pursued their own agendas.[295]

Mosaddeq not only refused publicly to support any specific candidate or to allow his name to be associated with any electoral list, but, curiously, he even maintained that the National Front as a single body should refrain from nominating candidates.[296] He feared that the National Front's presentation of a list of names and attempts to promote them could be construed as electoral manipulation by the government.[297] He also wanted to avoid further antagonizing and alarming the shah, who had always proved deeply averse to all attempts, other than court-sponsored ones, to control or affect parliamentary elections. In fact the court, many army commanders, local magnates, and Mosaddeq's various other opponents actively concentrated on ensuring that the Seventeenth Majles would be as uncooperative with Mosaddeq as possible, while the National Front pathetically squabbled over its tactics and failed to devise an effective strategy.

The National Front's various political segments jointly nominated a number of candidates, but the disagreements that existed between such groups, for instance between the Iran Party and the Toilers Party or between individuals such as Makki and Baqa'i, in addition to the complaints of the irascible and ever irritable Ha'erizadeh or the wrangling caused by the conduct of Kashani and his sons (Sayyed Mohammad, Mostafa, and Abolma'ali), added to the prevailing confusion.[298] The Iran Party had a longer record and a greater number of renowned and competent individuals than any other group within the National Front. Intensely jealous of the Iran Party, Baqa'i demanded that his party should have a role and opportunity equal to that of the Iran Party, and he wanted to put forward the same number of candidates. There was the likelihood that the Qanatabadi-led pro-Kashani Association of Muslim Warriors might have similar expectations.[299] The elections for the Seventeenth Majles precipitated the disintegration of the National Front.

It has been argued that the manner of conducting the elections for the Seventeenth Majles constituted Mosaddeq's most significant tactical error.[300] It was more than that; it was a strategic incapability and failure of leadership, rooted in and aggravated by the very configuration of the movement he represented. Mosaddeq's attitude to the elections for the Seventeenth Majles was molded and constrained by his peculiarly narrow understanding of free elections, his insufficient appreciation of the necessity for adequate organization, his desire to transcend partisan politics, and his hope that others like Kashani would follow suit. He wished to avoid accusations of improper electoral conduct. Mosaddeq could not have failed to appreciate the indispensability of a cooperative parliament but did not have the organizational means for its realization. His approach to the elections was largely rooted in the deep and self-evident limitations of the National Front as an organizational framework. Undoubtedly Mosaddeq desired a situation in which progovernment candidates competed effectively with others. The National Front was not, however, the appropriate organizational vehicle to render this possible; no substitute existed and no serious effort had been made to overcome this handicap; nor were its dangerous implications fully comprehended.

The National Front had been an undisciplined, intrinsically fragile coalition of mostly well-meaning but also self-centered individuals, as well as loosely organized small associations. It was not a political entity structurally capable of overcoming its crippling oppositional perceptual mold; it could not transform itself into a political party intent on self-perpetuation, dedicated to a program and strategy for furthering its influence and political aims, and playing a major role in governance. Both at the beginning and toward the end of Mosaddeq's premiership, efforts were made to form a political party, spearheaded in the beginning by Fatemi and later by the pro-Mosaddeq parliamentarian Ali Shayegan, but nothing concrete was achieved. Mosaddeq and virtually all of his supporters seemed pessimistic about the feasibility and prospects of a large-scale and durable political party. The prevailing political culture was averse to the emergence of viable political parties.[301] Prime ministers needed to display considerable restraint in not provoking the court, which had proved to be manifestly inimical to political parties.[302] The astonishing rise and rapid disintegration of Qavam's seemingly impregnable Democratic Party of Iran was too salutary a lesson to be forgotten. The Mosaddeqists were overwhelmed by their political preoccupations and discouraged by existing circumstances and constraints, including royal hostility to court-independent political associations. Nevertheless, without a firm organizational basis of support through which public backing could be both mobilized and channeled, they could not expect to maintain their tenuous hold on power.

The very Majles on whose support Mosaddeq was to rely in his dogged pursuit of an honorable oil settlement proceeded in an inauspicious act of defiance to elect the anti-Mosaddeq Hasan Emami as Speaker and later, in a deviously shrewd move, to opt for Kashani. Pro-Mosaddeq deputies, having organized themselves into the National Movement faction, constituted the largest bloc in the Majles and remained loyal in their support; following the departure of the defectors they became more homogeneous. Although dedicated to civic nationalist principles and common political aims, the faction members cooperated with and tolerated each other primarily because of the uncontested leadership of Mosaddeq. He was the only leader whose moral and political authority they did not defy. There was no consensus on who should be the second in command, and no readily accepted hierarchy. The Mosaddeqist faction continued to have the upper hand but not to the extent of being able to ensure that Mosaddeq continued confidently to enjoy the support of a solid majority. Spearheaded by the defectors, the heterogeneous parliamentary opposition, having overcome the shock of the July uprising, grew into an increasingly vociferous and serious threat.

The impossibility of procuring a reliably supportive Majles had helped to convince Mosaddeq further that were he to continue in office he needed to strengthen his position. Despite latent accusations of deviance from the Constitution, Mosaddeq was determined to acquire extra powers but entertained no illusion about overcoming obstacles. Soon after his assumption of office he had realized how the Parliament, or a minority of deputies and senators, could be manipulated or mobilized with the aim of debilitating him. He had previously survived such maneuvers primarily as a result of continued public support. In the course of his second year in office, and despite having acquired extra powers, many of his reformist measures were thwarted, and he remained vulnerable to the quasi-parliamentary and seemingly legal machinations of his parliamentary opponents, who were much bolstered by the defectors. Through sources such as Javad Ganjeh'i, a Tabriz deputy, and Abolfazl Tuliyat, deputy for Qom, who had abandoned opposition to Mosaddeq in favor of support, the prime minister was aware of moves on the part of foreign agents such as the Rashidians to procure collaborators among the deputies.[303] As he confided to Kazem Hasibi in late July 1953, Mosaddeq feared that the Majles could preemptively topple the government, a move that in his eyes was tantamount to formal legal surrender to foreign antagonists.[304] Dissolving the Majles through a referendum, justifiably described as Mosaddeq's political masterpiece,[305] was an ingenious countermeasure adopted by him to deprive his opponents of a quasi-legal vehicle for his ouster. The opposition capitalized on the referendum, denouncing it as another blatant violation of the Constitution. While Behbahani failed to find religious grounds for pronouncing it unlawful, Kashani declared it religiously impermissible and called on the faithful not to take part in it.[306] Mosaddeq did not falter, as he rightly believed that his defeat through parliamentary machinations, long pursued by his royalist and pro-British opponents, would irreparably harm the very ideals that he had long endeavored to promote. The dissolution of the Majles was to be followed by elections for the next Majles, which would have constituted an unprecedented challenge had Mosaddeq survived in office to face and conduct them.

Mosaddeq's avowed commitment to promoting and respecting political and civil rights and liberties and allowing the due process of law to take its course greatly benefited his enemies who, untroubled by any similar considerations, resorted to whatever measures possible to undermine his government. Existing legal loopholes, the evident inadequacy and inefficiency of the legal procedures, and the absence of adequate mechanisms for expeditious law enforcement meant that plotters continued to act unhindered. Mosaddeq had to operate within the confines of a cumbersome, corruption-ridden, ineffective, and vulnerable bureaucratic and legal apparatus. There was also no reliable and efficient government-controlled intelligence-gathering apparatus; police and security forces, traditionally controlled by the court or its appointees, largely operated outside the orbit of effective governmental oversight. Mosaddeq also had to contend with an army whose collective institutional interests were more congenial with close ties to the Crown than with the control of a financially overstretched government. Mosaddeq had experienced serious problems in exercising effective control over the army as well as the police; he had to rely on essentially unreformed police and security forces whose very ethos was scarcely congruent with Mosaddeqist objectives. He had tried to choose commanders who would not unnecessarily provoke the court, but he came eventually to appoint reliable progovernment officers such as Generals Riahi, Amini, and Afshartus. Afshartus's gruesome fate, however, constituted a grim warning to officers willing to serve the government loyally.

The question of the government's treatment of foreign agents such as the Rashidians, whose extensive activities could not have and had not gone unnoticed but who continued to act virtually unhindered, is mystifying.[307] In the crucial weeks before the coup, Asadollah Rashidian's opportunity to travel to Europe to meet SIS officials such as Darbyshire puzzled even the CIA.[308] Were such lapses due to bureaucratic or security failings and complacency, the absence of intelligence, or foul play? Why were the Rashidians' regular wireless communications with SIS headquarters in Cyprus not intercepted, despite the availability of the technical means to do so? Why did the activities around the court, the U.S. embassy, and the residences of the American personnel in Tehran remain unchecked or escape adequate notice? The government's opponents, whether from the Left or the Right, had continued with their demonstrations, associations, and publications with astonishing impunity. The remarkable lenience with which such active opponents, particularly domestic agents of foreign powers, had been treated emboldened them to intensify the scale of their activities. The Mosaddeq government's treatment of them, including those who took part in the February 1953 episode, verging on complacency, did not escape the criticism of his supporters.[309]

While some of his perceptive supporters, such as Khalil Maleki, "that most realistic of Iranian idealists,"[310] regretted Mosaddeq's "liberalism," which also implied a lax attitude toward subversive opponents,[311] Mosaddeq's opponents constantly accused him of antiliberal and heavy-handed measures. Mosaddeq was convinced that in the context of a society's democratic experiment, strife, factionalism, a vitriolic press, and other abuses and pathological manifestations of freedom could not be easily avoided; they constituted a price societies would have to pay in their march toward political maturity. Insistent on the dangerous implications of unchecked Tudeh militancy and the exploitability of its adventurist activities by Mosaddeq's foreign opponents, Maleki tried in vain to persuade Mosaddeq to deal with the Tudeh Party leadership with greater firmness.[312] While maintaining that the Tudeh Party was as entitled to its beliefs as other groups, Maleki advocated decisive security and legal measures to monitor and contain those of its activities that were detrimental to the government and the civic nationalist movement.[313] Right-wing or Islamist opponents of Mosaddeq also invoked his tolerance of the Tudeh Party to propagate and mobilize opinions against him. Refusing to condone or believe in the efficacy of suppression, Mosaddeq persisted, however, in his adherence to democratic values and insistence on proper legal procedures. Such an approach, in the absence of adequate laws and even less adequate means of law enforcement, in practice severely constrained the opportunity of his government to counter and neutralize his active opponents. Without his policy of tolerance, his domestic and foreign opponents would have found it nearly impossible to engage in their virtually unopposed and unhindered destabilizing and subversive activities.

Immediately following his assumption of office, Mosaddeq decreed that lofty titles should not be used by the media in referring to him and ordered that the press should not in any way be hampered on account of what it published about him.[314] This curious order could be interpreted not only as indicating Mosaddeq's belief in the necessity of press freedom but also as revealing a clear sense of confidence in the indestructibility of his public image and the virtual impossibility of publicly disputing his patriotic agenda. Mosaddeq and his agenda were, however, not invulnerable to modern techniques of propaganda and disinformation.

Not unexpectedly, and parallel with quasi-parliamentary tactics, the opposition press constituted an essential component of the campaign of destabilization against Mosaddeq; it was a significant strategic asset available to his domestic and foreign opponents in their campaign of propaganda against the government. Abolhasan Amidi-Nuri, the editor of *Dad,* was at the forefront of the expanding press campaign. He had been a member of the National Front but had turned against Mosaddeq and had been expelled after bitterly blaming the National Front for his failure to win a seat in the Sixteenth Majles. His role in anti-Mosaddeq activities earned him the position of deputy prime minister under Zahedi.

The opposition press was used by various agents, acting on behalf of the court, the AIOC, British intelligence, and the CIA, to plant articles damaging to the government. The anti-Mosaddeq propaganda campaign was greatly intensified toward the end of his tenure, when the CIA agent Donald Wilber was placed in charge of the extensive propaganda operations in which the foreign-subsidized opposition newspapers played a key role. Following the failure of the coup's initial military stage, the opposition press played an indispensable role in disseminating CIA and SIS propaganda and disinformation. Newspapers such as *Dad* and Baqa'i's *Shahed,* among others, helped to publish and spread manufactured rumors that either there had been no coup or that it had actually been stage managed by Mosaddeq in order to evict the shah; they published fabricated interviews with Zahedi and circulated the royal edict appointing him as prime minister. They implied that Mosaddeq's government was illegal, having in effect launched a coup by rejecting the royal decree. If, due to the government's vigilance, not enough domestic newspapers were able to reprint the royal decree appointing Zahedi, foreign correspondents were used. Occasionally, the large sums spent, such as the "personal loan" of forty-five thousand dollars paid to former senator Abbas Mas'udi, owner of *Ettela'at,* to ensure that the paper was "amenable" to CIA-SIS purposes,[315] did not produce the desired result, as the paper's editor, Ahmad Shahidi, followed a more neutralist stand.[316] There were, however, at least twenty newspapers subsidized by the CIA or SIS that unfailingly complied with their task of aggressively denouncing Mosaddeq.

Prior to August 18 only a handful of newspapers had been able to print the shah's edict appointing Zahedi, but on August 19 it was published and circulated extensively. Clearly the subsidized opposition press proved far more crucial in the final two months of Mosaddeq's term of office than it had prior to that time. In the words of Donald Wilber, "It must be admitted that in the years and months of working with a subsidized press and its venal (or patriotic) journalists in Tehran, the [CIA/SIS] station was still not sure whether it was achieving results comparable to the sums so spent. In July and early August every segment of the press with which we or the United Kingdom had working relations went all out against Mossadeq [*sic*]. As judged by the public reactions on the days following 16 August, there can be no doubt whatsoever that this campaign had reached a very large audience and had directly influenced their thinking in a most positive way." [317]

This revealing assessment fails to recognize the fact that had Mosaddeq's government not allowed a large number of opposition newspapers to exist and had it not tolerated a hostile press campaign, the propaganda machinery of his Anglo-American opponents would have been largely crippled. On average, out of a total of 370 newspapers and journals published during Mosaddeq's term of office, at least 70 publications were hostile to his government.[318] Without an atmosphere of tolerance, newspaper editors and journalists bribed by CIA and SIS agents would not have been able to reproduce material, including cartoons, provided by the CIA, and publish the kind of vitriolic articles that savagely ridiculed Mosaddeq and increasingly denounced him not only as leading the country to chaos and communism but also, and absurdly, as being a dictator.[319]

Although in his seventy-first year and in delicate health, Mosaddeq's stamina seemed inexhaustible. However, toward the end of his tenure as prime minister, the cumulative strains of governing against overwhelming odds fatigued him considerably.[320] What he had intended to accomplish was nothing short of revolutionary, but he was a man of reform. Averse to suppression of opponents, violence, and illegal or immoral means, he nonetheless was confronted by opponents who in their fervor to defeat him did not refrain from using virtually any measure irrespective of legality or morality. He faced severe financial constraints resulting from failure to reach an oil agreement. A corollary to this was the impossibility of initiating reforms that could forestall or alleviate popular frustrations and restlessness and would tangibly appeal to guilds, merchants, and business strata, the workers as well as the unemployed. Mosaddeq had undoubtedly enlisted the cooperation of colleagues who were mostly men of exemplary integrity and sustained dedication to civic nationalist goals. They were, however, not always endowed with commensurate political acumen and administrative ability. Although rarely revealing his inner thoughts, he did not refrain from bemoaning the absence of truly capable colleagues.[321] His colleagues and supporters possessed neither his charisma nor his political acumen; none remotely rivaled him in ability to muster genuine public support, and none commanded the comparable allegiance and respect of their peers. Moreover, the kind of selfless dedication Mosaddeq demanded from his colleagues and the spirit of self-sacrifice he hoped the general populace would display in continuing to support him in his aims were not easily reconcilable with the prevailing exigencies of Iranian society and politics, or the constraints of human frailty.

Mosaddeq had faced the unenviable task of fighting a two-pronged antiimperialist and anti-autocratic war with the certainty of encountering a combined, coordinated, and dogged counterattack. His anti-imperialist and anti-autocratic agenda and strategy accounted for the appeal and the moral hegemony of the National Front, but it was ultimately unlikely to result in success. The structural prerequisites for success were largely nonexistent. Neither the domestic nor the international situation, adversely and deeply affected by the cold war, was conducive to Mosaddeq's success in accomplishing real nationalization of the oil industry or creating and sustaining a credible democratic-constitutional polity. And yet the very struggle to achieve these ends, in Mosaddeq's eyes, was in itself a worthy end and not merely pertaining to the means. His strategy was to persevere in the anti-imperialist, anti-autocratic struggle, to endeavor to maintain the political momentum of the movement, and to overcome orchestrated oppositional machinations through a consistently defiant, transparent, morally unassailable, principle-driven stance. His clearly unconventional and visionary political modus operandi was not easily intelligible to his foreign and domestic detractors; hence the barrage of invective deployed by, among others, the British ambassador, Shepherd, and occasionally his American counterpart, Henderson, denouncing Mosaddeq's alleged irrationality, lunacy, absurdity, and so on.

Mosaddeq and his advisers could arguably have been more flexible on issues such as the vexed and convoluted subject of compensation due to the AIOC. Mosaddeq was fully committed to a dignified settlement of the oil issue that would involve the payment of fair compensation.[322] He was also far more realistically aware of the need for flexibility than his hard-line advisers such as Hasibi. However, it must not be forgotten that he was under tremendous propaganda pressure from both the Left and the Right; they ceaselessly accused him of willingness to compromise and surrender in defiance of national interests. Moreover, the ongoing and incessant British campaign to dislodge him did not help to foster an atmosphere of confidence, a belief in British good faith, or any real measure of trust needed for meaningful negotiation. Deeply distrusting Britain and convinced that the British were adamant in their intentions to undermine and topple his government, Mosaddeq believed that any concession on his part would not eliminate British hostility but could be exploited to extract more favorable terms from a successor government.[323] He was unwilling and unable to entertain any compromise that, in his view, infringed upon Iranian sovereign rights, and he received no offers from Britain that did not do so. Mosaddeq belonged to a generation that had fully experienced the conspicuous power and arrogance of the British Empire and was cognizant of the strategy and machinations the British deployed to sustain and extend their influence. In the context of the historically rooted British domination and Iranian subjugation, his negotiations with Britain had often amounted to little more than an asymmetrical discussion, permeated by deep mutual distrust, incomprehension, and dismissiveness. The stark reality that the British were relentlessly endeavoring to unseat Mosaddeq made it immensely difficult for him to believe that he was participating in sincere dialogue and meaningful negotiation. He and his British detractors were divided by an unbridgeable perceptual gap.

Mosaddeq had won several battles but, in the absence of the structural preconditions of success and in view of the eroded national solidarity partially symbolized by the activities of defectors, he could not feel optimistic about winning the war. He had long realized that the alliance of the United States and Britain, bolstering and acting through his domestic opponents, would overwhelm him. The coup that toppled Mosaddeq was the culmination of an intensified process that aimed not only to incapacitate Mosaddeq as an effective and credible leader and to crush those who supported him, but also to undermine the very ideals he had unfailingly championed. The aim of the coup, which would only succeed as the result of combined foreign and domestic support, was not only to settle the oil issue to the satisfaction of the West but also to subvert the very desires and struggles of the Iranians to achieve national sovereignty and move in a democratic direction. Iran was "saved" as part of "the free world' just as it began to deny its citizens basic political freedoms.[324] The oil issue was settled through systematically denigrating civic nationalism as dangerously fanciful and equating it with failure and chaos, and particularly through reaffirming the shah's pivotal role in the Iranian political process. Accused of treason, Mosaddeq, in his detention cell, could only have felt painfully vindicated in his belief that Western hegemony over Iran had proved sustainable only through revitalizing and endorsing royal autocracy or authoritarian trends. This could only be maintained by coercively suppressing ultimately insuppressible and resilient civic nationalist and democratic aspirations.[325] Despite their triumphalist clamor, his victorious enemies, whether domestic or foreign, did not escape unscathed. Whether in or out of office, Mosaddeq had permanently and crucially changed the Iranian political landscape.

3

The 1953 Coup in Iran
and the Legacy of the Tudeh

Maziar Behrooz

Newly available CIA documentation on the role of the United States and Great Britain in toppling the nationalist government of Mohammad Mosaddeq presents a single, all-embracing motive for the coup.[1] CIA analyst Donald N. Wilber's *Overthrow of Premier Mosaddeq of Iran: November 1952-August 1953* suggests that fears that the Tudeh Party might push Iran into the Soviet camp—geopolitical anxieties conditioned by the cold war—were of prime concern to the perpetrators of the plot and the main justification for Operation TPAJAX.[2] The new CIA documents argue that with the deterioration of Iran's economy under the nationalists, chaos and collapse were probable and would ultimately lead to the loss of Iran to the West. The oil issue is deemed to be of secondary importance in the new documents and is explained away by pointing to an oversupply of petroleum on the international market.

Other chapters in this volume discuss the political and economic state of Iran under Mosaddeq, the British and American programs to undermine his government, and the activities of various Iranian actors other than the Tudeh. This chapter evaluates the role and legacy of the Tudeh in the 1953 coup, examines the party's relationship with the National Front and Mosaddeq himself and the reasons behind its inaction during the crucial August 16–19 period, and attempts to explain why the party was so easily tossed aside during the coup.

Understanding the performance of the Tudeh has become even more important in light of the new evidence. According to the latest documents, the coup plot was successful only on the narrowest of margins. This suggests that a concerted reaction by either the nationalist government or the Tudeh (or both) could have prevented its success. Hence, a realistic portrait of Tudeh strength, the state of its leadership, and the party's relationship with Mosaddeq are the focus of this chapter. What assessment can be made of the Tudeh's organizational strength? Here, the party's abilities should be viewed from two perspectives: first, whether the party was a threat to the nationalist government—that is, whether the party had a plan to take over political power; and second, whether the Tudeh was in a position to counter the coup even if it had no plan to assume state power and was not in a position to do so. Dividing the question into two parts offers the benefit of allowing an assessment of the Tudeh's abilities on two levels. This chapter argues that while the party had neither a plan nor the capability to secure state power for itself in 1953, it could have strengthened its position had it reacted differently to the coup. The Tudeh's posture toward Mosaddeq and the coup was significantly affected by factionalism and the incompetence of its leadership, which translated into inaction and ultimately the decimation of the party.

The Tudeh Organization and Its Strength

Established in 1941, the Tudeh had become a popular political organization by the late 1940s. By 1951, when the oil nationalization movement culminated in the appointment of Mosaddeq as premier, the Tudeh had already managed to survive elimination from the political scene. Following an unsuccessful attempt on the shah's life in early February 1949, the government declared the party illegal and forced it to go underground.

With many of its leaders arrested or in hiding around the country, and with little experience in underground activity, this crisis was the most serious challenge to the party since its establishment. But state repression at this point was not systematic, and, compared to the post–1953 period, was clearly less severe. The party's activities in the early 1950s became semilegal, and it soon managed to reestablish itself by creating a number of front organizations and publications designed to fill the vacuum left by its inability to function fully in the open.

By 1950, the party was publishing three daily papers, *Razm, Mardom,* and *Besui-ye Ayandeh,* and had organized its supporters under the banner of the Iranian Society for Peace (*Jam'iyat-e Irani-ye Havadar-e Solh*). Furthermore, in December 1950 the Tudeh's military network managed to arrange for the escape of key members of the party leadership who had been in jail since early 1949.

By 1951, the nationwide Tudeh organization seems to have adapted to its semilegal status and become almost fully functional under the new political atmosphere of the nationalist government. The government crackdown, nevertheless, had a number of drawbacks for the party. First, while the Tudeh managed to reorganize itself as a semilegal force, it was still limited when it came to participation in legitimate, open political activity. The party was unable to participate in parliamentary elections or maintain official political clubs or headquarters, and its members could be arrested simply by virtue of being associated with the organization.

Second, some experienced party leaders were forced to flee the country, which in effect split control of the party into two groups, those who stayed in Iran and those who left, with real power remaining in the hands of those who stayed. With the departure of some additional top functionaries in 1952 and the cumbersome nature of communication between the two groups, the leadership in Iran ultimately proved unprepared to guide the party during the defining days of 1951–53.

The third impediment was a psychological one, which may have had a directly negative influence on the party's performance during the coup some three years later and may help to explain the leadership's failure to move decisively against the plot. One observer has suggested that in 1953 the top levels of the Tudeh believed that the party could survive the crisis, much as it had in 1949.[3] Nureddin Kianuri, one of the Tudeh's main figures, points in his memoirs to the leadership's false sense of self-assurance and even arrogance as a result of its ability to recover from the earlier crisis.[4]

What assessment can be made of the Tudeh's strength during 1951–53? According to one source, a CIA memorandum dated October 1952 suggested that the party had about twenty thousand hard-core members with eight thousand based in Tehran.[5] Other American intelligence reports during this period confirm this and add that the Tudeh had by then rebuilt its network, drawing its membership from among intellectuals and industrial workers.[6] These intelligence reports also note some of the Tudeh's shortcomings, such as the fact that its appeal was limited to urban dwellers, whereas the overwhelming majority of Iran's population lived in rural areas where the party had no apparent base. None of the reports seem to suggest that the Tudeh was viewed as an imminent danger in terms of its ability to topple the Mosaddeq government. Indeed, one U.S. embassy specialist on the communists has suggested that the party was "well-organized but not very powerful" and that its significance was greater "in the minds of certain U.S. officials than in reality."[7]

As far as the Tudeh threat is concerned, there is a clear difference between Donald Wilber's *Overthrow* and its appendixes and other American appraisals.

While the sources of information used in the other appraisals seem to be the same, Wilber makes much of the communist threat and uses it as an important justification for the coup. Other U.S. intelligence reports generally view the Tudeh factor as much less threatening than Wilber does.

Another asset of the Tudeh was its network within the Iranian military. It should be noted that U.S. intelligence was only partially aware of this network at the time *Overthrow* was produced in March 1954.[8] The Tudeh Party Military Organization of Iran, or TPMO (*Sazman-e Nezami-ye Hezb-e Tudeh-ye Iran*) was established in 1944. It is also sometimes referred to simply as the Officers Organization (*Sazman-e Afsaran*).[9]

The TPMO has generally been considered to be the party's strongest card in the years preceding the coup. Estimates on the number of officers involved in the network vary. All the estimates on the number of personnel involved in the TPMO were provided by the shah's regime after 1954, as the party did not have clear estimates of its own at the time.[10] The official Tudeh estimate of 466 members suggests that 429 people were arrested after the coup and that 37 managed to flee the country. On August 19, 1953, 243 officers were stationed in Tehran and only three or four were serving in the shah's Imperial Guard, the principal military unit counted on to execute the coup. Most of these personnel were in noncombat positions. A high-ranking officer in the TPMO has since given the number of pro–Tudeh officers as 491, which seems to be the most realistic figure.[11]

Had the party chosen to take military action, the TPMO could have counted on some six thousand or more party and Tudeh Party Youth Organization members in Tehran alone.[12] These party estimates are close to U.S. intelligence assessments of the party's strength in the capital. In addition, during August 1953 an officer in charge of a battalion from Hamadan that was brought to Tehran to take part in the coup and another in charge of a company in Chalus were both Tudeh members and able to distribute weapons to the party.[13]

During 1952–53 the TPMO, through its intelligence network in the armed forces, helped to uncover plots against the nationalist government. The TPMO was well aware of the August coup plot and gave the party leaders a warning to this effect that was subsequently passed on to Mosaddeq (see below).

What appraisal can be made of the combined strength of the Tudeh's non-military and military components? Some American intelligence reports did not see an immediate danger in the party's posture, and at least one Tudeh leader's assessment corresponds with this observation. Kianuri states that not only did the party have neither a plan nor the capacity to topple Mosaddeq, it was not even strong enough to defend the nationalist government against the coup.[14] Clearly, there is no evidence that the party had a plan for securing political power for itself in the foreseeable future. It is difficult to imagine how the party could have ousted Mosaddeq with no plan, no real base in the countryside, and with approximately five hundred army officers and between six and eight thousand members and supporters in Tehran.[15]

Does this mean, however, that the party did not have a realistic chance of defending the nationalist government against the coup and saving itself? It is clear that most of the Tudeh officers were in noncombat posts and would have had limited ability to provide the party and Mosaddeq with rapid military counteraction. It is also clear, however, that these officers were in a position to access and distribute weapons.[16] In their memoirs, TPMO high- and middle-ranking members have confirmed their ability to distribute weapons and even to assassinate key Iranian leaders of the coup.[17] Hence, with a disciplined party membership, backed by military officers with access to weapons, the Tudeh had a strong hand. It might not have succeeded in defeating the coup, but there was a strong possibility that it could have. For these party resources to translate into meaningful action, however, a coherent and thoughtful leadership—united and with a vision of how to prepare the party and its assets—was required. As we shall see, this was the area where the party had major shortcomings.

The Tudeh and Mosaddeq

Wilber's *Overthrow* makes much of Mosaddeq's relationship with the Tudeh. It argues that his tolerance of the party made it possible for the Tudeh to grow in strength and pose the danger that served as the partial pretext for the coup. On the other hand, any move by the party to counter the coup would have depended very much on the Tudeh's relationship with Mosaddeq. In the final analysis, it is difficult to imagine how the Tudeh could have moved against the coup without some sort of coordination with the National Front.

The Tudeh reaction to the oil nationalization movement, led by the National Front and Mosaddeq, was, at best, contradictory, in part because the party made its decisions with the interests of the Soviet Union in mind.[18] A fundamental difference between the nationalists, headed by Mosaddeq, and the Tudeh was over their approach to the concept of national sovereignty. For the

Tudeh, its fraternal obligations to the Soviet Union, a concept it also referred to as its international proletarian duty, were of prime significance in formulating its approach. From the party's perspective these commitments played an important role in the international battle between the capitalist and socialist blocs. In this context, if such obligations came into conflict with Iran's national interests, then the latter could be, and in many cases were, compromised.

The nationalists' approach was far removed from such a class-based and ideological approach. For Mosaddeq, national sovereignty of a country like Iran, for so long under foreign domination and occupation, meant national control over its resources and politics. In this context, international developments could be addressed only after national interests were secured. The issue of national sovereignty remained a major point of friction between the Tudeh and the nationalists for years.

In the 1940s and early 1950s, national sovereignty was increasingly connected to the oil issue. When nationalization of Iran's petroleum industry resurfaced in 1949, tensions between the Tudeh and the nationalists also reappeared. When the oil nationalization bill was passed in 1951 and Mosaddeq became prime minister, the communists once more proved unprepared for the challenge.

The Tudeh entered this new round of crisis by miscalculating the internal balance of power in Iran, misunderstanding the new wave of nationalism and patriotism unleashed by the oil nationalization act, and, once more, maintaining its close links to Soviet interests.

At this point the cold war was well underway, and the United States and the Soviet Union were engaged in a competition on a worldwide scale. The victory of the Chinese Revolution in October 1949 and the start of the Korean War in June 1950 only added fuel and intensity to the superpower struggle for control and hegemony. But the situation in Iran was very different from the rest of the world. Here, by taking on the British Empire, the oil nationalization act had become a manifestation of the nation's struggle for its national sovereignty. The emergence of mass support in urban areas that followed nationalization further pointed to the popularity of the actions led by Mosaddeq.

Oil nationalization put the Mosaddeq cabinet on a collision course with the British Empire but not necessarily with U.S. interests, or at least not right away. Initially, the Americans, under a Democratic administration, had their differences with the British, both on the way the petroleum crisis was being handled and on the issue of greater profit sharing for the U.S. oil companies. One observer of Iran–U.S. relations described the American approach, under the Democrats, in the following terms: "The Truman administration's policy as developed by Secretary of State Acheson was to attempt to placate the British while trying to convince Mosaddeq to agree on a compromise."[19] Mosaddeq was well aware of these differences and tried to exploit them to Iran's benefit. The presence of such figures as Gen. Fazlollah Zahedi (the future coup leader and Mosaddeq's successor) and Ali Amini in Mosaddeq's first cabinet and the support of such figures as Mozaffar Baqa'i attest to this fact. These were the people who supported Mosaddeq while he was on good terms with the Americans but began to desert him when he fell out of favor.

The Tudeh Party based its analysis of the nationalization movement not on internal Iranian realities but on the international situation, again keeping Soviet interests primarily in mind. Hence, while the National Front was engaging the British and its domestic Iranian supporters, the Tudeh viewed the situation in terms of the U.S.–Soviet rivalry. For example, after the start of hostilities on the Korean peninsula, the main Tudeh front organization, the Iranian Society for Peace, directed its propaganda against the United States. The society's tactics exposed the Tudeh leadership's lack of comprehension of Iran's internal realities.

From the very beginning of the oil nationalization movement, the Tudeh denounced it as an imperialist act and suggested that the only proper expression could be nationalization of southern oil. In analyzing the Sixteenth Majles, where the National Front had a minority presence yet eventually managed to pass the nationalization bill, the Tudeh divided the members into three categories: first, the opportunists, who had no stand of their own and would change their vote in accordance with the position of the most powerful alignment of the moment; second, those who depended on foreigners and carried out their wishes; and third, the deceivers who had all the characteristics of the first two categories but pretended to care for the people, whom they never really understood.[20] Of course, this third group was the National Front.

In June 1950 the daily *Mardom* described the oil nationalization attempt in the following terms: "Already we can be sure that revisions in the southern oil contract will not be in favor of our people and will only result in the consolidation of England's position in our country. The only time our people may realize their rights in the southern oil resources is when they can determine their destiny. Hence, the solution of the oil question is related to the victory of our party, that is, the people of Iran."[21]

When the Majles subcommittee on oil rejected the Gass-Golsha'iyan bill, the Tudeh attributed it not to the efforts of the National Front but to the people of Iran: "[The bill] was rejected by the people of Iran and not by the disgraced National Front." [22] Even Mosaddeq's rejection of the American offer of a compromise, put forward by Averell Harriman in July 1951, failed to convince the party of the genuinely patriotic nature of the movement. The Tudeh's position from the start of the second round of the oil debate in Iran in the summer of 1950 to mid-1952 was one of antagonism toward the authors of the movement, namely Mosaddeq and the National Front.

While the party formulated its policy on the oil nationalization question with Soviet interests in mind, this did not mean that Moscow's policy on the matter was the same as the Tudeh's. The Soviets, while not doing much to help Iran at a time when it was under a British embargo, did recognize the importance of the nationalization act. The Soviet media supported nationalization and gave positive coverage to Mosaddeq and the National Front. [23] This meant that at this point the Tudeh was acting on its own perception of what its international duties (i.e., Soviet interests) were.

The party's antagonism toward the Mosaddeq cabinet continued into the second year of his term in office. The party leadership's reaction to the July 1952 events was confused and ineffectual. It was unfazed by Mosaddeq's resignation on July 16. The party press continued to attack him and to refer to his dispute with the shah as merely one between different factions of a reactionary ruling elite. [24] But the popular explosion inevitably involved many rank-and-file party members and supporters who could see firsthand Mosaddeq's popularity and became persuaded of the justness of his cause. These members began to join in the demonstrations and put pressure on the party leadership to reconsider its position. Reluctantly, the party finally joined the drive for Mosaddeq's reinstatement on July 21. [25] For obvious reasons, the Tudeh lost all initiative in this round of the confrontation. While some experienced party members managed to lead some local demonstrations, the Tudeh in effect joined spontaneously, without preparation. The TPMO, which had many officers among the military units assigned to suppress the revolt, also likely remained inactive. [26]

The July 21 events put the Tudeh leadership in a rather odd situation. Up to this date the party had been attacking the nationalist movement and Mosaddeq as reactionaries and deceivers. Now the turn of events and political realities had put the party in the position of joining in to defend the very movement it had mocked. From this point on, the Tudeh's policy began gradually to back Mosaddeq at the expense of maintaining the party's independence. This gradual change in party policy was linked to a changing factional balance within the party leadership and was qualified at the beginning. Following the July 1952 events, the party accepted the slogan of oil nationalization in place of its own calls for nationalization of the southern oil fields only. This was a major policy adjustment, and was a clear admission of error in connection with the Tudeh's policy toward the nationalists. Furthermore, the party began to tone down its attacks on Mosaddeq, although they did not stop altogether.[27]

The Tudeh's relationship with the nationalist government during the second year of Mosaddeq's tenure should be understood in light of the fluidity of the period. CIA documents show that American officials feared Mosaddeq would have to rely increasingly on the Tudeh to mobilize the crowds on his behalf. Their fear was further strengthened by Mosaddeq's refusal to suppress the Tudeh, even though the party had already been declared illegal in 1949. Much of this perception seems to have been based on the perception of National Front-Tudeh cooperation during the July 1952 events. But, as noted above, the party's participation in those events was spontaneous and came at a time when the party leadership was disoriented and out of touch with realities on the street.

The Tudeh's relationship with the National Front between July 1952 and August 1953, even as the party was readjusting its policy, was far from harmonious. Because of intense internal factional struggles, the party was losing its cohesion and often adopted contradictory policies toward Mosaddeq. It is clear that the type of coordinated cooperation and mutual reliance the Americans feared existed between Mosaddeq and the Tudeh could not have existed. On the other hand, the type of confidence building necessary to establish a more cooperative and harmonious relationship between the party and Mosaddeq also did not materialize.

Tudeh Factionalism

To understand the party's behavior toward Mosaddeq and its lack of a meaningful reaction to the coup, it is necessary to understand its internal dynamics and factionalism at the highest levels.[28]

Different labels could be used to identify the two factions. Sources published by the coup leaders called them, rather inadequately, the old guard and corrupted faction versus the critical and compromising faction.[29] Better designations would perhaps be moderate versus hard-liner. Both factions shared an admiration for the Soviet Union and adhered to Moscow's interpretation of Marxism-Leninism. But they also had major theoretical and other differences.

The oil nationalization movement brought the two factions deeper into conflict.

The hard-line faction's principal members were young activists such as Nureddin Kianuri, Ehsanallah Tabari, Amanallah Qoraishi, Ahmad Qasemi, Maryam Firouz, and Gholam Hossein Forutan, as well as older members such as Ardeshir (Ardashes) Avanissian and Abdul Samad Kambakhsh. This group presented a more dogmatic perception of Marxism and was more insistent on the leadership of the working class and on adherence to party rules, and was generally opposed to the nationalist government of Mosaddeq. The policy of confronting the Mosaddeq cabinet, which lasted until July 1952, was largely a result of this faction gaining the upper hand. The hard-liners considered Mosaddeq and the National Front as part of the Iranian bourgeoisie who enjoyed close ties with the Americans. The oil nationalization movement was explained away as a conflict between the bourgeoisie and the imperial court and the landowning class, which maintained close ties with the British. Because of this two-sided understanding of international and domestic alliances, the hard-liners viewed the dispute between the National Front and the British as being in reality one between British and U.S. policy in Iran.

The differences between the two factions were clearest when it came to the party's proposal for a united popular front against imperialism and domestic reactionary forces. The united front policy was a replica of the Soviet-led approach to the Third Communist International (Comintern) in the 1920s and 1930s. Its essence was to form a coalition between the communists and noncommunist progressive political parties in order to establish a strong opposition force against those deemed to be reactionaries. On the international level, results of the policy had been mixed by the time of the 1951–53 events in Iran.

The key question was who should lead such a coalition. In the mid-1920s, the Comintern, influenced by Nikolai Bukharin and Joseph Stalin, proposed that the leadership did not have to be communist where the communist parties were weak. This led to the 1927 disaster of the Goumindang massacre of the communists in China. After this episode, the Comintern, now firmly under Stalin, made a turnabout and took a rather dogmatic and uncompromising position. Accordingly, communist parties around the world were ordered not to make alliances unless they featured communist leadership. This policy led to the rout of the German Communist Party as it refused to unite with the German Social Democrats until the Nazis destroyed both. The united popular front policy did have its successful moments as well. In China in the 1930s and early 1940s, and in Indochina in the 1940s and 1950s, the respective communist parties of these two regions used the policy to their advantage.

When the Tudeh proposed a united popular front policy, the hard-liners insisted that any such coalition with noncommunist forces should come under party leadership. This faction considered the Tudeh to be the working-class party, a perception that became a major point of dispute with the moderate faction. The hard-liners used their considerable organizational might within the party to win many converts to its cause. Leftist and extremist policies against the nationalist government were mostly, but not all, the result of this faction's courses of action, which changed only after the tide began to turn against them following the July 1952 uprising.

The moderate faction's principal members were Morteza Yazdi, Iraj Iskandari, Reza Radmanesh, Fereydun Keshavarz, Hossein Judat, and Nader Sharmini, the head of the party's Youth Organization. This group, although initially opposed to Mosaddeq, gradually came to accept his leadership. The moderates deemphasized the leadership role of the working class and the party, and believed that a united front with noncommunist forces did not necessitate party leadership. They had a more populist view of Marxism and considered the Tudeh not as the party of the working class but as a toilers party that included other deprived classes. In contrast to the hard-liners, they were open to leadership by the nationalists. The gradual change in Tudeh policy toward support for the nationalists at the cost of losing initiative after July 1952 was the result of this faction gaining the upper hand.

The moderates' gradual assumption of party leadership from July 1952 onward not only clarifies the change of policy toward the nationalist government but also may partially explain the party's ineffectual response to the coup. While much attention has been paid to the Tudeh's hostile reaction to Mosaddeq before July 1952, not much has been said about the consequences of the Tudeh's gradual shift, under the moderate faction, in support of Mosaddeq.[30] Under the moderate faction, particularly after March 1953, the Tudeh in effect delegated all initiative to the Mosaddeq government to the point where it was left with none of its own. When asked why the party had stored no weapons before the coup, Kianuri suggested that the party did not want to be seen as attempting to overthrow Mosaddeq.[31]

Sharmini and Kianuri were the two most controversial figures among the Tudeh leaders. Sharmini was the head of the party's Youth Organization until 1952 and maintained his influence over it through the time of the coup. The controversy surrounding him is that as the head of the Youth Organization he proposed some of the most radical slogans, while at the same time he sided with the moderate faction on most issues. Under him the Youth Organization undermined the authority of key personalities of the hard-line faction, attacking them for being soft and not revolutionary enough. These attacks were accompanied by the proposal of radical actions at party gatherings. At the same time, there are strong indications that Sharmini worked closely with the moderate faction on strategic party policies. Documents published by the shah's regime after the coup clearly mention this.[32] Internal party leadership correspondence also indicates that the moderate faction was hesitant to remove Sharmini as the head of the Youth Organization and used the issue as a bargaining chip to extract concessions from the opposite faction.[33] Hence, Sharmini, who was a maverick of sorts, played a crucial role for the moderates in disarming the hard-liners by undermining their radical appeal. But by attacking the hard-liners, Sharmini and his followers also took a radical posture toward Mosaddeq. This factional struggle within the party overshadowed efforts at coordination with Mosaddeq during 1952–53, which would have been an important aspect of any Tudeh move against the coup in August 1953.

Throughout his memoirs, Kianuri claims he was a proponent of Mosaddeq after the July 1952 uprising, although he does admit that he, along with the other members of the leadership, opposed the oil nationalization movement before July 1952. Indeed he suggests that he was the one who warned the prime minister of the impending coup. Kianuri's claim is only partially true.[34]

Among key hard-line personalities Kianuri ranked third, after Kambakhsh and Qasemi. Kambakhsh was not a theorist but a party functionary with strong personal connections to the Soviets. Qasemi was a staunch Stalinist and a dogmatic theorist who was the main force behind the party's anti-Mosaddeq policies during 1951–52. Both of these men had to leave the country by mid-1952. Hence, during the year before the coup Kianuri was the only hard-liner left in the party's five-man executive committee.

The key to understanding Kianuri's role is to note his theoretical differences with Qasemi. Kianuri believed in the hegemony of the proletariat in any coalition with nonproletariat forces, while Qasemi did not envision any coalition with the bourgeoisie, which he deemed as having betrayed the anti-imperialist movement. Qasemi's view was closer to Stalin's, while Kianuri was more moderate in this respect and closer to Mao Zedong; both, though, were at odds with the moderate advocates who proposed closer cooperation with Mosaddeq after July 1952, with or without party leadership.[35]

To the above political differences between the two Tudeh factions must be added personal differences that helped fuel factionalism within the party. Jealousy of individual leaders was among the most significant of these factors. Documents related to the party's Fourth Plenum mentions the factions and personal differences between individual party leaders.

On differences within the central committee, the plenum identified two factions, one dominant and centered around Iskandari and Radmanesh and the other in opposition around Kianuri and Qasemi, but suggested that the disputes were mostly personal and due to character flaws. Nevertheless, the plenum placed general responsibility for the party's failure collectively on the executive committee of the time.[36]

After the February 1949 attempt on the shah's life, there was no systematic contact between those party figures who fled abroad and those who remained inside the country. After the jailbreak of Tudeh leaders in December 1950, an executive committee was created in order to run the party's day-to-day affairs and to coordinate operations with the leadership abroad. Between 1950 and 1952, this eight-member committee was under the clear hegemony of the hard-liners, with Kianuri, Qasemi, Forutan, and Mahmud Buqrati forming a united bloc against Judat, Mohammad Bahrami (the party's first secretary), and Yazdi. Ali Olovvi, the eighth member of the executive committee, seems to have had his own independent line and often wavered between the two. In 1952, Qasemi, Buqrati, and Forutan were sent to Moscow to represent the Tudeh's leadership based inside Iran at the Nineteenth Party Congress of the Communist Party of the Soviet Union (CPSU). This development changed the balance in the executive committee in favor of the moderates. The party's misjudging of the oil nationalization movement and the events of summer 1952 may have helped remove the hard-line members of the executive committee. At any rate, as the 1953 events approached, the hard-line position within the executive committee was weakened considerably, with only Kianuri remaining as the faction's representative.

The two factions divided control over various party organs, which added to the general disorganization and inefficiency as factional competition grew more intense. While in a minority in the executive committee, Kianuri and supporters had a controlling presence in the Tehran Provincial Committee, the nerve center of the party network led by Amanallah Qoreishi, and in many of the neighborhood committees. They also had the ear of the TPMO's leadership, which meant effective control of that organization.[37] Kianuri was the person in overall charge of party organization, but the party liaison with the

TPMO was Judat, a member of the moderate line. Kambakhsh and Qasemi were the previous party liaisons, which suggests the hard-liners had control up to 1952. Nevertheless, it seems that the TPMO kept up its ties with Kianuri and bypassed Judat as he was accused by Kianuri, and later by the Tenth Plenum, for his incompetence in providing effective leadership.[38]

It is clear that the moderates' control of the executive committee did not translate into overall control of the party. Nevertheless, the moderates did determine the Tudeh's general policy (e.g., toward Mosaddeq). It seems that much of the factional conflict during 1951–53 was focused on which wing presented the more radical and leftist view. It did not really matter what the real policy was as long as a leftist posture could be maintained to satisfy the many young party cadres. Thus, the hard-liners systematically attacked the moderates as being too soft, too rightist, and too willing to compromise with the enemies of the party and the working class. In this context, the moderate faction's control of the party's Youth Organization was important. The Youth Organization played a pivotal role in balancing the hard-line attack. The Tenth Plenum made a point of criticizing the Youth Organization and Sharmini.

Factionalism within the Tudeh had a number of consequences that significantly contributed to the party's behavior toward the oil nationalization movement and the 1953 coup. First, while the hard-liners were dominant in the leadership of the party (1951–52), the party completely missed the significance of the movement led by Mosaddeq and thus contributed to weakening the National Front. The hard-liners' dogmatic understanding of Marxist-Leninist doctrine and inflexible interpretation of the CPSU's guidelines were prime factors in determining the policy regarding Mosaddeq and the National Front.

Second, with the moderate arm's domination (1952–53), the Tudeh began slowly to see events in a new light and gradually changed course. This development meant that the party began to align its activities with those of the nationalist government at the cost of losing all independent initiative. Not wanting to alienate the Mosaddeq government, the Tudeh failed to prepare a contingency plan for coordination with the nationalist government to help it face off the coup. The party also failed to plan for a situation where it would have to continue without Mosaddeq.

Third, factional competition meant that the party leadership and various party organs became almost paralyzed at times and unable to perform with suitable efficiency. Much time and energy was wasted over professional and personal rivalries. Factionalism at the highest levels also meant that the leadership was unable to put forward resolute and effective policies in a timely manner, which worked to the party's disadvantage during the coup.

The Road to the Coup

While American intelligence reports for 1951–53 did not view the Tudeh as an immediate threat, the coup planners underscored the danger from communism in their preparations for Operation TPAJAX. Both the drafts of the operation and Donald Wilber's *Overthrow,* which was written a few months after the coup, note the expected violent reaction of the Tudeh and suggest steps to counter it. Wilber's history points to the July 21, 1953, demonstrations commemorating the events of the previous year as being dominated by the Tudeh, and states that party "participants far outnumbered those assembled by the National Front." [39]

The American coup organizers used the threat of the Tudeh to woo more conservative elements in society to the anti-Mosaddeq camp and throw Mosaddeq and his cabinet off balance. For example, they arranged for threatening phone calls to be made in the Tudeh's name to religious leaders. [40] Likewise, they arranged for "black" mobs pretending to be Tudeh crowds, as we shall see below.

The Tudeh had intelligence throughout 1952–53 about a number of plots to overthrow the government. The Tudeh's assessment from the summer of 1952 was that a coup attempt was probable. As early as March 1953, the party had clear reason to suspect that preparations were being made for an overthrow. [41] This suspicion became undeniable fact eight days before the first coup attempt on August 16. As early as winter 1952–53, the Tudeh leadership ordered the creation of vanguard cells made up of experienced party members working closely with the TPMO. According to an officer's memoirs, the TPMO identified key military installations, army depots, and command and control centers in the capital. [42] The vanguard cells, equipped with the intelligence provided by the TPMO, were to react violently to any coup attempt. However, the leadership dismissed the cells before the coup, and the TPMO remained passive as the covert operation consumed the nationalist government. Lack of determination and factionalism among Tudeh leaders were the reasons behind this failure to prepare the party. While the Tudeh's intelligence reports lacked detail, particularly on the events leading to the August 1953 coup, they should have prepared the party for an eventual showdown. [43] Instead, the Tudeh refused to prepare and arm itself. According to one source, the main reason for this was that they did not want to appear as if they were preparing to overthrow Mosaddeq.[44]

It is clear that the Tudeh passed its intelligence on the pending coup to the prime minister on August 15. TPMO members had infiltrated the ranks of the coup organizers and had people in key positions. For example, Col. Mohammad Ali Mobasherri, a member of TPMO's three-man secretariat, was an active member of Tehran Military Governor, the center of the coup operation; Maj. Mehdi Homaouni of the shah's Imperial Guard actually discovered and reported the August plot; Capt. Mohammad Pulad-dezh, an officer in the national police, who is in fact mentioned in *Overthrow,* was another TPMO member.[45]

While the TPMO acquired the information, Kianuri, whose wife was a relative of Mosaddeq and thus gave him access to the inner quarter (*andarun*) of the premier's household, was the executive committee member charged with contacting Mosaddeq by telephone.[46] Kianuri claims that he communicated with the prime minister on a number of occasions before the coup, including on August 13 and late on the night of August 14. The first contact led to postponement of the coup and the second to its failure on August 16. Other Tudeh leaders have questioned some of Kianuri's claims.[47] But Mosaddeq, who probably had his own independent sources as well, makes mention in his memoirs of at least one such telephone call.[48] Wilber's reference in *Overthrow* to postponement of the coup on August 14 due to the "indiscretion of one of the Iranian officers" is probably linked to the Tudeh's information on the coup received on August 13.[49] Wilber also notes Brig. Gen. Taqi Riahi's later remarks to the effect that he was informed of the coup at 5 P.M. on the evening of August 15, which corresponds to the second and most important piece of Tudeh intelligence on the coup, which was passed on to Mosaddeq. A TPMO officer also played a crucial role in the physical defeat of the coup on the evening of August 15. Lt. Ali Ashraf Shoja'ian had accompanied Col. Ne'matallah Nasiri and his Imperial Guard unit to Mosaddeq's residence to arrest him. Apparently on his own initiative he changed sides at the crucial moment and aided Mosaddeq's guards in arresting Nasiri and his men.[50]

The period from August 16 to August 19 was a brief but crucial one, and the Tudeh leadership needed to react speedily and with focus and determination if the situation was to be turned around. Instead, chaos and a lack of resolve prevailed. On August 16, the morning after the initial coup attempt failed, the general situation in Tehran was tense and electric. The shah had fled the country and was implicated in the attempt to overthrow the constitutional government. At this point, TPAJAX seemed doomed as supporters of the National Front and the Tudeh poured into the streets in defense of Mosaddeq. A broad array of emotionally charged, spontaneous activities took place during the fateful days of August 16–18.

The popular sentiment expressed in the streets of Tehran on August 16 may be divided into three categories. All three groups of demonstrators had come to support Mosaddeq but with different perspectives. The first group consisted of supporters of the National Front whose slogans typically targeted the shah, the Pahlavi dynasty, and the coup, but not necessarily the monarchy. Certainly, Hossein Fatemi's fiery speech that day, in Baharestan Square in front of the Majles, radicalized the front's supporters. Fatemi had always been somewhat more radical than other front and Mosaddeq cabinet members. His speech, which attacked the shah and called for his abdication, fired the crowd to the point where even some antimonarchy slogans were heard. But even he apparently did not directly call for the overthrow of the monarchy or the establishment of a republic.[51]

The second group was comprised of Tudeh supporters who were already more radical and who more openly targeted the monarchy, demanding sovereignty for the people in light of the new situation. But even here there was no sign of widespread demand for a republic. The third group constituted ordinary people who could have been attracted to either of the above two according to the situation.[52]

Here, the "black" crowds can be put in perspective. In *Overthrow,* Wilber suggests that the coup planners had thought of using such a device as part of the overall scheme to destabilize the situation.[53] But it is not clear to what extent they were actually used or how effective they were. According to Mark Gasiorowski (see his chapter in this volume), by distributing fifty thousand dollars a phony Tudeh mob was created. This crowd then began to attack symbols of monarchy on August 17. Gasiorowski also asserts that the black crowd was joined by actual Tudeh supporters and others.

While the situation was highly charged and chaotic at this point with no clear indication as to who was actually in charge, it seems apparent that the Tudeh had no idea that the black crowds existed. Clearly, the Tudeh leadership was unaware of such activities.[54] Interviews with six rank-and-file Tudeh and Youth Organization members also suggest that there was no Tudeh awareness of black crowds on the street level. All those interviewed were either in the streets of Tehran during August 16–19 or were well connected to the party.[55]

This lack of awareness strongly suggests that the CIA appraisal of the crowd's role is probably exaggerated. While no certain conclusion can be made on this point, it is difficult to see how the crowds could have materialized in any significant and determining manner without the Tudeh picking up some signals along the way.

Whether with the help of the black mobs acting as a trigger mechanism or purely due to the genuine spontaneity of the crowds in the streets, the general situation after the failure of the first coup attempt turned radical. At this point the Tudeh and the National Front were on the same side regardless of their rocky relationship during the previous period. On the morning of August 17 the angry crowd began to attack symbols of the monarchy and demanded its abolition. This was a major shift and a challenge to the National Front and its constitutional premier.

An anti-shah crowd tearing down a statue of Reza Shah on August 17 or 18, 1953. By August 19, the tide had completely shifted as pro-shah forces took control of the streets of Tehran. Copyright © 2002 AP/Wide World Photos.

Meanwhile, on August 18 the Tudeh leadership opened a decision-making process that led to the party's fateful demand for the elimination of the monarchy and establishment of a "democratic republic." Posing the latter demand seems to have been a major blunder because, coming from a pro-Moscow party, it smacked of the Soviet-dominated satellites of Eastern Europe. Demanding a republic of any kind would have been problematic and would have alienated Mosaddeq since he had never suggested he was in favor of abolishing the constitutional monarchy. How did this gaffe occur?

According to one source, the party's Tehran Provincial Committee, a hotbed of the hard-line faction, proposed the "republic" slogan to the party executive committee on August 17.[56] It seems that the events unfolding in the streets had a direct bearing on this decision. The Tudeh considered itself the vanguard party and, as such, had to try to stay one step ahead of the masses in order to be able to lead them. Certainly, the hard-liners within the party emphasized this role more than the other faction.

A few hours later, still on August 17, the party's executive committee gave its response to the "republic" proposal. The counterproposal was even more radical and called for demanding a "democratic republic." Subsequently, Tudeh members were instructed to join demonstrations for the new cause.[57] By late August 17 and August 18, the role of the Tudeh in street demonstrations was more pronounced, making it even more difficult to assess the impact of the fabricated crowds even if they did exist.

The Tudeh's new policy of demanding a democratic republic was announced on the morning of August 18 just before impending street battles and chaos. This new slogan was a major change for the party. It contradicted the policy, in effect since March 1953, of strengthening the nationalist government. Overnight, the Tudeh shifted from supporting the constitutional monarchy through Mosaddeq's government to demanding its overthrow. Moreover, the Tudeh demanded that the constitutional premier go against his own mandate due to the extraordinary situation. This led to panic by the nationalist regime, which did not really intend to generate such a radical reaction. The government therefore ordered the military into the streets on August 18, resulting in the arrest of many Tudeh activists, the withdrawal of progovernment supporters, and a hostile military in control of the city. One Tudeh estimate suggests that on that day up to six hundred mid- and low-level Tudeh activists were arrested in Tehran alone, severely damaging the party's network.[58]

Why did the moderate faction, comprising a majority in the executive committee, accept the new policy? Did the Tudeh not fear that Mosaddeq might not accept the party's demand for a democratic republic? It seems that for a brief moment the party leadership, influenced by the radicalized political atmosphere, opted for attempting to pull the nationalists to their side. Militant street demonstrations and Fatemi's more radical posture may have helped cause the leadership to change course for a brief moment. Furthermore, Fatemi's radical tone could have persuaded some party leaders that a split had developed within the ranks of the National Front that was worth exploring. One party document shows that the Tudeh was aware that Mosaddeq might not accept the party's demand, but it opted for convincing the premier to accept the new policy through resistance and pressure.[59] As suggested, this change of course was brief and the Tudeh soon shifted directions again and stopped its challenge of Mosaddeq. This episode should be understood in the context of the charged political atmosphere of the time.

On the evening of August 18, fearing a loss of control, Mosaddeq ordered the military to clear the streets of all demonstrators. Having a large number of its activists arrested and not wanting to alienate the premier any further, the party vacillated again and ordered a demobilization. On the morning of August 19, it became clear that the coup had been rejuvenated and the nationalist government was in danger. One Tudeh leader has suggested that the party contacted Mosaddeq and offered to resist the coup but that Mosaddeq declined and suggested that he had things under control.[60]

Published correspondence between the party's executive committee inside Iran and the leadership abroad sheds more light on the condition of the party's top levels and their reaction to the August 19 coup.[61] According to these documents, on the morning of August 19 Ali Olovvi, a member of the executive committee, suggested holding demonstrations and a national strike in opposition to the coup. At this point the party's Tehran Provincial Committee was notified to prepare the ground.[62] Olovvi's proposal, however, was deferred by the other members until Mosaddeq's approval could be secured.[63] By noon, however, no contact with Mosaddeq had been established. By afternoon, when the party finally began discussing whether to take action, Mosaddeq's government had been overthrown.

How can the Tudeh's overall reaction to the coup and its vacillation be explained and put within the context of Tudeh factionalism? The party's policy clearly fluctuated from strengthening Mosaddeq in March 1953, to pressuring him to declare a democratic republic on August 17–18, to demobilizing late on August 18 and taking no action pending Mosaddeq's consent.

One overall explanation is that the five members of the party's executive

An anti–Mosaddeq crowd on Shah Reza Avenue, August 19, 1953. Stephen Langlie Collection, GB165–0351–2.1.3, Middle East Centre Archive, St. Antony's College, Oxford. Courtesy Stephen Langlie USAF/MAAG.

committee may at some point have come to the conclusion that the party could survive the storm, as it did in 1949. Bizhan Jazani, some twenty years later, made the following important observation: "The leadership of the party thought that the 1953 [coup] was only a defeat for the nationalist movement . . . and that the party, and its underground organizations, could continue underground activities." [64] This, however, only partially answers the problem of a lack of resolve and coherent policy within the party leadership. Factionalism and a state of paralysis at the top complete the picture.

The party leadership collectively was suspicious of Mosaddeq, but a subset began to change policy after the summer of 1952. The hegemony of the moderate faction contributed to the party's loss of initiative vis-à-vis the nationalist government, particularly after March 1953. As if wanting to compensate for its attacks on Mosaddeq during 1951–52, the party leadership refused to prepare for the coming showdown and left all initiative to the nationalists. While the moderate faction's control over the party was not absolute, it could and did initiate general policy. Thus, while the Military Organization was ready to take steps to prepare the party and the Youth Organization in the months preceding the coup, the order arrived from the Tudeh leadership to cease activities so as not to alienate the Mosaddeq government.

The Tudeh clearly lost its balance due to the speed of events and, even more importantly, due to a lack of internal unity and cohesion. Only a unified leadership could have processed the incoming information and come up with an appropriate decision. In the absence of such conditions, the party leaders were reduced to fighting among themselves while trying to maintain their revolutionary posture and choose a proper course of action.

The Coup Aftermath

It was only after Mosaddeq's overthrow that the Tudeh leadership began to take a number of steps to prepare the party for armed resistance. These included the creation, in September 1953, of a center for resisting the coup. Three members of the party's executive committee and three members of TPMO were assigned to command the center.[65] The idea was for the TPMO to train and arm some two thousand party members and to establish contacts with the Qashqa'i tribe's leaders in order to wage guerrilla war in coordination with them in the northern and central parts of the country. None of these measures resulted in any concrete action. The Qashqa'i chiefs ultimately refused to cooperate, and the TPMO was unable to obtain adequate armaments due to the repressive atmosphere of the postcoup period.

The official Tudeh reaction to the question of the causes of the party's failure came during its historic Fourth Plenum, held in Moscow in July 1957. The plenum criticized the party for its policy toward the National Front and for not recognizing the progressive nature of the oil nationalization movement.[66] Calling its policies toward the nationalist government sectarian and leftist, the party also suggested that its policy between August 16 and 19 had been incorrect when party demonstrators pulled down the shah's statues and asked for a people's democratic republic.[67] The party admitted to its state of paralysis and blamed it on the leadership inside Iran while suggesting that the leadership abroad had failed to provide help and guidelines. The party attributed the leadership's weakness to the lack of internal democracy within the Tudeh, the absence of close bonds between the leadership and rank-and-file members, the leadership's low level of theoretical knowledge, and the existence of deep differences at top levels of the party.

With the discovery of the TPMO and arrest of its members in the summer of 1954, the fate of the Tudeh was sealed. Through its intelligence network, the TPMO had acted as a shield for the party and had played a determining role in preserving the Tudeh immediately after Mosaddeq's overthrow. During 1954–58, with the decimation of the TPMO complete, the Tudeh network was compromised and wiped out as well. Many high- and middle-ranking Tudeh leaders were arrested or forced to flee the country. The arrest and execution of Khosrow Roozbeh in 1957–58 signaled the end of this process.

Based on the above analysis of the Tudeh's forces on the ground and its internal divisions, it seems clear that the perceived Tudeh threat, as feared by the perpetrators of the coup, was not real. The party had neither the numbers, nor the popularity, nor a plan to take over state power with any hope of holding on to it. Similar to any fraternal communist party, the Tudeh had a long-term goal of seeing Iran, and for that matter the rest of the world, join the socialist camp led by the Soviet Union. But this did not have much to do with the concrete case of Iran where, in the Tudeh's terminology, objective conditions for a takeover did not exist. At best the party had come to conclude that to ward off imperialist domination of Iran, it had to throw its support behind Mosaddeq's government. One Tudeh leader at the time has explained the party's policy as follows: "[T]he reality is that we did not want Mosaddeq to be overthrown. . . . well, we understood that there is no possibility for the party to come to power, we did not have the strength." [68] Even the party's demand for a democratic republic, misguided as it was, was an attempt to pull Mosaddeq into the Tudeh camp, not overthrow him.

The fact that the Tudeh neither had the intention nor the power to oust Mosaddeq does not mean it could not have reacted to, and even reversed, the coup. We now know that the 1953 coup was successful only by the narrowest of margins. Rarely does one witness the fate of a nation depending on such tenuous circumstances. Supporters of the coup in the military were not sure of their own strength until the final moments. The American operatives were ordered to leave the country. Many military units and their officers became fence sitters, waiting to see who would win in order to be sure to join the right side. The Tudeh had adequate support in Tehran and in the military to react effectively. Of course, it was impossible to predict whether the party would be successful or not, particularly during such tense and stressful moments as existed between August 16 and August 19. But the Tudeh considered itself a revolutionary vanguard party and, as such, was expected to react forcefully. Considering the fact that the organization was decimated and in a state of inaction between 1953 and 1958, any other fate would have been preferable.

For the Tudeh to have been effective in August 1953, it would have had to take care of two prerequisites. It needed a resolute, cohesive, and insightful leadership. It also required a more trustful and amicable relationship with the National Front. The Tudeh lacked both. In other words, what the Tudeh lacked in 1953 was competent leadership.

Because U.S. field intelligence suggested that the Tudeh was not an immediate threat to Iran, it seems that the decision to launch TPAJAX must have been made at higher echelons of the U.S. government. This decision seems to have had little to do with on-the-ground realities and much to do with the ideological imperatives of the period: the cold war.[69]

Other chapters in this collection cover this aspect of the puzzle thoroughly. Here, it should briefly be noted that the U.S. perception of the Tudeh and Soviet threat, or communism in general, should be seen from three angles. First, the American competition with the Soviet Union after World War II had already triggered the cold war. Episodes such as the Soviet take-over and domination of Eastern Europe, especially the 1948 crisis over Czechoslovakia, and the Berlin airlift were all events within this drama. The success of the Chinese Revolution, the launching of the Korean War, and the outbreak of war in Indochina only fueled the cold war mentality.

Second, the American perception of the Tudeh and communism in Iran did not help Iran's case. The Azerbaijan crisis of 1945–46, where a Soviet-backed regional party tried to secede while Iran was under Soviet occupation, diluted the U.S. view. The Tudeh did not have much to do with this episode and was itself a victim of events as the Soviets forced the party to support the movement.[70] Outright Tudeh identification with Soviet policy in Iran between 1944 and 1951 also added to Washington's negative assessment. Finally, in the United States the 1953 coup in Iran coincided with the anticommunist hysteria commonly identified with the activities of Sen. Joseph McCarthy. This anticommunist atmosphere ruined many careers and lives, both inside and outside the United States.

The 1953 coup in Iran cannot simply be understood, as portrayed in Donald Wilber's history, as an attempt to save Iran from falling into the Soviet orbit. There were many other variables involved. An important aspect of the equation is that the main justification for the coup—the Tudeh, and by extension Soviet, threat—in retrospect seems implausible.

4

Britain and the Overthrow
of the Mosaddeq Government

Wm. Roger Louis

The overthrow of the Mosaddeq government by the intelligence agencies of the United States and Britain in August 1953 is a subject that invites periodic reassessment.[1] The archive of the British Secret Intelligence Service (SIS) remains even more tightly sealed than that of the CIA, but the publication by the *New York Times* of a CIA historical study on the 1953 operation written shortly after the event by Donald N. Wilber, an historian of Islamic architecture and art as well as an undercover agent, throws considerable new light on the British as well as the American side of the story.[2] In some ways the episode resembles a mosaic. The small pieces of evidence have long formed a general pattern, even though many of the British parts remain elusive and will probably remain so until sometime in the remote future when SIS disgorges its secrets of the 1950s. Nevertheless it is worth the effort, even on the basis of fragmented evidence, to reconsider the subject from a British vantage point. Significant parts of the mosaic have become more distinctly visible in the last decade.[3] The post–cold–war era, moreover, offers an opportunity to the historian to approach the subject from a different angle of vision. Greater distance in time and greater access to archival material encourage a more dispassionate view of a subject still riddled with ideological assumptions. Thus the purpose of this essay will be to reflect on the British involvement with Iran from the time of Mohammad Mosaddeq's advent to power as prime minister in April 1951 to his overthrow in August 1953, and in a more general sense to restore British perspective to a story that has, on the Western side, been dominated by American comment.

One thing that intrigues the historian is how little is known of British intelligence activities as conducted by the British Labour government 1945–51, and how little the underlying assumptions have been studied.[4] Did the Labour government, when confronted with the issue of covert action, differ in principle from the successor Conservative government? If so, then what led Herbert Morrison, who succeeded Ernest Bevin as foreign secretary in 1950, to endorse plans for subverting the Mosaddeq government? Did the prime minister, C. R. Attlee, lose his grip, or had Attlee himself come around to the view that Mosaddeq had to be removed from office? Who besides the prime minister and the foreign secretary made the decisions on covert operations during the time of the Labour government? What of the influence of the local British experts in Iran? How did the chain of command differ from that of the Conservative government under Sir Winston Churchill, who again became prime minister in late 1951? What comparisons can be made between MI6—the overseas arm of the British Secret Intelligence Service—and the CIA?

The key to British thought from the time of Mosaddeq's ascendancy in April 1951 can be summed up in the description of him as a fanatically anti-British nationalist. But even the British granted that Mosaddeq possessed certain qualities of leadership. First and foremost he was an Iranian patriot. When he became prime minister in 1951, he was seventy years old. His family belonged to the landed ruling class. He championed the Iranian constitutional movement and was a long-standing member of the Majles, the Iranian Parliament. He was not corrupt. The British and, for that matter, the Americans often misunderstood his principal motivation. The crucial set of events that determined his outlook was the virtual occupation of Iran by the British and Russians twice in less than fifty years. Although he was often described in the West as a demagogue, and he did sometimes add drama to his oratory by pretending to faint, he consistently held that the shah should reign and not rule and that the army and police should be subject to civil control. Mosaddeq aimed to make the Majles supreme. He passionately opposed foreign intervention in Iran and above all wanted to end the domination of the Anglo–Iranian Oil Company (AIOC). In this sense his goals were mainly negative. Although he worked for social, judicial, and economic reform and did possess gifts for constructive and creative work, he is remembered above all for his crusade against the British. In 1949 he became the architect of the plan to nationalize the oil industry and led a loose alliance known as the National Front, which in the Majles consisted of representatives from most political parties in Iran, not least of whom was one of the most politically active clerics, Ayatollah

Abolqasem Kashani. Mosaddeq eventually broke with Kashani, but intermittently there existed an uneasy partnership. The British viewed both of them as irreconcilably anti-British. In fusing religion and politics, Kashani in a sense was a forerunner of Ayatollah Khomeini. Mosaddeq by contrast was a secular nationalist.

According to the British "Oriental Counsellors"—the officials who spoke Persian and whose job it was to follow Iranian politics in the embassy in Tehran—Mosaddeq drew his strength from Iranians who not only shared his anti-British sentiment but also his vision of constitutional democracy.[5] As a populist leader, he had solid public support because of his stand on civil rights as well as his unswerving protest against foreign exploitation of Iranian oil. He fused the constitutional movement with that of anti-imperialism. The shah found it difficult to oppose openly a populist prime minister who championed Iranian sovereign rights and freedom of the press. Mosaddeq's dual stand on constitutional liberties and anti-imperialism appealed especially to the urban middle and working classes. His supporters also included some of the more important guilds and, in the business community or bazaar, owners of coffee- and teahouses. Most important of all—especially for the British in their calculations of how to undermine a fanatic—he controlled the police and had wide support in the army at all levels. He was in short a formidable political leader, one who presented the British and the Americans with a paradox. Why should Britain and the United States want to get rid of a statesman who stood for constitutional democracy and, according to Mosaddeq himself, a fair-minded settlement of the oil issue?

Mosaddeq was not a communist. There was no alliance between him and the Tudeh (the Iranian Communist Party) to achieve his goals. Nevertheless, Western contemporaries in Iran often portrayed him as sympathetic to communist aims. Such was his anti-British obsession, in the view that the Americans as well as the British came to espouse, that it blinded him to the dangers of communism through a takeover by the Tudeh Party, which the British estimated to have some twelve thousand members and perhaps fifty thousand sympathizers. To the British the danger was that the communists would gain control over Mosaddeq and then Iran. Mosaddeq might thus wittingly or unwittingly enable the Soviet Union—in the words of C. M. Woodhouse, the head of MI6 in Iran in 1951–52—"to take the country over as it [the Soviet Union] had just taken over Czechoslovakia."[6] Some within the British government thought from the outset that it would be impossible to do business with the Mosaddeq regime and that plans should be made as soon as possible for his removal from office. On the other hand, a few sympathized with his aspirations as an Iranian patriot and in any event believed it to be unethical to intervene in the affairs of other nations by covert means, at least in normal times. A good example is (Sir) Sam Falle, later high commissioner in Singapore and then Nigeria. In 1949–52 Falle was a young foreign service officer in Iran.[7] "In the Foreign Service I was known as 'Red Sam' because I believed in liberal causes, resurgent nationalism and the like. . . . Thus Dr Mosaddeq was initially a man after my own heart. . . . So the fact that even I eventually became convinced that he had to go says something."[8] It was the circumstances of the cold war that brought even well-wishers such as Falle around to the view that Mosaddeq must be toppled. By August 1953 there existed a virtual consensus within government circles that covert action was politically necessary and morally justified.

There is a vital chronological point within the 1951–53 period. In October 1952 Mosaddeq expelled the British diplomatic mission from Iran on grounds of interfering in domestic politics. Thereafter, there existed no official British presence in the country. In October 1952 MI6 relinquished control of its intelligence network to the CIA. The British continued to monitor the situation in Iran from Cyprus as well as from London and Washington, but in the last part of the covert action the British participated only indirectly. On the other hand, an equally emphatic point needs to be made about the origins of the operation. Before October 1952 the plan to destroy the Mosaddeq government was British in inspiration, British in the covert financial assistance proffered to Mosaddeq's enemies, and British in the actual attempts to replace him.

The historic British connection with Iran was based on India and on oil. The AIOC refinery at Abadan, an offshore island at the head of the Persian Gulf, was the largest installation of its kind in the world. It was Britain's single largest overseas asset and a source of national pride in the England of Attlee, Bevin, and Morrison. Even in the late 1940s and early 1950s some high British officials still believed that Persian oil was actually and rightly British oil because it had been discovered by the British, developed by British capital, and exploited through British skill and British ingenuity.[9] Hence the degree to which Mosaddeq's nationalization of the AIOC in 1951 outraged the British.[10] His action had implications worldwide. If Mosaddeq could get away with nationalizing the oil industry in Iran, might not Naser be inspired to nationalize the Suez Canal Company? Mosaddeq's challenge was basic in another sense. He held the foundation of Britain's position in Iran, the concession agreement of 1933, to be both illegal and immoral. Mosaddeq stands as one of the forerunners of a later generation of Asian and African nationalists who believed that the Western powers had no right in the first place to impose conditions of economic exploitation.

In the political domain, the British embassy in Tehran occupied fifteen acres in the heart of the city. The staff included political officers, consuls, economic and commercial officers, military attachés, and, not least, intelligence officers and cipher clerks. In short the British compound was almost as much a world within itself as the cantonments of the Anglo-Iranian Oil Company. The British diplomatic enclave symbolized foreign dominance. The British in 1952 could still joke that the Iranians believed its water supply contained miraculous life-invigorating qualities.[11] The power of the British Empire seemed to be all-pervasive, even though Iran was never a British colony. British influence in this sense was more subtle but not less potent for being indirect. There were good reasons why Iranians as well as the British themselves regarded Iran as part of Britain's "informal empire," in other words within the compass of the British Empire yet receiving none of the benefits of direct British colonial administration that would have been conferred by accountability to the British Parliament.

Mosaddeq's own cosmology certainly held British political hegemony and economic exploitation to be a certainty. His belief in the British as a source of "evil" helped to explain his outlook and indeed his political philosophy. "You do not know how crafty they are," he once said in characteristic vein. "You do not know how evil they are. You do not know how they sully everything they touch."[12] Melodramatic or not, Mosaddeq thus expressed a deeply felt sentiment, although he meant it collectively and not individually. There could be no mistake that he was to the core an anti-British nationalist. Although he opposed all foreign intervention, he believed specifically that the British had exploited Iran through the Anglo-Iranian Oil Company and had exerted political control over Iran that had to be broken before Iran could be truly free and independent. There could be no compromise with the British. For the most part the Foreign Office in London as well as the embassy in Tehran took Mosaddeq's unremitting hostility as an axiom. In the British view, little or no reconciliation was possible. From 1951, plans to overthrow him were set in train.

The architects of the plan were no less than two distinguished British academics, Ann K. S. (Nancy) Lambton, author of the famous book *Landlord and Peasant in Persia* (1953), and Robin Zaehner, who later became Professor of Eastern Religions at All Souls College, Oxford. Nancy Lambton believed that covert operations to overthrow Mosaddeq would be the only way to achieve a stable and pro-Western government in Iran; and she not only moved in high circles within the Foreign Office but was a friend of Anthony Eden, who again became foreign secretary in late 1951. In the early 1950s she was reader in Persian at the School of Oriental and African Studies at the University of London. She had served in an official capacity during the Second World War as press attaché at the embassy in Tehran. She was respected not only as a scholar but also as an authority on contemporary Iranian affairs.[13] In her view, the "stupidity, greed and lack of judgment of the ruling classes in Persia" caused the government to be corrupt and parasitic.[14] The wealth of the country was entrenched in the hands of large-estate owners, who were linked by marriage or family with an elite of rich merchants and ranking military officers. Unless the social and economic system of the country could be reformed, Iran faced a revolutionary catastrophe.

Lambton believed that revolution might be averted because certain patriotic and intelligent Iranians held views that coincided with British concepts of national self-interest based on effective and responsible government, professional integrity, and respect for the rule of law. Yet they would be regarded as traitors if they publicly denounced Mosaddeq. Hence there was a need for covert cooperation with those public-spirited Iranians who would work toward reform in concert with the British. She thus expressed a fundamental aim of the Labour government: to sustain Britain's own influence in Iran by economic and social reform. A harmony of interests could exist between the British and enlightened Iranians. Since the initiative had passed to Mosaddeq, the collaboration had to be covert rather than open. Propaganda would play an important part. "We discussed . . . with Nancy Lambton," wrote the head of the Eastern Department of the Foreign Office, Geoffrey Furlonge, "effective lines of propaganda and . . . we decided that we should try to show that responsibility for failure to improve the lot of the ordinary Persian lies not with the AIOC nor with the British Government but with the successive Persian Governments, who, while professing to be interested in economic development, have done little or nothing to bring it about."[15]

Robin Zaehner was the official in the British embassy in Tehran appointed by Herbert Morrison in 1951 to plan and carry out the operation against Mosaddeq. Zaehner was an improbable figure for such a job. He qualified for it because he had worked in covert operations in Tehran during the Second World War and thereafter with MI6 in Albania. He was fluent in Persian, indeed bilingual, and possessed an intimate knowledge of Iranian politics. According to a Foreign Office minute in 1951: "Dr Zaehner was apparently extremely successful in covert propaganda in 1944 at the time that there was a serious threat that the Russians would take over Azerbaijan. He knows almost everyone who matters in Tehran and is a man of great subtlety. The line then was, of course, to mobilise public opinion from the bazaars upwards about the dangers of Russian penetration."[16] Zaehner regarded Iranian politicians and political parties as part of a fascinating game, a constant jostling for supremacy in which the British, although in the background, played an almost natural part. As he saw it, the British and their allies in the internal political struggle could win out if they had the willpower and the skill to prevail in the perpetually shifting set of alliances and personalities. Like Lambton, Zaehner believed that he and his colleagues in the British embassy had to align themselves decisively with influential and patriotic Iranians who perceived their own self-interest to be identical with that of the British. Zaehner possessed extraordinary capacity to combine high thought with low living. He relished the lighter side of his duties. He held his own in gossip or discussion, whether about philosophy and religion or about human foibles. He drank heavily.[17] To those who wished to learn about Iranian politics he recommended Lewis Carroll's *Through the Looking-Glass.* He tended to tell his superiors what he believed they wanted to hear. His temperament did not draw him to the more sinister side of intelligence operations, nor did he have the discipline for rigorous secrecy. Zaehner was an Oxford bon vivant transmogrified into a quasi secret service agent.

The word "quasi" is necessary to understand Zaehner's brief and the nature of his appointment. Although he had previously served in MI6, in 1951 he held a Foreign Office appointment as acting counsellor in Tehran.[18] In a strict sense the Foreign Office charged Zaehner to work for the overthrow of the Mosaddeq government through legal and constitutional methods; but in fact a gray area existed in which Zaehner moved between intelligence and Foreign Office activities. Zaehner worked so closely with MI6 officers that he was often mistaken for one of them. He made no secret of his assignment to have Mosaddeq replaced by whatever means possible short of force. Here is an important difference between the British Secret Intelligence Service and the CIA, for the lines between MI6 and the Foreign Office were more fluid than those between the CIA and other parts of the American government. The same might be said about the circumstances of his appointment, for it is difficult to imagine, for example, Dean Acheson (secretary of state in the Truman administration) charging a member of the U.S. foreign service with such an assignment. Zaehner's brief came directly from the foreign secretary, Herbert Morrison.

Morrison's advent as foreign secretary occurred at the same time as Mosaddeq's rise to power in the spring of 1951. The Persian oil crisis preoccupied

Morrison during the eight months of his tenure. Famous for his leadership in the House of Commons, he failed to complement his mastery of domestic politics with a command of foreign affairs.[19] His interests did not extend much beyond British politics, although he did possess an aggressive attitude and a contempt for non-European peoples that put him at odds with some of his colleagues, not least Attlee. In 1943, while home secretary, Morrison had dismissed as 'nonsense" the possibility of granting independence to dependent territories under British sway: "It would be like giving a child of ten a latch-key, a bank account, and a shot-gun." [20] Morrison held the same paternalistic attitude toward Iran. After the nationalization of the Anglo-Iranian Oil Company on May 2, 1951, he took the lead in urging British retaliation by launching an expeditionary force to seize the island of Abadan. In an operation planned under the code name "Buccaneer," the Royal Navy, the Royal Air Force, and the army assembled a virtual armada, ready for attack.[21] The plan reached an advanced stage when an MI6 officer, Norman Darbyshire (who, as will be seen, played an important part in the unfolding story of the 1953 operation) bribed the Iranian commander in chief to put up only token resistance.[22] Attlee himself now took charge, bringing the cabinet to the conclusion that an invasion would not end the nationalization crisis but on the contrary would mobilize the Iranian nationalist movement against Britain. Attlee acted in part on a consistent noninterventionist principle of the Labour government, but in this case realpolitik assisted virtue because the U.S. government opposed British military action. In effect Attlee vetoed the plans for an invasion. Morrison suffered a humiliating setback.[23]

It is useful to place the decision in the broader setting of the cold war. To the British chiefs of staff and those on the military committees who drew up the series of contingency plans culminating in Buccaneer, there were grave issues of timing, manpower, and priorities. In this time of international crisis, as in others, intervention would be most effective if done expeditiously. Apart from doubts within the cabinet about the legal basis for action, the chiefs of staff lamented the lack of flexibility that had once allowed quick and decisive strokes by the Indian army, a resource no longer at their disposal. Political as well as military decisions proved to be protracted. The Iranian crisis had to be seen against the background of the Korean War, where the number of British troops ranked only behind that of the United States and South Korea. What would be the extent of British intervention in Iran? Could the British deploy troops there without weakening their commitment in Korea? Would British forces occupy the entire region of the oil fields, thereby requiring the call-up of reserves in Britain at a time of an economic crisis? Or, if the aim were limited to the seizure of the island of Abadan, might not the British in any event be drawn into a larger operation? Would the British occupation trigger a Soviet invasion in the north?

Mosaddeq himself declared that British aggression would signal the start of World War III, an eventuality that had a certain edge to it in view of the open question in Korea of whether American bombing would extend to Manchuria. In the event, Buccaneer focused on the capture of Abadan island. Even this limited aim might have the reverse of the intended effect by unifying the Iranian people against British imperialism. What would be the purpose of holding an enclave while a hostile hinterland held the oil reserves? The prime minister had those broad considerations in mind when he explained to the cabinet that the U.S. president refused to endorse the use of force. It was the American opposition to the British plan that proved to be decisive in Attlee's own calculation of a complex problem. He firmly led the cabinet to this conclusion: "We could not afford to break with the United States on an issue of this kind."[24] Dean Acheson later remarked emphatically that it had been "to the great credit of the Labour Government" to stand "against jingo pressures."[25] He had in mind not only Churchill but specifically Herbert Morrison as well.

From Morrison's point of view, the entry of Robin Zaehner into the story represented a small but significant step. It is evidence of the seriousness with which the foreign secretary viewed the situation. The appointment passed virtually unnoticed because it involved only a relatively obscure assignment to the staff in the British embassy in Tehran. Yet it eventually had ramifications that affected the British government as a whole as well as the Anglo-Iranian Oil Company and even the United States. Zaehner's name eventually came to symbolize subversive activity. It is important, however, to note some of the subtleties of distinction between covert and overt intervention, and to establish the nature of the debate within the Labour government in 1951. In the cabinet, Attlee restrained the foreign secretary's impulse openly and forcibly to punish Iran and thereby to bring about a change in government. But Morrison by no means stood alone in believing that Mosaddeq had to be toppled. The minister for defense, Emmanuel Shinwell, spoke just as aggressively in favor of intervention. In slightly different circumstances, Morrison's line of "sharp and forceful action" might have prevailed.[26] As events transpired, Morrison had to rely on covert means to achieve his goal. But even at the local level Zaehner's course of covert activity in attempting to unseat Mosaddeq did not necessarily contradict Attlee's high policy. On the whole, Zaehner adroitly stayed within traditional Foreign Office boundaries of influence or manipulation and not force.

There was tension within the Labour government, as in the U.S. government, between those who favored covert action as an extension of policy by other means and those who did not. In the Attlee era, the balance rested with those who did not, thereby making the Zaehner episode all the more significant by providing a small but vital element of continuity from Attlee to Churchill and from Morrison to Eden. In tracing the origins of the 1953 covert action against Mosaddeq, however, it is necessary to place the problem in the general context of the British and the politics of Iran. Otherwise the issue of intervention is likely to be distorted. It is also necessary to bear in mind from the beginning that the Anglo-Iranian Oil Company played no part in either the origins of the intervention or its execution. Otherwise the covert action of the intelligence agencies is obscured by the persistent myth that the company participated in Mosaddeq's overthrow.[27] In the British government, as in the American, covert action had its origin entirely within official circles.

The British and Iranian Politics

Almost from the beginning of the crisis in 1951 a strong current of thought in the Foreign Office held that Mosaddeq's "pathological" but shrewd anti-British attitude would make any discussion futile. In British eyes Mosaddeq himself was responsible for this deplorable state of affairs. Sir Francis Shepherd, who served as ambassador in Iran from March 1950 through the crisis of 1951, regarded him as on the fringe of irrational or "lunatic" behavior.[28] Shepherd's view was representative. George Middleton, who acted as chargé d'affaires in 1952 and who was universally regarded as a man of balanced judgment, wrote that Mosaddeq was "no longer capable of rational thought."[29] In London the prime minister himself referred to "the emotional state of the Persian Prime Minister (who appeared to be on the lunatic fringe)."[30] According to the *Observer*'s "Profile": "Moussadek is wholly impervious to common sense arguments of expediency. . . . He is surrounded by crooks, adventurers and madmen. . . . He is truly a Frankenstein."[31] Nor was this view restricted to British circles. The U.S. ambassador in Tehran, Loy Henderson, referred to Mosaddeq as "a madman"—and in virtually identical vein the secretary of state, John Foster Dulles, exclaimed, "That madman Mossadegh!"[32] The growing consensus on Mosaddeq's irrational behavior is basic to understanding one of the reasons the British and American governments eventually decided to intervene.

In view of Shepherd's low opinion of "Oriental character" and of Iran itself as a country of "Oriental decadence," it is hardly surprising that he and Mosaddeq found conversation difficult. He impressed upon Mosaddeq, and, it seems, on all other Iranians he met, that Iran had not been allowed to develop "at the hands of a virile and civilised nation." The Iranians lacked the benefits of a nationalist movement that British imperialism might have inspired. There were at least two major, underlying assumptions in Shepherd's quintessential British outlook: Iranian politics were irrational, and the nationalist movement was not authentic but merely a "preliminary flicker" of genuine nationalism.[33]

Both in Tehran and London the old Middle East hands of British official-dom developed more sophisticated interpretations of Mosaddeq and Iranian na-tionalism. Shepherd's ideas "may well have been sound at the time of Mosaddeq's rise to power," wrote R. F. G. Sarell of the Eastern Department of the Foreign Office, but some nine months after Mosaddeq's advent those assumptions no longer held true. Shepherd had believed that Iranian nationalism was a "spuri-ous" movement concocted by Mosaddeq and a few other anti–British extremists in order to divert attention from the corruption of the ruling propertied classes. It had no roots and commanded no genuine popular support. Sarell took issue with that superficial analysis. Paraphrasing from an article by Nancy Lambton, he penned the most searching estimate of Iranian nationalism in the "post-Shepherd" era (in fact he wrote in the same month that Shepherd left Iran to be-come ambassador to Poland, January 1952).[34] Sarell (closely following Lambton) argued that Shepherd was correct in holding that only a minority of the popula-tion supported the nationalist movement. But the explanation of Mosaddeq's popular appeal lay in the genuine sentiment that existed against the Anglo-Iranian Oil Company. Mosaddeq wished to expel the parasite of Western capi-talism, and he exploited the "xenophobia" and latent nationalism already present. He had been able to create a coherent national movement only because the religious leaders, especially Ayatollah Kashani, had already expressed the sense of dissatisfaction in Iranian society. Mosaddeq and Kashani roused nation-alist sentiment and transformed the situation: "By claiming to represent the real spirit of the nation against alleged foreign exploitation he [Mosaddeq] and the other leaders of the movement, notably Kashani, were able to produce a state of emotional excitement in which criticism could be stifled."[35]

By closely relying on Lambton's analysis, indeed her very language, Sarell helped to shape the collective estimate of the Eastern Department of the For-eign Office. The assessment included a historical analysis of the forces in Iran-ian society that had produced Mosaddeq and the tensions between the "classes" that might, or might not, sustain him:

In the early period of the Nationalist movement as now many of its leaders in fact belonged to the religious classes. The other class from which the Nationalist leaders were drawn in the past was the middle-class bazaar merchants, to whom the exclusion of the West and restriction of competition offered the promise of financial gain; between this group and the religious classes there has been a traditional connection, and the support of leaders such as Kashani is still drawn largely from the bazaar.

Calculations about the response of the bazaar, as will be seen, played a critical part in British plans to topple Mosaddeq. The Foreign Office (Lambton) assessment next discussed the "classes" from which Mosaddeq drew his support:

> The main support for the nationalist movement . . . comes from the military, professional, and bureaucratic classes, to whom nationalism opens the way to political power. In so far as nationalism is accepted by the masses it is probably because of their intuitive clinging to the Shia'. Nationalism appears to them as a reaction against the West, that is the non-Islamic world, but in so far as it penetrates to the masses it is transformed by their social traditions, and differs from the nationalism of the intellectuals. . . . Any alliance between the intellectuals and the masses is likely to prove unstable, because the former are out of touch with the latter, and the intellectuals, failing to understand the masses, despise them.[36]

Such was the drift of British official thought as of January 1952.

Lambton's view of Mosaddeq as a dangerously irrational, anti-British nationalist also found expression in minutes written by Eric Berthoud, the assistant undersecretary supervising economic affairs. Berthoud did not, however, usually address himself to day-to-day Iranian questions. Indeed, by a sort of gentleman's agreement he remained one step removed because early in his career he had been an employee of the Anglo-Iranian Oil Company. But whenever the occasion arose he freely ventured his opinion. It usually reinforced the judgment of Nancy Lambton, who characteristically urged the Foreign Office to boycott Mosaddeq as far as possible and to deal with him only when necessary to preserve public order. This was an attitude she maintained consistently. "Miss Lambton spent last weekend with us," Berthoud wrote a year and a half after Mosaddeq had been in office. She still held, as she had from the time of Mosaddeq's ascendancy, that it was impossible to negotiate with him because his entire position was based on anti-British sentiment. If he began making concessions he would destroy the foundation of his own power. Thus, in Lambton's judgment, "It is still useless to accept any settlement with Dr. Mosaddeq" because he would immediately renege.[37]

Like Lambton, Zaehner believed that the British embassy in Tehran had to align itself decisively with influential Iranians who perceived their own self-interest to be identical with that of the British. Zaehner's extensive minutes reveal that he regarded the wealthy Rashidian family—the brothers Saifollah, Qodratollah, and Asadollah—as allies of that kind. They are well described by the leading historian of American-Iranian relations, James A. Bill: "Seyfollah, the eldest and a musician and philosopher, was the brains of the triumvirate and a superb conversationalist and host. He was a student of political history and liked to quote verbatim from Machiavelli. Asadollah was the organizer, political activist, and confidante of the shah, while Qodratollah was the business man and entrepreneur." [38] Asadollah became the key British contact—in the words of Donald Wilber's CIA history, *Overthrow,* "the principal SIS agent." [39] The father of the three brothers had built a family fortune based on shipping, banking, real estate, and an array of business ventures including cinemas. During the Second World War, Zaehner had established contact with the Rashidian brothers in covert anticommunist activities.

By the early 1950s the Rashidians represented the operational arm of MI6 in Iran. From Zaehner they received a monthly sum of ten thousand pounds, which was used in part to influence attitudes in the bazaars but also in part for anti-Mosaddeq articles and lampoons in the daily press. [40] The Rashidians were staunchly pro-British quite apart from the money. They were also anti-American. One of the questions in the 1953 operation against Mosaddeq was whether they would transfer their loyalty to the CIA. Until the British eviction in November 1952, they played the leading part in Zaehner's efforts to destabilize the Mosaddeq government. *Overthrow* correctly notes that they had contacts "in such fields as the armed forces, the Majles (Iranian Parliament), religious leaders, the press, street gangs, politicians, and other influential figures." [41] Their view of Mosaddeq coincided with Zaehner's. Saifollah Rashidian told Zaehner in January 1952: "Even if Mosaddeq were offered everything he wanted plus £100,000 he would still say 'no.' " [42]

As Zaehner saw it, much would depend on the shah, whom the British at this time regarded as an unreliable ally, at once vacillating, indecisive, and opportunistic. It would be a mistake of the first magnitude to regard the authoritarian shah of later decades as the same as the weak figure of 1951–53. The shah, like Mosaddeq and indeed like many other prominent Iranians, was suspicious of British influence. *Overthrow* refers to the shah as "a man of indecision," but it also describes his "pathological fear of the 'hidden hand' of the British." [43] In any event the shah did occupy a position at the center of the Iranian political world. Any action on his part could help to determine the course of events, but so also would inaction. Thus the British attached importance to the shah's twin sister, Princess Ashraf, who had a stronger personality than her brother and often influenced him.

The British, in particular Zaehner, were well informed of palace politics through the shah's private secretary and éminence grise, Ernest Perron, a Swiss of long-standing influence with the royal family and "probably the shah's closest friend."[44] Perron did not use his position to acquire money, but he relished the glamour of the court and the social prestige as well as the status of poet and philosopher conferred on him by the shah. Others in the shah's circle regarded him as "slippery as an eel."[45] It was commonly known that he was a homosexual. He dressed "like a musical comedy Bohemian."[46] His lifestyle gave a certain racy reputation to the shah's entourage. He cultivated the military officers and politicians close to the shah as well as the prominent families who moved within the social circles of the court. On political issues he calculated that the shah's self-interest often coincided with that of the British and he thus was an invaluable British source of delicate information. Like Zaehner, he loved to gossip. The two were compatible, although one can detect an element of wariness on both sides. "Perron is admittedly not the ideal link" with the shah, Zaehner noted in August 1951, "but I can see no harm in keeping in close contact with him."[47] Perron was the shah's man, but he was also a vital British contact.[48]

There were two politicians whom the British regarded as possibilities to replace Mosaddeq. They were Sayyed Zia and Qavam al-Saltaneh, both of whom had long political careers and still commanded "about an equal amount of support in the Majles."[49] Sayyed Zia was the British favorite. He had served briefly as prime minister as long ago as 1921 and had consistently aligned himself with the British in Iranian politics. One of Shepherd's predecessors, Sir John Le Rougetel, in 1949 had described Sayyed Zia as "one of the few, in fact the only, outstanding personality in public life who is both competent, honest and sincere."[50] 'The best man," commented the Oriental Counsellor.[51] In 1951 Sayyed Zia had emerged as one of Mosaddeq's principal rivals, but he failed to receive the shah's endorsement as prime minister. The British thus held the shah partly responsible for Mosaddeq's advent to power and saw the shah's refusal to act as characteristically feckless. But the shah had his reasons.

Sayyed Zia's strength was also his weakness. He was so pro-British that the Iranian public would have regarded him as no less than a traitor on the issue of oil. He did indeed offer assurances that he would attempt to reach a "sensible" settlement. From about September 1951, however, the British learned that the

U.S. embassy in Tehran increasingly had reservations about him for the same reasons that the shah had opposed him. Sayyed Zia had so committed himself to the British that his ascendancy would be denounced as the high noon of U.S.-British hegemony in Iran. Nevertheless he remained invaluable to Zaehner and others not only as a source of information and advice but also as an important pro-British, yet independent, figure in Iranian politics. Sayyed Zia could not be ordered about. He advised the British on how to conduct their affairs in Iran rather than passively seeking their advice. In different circumstances he might have been, from the British vantage point, an excellent replacement for Mosaddeq.[52]

A tantalizing mention of a possible bribe to Sayyed Zia occurs in one of the British documents. It is in a telegram from the ambassador to the Foreign Office in September 1951: Sayyed Zia expected "to be helped with some fairly generous payment."[53] In fact no evidence exists that money changed hands, although Sayyed Zia may have expected, had he become prime minister, substantial but indirect financial gifts raked off from defense contracts. Nor is there any evidence of payments to the other two British candidates for high office in the 1951–54 period, Qavam al-Saltaneh and Gen. Fazlollah Zahedi. There was no secret that all three, at different times, had British sponsorship and that the British would have preferred any of them to Mosaddeq. They were called the "open opposition." As public figures they had their own reasons for being associated with the British, but to everyone concerned, the British as well as the Iranians, bribery at that level was dangerous, even in a culture that matched Chicago politics in its easy acceptance of bribery.

There was an underlying principle in the British method.[54] With prominent politicians, the more the British could stay in the background, the better. Bribery, under whatever name, almost always took place indirectly through the Rashidian brothers, but they in turn regarded Sayyed Zia, Qavam, and Zahedi as off-limits and left them to their political masters, at different times Zaehner, Woodhouse, and Falle. The Rashidians possessed a genius of sorts for securing political patronage. MI6 officers, particularly Norman Darbyshire, would occasionally make payments directly to deputies in the Majles, but bribery was the domain of the Rashidians, who had a monthly retainer of ten thousand pounds and could request more if necessary. So wealthy were the Rashidians, however, that they appeared to have viewed the MI6 payments mainly as operational funds and did not hesitate to use their own bank accounts to promote operations against Mosaddeq. At one time Mosaddeq himself guessed that at least one-third of the deputies in the Majles were on the Rashidian payroll. The three brothers controlled, or at least manipulated, some twenty newspapers.

They had contacts in the military and the police. Clerics as well as politicians and army officers were susceptible to their bribes. Asadollah Rashidian once spoke of his ability to promote a coup d'état against Mosaddeq by enlisting "the Army and the mullahs."[55] The influence of the Rashidians was thus far reaching. But it was by no means all-embracing, and the three brothers probably sometimes exaggerated their ability to influence events, as did, perhaps, the MI6 officers who worked with them. The CIA, for example, believed that MI6 overestimated Rashidian capability.[56] Nevertheless, it is difficult to imagine how the 1953 operation against the Mosaddeq government could have taken place without the Rashidian network.

Despairing of the prospect of replacing Mosaddeq with Sayyed Zia, the British from the autumn of 1951 believed that the next suitable alternative was Qavam al-Saltaneh. In a famous chapter in his long political career, Qavam had been premier at the time of the Azerbaijan crisis in 1946. He had managed to secure the withdrawal of Soviet troops by promising Stalin an oil concession in northern Iran. The Majles later canceled the concession. Whatever lessons the British might have derived about Iran and the Soviet Union from that episode, which the Russians regarded as treacherous, it nevertheless seemed obvious that Qavam was far preferable to Mosaddeq. Qavam, in the British view, was just as much a nationalist as Mosaddeq, but more anti-Soviet and less anti-British. He had the positive advantage of not having a pro–British reputation. But the British approached him with a certain wariness. The overt campaign in favor of Sayyed Zia had proved to be counterproductive. They now tried not to support Qavam too openly. Qavam himself merely regarded the British as a means to gain power, and was willing to do whatever was necessary toward that end.

The following minute by Zaehner records a conversation with one of Qavam's supporters, Abbas Eskandari, and gives a clear indication of the mounting British intention, as of late 1951, to get rid of Mosaddeq: "After concluding our discussion on the ways and means of overthrowing Mosaddeq, Iskandari went on to assure me (in Persian) that it was Qavam's desire to work in closely with the British and to preserve their legitimate interests in Persia without jeopardising Persia's political and economic independence."[57] In the complex interplay of forces known as "economic imperialism," Qavam could be expected to follow the British lead despite the past experience of the Anglo-Iranian Oil Company:

> I said that the independence of Persia had always been the corner-stone of our policy, but we were prepared to admit that economically Persia had been

largely dependent on the A.I.O.C. just as we and Europe in general were dependent on American aid. In the modern world no such thing as economic independence existed any more: and Persia must face this fact.

Iskandari said that this was understood and that Qavam-us-Saltaneh greatly preferred that British influence should be exercised in Persia, rather than that of the Americans (who were foolish and without experience), or of the Russians who were Persia's enemies.

There was to be a firm, if implicit, alliance between Qavam and the British. Qavam would have a free hand and, with patience, the legitimate commercial interests of the British would be restored:

> If we were prepared to accept Qavam-us-Saltaneh's assurance that he would come to an agreement satisfactory to both sides [i.e., the Iranians and the British], we must give him a free hand in the use of methods. Public opinion had been worked up to such an intensity of anti-British feeling that it would need a month or two to change it. Qavam-us-Saltaneh did not wish to disclose in advance exactly what his methods would be, but we knew by experience that with him everything came out right in the end, however curious the beginning might be.[58]

All of this, according to Zaehner, seemed to be "very much on the cards."

Here a general observation should be made about the British, Qavam, and Mosaddeq. Zaehner was accurate in his estimate of Mosaddeq. Economic dependence was precisely the point Mosaddeq was not prepared to admit, at least to the British. In Qavam the British hoped they had found a collaborator, perhaps a devious one, in the traditional mold.

In the circumstances of 1952, the youngest of the "Oriental Counsellors," Sam Falle, consistently argued that the British would be acting in the best interests of the Iranians (as well as in legitimate self-interest) by promoting Qavam. Falle wrote in April: "If Qavam comes to power he will try to act as a dictator—dissolve the Majles and arrest dissident elements, among them probably Mosaddeq and Kashani. On oil he is keen to reach an agreement with us."[59] Through Falle's minutes may be traced the mounting excitement during the spring and summer of 1952 when it seemed to be a question not *if* Mosaddeq would fall but only a question of *when*. Having brought the country to the brink of economic ruin, Mosaddeq, it now appeared, would be replaced by Qavam. The problem was the shah's attitude. The shah feared, rightly in the judgment of Zaehner and Falle, that he could not dominate Qavam. The British were indeed uncertain whether the shah would support him. According to Falle:

> Even if Mosaddeq falls the immediate future leaves plenty of room for anxiety. The Shah wants Mosaddeq to go quietly without any fuss and seems to be determined that the new Prime Minister be a weak man. . . . Such an appointment would in all probability be catastrophic and could not lead to the order and security which are vital if the country's problems are to be solved. Hence we come back to our problem which is that Qavam is the only man who can deal with the present situation, but that the shah will not have him. . . . The Shah's irresolution is extremely dangerous in these critical times.[60]

As the critical time of July 1952 approached, it looked as if Mosaddeq might collapse mainly because of Qavam's own initiative. Falle judged that, whatever the shah might do, the British should throw their weight behind Qavam: otherwise, "there is a chance that the whole work of the country might be paralysed for a time and render an oil solution more difficult. . . . My conclusion is that at the moment Qavam is the only man who can work effectively."[61]

After much hesitation the shah decided to accept Qavam as prime minister after Mosaddeq abruptly resigned in July in what proved to be a skillful attempt to reconsolidate his authority. Here was the test of the Zaehnerian interlude in Iranian politics: could British influence still be decisive? If so, the episode was an attempt to revert to the British doctrine of "Masterly Inactivity" because the British did very little. They remained aloof. As Zaehner himself explained the rationale, "I think it would be a tactical mistake to do any overt campaign on behalf of Qavam; we did this with Sayyid Zia and this did him no good."[62]

Qavam remained in power for less than a week. If the incident proved anything at all from the British side, it was that calculations could go radically wrong, not least from Zaehner's perspective. No one had championed Qavam as an anti-Soviet, anti-Mosaddeq statesman more than Zaehner, but when Mosaddeq triggered the crisis by his resignation, thus providing Qavam—and the British—with the opportunity to forge an anti-Mosaddeq combination, the intelligence community as well as Zaehner himself was caught off guard. Woodhouse and Roger Goiran, the CIA chief of station, had left Tehran together on a trout-fishing holiday in the northern mountains. They returned to find that Mosaddeq had been restored to power on a wave of popular support.[63] Woodhouse lamented in retrospect that the British had given Qavam virtually no assistance. Why had the British failed to rally to such a staunch anti-Mosaddeqist? The Rashidians for example played no part at a critical juncture in which they could have made a difference, if not a decisive one.

The political crisis of July 1952 proved that British policy had been based on a drastic miscalculation. Zaehner and others had assumed that Qavam as a national hero would have far-reaching popular appeal. But the Qavam of 1952 was not the Qavam of 1946. He had neither the military nor the public support to sustain himself in office. He was ousted by pro-Mosaddeq forces within a few days, on the twenty-first of July. Mosaddeq himself returned to power following mass demonstrations in which seventy-nine people were killed. In this test of strength, the remarkable outcome demonstrated the loyalty and perseverance of Mosaddeq's followers as well as the skill of Mosaddeq himself in consolidating his position against both the shah and the British. By acquiring new plenary authority on an emergency basis after his return to power, Mosaddeq now resolved to move forward not only in reforming the political economy of Iran in tax and land laws but also in matters that had popular appeal, such as an increase in the education budget, more road construction, rent control, the nationalization of telephones, and the creation of a uniform bus service. Mosaddeq had greatly enhanced his popularity and authority while the shah's had diminished. It is true that Mosaddeq's euphoria was brief. He soon began to quarrel with Kashani and other members of the National Front about his emergency powers and about cabinet appointments. The morale of the army plummeted when Mosaddeq purged officers sympathetic to Qavam. The communists were now beyond Mosaddeq's influence. The British were greatly discouraged at the time, above all because the shah had proved to be an even more negligible force in Iranian politics than they had previously assumed.

George Middleton immediately described the events of July 21 as "a turning point of Persian history." Mosaddeq had reconstituted his support by "mob riots," which seemed to reveal a close coordination of forces within Iranian society that previously had regarded each other with hostility. Middleton wrote the day after:

> It seems clear to me that the bloody riot of the 2lst July was a highly organized affair. . . . The National Front demagogues, notably Kashani, gave an outward appearance of a spontaneous popular surge of feeling to these riots. But in fact I believe these were almost certainly organised by the Tudeh. Reports reaching me are that the demonstrations were as much anti-monarchical as anti-"imperialist". . . . Moreover there was a cold determination and ruthlessness behind the manifestations which is typically communist. . . .

Mob rule, according to Middleton, now prevailed. The constitutional position of the shah had been weakened. Middleton believed that the shah himself bore large responsibility.

> The mob successfully defied the security forces and from now on the consent of the mob will be the decisive factor in judging the acceptability of any future government. . . . In all this it seems to me that the influence and prestige of the Court has been fatally weakened. The Shah has I suppose been anxious to avoid bloodshed and to act in every respect as a constitutional sovereign who must bow to the majority of public opinion. In fact by his vacillations and weaknesses and in the absence of an informed and educated public he has allowed the initiative to pass to the Tudeh and to the mob which the Tudeh controls.[64]

This was a black week, in Middleton's judgment, for the future of Western influence in Iran. The shah and "a small section of educated Persians" would probably continue to look to the United States and Britain for help, but, Middleton warned, "I fear that their influence and consequently ours will be a declining one and that it may be beyond our power now to stop the drift towards communism."[65]

Zaehner played a critical part in the Qavam episode, which in turn contributed to the expulsion of the British from Iran and the bringing together of MI6 and the CIA later in the year. The July crisis revealed not merely a lack of coordination but an uncertainty in estimating the extent of British power. In tracing the origins of British support for Qavam, it is clear that one of the motives was the search for a collaborator who would be able to conclude an agreement on oil satisfactory to the AIOC as well as to bring stability to the internal affairs of the country. This was a discussion that took place in London as well as in Tehran. One of Qavam's supporters had been Julian Amery, a Conservative member of Parliament who had served in MI6 during the war.[66] He had long-standing contacts in the Middle East and elsewhere because of his father, Leopold Amery, who had served as Churchill's secretary of state for India. Julian Amery is of interest not only because of Qavam's contacts with him but also because of his perspective from the hard right of the Conservative Party. Amery believed that Britain still possessed the military and intelligence capacity to stand apart from the United States and to exert an independent influence that would allow Qavam to dominate Iran. The trouble with this view was that it ascribed to the British in Iran much greater power than they possessed. It also assumed that the shah would fall in with British plans. In the case of Qavam he did not. In Zaehner's calculation, and especially Sam Falle's, it was the shah's indecisiveness that undermined Qavam.[67] As has been mentioned, Qavam lasted only five days. The episode unnerved Zaehner, who decided shortly thereafter to return to academic life.

Since Robin Zaehner's name has acquired almost symbolic significance in the history of clandestine operations in Iran, it is worth briefly contemplating his achievements and his limitations. First and foremost he forged the Rashidian organization into a reliable and effective British undercover network. He established an inside track to the Palace through Perron. Not least Zaehner developed firm friendships with younger members of the embassy. He assisted the rise of Sam Falle, the junior foreign service officer who would play a critical part in the plans leading to Mosaddeq's overthrow in 1953. Zaehner's legendary status as a hard-drinking, opium-smoking éminence grise and bon vivant is entirely justified, but for those reasons Woodhouse, Falle, and others regarded him as an eccentric and ultimately unreliable academic who was unsuited for operational intelligence work.

Zaehner's lieutenant, Sam Falle, was fluent in Persian. Falle's specific assignment was to cultivate the younger anti-Mosaddeqists. He sympathized with their nationalist aspirations. He had assisted Zaehner in sustaining contact with the Rashidians and increasingly became the principal point of contact with them. Although he had no doubt that they represented the equivalent of the Mafia in their gang-like tactics and criminal activities, Falle liked them and regarded them as patriots. This may seem paradoxical. How could any Iranian recruited by the British secret intelligence be regarded as an Iranian patriot? In Falle's view no less than Zaehner and Lambton's, the Rashidians believed that Mosaddeq's anti-British obsession would lead Iran to a communist takeover and with it the destruction of Iran itself. Iran's salvation as well as the Rashidians' fortune lay in cooperation with the British. In any event Falle regarded them realistically as a means of getting rid of Mosaddeq. It is not surprising that in late 1952 he was brought into the discussions with the CIA. Though only a junior officer, Falle's full-blooded and decisive views carried influence with his superiors, of whom the most significant was George Middleton, the chargé d'affaires from January 1952 until the rupture of relations between Iran and Britain in October.

Middleton had a broad outlook. By examining his assumptions, it is possible at the same time to return to the larger themes of Iran's future in relation to the United States and the Soviet Union as well as the Anglo-Iranian Oil Company, and above all the conundrum of Mosaddeq himself. While Middleton's colleagues often became caught up in Zaehnerian "intrigue" (one of Zaehner's favorite words), usually with the anti-Mosaddeqists, Middleton himself remained uncommitted to the view that Mosaddeq was essentially irrational. Indeed Middleton stood out conspicuously as recognizing in Mosaddeq the qualities of a highly cultivated and intelligent human being. Among the British in Tehran, Middleton was almost alone in regarding Mosaddeq not only as an anti-British nationalist but as a nationalist figure attempting to bring about an Iranian renaissance. Mosaddeq in his view had an almost mystical feeling toward nationalization. Both Mosaddeq and Middleton had been educated in France, and they conversed easily in French. Middleton was then forty-two while Mosaddeq was seventy-one. The older man was cordial to the younger, even though they disagreed on almost everything. "He was a highly civilised person," Middleton recalled much later, in 1985.[68]

Mosaddeq had such an inveterate mistrust of the British that no one who listened to his animated conversation could doubt that he actually believed the British to be somehow responsible for the poverty and general malaise of Iran.[69] Some remarks recorded in a confidential letter by Middleton in February 1952 well convey the flavor of Mosaddeq's sentiments. As Mosaddeq "bounded up and down excitedly," he dwelt on the corruption of previous governments, the danger of Iran falling to the communists, and the interference of the Anglo-Iranian Oil Company in the internal affairs of Iran. Corruption could be combated. Even the disaffected intellectuals, whom he denounced with contempt, could be prevented from turning communist by providing them with a "dole." But the secret "agents" exploiting the divisions of Iranian society seemed genuinely to worry Mosaddeq. He held, according to Middleton, that Iranian society had certain distinct components:

> The Iranian people could be divided into three classes: communists, agents of the ex-Anglo-Iranian Oil Company and patriots. He would eliminate the first two and the nation would then be united and strong as never before. I remarked that the A.I.O.C. had already left. Mosaddeq replied that their agents were still everywhere and because they were all self-interested they were perhaps an even greater danger than the communists.[70]

Did Mosaddeq actually believe his own conspiratorial rhetoric? If not, some sort of accommodation with the British might still be possible. Or was the anti-British obsession so integrated into his political personality (as Zaehner held) that Mosaddeq could never come to terms with the British oil company? If so then further discussion was virtually useless. Middleton, who probably knew him as well as any Englishman, had to admit that he saw no clear-cut answers. But he was willing to give Mosaddeq the benefit of the doubt. The anti-British rhetoric was part of Mosaddeq's political armor. The real question was whether Mosaddeq intended to come to terms on the oil question.

Mosaddeq to the British may have been irrational about certain things, but at least he was consistent. He saw in the Anglo-Iranian Oil Company the personification of the evils of economic imperialism, and he never deviated from that view.[71] The British for their part were also consistent. From the outset of the crisis in 1951 they had been prepared to admit the principle of nationalization. With a Labour government dedicated to nationalization, they could hardly do otherwise. But they insisted that the Anglo-Iranian Oil Company was entitled to fair compensation. Mosaddeq himself agreed that the company should be compensated, but he flatly disagreed on the more fundamental point of the legality of the 1933 concession. By viewing the contractual arrangement as immoral as well as illegal, he challenged every aspect of the British commercial presence in Iran. It was difficult to see where there might be common ground. For the British, the Iranian oil dispute brought to a head the conflicting outlooks as represented by Mosaddeq and the Anglo-Iranian Oil Company. The controversy brought home a basic point to the British, one they could not afford to concede. If Mosaddeq's view prevailed, especially on the validity of the 1933 concession, then nationalists throughout the world could abrogate British concessions with impunity.

To George Middleton the significance of the oil dispute was the sanctity of treaties. He was never in any doubt that the British had to hold firm on that point in all respects, legally, politically, and morally. But he did not think that the British could simply maintain a negative attitude, if only because the United States, while agreeing on the need to uphold the sanctity of treaties, would expect some kind of compromise. "We cannot indefinitely maintain a basically negative attitude," Middleton wrote in early 1952, "nor do I suppose the Americans will easily acquiesce in a policy of passive resistance to Mosaddeq."[72] As if those things were not difficult enough, Middleton judged that there was a further, insidious, psychological stumbling block. The British recognized the principle of nationalization, but they continued to protest the way it was carried out. They would accept nationalization as an accomplished fact if the Iranians agreed to provide acceptable compensation. But they also insisted that the oil industry be run "efficiently." Virtually no British expert believed that the Iranians could manage a refinery as complex as the one at Abadan.

Therein lay Middleton's point about national psychology. The Iranians knew that the British regarded them as inefficient if not incompetent—even more, that the British thought of them as inferior human beings. This was a psychological reality that bore as much on the actual negotiations as the abstract debate about the validity of the 1933 agreement and the practical amount of compensation to be paid to the company.

According to British calculations, the Iranian economy would take a serious turn for the worse in the spring of 1952. Within a year after Mosaddeq's rise to power, British economic sanctions—the boycott of Iranian oil and the successful denial of it to almost all foreign markets—would demonstrate the futility of the Mosaddeq regime. Or so it was hoped. According to Middleton's reports the economy was sagging but not collapsing. If Mosaddeq did not respond soon to economic pressure, there would be the danger that he might be replaced by something worse, either a communist regime or the fundamentalist religious faction led by Kashani, whom Middleton described as "a sly, corrupt and anti-Western demagogue."[73] The spring and early summer of 1952 was also the time that the British awaited the result of Mosaddeq's case against the Anglo-Iranian Oil Company before the International Court of Justice at The Hague.[74] When the court decided in July 1952 that the dispute lay beyond its jurisdiction, the ruling increased rather than alleviated the tension. The international legal action coincided with rapidly developing events within Iran.

Middleton had always been skeptical of Mosaddeq. Skepticism now hardened into disillusionment. "His strength lies in his powers of demagogy," Middleton wrote in his report to the Foreign Office, "and he has so flattered the mob as the source of his power that he has, I fear, made it impossible for a successor to oust him by normal constitutional methods."[75] Middleton believed that the sense of power deriving from the mob had gone to his head. Mosaddeq thought he could control the Tudeh as well as Kashani. He was now more than ever incapable of "reasonable" discourse: "[H]e is surrounded by a gang as little amenable to reason as himself and there does not appear to be a single person in his entourage with whom one can discuss matters in a rational way. . . . I think that his principal motivation just now is spite against the Americans and ourselves and he will stop at nothing to vent his dislike even though in effect it means alliance with the communists."[76]

Middleton wrote those lines during the July crisis in the immediate aftermath of Mosaddeq's restoration. The chronology is significant because it marks, in the testimony of the British official most willing to cooperate with him, Mosaddeq's point of no return: "Mosaddeq appears to be beyond reasonable thought and to be swayed entirely by emotion." In other words, he had crossed the rubicon into irrationality: "His megalomania is now verging on mental instability." [77]

Mosaddeq had been well aware of the British attempt to dislodge him by aiding Qavam. Their days were now numbered. The opportunity for expelling them came in September with the presentation of a joint offer made by Britain and the United States to settle the oil controversy. Mosaddeq found the offer unacceptable. The British explanation was quite simple. Whatever they held out, he demanded more. As the economy of the country deteriorated, he played on the emotions of the mob to retain power. The British in Tehran believed they were witnessing the virtual collapse of the Iranian state, a debacle that could be fatal because Mosaddeq was playing the game of the communists:

> Dr. Mosaddeq by his own action has largely implemented the known pro- gramme of the communist Tudeh Party; the shah has been reduced to a cypher, the Army fatally weakened, the British "imperialists" dispossessed, the central authority of the Government weakened and the economic and finan- cial structure of the nation reduced almost to chaos.
>
> Without having had to commit their forces in strength, the communists are in the fortunate position of seeing Persia reduced to the point where the advent of a communist régime seems almost to be part of the logic of history. [78]

Mosaddeq now demanded fifty million pounds in unpaid royalties from the Anglo-Iranian Oil Company. He argued more dramatically than ever that the concession of 1933 was invalid. "The popular belief has been carefully fostered," Middleton reported, "that the A.I.O.C. is responsible for the existing ills of Per- sia and indeed for the miseries which the country has suffered during the past 50 years." Thus Britain owed Iran reparations for past wrongs rather than Iran owing an indemnity for nationalizing a British company. [79] *Through the Looking- Glass* now seemed to be an entirely accurate way of viewing the situation in Iran.

One year to the month after the eviction of the Anglo-Iranian Oil Com- pany, Mosaddeq "kicked out," in Middleton's explicit phrase, the official British diplomatic mission in October 1952. Mosaddeq had become the victim of "his own brand of jingoistic nationalism." Polite yet melodramatic to the end, he explained to Middleton that "he was a fatalist," and things would now have to take their own course. He had "tears in his eyes" as he wished Middleton suc- cess in his future career. [80] Middleton himself, on the eve of his departure, re- flected that it might have been a false assumption all along to believe that rationality could prevail and that Mosaddeq might come to terms. Lambton and Zaehner, it may be inferred, had proved to be right. "Perhaps it was a mistake," Middleton wrote, "to fall in at all with the American view that Mosaddeq is 'negotiable.' "[81] Lambton expressed the point even more emphatically: "The United Kingdom policy of not making unjustifiable concessions to Dr. Mosaddeq was right and would have been successful had it not been for American vacillations."[82]

The American Connection, the Anglo–Iranian Oil Company, and the Dilemmas of the British Government

Until the political crisis of July 1952 there had been a fundamental difference in outlook between the British and the American governments. From the outset the Americans feared that the economic collapse of the Mosaddeq regime might bring about the advent of communist rule. Economic assistance was necessary to counter Tudeh exploitation of chaos, poverty, and despair. The British were skeptical. They did not minimize the danger of a Tudeh coup, but they did not believe that Mosaddeq could be appeased. Nor would economic assistance have any tangible effect on the political situation. If anything it would merely delay the fall of Mosaddeq. According to a Foreign Office assessment in early 1952:

> The State Department's repeated reference to impending economic collapse in Persia seems to us to betray a misreading of the Persian situation and a diagnosis too much in terms of a Western industrial state. Their theories on this subject have no doubt been sedulously fed by Dr. Mosaddeq's own propaganda . . . forecasting "collapse in about 30 days."
>
> It is our view that such terms are meaningless in Persia. A primitive agricultural community such as Persia, where some 80% of the population are estimated to live off the land at bare subsistence level does not "collapse" economically. It sags, and no doubt more of the population will die of starvation than usual. We do not believe in the imminence of the catastrophic phenomenon forecast by the State Department.[83]

The crisis of July 1952 brought the British closer to the American assessment. To reiterate George Middleton's emphatic point, Mosaddeq had now "worked himself up to a pitch of excitement" and was no longer capable of "rational thought."[84] He might well play into the hands of the communists. The British thus now believed, again in Middleton's words, that something was necessary "to check Communist activity in Persia."

Nevertheless the British and the Americans remained poles apart in their assessment of Mosaddeq. The British continued to hold that the end of the Mosaddeq regime would not necessarily lead to communism, while the Americans believed that Mosaddeq, for all his faults, was the only person who might prevent a communist revolution. In the immediate aftermath of the July crisis, Bernard Burrows (a former head of the Eastern Department of the Foreign Office now serving in Washington), reported a conversation with Charles Bohlen, a State Department official for whom the British had high respect. Bohlen had delivered an "emotional tirade about Persia. . . . his view seemed to be that Mosaddeq and Co. were the only people left who could conceivably save Persia from Communism and we ought, therefore, to make up our minds that we must make a deal with them." [85]

The British thought the Americans were responding excessively. Whatever might be happening in Iran could be explained more plausibly within the framework of Iranian politics than by the paramount American preoccupation at that time, the loss of China. Nor did the British believe that the fate of Mosaddeq would set off a chain reaction. Yet, according to Bohlen, "if Persia went Communist, Iraq and probably the rest of the Middle East would also, and our position would be lost anyway. We ought therefore to concentrate on saving Persia from Communism at all costs." [86] This "domino" theme also appeared in the American press, notably in articles written by Joseph and Stewart Alsop (a pair of reporters the British followed closely because their writing often revealed underlying assumptions of high American officials). The Alsops wrote after Mosaddeq's return to power: "This country [the United States] may be faced with the choice of allowing Iran to go the way of China, or intervening forcefully to support any anti-Communist forces in Iran, however reactionary and blindly nationalist. It is believed in Washington that a Communist takeover in Iran must be averted at whatever cost, even the cost of a break with Britain on Middle East politics." [87]

The Americans seemed to believe that the British would rather see Iran go communist than make an "unsatisfactory" oil agreement with Mosaddeq. This was the explicit challenge: "whether we were now more interested in stopping Communism than in an oil settlement." [88]

If there were to be an oil agreement, it would probably have to be based on the premise that the return of the Anglo-Iranian Oil Company was impossible. This was an American assumption as well as an Iranian one. But it was not necessarily a British assumption. As long as there seemed to be the prospect that Mosaddeq might fall for reasons of his own making (because, for example, the Iranians themselves might see that he was leading the country to economic ruin), then there was hope that the AIOC might be reinstated under the façade of a new management company. In the first half of 1952 British policy pursued the hallowed course of "Masterly Inactivity"—keeping the Americans in play (for example through joint discussions with the World Bank as an intermediary with Mosaddeq) and putting forward no constructive solution. There were good reasons for this negative approach. Any alternative to the AIOC would mean a breaking of the British monopoly. Thus the Americans were justified in their standard criticism that the British were merely "standing pat." Even before the July crisis, however, certain officials in the Foreign Office began to recognize that something had to be done, if only to counter the American suspicion that the British would allow Iran to drift into communist revolution before giving up the concession. The driving force behind the effort to arrive at some solution, however unpalatable it might be to the company and the champions of privileged position, was the deputy undersecretary at the Foreign Office, Sir Roger Makins (later Lord Sherfield). It came as a revelation to him that both the Treasury and the Ministry of Fuel and Power seemed to be just as hostile to compromise as the AIOC. "We are indeed faced with a solid wall of Bourbonism and Micawberism in dealing with this question," Makins wrote in June 1952, "of which the failure to deal with the re-organisation of the A.I.O.C. in the last six months is a symptom."[89]

The actual architect of the reorganization of the Iranian oil industry on the British side was Peter Ramsbotham, then at the "oil desk" of the Foreign Office. Through his minutes may be traced the steps that eventually led to the consortium agreement of 1954. Ramsbotham approached these problems with an eye toward a realistic settlement and with a sense of humor. "A concession is probably neither definable in law nor as a term of art," he once wrote.[90] Whatever a "concession" might once have amounted to in Iran, it now had to be replaced. He had in mind a "contractual arrangement" whereby a new company would negotiate a fifty–fifty principle of profit sharing with the Iranian government. The Anglo–Iranian Oil Company would receive compensation for losses (possibly through arbitration). Ramsbotham's language made explicit the nature of the proposed arrangement: the new managing company would be a "façade" that would enable the Iranians to save face, and the new agreement would include a guarantee that would prevent them from interfering "in the company's day to day operations." He was well aware of the danger of attempting to make this fabrication a purely British façade: "A reconstructed British company would not be able to operate as the sole company inside Persia as this would be too transparent a restoration of British monopoly."[91] Therefore American and perhaps other foreign oil companies would have to be allowed into the new arrangement. This proposal drew a protest from the foreign secretary himself. "I do *not* like the idea of bringing American companies in," Anthony Eden wrote in May 1952.[92]

Eden's past experiences help to explain his attitude toward Iran in 1952. At Oxford he had studied Persian, which he continued to refer to as "the Italian of the East." He had served as parliamentary undersecretary at the Foreign Office at the time of the Iranian oil crisis of 1933. He had been to Iran and had seen the oil fields. In 1951 he had denounced the Iranians for stealing British property. Upon becoming foreign secretary again after the fall of the Labour government, one of his first major anxieties became "Old Mossy." Behind the caricature of Mosaddeq as a buffoon in pajamas negotiating from an iron bedstead, Eden saw a shifty operator who was impervious to reason because of his antipathy to the British. He occasionally referred to Mosaddeq as a megalomaniac (a word he usually reserved for Naser). He certainly regarded him as one of the shrewdest and most devious "Orientals" he had ever encountered. Eden wrote in his memoirs: "Interviews with Mosaddeq, whether in bed or out of it, affable or corrosive, did not advance us one jot."[93] The problem of Iran was of course only one of many that Eden faced, but in retrospect he regarded it as the most difficult to resolve. He wrote at the end of the critical year 1954, after the successful conclusion of negotiations on the consortium: "It is a strange thing about this year that though many people have written about the problems which we have, we hope, solved, Western European Union, Egypt, Indo-China, Iran, Arabia (Buraimi), very few have given much credit to Iran, which was, I believe, the toughest of all."[94]

Eden's success in dealing with the Iranian crisis in fact derived in large part from delegating responsibility and listening to the advice of his permanent officials. In 1952 it was Sir Roger Makins, probably more than anyone else, who convinced him that he was wrong in his initial response to the question of the American oil companies. Makins held that the Americans would have to be allowed into the Iranian oil industry or there would be no hope of a settlement.

The principal opponent to radical reorganization was Sir Donald Fergusson. From his position as permanent undersecretary at the Ministry of Fuel and Power, he was in a position to block any proposal the Foreign Office might put forward, or, conversely, to shape an outcome that would, in his view, correspond to the British national interest. Fergusson had been a member of the Stokes mission to Iran in 1951, when the British made certain proposals to Mosaddeq The British would recognize the principle of nationalization and would relinquish the concession in favor of a contractual arrangement. In return for compensation, the British would help to establish a new management company that would efficiently run the Iranian oil industry on the basis of a fifty-fifty division of profits. This compromise represented the limit of Fergusson's generosity, which scarcely included the Americans. He was almost as distrustful of them as he was of the Iranians. After Makins wrote to him of the possibility of reopening discussion with both the Iranians and the Americans in the spring of 1952, Fergusson responded:

> I fear that we are in some danger of finding ourselves in a position where, having talked vaguely about resuming negotiations and making concessions, we shall be accused by the Americans of bad faith because we are unable to agree to specific concessions which their backroom boys will produce at short notice and in large quantities.
>
> The fact of the matter is that there is very little that we can do by way of making concessions.[95]

Only with extreme reluctance did Fergusson concur that somehow the Americans had to be accommodated, but not at the expense of the legitimate interests of the Anglo-Iranian Oil Company. He held that the British and American governments were not the appropriate parties to negotiate a settlement. The AIOC itself, in his view, was the only competent body to reach an agreement with the Iranians. Fergusson's attitude well represented what Makins referred to as "Bourbonism."

"I suppose one can never be certain of anything in Persia," Makins wrote, but waiting like Mr. Micawber for something to turn up would surely not yield results favorable to the British. Makins and Fergusson could both agree that there was no room for false optimism. Yet they were pulling in quite opposite directions, Makins toward collaborating with the Americans, Fergusson toward aligning the government's policy with the company's, or at least remaining true to sound British business principles. This developed into a first-class bureaucratic row. Makins eventually prevailed. He did so because of Eden's influence within the cabinet and because of the transcendent importance of the political issue at stake. In Eden's own words, "It is our national interest to obtain a settlement, not on account of the oil but because Persia's independence is very much our concern."[96] Eden thus demonstrated the qualities of a statesman. And he exerted pressure on his colleagues. He spoke to the chancellor of the exchequer, R. A. Butler, and the secretary of state for coordination of transport, fuel, and power, Lord Leathers. The latter, of course, was Fergusson's minister. Fergusson was a loyal, efficient, and extremely tenacious civil servant. From about mid-1952 onward he began to redirect his energies toward bringing the AIOC into line with government policy, the Eden policy. He was exceedingly skeptical whether the chairman of the company, Sir William Fraser, was capable of seeing beyond the strictly commercial limits of the problem. Fergusson minced words with no one. He told Fraser himself that he was "a damn bad negotiator."[97] After reading a report of one of Fergusson's conversations with Fraser, Eden made a memorable comment that will probably always be associated with the Iranian oil controversy: "Fraser," noted the foreign secretary, "is in cloud cuckoo land."[98]

Sir William Fraser (Lord Strathalmond) holds a unique place in the history of British overseas expansion not only because he dominated the Anglo-Iranian Oil Company but also because of his autocratic personality. An exceptionally rugged Scottish individualist, he had been born and bred in the British oil industry. His father had been founder and managing director of the Pumpherston Oil Company, the leading Scottish shale oil company. The younger Fraser personified the sense of adventure and enterprise that the British public associated with "Anglo-Persian," as the company used to be called. He had been chairman since 1941. According to a notice in the *Times* after his death, he was "a Scotsman to his fingertips. . . . He had a razor-keen business brain combined with a Scottish sense of caution such that few, in an industry where tough bargaining is an accepted way of life, were likely to get the better of him."[99] In business affairs he was accustomed to having his way. He must therefore have found it galling to confront Mosaddeq's brand of Iranian nationalism that aimed to repudiate everything the AIOC represented—even though Fraser maintained that nothing other than ingratitude should ever be expected from "the Persians." In fact Mosaddeq's estimation of him was probably not much different from that of Fergusson, who believed that Fraser intended to exact as much as possible from Iran whatever the consequences. Fergusson believed that Fraser should be removed from the chairmanship of the company. So did most other officials, including the governor of the Bank of England. Even the National Provincial Bank, the AIOC's bankers, believed that he had outserved his time.[100] Fraser, however, had great staying power. "[T]he retirement of Sir W. Fraser has been under consideration at various times in the past 2 years," wrote Christopher Gandy of the Eastern Department in 1954: "He is still there."[101] He did not retire until 1956, and did not die until 1970, long enough for his friends to maintain that he had understood Iranian nationalism better than his critics and to claim credit for his reorganizing the Iranian oil industry in the form of the consortium arrangement of 1954.[102]

In fact Fraser resisted from beginning to end. Part of the problem was his open contempt for civil servants. He was generally scornful of those who chose to earn their living by working for the state, and he was specifically disdainful of their knowledge of the oil industry. "We had a pretty sticky meeting with Sir William Fraser last night," Makins wrote on July 19, 1952.[103] The date is significant because this was the time of Qavam's brief advent to power. Fraser argued that Qavam would come to a reasonable agreement. The company did not wish to rush; indeed, as Fraser explained, there was no particular need for the AIOC to return to Iran. The losses at Abadan had already been more than recovered by the Kuwait fields. By the early 1950s Kuwait reserves were estimated at 16 percent of the world's total compared with Saudi Arabia at about 10 percent.[104] Thus the Foreign Office did not have a strong hand to play against the company. Fraser was not unresponsive to patriotism, but it was probable that his business instinct would prevail.[105] Nevertheless there was progress. By July 1952 Fraser had agreed in principle to a management company in which the major American oil companies might participate. The more he thought about it, the more Fraser believed it would be best for the AIOC to retain the initiative in this new arrangement. He himself would go to Iran to discuss the matter with Qavam. The following Foreign Office minute indicates Eden's response to Fraser's proposal: "The Secretary of State had been horrified at the suggestion that Sir William Fraser should go out to Persia to conduct negotiations."[106]

Speculation about Fraser bartering with the Iranians was short-lived. After Mosaddeq's restoration in late July 1952, the calculations changed. During this period, American and British outlooks began to converge. The longer Mosaddeq remained in power, the greater would be the danger of an eventual communist takeover. There remained, however, serious differences in the American and British points of view. According to the British ambassador in Washington, Sir Oliver Franks, the Americans distrusted the Anglo-Iranian Oil Company to the extent that they doubted whether any solution would be possible if Fraser remained a part of it. The Americans and the British also continued to disagree in assessing the stability of the Mosaddeq regime. In the British view economic assistance would sustain the Mosaddeqists while in the American outlook economic aid was necessary to prevent a communist takeover. "We must go on trying to restrain them," Makins wrote of the Americans in August.[107] "[T]hey are agog for action," reported Franks.[108] The result was the Truman Churchill proposal of September 1952 whereby the amount of compensation would be arbitrated. The AIOC would negotiate with the Iranian government for the resumption of oil production; and the United States would grant $10 million in budgetary aid. "It is very important that we should not lose momentum," wrote R. J. (later Sir James) Bowker, the assistant undersecretary supervising the Eastern Department. "At any minute Musaddiq or the State Department may have another bright idea."[109] The offer was presented. Mosaddeq responded with a demand for £50 million as an advance against oil.[110] This was another turning point. The Americans now moved still closer to the British assumption that it was impossible to do business with Mosaddeq.

The autumn and winter of 1952 marked the critical period when the British and Americans began together to plan covert operations. Here a word must be said about the nature of the archival evidence. In late 1952 and early 1953 there occurs something like a sea change in the British documentation. It is not merely a coincidence that this was the beginning of the Eisenhower administration and the advent of Allen Dulles as head of the CIA. Until this time British intelligence operations, if impinging on foreign policy, were discussed fully and candidly within the secret councils of the Foreign Office. One can read minutes, for example, about the possibility of assassinating the mufti of Jerusalem during the Second World War. For the Mosaddeq period the records have been suppressed. With the beginning of the Eisenhower presidency, the cold war was stepped up several pitches. Even within the Foreign Office, officials stopped writing about matters they previously had debated in the ordinary course of minutes and private correspondence. The nature of historical analysis is thus affected. British policy remained constant; but it now had a deeper, subterranean dimension. Nevertheless, detailed points have emerged from accounts of the cold war and, not least, from *Overthrow.*[111]

The British in 1953 detected a change in mood as well as a shift in policy in Washington. The Truman administration, in the British view, had been exceedingly cautious in dealing with Mosaddeq. Indeed, Dean Acheson, the secretary of state, and George McGhee, the assistant secretary who dealt with the Iranian question, seemed to the British to err in judgment by treating Mosaddeq as a sort of charming Oriental gentleman, rather than as a demented and extraordinarily devious and dangerous anti-British extremist. "The difficulty with the previous administration," wrote Sir Pierson Dixon (the deputy under-

From left: John Foster Dulles, Winston Churchill, Dwight Eisenhower, and Anthony Eden during a summit meeting in Washington in June 1954. The two heads of state, along with their top foreign policy advisers, had agreed the previous year that Mosaddeq had become a liability to Western interests and would have to go. Courtesy Dwight D. Eisenhower Library.

secretary who succeeded Makins when the latter became ambassador in Washington in January 1953), "was that we were continuously being pushed to make new concessions whenever Mosaddeq shifted his ground. The new Administration, however, seem to realize that we have now reached the limit of concession." This was a decided improvement over the "vacillation" described by Lambton and Zaehner. "Much more robust" were Dixon's words to sum up the change.[112]

It would suit one's taste for historical symmetry if a similar contrast could be made between the Tory government and its Labour predecessor. For better or worse, it was a Labour foreign secretary, Herbert Morrison, who had instructed Robin Zaehner to work for Mosaddeq's overthrow by covert means, and it was Churchill himself, as will be seen, who sustained that course of action to its logical conclusion. On the other hand Eden proved to be just as cautious and capable in his handling of the Iranian question, as distinct from the

Egyptian, as any Labour foreign secretary might have been. There are no generalities that can be drawn other than that personalities and the quirks of fortune played a large part in the outcome of the Iranian question in 1953. So much has been made of the conspiracy to overthrow Mosaddeq that it is well to bear in mind that things might have turned out quite differently with only a slight variation of circumstance. Indeed, as C. M. Woodhouse points out in his autobiography, *Something Ventured,* Mosaddeq might well have fallen without any assistance from the British and Americans. Even so, Iran might have been doomed. Woodhouse's basic assumption was identical to that of Wilber's *Overthrow.* "Iran was in real danger of falling behind the Iron Curtain."[113]

The British and the 1953 Covert Operation

From the vantage point of the CIA, "Monty" Woodhouse was indispensable in planning the overthrow of the Mosaddeq government because of his reputation, his competence, and his contacts, which extended to Churchill. Woodhouse was one of MI6's "most highly esteemed officers," according to *Overthrow.*[114] He had fought with the Greek resistance during the Second World War. He was a colonel at the age of twenty-seven. He later became Conservative member of Parliament for Oxford, chief editor of Penguin Books, director of Chatham House, and a distinguished historian of Greece. In 1951–52 he headed MI6 in Iran. He was trusted by the U.S. ambassador in Iran, Loy Henderson, and by certain key figures in the CIA including Walter Bedell Smith (director of the CIA until 1953) and Allen Dulles (the deputy director who himself became director in the Eisenhower years). Woodhouse got on well with Frank Wisner (director of operations) and Kermit Roosevelt (head of CIA operations in the Middle East). In his general approach Woodhouse took care to avoid the impression that the British aimed merely to reverse Mosaddeq's decision to nationalize the oil industry and to restore the Anglo-Iranian Oil Company. Since Woodhouse himself regarded the AIOC as "stupid, boring, pigheaded and tiresome," this was not difficult.[115]

In Woodhouse's assessment, joint action by Britain and the United States would be the only way to prevent the Soviet army from marching southward and forging a satellite state in Iran on the model of Eastern Europe. Stalin might not actually have had that in mind, Woodhouse reflected later, but in the early 1950s it had certainly seemed possible. With the shah and Kashani playing the respective parts of Hamlet and Thomas à Becket, Mosaddeq appeared to Woodhouse as "a wily theatrical, tragi-comic figure . . . [whose] abiding enemy . . . was Britain." [116] The principal danger was not Mosaddeq's crusade against the Anglo-Iranian Oil Company, which was serious enough from the British vantage point but was not Woodhouse's main concern. From his background of the Greek civil war the overarching menace was that of a communist takeover: "The longer he [Mosaddeq] held office the more probable it became that Iran would pass under Soviet control." [117] This of course was close to the American view, specifically the one held by Loy Henderson, who had long experience with the Russians and played a critical part in aligning the American and British positions: "Loy Henderson changed the atmosphere in the U.S. Embassy towards sympathy with the British case." [118]

By late 1952 there was a convergence of British and American views in Tehran, but with a dissenting voice. The CIA chief of station in Tehran, Roger Goiran, believed that intervention would be a mistake. Goiran had carefully and skillfully built up an intelligence network in Iran, but its purpose in his judgment should remain anti-Soviet. He believed that intervention would not only be disastrous in the long run but would also create the short-term impression that the United States supported "Anglo-French colonialism." [119] He was sensitive to that point because, among other reasons, he was a second-generation French American. He was also a man of principle and of religious commitment. Woodhouse respected him, and the two of them worked in harmony despite a profound difference of outlook. He was an "invaluable ally," Woodhouse commented in retrospect. [120]

Woodhouse became head of MI6 in Tehran during the last months of the Labour government in 1951. It is convenient at this point to review the relationship between MI6 and the Foreign Office at that time, and to inquire into the ways in which the Conservative government did or did not change things under the leadership of Churchill and Eden. Woodhouse owed his assignment to George Young, who had only become head of MI6 operations in the Middle East earlier in the same year. Young has legendary status in MI6 lore as a man of unabashed contempt for Labour politicians as well as for Arabs and Iranians. "A depressing experience," he once commented on the Attlee government. He remarked about the 1951 election that "the pall of negation" had lifted. [121] Those were revealing comments. Attlee and Bevin held MI6 in check. There existed in any event a tension between MI6 and the Foreign Office, with officials of the latter generally reluctant to endorse covert action. The permanent undersecretary, Sir William Strang, held the responsibility for coordinating intelligence operations with the head of MI6, "C," Maj. Gen. Sir John "Sinbad" Sinclair. Since Sinclair played such a major part in the events of

1952–53, the following description of him is of interest: "a tall, lean Scot with the angular, austere features of a Presbyterian minister, blue eyes behind horn-rimmed spectacles and a soft voice [that] gave him a kindly demeanour."[122] Strang was the stronger of the two personalities. Sinclair often deferred to him on the Middle East, a region with which Strang had much greater experience. Strang submitted minutes to Bevin, who in turn, characteristically and without fail, consulted Attlee on matters of importance. It is certain that Attlee directly concerned himself with intelligence operations during Morrison's tenure as foreign secretary (although Zaehner's appointment probably did not attract Attlee's attention). After the Conservative victory in 1951, the structure of decision making remained the same, but Eden acted with a much greater degree of independence than Morrison had been allowed. Indeed Eden reasserted the prerogatives of covert action that he had held during his earlier term as foreign secretary during the wartime years 1941–45. When he fell ill in 1953, the prime minister took charge. Churchill had an enthusiasm for clandestine operations that was entirely alien to Attlee. In such a way did the change of regime make a difference.

Within the Foreign Office, only a handful of officials knew of the plans to overthrow Mosaddeq. These included the deputy undersecretary, Sir Roger Makins, and his successor in early 1953, Sir Pierson Dixon, both of whom had strong reservations about the wisdom of covert action. Dixon objected not so much as a matter of principle but because he doubted the efficacy of political intervention in Iran both in the short and the long term. As will be seen, he nearly throttled the Mosaddeq project. Below Dixon in the chain of command was (Sir) George Clutton, who acted as the Foreign Office liaison with MI6. Astigmatic and austere, Clutton before the war had worked as an officer in the British Museum. He was both efficient and humane, and his colleagues held him in esteem. Clutton controlled the circulation of intelligence papers, of which the further recipients included the assistant undersecretary supervising the Middle East, Sir James Bowker; the head of the Eastern Department, Geoffrey Furlonge; and the officer in charge of the Iran desk, Christopher Gandy.

In Tehran, Woodhouse's predecessor, in practice and spirit if not in direct employment in MI6, was Col. Geoffrey Wheeler, a former officer in the Indian army whose intelligence career in Iran had begun during World War II.[123] Wheeler was a friend of Nancy Lambton. He had no more faith than she in the capacity of the Anglo-Iranian Oil Company to adjust to postwar circumstances, and he was in advance of most of his colleagues in recognizing the soundness of the fifty-fifty principle of profit sharing.[124] Not least, he was a source of inspiration to younger members in the British official community in Tehran. Woodhouse identified Wheeler as a man of kindred intellect and disposition, and often conferred with him in London. In Tehran, Woodhouse at the beginning of his tenure found the British mission to be efficient and reliable, although he quickly developed doubts about both Zaehner and the ambassador, Sir Francis Shepherd, who, he thought, perhaps unjustly, failed to rise to the challenge of the job.[125] Woodhouse got on well with Middleton and kept him fully apprised of MI6 activities.

When Woodhouse arrived in Iran, there were standing plans to defend Iran from the threat of internal communist subversion and from possible Soviet aggression in the event of another world war. Woodhouse himself was skeptical about the possibility of protecting the western position in Iran in the circumstances of all-out war against the Soviet Union, but he saw it as one of his duties to carry forward such activities as surveillance on the Caspian. In the Qavam crisis in July 1952, when the British feared the destabilization and possible collapse of the Iranian government, Woodhouse flew to Iraq to secure weapons for possible use by the tribes in northern Iran to prevent a Soviet invasion.[126] There was also a tribal dimension to his work in southern Iran, roughly in the oil-rich area of the Abadan region controlled by the Bakhtiari. With long, pre–World War II antecedents, the plan involved the creation of an autonomous southern breakaway state under British overlordship. In the event of a collapse of the Iranian government, or the partition of Iran into informal spheres of Soviet and British influence, British control over the oil fields would remain intact. This plan carried over into the Woodhouse era. Although Woodhouse himself doubted its practicality, it remained part of his contingency planning in 1951–52.

Woodhouse devoted his principal attention to the danger of communist or Tudeh subversion. He was assisted by Norman Darbyshire, a hard-drinking but able intelligence agent who had worked with Robin Zaehner during the war and was fluent in Persian. Darbyshire's reputation later became clouded because of drunkenness, reckless behavior, and abuse of his second wife, but at the time of his association with Woodhouse he was an energetic and exceedingly competent MI6 officer. The two of them divided their Iranian contacts roughly into those who spoke English and those who did not. Woodhouse engaged those who spoke English and identified members of the professional class willing not only to convey information but actively to work against the Mosaddeq regime.

As Nancy Lambton had anticipated, a significant number of lawyers, journalists, doctors, professors, bankers, and businessmen believed it to be in Iran's interest to bring about the fall of Mosaddeq. Many of them, it seemed to Woodhouse, were motivated above all by a sense of patriotism. This was certainly true of Woodhouse's three principal contacts. One bore the code name "Omar" and was the director general of a government department and eventually a member of Mosaddeq's cabinet.[127] From "Omar" Woodhouse gained innermost secrets of the Mosaddeq government. He had two other major contacts. One was Abbas Quli Neysari, chairman of the Irano-British Bank.[128] The other was an ophthalmologist of international reputation, Hassan Alavi, who was also a deputy in the Majles and never disguised his links with the British. Darbyshire helped in winning the support of other members of the Majles, some with less than lofty motives, by distributing packages of biscuits, the centers of which had been removed and filled with bank notes.

When Woodhouse arrived in Tehran in August 1951, Robin Zaehner had already reestablished the alliance with the Rashidian brothers. Zaehner was now in the twilight of his Iranian career. Woodhouse recognized his skill in dealing with the Rashidians, but he regarded him as a dangerous amateur so far as serious undercover work was concerned. Zaehner did not possess the stamina or the ruthless determination to see his anti-Mosaddeq plans through to completion. Nor did he prove to be especially adept in coordinating the activities of his branch of the embassy with those of MI6. Before his departure he turned over the control of the Rashidian brothers to Woodhouse.[129] What Woodhouse would demonstrate was that the British, with careful planning, could still play a decisive part in Iran if they worked in concert with the Americans.

After Mosaddeq evicted the British diplomatic mission in October 1952, Zaehner played his last hand, nearly upsetting Woodhouse's carefully laid plans. Having returned to London, Woodhouse made the mistake of inviting Zaehner to meet with him and Eden and other high officials, including George Young, to discuss future operations. Zaehner gave a gloomy account. Plagued with self-doubt, he had been disillusioned with Qavam and now mistrusted the capacity of the Rashidians to dislodge Mosaddeq. A late convert to the principle of nonintervention, Zaehner now emphatically believed that the British should let Iranian affairs take their own course. Woodhouse was appalled at Zaehner's defeatism. He responded to a casual remark made by Eden, who said that nothing could be done anyway without the help of the Americans. A less enterprising person than Woodhouse might have let things go at that. If Woodhouse himself had not seized the initiative at this point, there might never have been a coup against Mosaddeq, at least not one partly sponsored by the British.

Woodhouse interpreted Eden's comment to mean that he should explore possibilities with the Americans. He went to Washington in mid-November 1952. Before his departure, he conferred with Nancy Lambton, not Zaehner. Woodhouse was accompanied by Sam Falle, who had an intimate knowledge of Iranian politics and, since he had become the principal contact with the Rashidians, a familiarity with the "three larger-than-life brothers." [130] In Washington, Woodhouse and Falle met with John Bruce-Lockhart, the MI6 station chief, who went with them to some of the meetings and cheerfully talked about the intricate relations between the State Department and the CIA but otherwise made no significant contribution to the discussions. Bedell Smith (Allen Dulles's predecessor) told Woodhouse, "You may be able to throw out Mosaddeq, but you will never get your own man to stick in his place." [131] The question of Mosaddeq's successor was by no means the only problem. The Rashidians were no less anti-American than previously. Woodhouse did not know how they would react until events actually unfolded. The Americans for their part generally did not rule out the possibility of a combined move against Mosaddeq, nor did they flinch at the price, which Woodhouse described as perhaps half a million pounds plus the ten thousand pounds a month already being paid to the Rashidians. Not all of the American bureaucracy, however, fell in so wholeheartedly with these ideas. Woodhouse found the CIA officials ready to carry the discussions forward even though they had been caught off guard by his raising the issue.[132] Those representing the State Department were hesitant to become involved. There was a lingering "silliness" among some Americans, who felt, Woodhouse wrote later, "that Mosaddeq could be retained and manipulated, and who dreaded the consequences of his downfall." [133] This was at the end of 1952, a significant time because, among other reasons, the British had made contact with Kermit "Kim" Roosevelt, who proved to be as enterprising on the American side as Woodhouse had been on the British.[134]

Woodhouse had made progress at the undercover level. Allen Dulles, though he could make no commitment in the transition between administrations, had seemed receptive to the idea of a combined operation against Mosaddeq. And Woodhouse had found a powerful ally in Frank Wisner, a key figure in the CIA. At the other level, the one of high policy, the British were content to let things drift. "We are in no hurry," wrote Sir Pierson Dixon in December. "Our Policy is to play the hand along until we can sound out the attitude of General Eisenhower's Administration to the Persian Oil problem." [135]

In one of Eden's first conversations with Eisenhower in late 1952, the president-elect kept repeating, "Then you don't think there is anything that can be done in the next sixty days?" Eden said he feared not, then and thereafter.[136] In his judgment the risks of intervention were too great. Yet the Americans insisted on some sort of action. "The President kept repeating that we could not do nothing," Eden reported to Churchill several months later, in March 1953. This was a ringing and persistent theme. "The difficulty of this situation," Eden went on, "remains that the Americans are perpetually eager to do something. The President repeated this several times."[137] The British again acquiesced in another "package deal" (as Eden described it to the cabinet), whereby they once more adjusted their terms but maintained their position that the company would have to receive "fair compensation."[138] The sticking point was now Mosaddeq's reluctance to guarantee the AIOC compensation for future losses. Mosaddeq himself seemed genuinely anxious to restore Iran's business reputation, and by all accounts, including his own, he desperately needed the money. But the Foreign Office believed that his anti–British attitude would preclude his acceptance of any joint Anglo–American offer. This was probably an accurate judgment. As for Eisenhower, Eden concluded that he was "obsessed" with the danger of a communist Iran, and far too solicitous of Mosaddeq. When the final stalemate approached in the spring of 1953, Dixon reflected: "The plain fact is that we don't care how violent and unreasonable Mosaddeq may be in announcing a breakdown. In fact the more unrestrained he is the more clearly our proposals will stand out as reasonable in the eyes of Persia & the world."[139] On March 10 Mosaddeq rejected the final offer. The "high policy" of aligning American and British action in order to give Mosaddeq a last chance had now come to an end, much to the relief of the British.

With such a concern for the reputation of Britain in "the eyes of Persia" and the world at large, it is not surprising that Dixon and his Foreign Office colleagues were exceedingly wary of the other level of British policy, that of covert operations. In February 1953 Woodhouse's plans were called to a halt. The principal influence in this decision was Dixon's. As deputy undersecretary he was proving himself to be just as "robust" (one of his favorite words) as his predecessor, Makins, and just as influential with Eden. Dixon believed that if the British and Americans sat tight then the Mosaddeq regime would fall of its own accord and they could then devise a solution to the oil problem with its successor. He was clear about priorities: "[T]he continuing tension in Persia," he wrote, "is probably doing more harm in the M.E. than a 'bad' settlement would cause."[140] The Ministry of Fuel and Power and the treasury did not agree. Here too Dixon saw a strong argument for biding one's time. The other departments would eventually concur in a settlement because the oil embargo could not be indefinitely sustained. He wanted to hold a steady course, "always," in his own words, "on the basic assumption that there must be a fair basis for compensation."[141] He was a man of principle. He demanded respect for the British position. He wished above all to avoid the compromise of Britain's good name by underhanded actions of uncertain effectiveness and doubtful morality. Those were some of the reasons why, on the twenty-first of February, he curtailed the anti–Mosaddeq conspiracy.[142] Yet his decision was shortly reversed. One cannot but pause to wonder how events would have transpired had Dixon not been overruled, or had Eden played a more aggressive part. Eden at the time was plagued with ill health and would be hospitalized in April for a gall bladder operation. He did not return to the Foreign Office until after Mosaddeq's fall. What then was the reason for deciding not merely to resume covert operations but to pursue them with a vengeance? The answer can be summed up in one name: Churchill.

Churchill had been involved in the high politics of Persian oil since the days before the First World War. It was he who had championed the conversion of the Royal Navy from coal to oil and had played a major part in the purchase by the British government of a majority of shares in the Anglo-Persian Oil Company. He had calculated at the time that the saving on the price paid for oil alone would amount to about £40 million. And he had stated:

> On this basis it may be that the aggregate profits, realised and potential, of this investment may be estimated at a sum not merely sufficient to pay all the programme of ships, great and small of that year and for the whole pre-war oil fuel installation, but are such that we may not unreasonably expect that one day we shall be entitled also to claim that the mighty fleets laid down in 1912, 1913, and 1914, the greatest ever built by any power in an equal period, were added to the British Navy without costing a single penny to the taxpayer.[143]

Churchill therefore had every reason to take a renewed interest in the fate of Iranian oil in the early 1950s. After Eden became ill, Lord Salisbury assumed responsibility for foreign affairs but, in clandestine operations, he acted in effect as Churchill's lieutenant. As Woodhouse points out, it was Churchill who reversed the course: "Churchill enjoyed dramatic operations and had no high regard for timid diplomatists. It was he who gave the authority for Operation Boot to proceed."[144]

Operation Boot was the British term, Operation Ajax the American phrase, for the anti–Mosaddeq plan.[145] It is certain that Eisenhower was fully aware of Operation Ajax and gave it his endorsement.[146] Like Churchill, Eisenhower worked from documents and mastered details. He knew his own mind and, contrary to the political mythology of the period, was by no means the captive of either Dulles brother, John Foster or Allen, although the latter certainly had his ear on this question. This is not the place for a discussion of the American side of the problem, but one point should be stressed. There was still an air of old-fashioned espionage about Operations Boot and Ajax. Mosaddeq would be toppled. But neither Churchill nor Eisenhower was in the business of assassinating a fellow head of state. Specifically, there is no evidence that MI6 made plans for the assassination of Mosaddeq as developed three years later in the case of Naser.[147]

Churchill merely endorsed plans that had developed since the meeting of Woodhouse and Falle with the officials of the CIA and State Department in November–December 1952. Despite Eden's ambivalent attitude, MI6 continued systematically to plan for Mosaddeq's overthrow. Sir John Sinclair, "C," in January 1953 lent his direct authority to Woodhouse, Darbyshire, and the Foreign Office liaison, George Clutton, to continue pursuing the possibility of a joint action with the CIA. Kermit Roosevelt attended some of their meetings in London. At almost the same time that Dixon attempted to stop the operation, Sinclair and Clutton met in Washington with both CIA and State Department officials on February 18 and proposed that Kermit Roosevelt be the "field commander."[148] A month later, on March 18, MI6 received a message from Frank Wisner, director of plans, that the CIA would be prepared to discuss detailed tactics. The calendar now had a monthly ring to it. In mid-April the Foreign Office finally endorsed the project after a period of continued vacillation. In view of the combined pressure of the prime minister, on the one hand, and of the CIA offering the equivalent of a full-blown Anglo-American alliance, on the other, the Foreign Office now came aboard. George Clutton took the decisive step in giving the go-ahead to the Rashidian brothers. The coup was now underway.[149]

The candidate to replace Mosaddeq was Gen. Fazlollah Zahedi. He had figured prominently in British and American discussions in Tehran after the collapse of the Qavam regime in July 1952 as the only alternative to Mosaddeq. During the Second World War Zahedi had been seized by the British at gunpoint and interned as a pro-Nazi, which now turned out to be an advantage since he was not tainted with a pro-British reputation.[150] Sam Falle had written about Zahedi:

In this country of weak men he is comparatively strong.

He is strongly anti-communist.

He was imprisoned by the British during the war and is not considered to be a British stooge.

He is on good terms with some members of the National Front—among these is Kashani. . . .

He should be able to count on the support of a section of the Army.[151]

The British analysis as expressed by Falle coincided with the CIA assessment: "Zahedi alone of potential candidates had the vigor and courage to make him worthy of support."[152]

The British supported Zahedi in the same manner as they had Sayyed Zia and Qavam. Zahedi now represented the "open opposition," in Falle's phrase, but too warm an embrace by the British would prove to be fatal because he would be regarded as a puppet. The British expulsion from Iran in October 1952 worked to Zahedi's advantage. In the preceding months the British tried to keep their support for Zahedi as discreet as possible. Falle made no secret that he was the British candidate, but there were no direct bribes. Zahedi later received large amounts of money from the CIA—$1 million in cash after Mosaddeq was ousted—but in the summer and autumn of 1952 the Rashidians conducted the campaign of bribery and other means of persuasion at a lower level. As with Sayyed Zia and Qavam, so with Zahedi: he was beyond the patronage of the three brothers. They had no contact with him up to the time of the British eviction.

One of Zahedi's principal virtues, in British eyes, was simply that he was willing to put himself forward. He was the only leading figure in public life bidding for the premiership. He attracted increasing support from disaffected members of the National Front including clerics and merchants as well as the military. Nevertheless the shah distrusted him, and Zahedi himself seemed incapable of putting forward a plan of action (in the end the CIA had to provide him with a military plan).[153] Mosaddeq's coalition had become increasingly fragile, but he still commanded the general loyalty of the army and police. It was an open bet whether Mosaddeq's enemies could combine to overpower him.

The Rashidians themselves were arrested and briefly imprisoned when Mosaddeq cracked down on the pro-Zahedi movement shortly before the British expulsion. "This in no way disconcerted the brothers, who continued to operate from jail, where they also obtained all the good food they desired."[154] They were set free because of insufficient legal evidence to prosecute them, although as always in the case of the Rashidians one suspects that a certain amount of bribery eased their release. To what extent did Mosaddeq himself perceive the mounting danger? Mosaddeq always had a fatalistic streak in him, but in the autumn of 1952 fatalism seemed to merge with a certain complacency. When he finally acted to expel the British, his ruling coalition had already been fatally weakened by the rift between him and Kashani. In 1951 the clerics had helped Mosaddeq to power; they now played a vital part in his fall. In April 1953 Kashani helped Zahedi avoid arrest by providing him sanctuary in the Majles. At an advanced stage of the planning for the coup, a joint MI6-CIA assessment concluded that "nearly all the important religious leaders with large following are firmly opposed to Mosaddeq. Both the U.S. field station and the British group have firm contacts with such leaders." [155]

It is important to bear in mind that after October 1952 the British operated in Iran only indirectly. "It's always unfortunate and makes things more difficult," Falle recalled with understatement in 1985, "if you don't have diplomatic relations. . . . [W]e couldn't negotiate on the spot, nor could we continue our contingency plan from an Iranian base." [156] Anti-Mosaddeq activities were now monitored from Cyprus, where Darbyshire kept in touch with the Rashidians by means of triweekly radio exchanges. The Rashidian organization swelled to full strength. It embraced not only deputies and senators of the Majles but also ranking officers in the army and police, mullahs, merchants, newspapermen, and, not least, mob leaders. And, as has been mentioned, there was another dimension to the British plan. In southern Iran the tribal leaders had maintained good relations with British consular officers. Both the urban and the rural components would be activated simultaneously in order to counter Tudeh support of Mosaddeq. Here a major stroke of luck played to British advantage. The prelude to the Iranian crisis coincided with Stalin's death on March 25. In the subsequent period of indecision the Russians failed to succor the communists in Iran. The Tudeh organization was cast adrift, leaving among other things a packing case of postage stamps overprinted with the words "Republic of Iran" as a reminder of what might have happened had the Soviet Union intervened.

The key British figure to emerge on the operational side of the project was Norman Darbyshire, who after October 1952 became head of the MI6 Iran station-in-exile in Cyprus.[157] It fell to Darbyshire to make the preliminary contact with the CIA operatives in the field and to draw up the preliminary plan with his counterpart, Donald Wilber. It will be recalled that Wilber is the author of the CIA history *Overthrow*. From the history there emerges a clear account of MI6 as a "junior partner" entirely willing to follow the American lead.[158] There were good reasons for this unaccustomed acquiescence. The

CIA not only had the tactical advantage of a base in the U.S. embassy in Tehran but also possessed incomparably greater resources. Wilber describes his initial encounter with Darbyshire:

> Mr. Darbyshire held quite similar views of Iranian personalities and had made very similar estimates of the factors involved in the Iranian political scene. There was no friction or marked difference of opinion during the discussions. It also quickly became apparent that the SIS [Secret Intelligence Service—MI6] was perfectly content to follow whatever lead was taken by the Agency.

In letting the CIA take the initiative, Darbyshire and his colleagues betrayed hints of simultaneous satisfaction and jealousy:

> It seemed obvious to Wilber that the British were very pleased at having obtained the active cooperation of the Agency and were determined to do nothing which might jeopardize U.S. participation.
>
> At the same time there was a faint note of envy expressed over the fact that the Agency was better equipped in the way of funds, personnel, and facilities than was SIS.[159]

Overthrow notes a pattern that recurred during the drafting of the two critical plans, the preliminary Cyprus plan prepared in Nicosia on June 1, and the major operational plan completed two weeks later on June 16 in London. On both occasions the British followed the American initiative.

In both meetings the British representatives carefully studied the language but merely endorsed the CIA version. Since the two views coincided, there was no need for elaborate exchanges, but American dominance was clear. At the meeting in mid-June in London, the CIA agents met with their counterparts at SIS headquarters at 54 Broadway, the inside of which was "notable only for a large sign with the legend in red, 'Curb Your Guests.' " The CIA officials produced an expanded draft based on a conference in Beirut presided over by Kermit Roosevelt. Although Woodhouse was present, Darbyshire represented MI6 on the operational side.[160] *Overthrow* describes again the relatively passive part played by the British:

> From the moment the discussion began, it was clear that the SIS had no major comments of their own on the draft plan. Nor did they have much to say on the Beirut version beyond a certain close attention to phraseology.

As at Nicosia it was apparent that the Americans were to be placated and allowed to run things as they pleased.[161]

In the discussion of the "assets" of the two organizations, it became clear that both MI6 and the CIA were rooted principally in the bazaar or business community, with the British stronger in contacts with the shah, the military, and clergy but with the Americans effective in slightly different ways. The two networks now meshed.[162]

The approval of the operational plan took place on the British side on July 1, with Churchill along with Salisbury and Sinclair giving formal endorsements. Eisenhower, John Foster Dulles, and Allen Dulles followed on July 11, but not without extracting a further formal letter from the British ambassador in Washington stating that the British government would submit to international arbitration the issue of compensation for the nationalization of the Anglo-Iranian Oil Company. The company had "not been consulted," wrote the ambassador, Sir Roger Makins, but he was convinced that "a generous attitude" would be adopted.[163] This was a major statement because it meant that the British government would, if necessary, confront the AIOC and prepare the way for a settlement based in part on arbitration. According to *Overthrow,* the purpose was to confirm that the British government would not rigidly follow the line of the AIOC but would be "flexible" with Mosaddeq's successor.[164] Lord Salisbury, who presided over the Foreign Office during Eden's illness, endorsed that principle and moreover stated to his colleagues in the cabinet that it would be "disastrous" to give the Americans the impression that "we are only concerned with our oil."[165] Arbitration seemed a small price to pay for American cooperation, and, in the event, did not prove to be necessary.

When the plan for intervention became operational, no one knew how the shah would react. This was the critical point. An earlier assessment of the part he might or might not play in the confrontation continued to hold true: "The Shah still has some symbolic standing with the public throughout the country and the Army although the latter are angry with him because they think he has let them down. If he does not show some signs of decisiveness and manliness in the near future he will lose what little is left of his prestige."[166] Whether the shah would now steel himself for the showdown with Mosaddeq, no one could predict. "There still remained the problem of persuading the nervous Shah to play his role," Woodhouse wrote in getting to the heart of the matter, "which would consist simply of signing two decrees (*farmans*), one dismissing Mosaddeq and the other appointing Zahedi in his place."[167] Much would depend on

Kim Roosevelt, who in turn relied on the Rashidians as well as the CIA network. The Rashidians would be Roosevelt's means of access to the shah and, from the British perspective, the key to his success.

Roosevelt secretly crossed the border into Iran on July 19. It is at this stage worth reflecting on the balance of forces in Iran, the way they had shifted in the spring and summer of 1953, and the British and American calculation of the odds at the time. Part of the irony of the story is that the Mosaddeq government was still popular, nationalist, and anticommunist. Mosaddeq remained a figure who touched a basic chord of Iranian nationalism. According to one of the leading historians of Iran: "Mosaddeq's single-mindedness and intransigence were matched by his affectivity, compassion and sincerity, which made him the object of popular affection and esteem."[168] He had powerful support from the population at large, in part because his social reforms had now begun to take hold.[169] But some of the debate over social legislation increasingly antagonized the religious conservatives, not least Ayatollah Kashani, with whom Mosaddeq's relations by the spring of 1953 had deteriorated irretrievably. The National Front had cracked, and with it Mosaddeq's precarious control over the Majles. In April his chief of police, Mahmud Afshartus, had been assassinated. At least indirectly the Rashidians were involved in his murder, which contributed to the instability of the Mosaddeq government.[170] Mosaddeq nevertheless remained in control of the police and the army, although the latter included officers who might declare themselves loyal to the shah if it came to a showdown.

The story of the actual intervention has been told many times, but there are two points of interest from the British vantage point that emerge from *Overthrow* and other documentary evidence that has become accessible in the last decade. They concern Darbyshire and the Rashidians, who from beginning to end played a vital part in the unfolding events. Far from being reluctant to transfer their loyalties to the CIA, the Rashidians proved to be stalwart and indeed irrepressible in their anti-Mosaddeq drive. When Dixon in February 1953 temporarily managed to call a halt to the MI6 activities, therewith curtailing the flow of money to the brothers, they carried on out of their own pocket. In the discussions with the CIA, Darbyshire gave assurances that the Rashidians would be willing "to risk their possessions and their lives in an attempt against Mosaddeq."[171] *Overthrow* concludes: "In the critical days of August 1953 the Rashidians did display such a willingness."[172] Darbyshire himself was everywhere at once, in Nicosia, Baghdad, Geneva, and London. When the crucial events began to unfold in mid-August, he requested authorization to return to Tehran, but MI6 headquarters refused permission. If the operation failed, it would be just as well not to have had direct MI6 involvement.

The basic weakness in the CIA–MI6 plan was the indecisiveness of the shah. So feckless was he that MI6 and the CIA believed that the only way to goad him into signing the two decrees, the one dismissing Mosaddeq, the other replacing him with Zahedi, would be for his twin sister, Princess Ashraf, to persuade him to take the plunge. Ashraf had been forced into exile. She lived mainly in Switzerland, but she often went to the Riviera. Asadollah Rashidian now made contact with her, but he left it to Darbyshire to provide a compelling lure.[173] When Darbyshire presented her with a mink coat and a substantial though unspecified amount of cash, "her eyes lit up."[174] She returned to Tehran on July 25 and left again five days later for Europe. She was confident, according to Darbyshire, that she had persuaded her brother to take a decisive stand. But not quite. The shah still insisted on guarantees from both the British and the Americans that they would come to his assistance. Darbyshire and Woodhouse helped to arrange for the routine BBC Persian-language news broadcast to begin not with the usual "It is now midnight in London" but with the phrase "It is now exactly midnight"—a signal to the shah that Britain would stand behind him.[175] He received similar assurance from Eisenhower himself. Everything then went off the track. After the shah finally decided to issue the *farmans*, Mosaddeq arrested the emissary handing him the decrees, thus preventing Zahedi from receiving the royal designation. The shah fled the country. Zahedi went into hiding. The CIA MI6 intervention seemed to have collapsed. Gloom and failure pervaded the two headquarters in Washington and London. Roosevelt was sent instructions to leave Iran, which he ignored. Churchill later referred to Nelson's blind eye.[176]

Again, the story has been related many times with different nuances of detail, but Roosevelt managed to twist victory from defeat by rallying the anti-Mosaddeq forces.[177] There is one passage that is frequently quoted because it vividly catches the bizarre mood as well as the technique used to rouse the mob to bring down the Mosaddeq government on the morning of the nineteenth of August. It bears repeating here because it can now be placed in a British context:

[W]ith the army standing close guard around the uneasy capital, a grotesque procession made its way along the street leading to the heart of Tehran. There were tumblers turning handsprings, weight-lifters twirling iron bars and wrestlers flexing their biceps. As spectators grew in number, the bizarre assortment of performers began shouting pro-Shah slogans in unison. The crowd took up the chant and there, after one precarious moment, the balance of public psychology swung against Mosaddeq.[178]

Darbyshire's reaction to those events was immediate and joyous, and he knew the underlying reason for the success: it had been the Rashidians who had bribed and manipulated the mob, and it was they who had "saved the day."[179]

More than three hundred Iranians were killed in heavy street fighting. Mosaddeq, true to style, carried on to the end by proclaiming that he would defend Iran against British and American tanks in the streets of Iran, but he acquiesced melodramatically in his arrest. At his trial he eloquently stated that he was being judged by the agents of foreigners for having struggled against the enemies of Iran. As the narrative of this essay has made clear, his accusation was not untrue, although British and American involvement in the coup was only one element in Iranian politics and did not determine the subsequent set of

Soldiers and onlookers outside Mosaddeq's house after it was destroyed, August 19, 1953. Stephen Langlie Collection, GB165–0351–2.2.6, Middle East Centre Archive, St. Antony's College, Oxford. Courtesy Stephen Langlie USAF/MAAG.

events over the long run. Few at the time could have anticipated the shah's later tyranny. Historians will long debate the connection between the intervention of 1953 and the origins of the Iranian revolution.

In 1953, at least to MI6 and the CIA, the story appeared to have an entirely happy ending. Roosevelt arrived in London on August 25. He was escorted immediately to Major General Sir John Sinclair, the head of the Secret Intelligent Service, MI6. "From the very beginning," according to *Overthrow*, "it was made plain to him that SIS was grateful not only because of the success of the operation per se, but because of the effect its success had already had and would continue to have upon SIS's reputation and relations with its superiors." [180] At the Foreign Office Roosevelt received a frosty reception from Bowker, the assistant undersecretary supervising Middle Eastern affairs, who probably represented traditional Foreign Office mistrust and disapproval of clandestine operations. "It appeared that their [MI6] relationships, at least in this [Foreign Office] area, were neither close nor cordial at that level." [181] On the other hand, the permanent undersecretary, Sir William Strang, extended a warm greeting to Roosevelt and listened sympathetically to him explain the reasons why it had been necessary to take things into his own hands and, for four or five critical days, not to report to headquarters. This was a sensitive point. Had the intervention failed, Roosevelt would certainly have been held accountable not only for failing to communicate but for not obeying orders to leave and thus risking capture. But in this case success justified local initiative and inspiration. *Overthrow* provides a fascinating account of the relationship between the Foreign Office and MI6 on that very point:

> He [Sinclair] explained that Strang was the source of his political guidance and such authorizations as were required from the Foreign Office. . . . In the course of the conversation it became apparent that the portion of particular interest to Sinclair was the reason why the station had not reported more fully from Tehran between August 15 and 19.
>
> Sinclair is not a demonstrative person, but there was a definite glow emanating from him when Strang with apparent heartiness responded to the explanations, remarking that Roosevelt had done the only possible thing and that in matters of that sort decisions could only be made on the spot. [182]

Lord Salisbury, as acting secretary of state for foreign affairs, also greeted Roosevelt with a combination of courtesy and warmth of feeling that was memorable. "As requested by Sinclair, Roosevelt gave Lord Salisbury the full treatment, and he appeared to be absolutely fascinated." [183]

Salisbury in fact was one of the principal figures in a secret caretaker government, for Churchill along with Eden was incapacitated. Unknown to the CIA—and to the public—Churchill had suffered a stroke. But he rallied sufficiently to receive Roosevelt and to launch into a tirade against the Anglo-Iranian Oil Company, which, Churchill said, had "fouled things up" and would no longer be allowed to do so. According to *Overthrow,* "this was a most touching occasion."

> The Prime Minister seemed to be in bad shape physically. He had great difficulty in hearing; occasional difficulty in articulating; and apparently difficulty in seeing to his left.
>
> In spite of this he could not have been more kind personally nor more enthusiastic about the operation. He was good enough to express envy of Roosevelt's role and a wish that he had been "some years" younger and might have served under his command.[184]

Apart from Sir James Bowker, everyone seemed pleased, especially Churchill. From the vantage point of half a century later, the CIA MI6 operation appears to have been basically misguided—indeed disastrous—because it strengthened the shah and led not only to dictatorship but to revolution. But that was not the contemporary judgment, which could be summed up in the contemporary view that the world had been spared "a Communist Iran" and "a second Korea."[185] Churchill probably expressed the consensus as well as anyone when he said that it was "the finest operation since the end of the war."[186]

5

The International Boycott of Iranian Oil and the Anti-Mosaddeq Coup of 1953

Mary Ann Heiss

In September 1951, five months after the government of Prime Minister Mo-hammad Mosaddeq nationalized its Iranian operations, the Anglo-Iranian Oil Company (AIOC) issued the following statement:

> It has been brought to the Company's notice that the Government of Persia in disregard of its solemn obligations to the Company, . . . attempts to sell oil products derived from the area covered by the Convention of April 29, 1933.
>
> The Company is confident that no oil company of repute or any tanker owners or brokers of standing will countenance any direct or indirect participation in the unlawful actions of the Persian Government. Should, however, any concerns or individuals enter into transactions with the Persian Government in regard to the oil products concerned, they are warned that this Company will take all such actions as may be necessary to protect its rights in any country.[1]

Thereafter, the company solidified an informal boycott of Iranian oil sales that had begun earlier that summer and declared what amounted to economic warfare against Mosaddeq's government in Tehran. The AIOC's boycott was part of a larger plan to destroy the Iranian government economically and was accompanied by the British government's own sanctions. The aim of these various measures was to bring Iran to its knees and thus force Mosaddeq into an oil settlement that suited Britain's purposes. The AIOC's boycott was supported by the U.S. oil companies, large and small alike, and by the U.S. government, and had the effect of cutting Iranian oil production to a mere fraction of its previous levels within a matter of months. It generated serious financial difficulties for the government, forcing the prime minister into various strategies for increasing revenue, conserving foreign exchange, and ultimately finding other customers for Iranian oil. This essay explores the motivations for the boycott, its implementation, and the support it received from the U.S. government and the U.S. oil companies. It also explores the effects of the boycott on the Iranian economy and especially on the Mosaddeq government and speculates on what role the boycott might have played in leading to the coup that overthrew the prime minister in the summer of 1953.

The AIOC's boycott of Iranian oil sales was by no means the only cause of the downfall of the Mosaddeq government. As other essays in this volume make clear, a host of things came together in August 1953, some of them external to Iran and some of them originating within the country itself, to bring Mosaddeq down. Not all of these elements were equally important in forcing Mosaddeq from office, of course, nor have all of these elements received equal attention in the historical literature on the origins and implementation of the 28 Mordad/August 19 coup. One of the more neglected aspects of the coup is the role of the British boycott. Although this neglect is not surprising, given the more visible roles played by other actors, it is nonetheless lamentable, because it has thus far prevented a complete understanding of the myriad forces that came together to bring about the coup that forced Mosaddeq from office. In delineating the workings of the boycott and its contribution to the coup against Mosaddeq, this essay not only broadens our understanding of the events surrounding the coup but also illuminates the power that important multinational corporations, and their governmental allies, can exert on international affairs. The formulation and execution of the boycott required close cooperation between the AIOC and the other oil giants and the British and American governments, cooperation that demonstrated the coincidence between governments and private corporations, in this case the multinational oil companies. The public–private cooperation in launching and sustaining the boycott makes clear how governments and corporations can come together to help shape foreign policy, demonstrating in the process the interplay between economics and politics.[2] Although Mosaddeq proclaimed repeatedly that the two were entirely separate, the boycott and its effects on his government make clear that this was far from the case.

Putting the Boycott into Place

Throughout the Anglo-Iranian oil dispute, the British position was based in large part on the rule of law and the sanctity of contracts. Both the British government and the AIOC insisted that Iran had no legal right to cancel the company's concession unilaterally, and both were determined that Iran not profit from what was in their eyes an illegal action.[3] To this end, the British government instituted an array of economic measures designed to punish Iran for moving against the AIOC, including freezing Iran's sterling balances in London, withdrawing Iran's previous right to freely convert sterling into dollars, and halting exports to Iran of such scarce commodities as sugar and steel. From London's perspective, Iran's nationalization had created severe economic and financial problems for Britain, notably the need to find alternative—and more expensive—sources of oil, primarily from the United States. The hardships thus created could be partially offset by economic measures on the Mosaddeq government that would help to conserve dollars and preserve supplies of goods that could be sold for dollars, since that currency was now needed to pay for oil imports. In addition, because the measures would have a deleterious effect on the Iranian economy, they could also help to convince the Iranians of the folly of nationalization and force them into a settlement that allowed for continued British control of Iranian oil. As British officials made clear, their restrictions would be lifted once an acceptable oil agreement had been reached.[4]

The AIOC imposed its boycott for much the same reason: to show Iran that the AIOC would not sit idly by and allow its property to be confiscated illegally and without adequate compensation. The company first indicated its determination to protect its Iranian property—which it considered to include not only the oil industry's physical plant and equipment but also all the oil that remained in the ground—early in the summer of 1951, when it balked at Iranian demands that tanker captains sign receipts acknowledging the Iranian government's National Iranian Oil Company (NIOC) as the true owner of the oil they were loading. Allowing tanker captains to sign such receipts, of course, would legitimize nationalization by negating the AIOC's own claims to ownership of the oil and destroy the company's hopes of retaining control of the Iranian oil industry. After Iranian officials blocked ships from leaving port unless their captains had signed the new receipts, the AIOC concluded that it had no choice but to halt loadings from Iranian ports. Ultimately, in a move that was described as Britain's "M[iddle] E[ast] Dunkirk," the company decided to shut down its Iranian operations and withdraw its personnel. The AIOC's personnel left Abadan in October 1951, amid much fanfare and "funeral headlines" in London.[5]

Company officials and members of the British government seemed gen-

The oil refinery complex at Abadan, Great Britain's largest
overseas commercial operation at the time. Copyright ©
AP/Wide World Photos.

uinely and openly distressed at the turn of events in Iran. The AIOC's operations in Iran provided Britain with £100 million annually in foreign exchange,
as well as twenty-two million tons of oil products and seven million tons of
crude oil per year. Clearly, neither the company nor the British government
was going to give up these assets without a fight. In addition to the important
practical benefits that came from the AIOC's operations in Iran, British leaders,
public and private alike, also believed that the company's decades of investment
in the Iranian industry, decades marked by what they considered to be "generous and enlightened treatment," gave it a vested stake in that industry's operations that could not be wiped away with the simple passage of the
Nationalization Laws.[6] All of that investment had to count for something, and
when early efforts to reach a negotiated settlement that protected the
company's rights and allowed it some modicum of influence in a future Iranian
oil operation failed, the company withdrew its personnel and solidified its boycott. AIOC officials were confident that once the Iranian government realized
the impossibility of marketing oil on its own, it would beg the company to re-
take control of the industry. In other words, the AIOC saw the boycott as a tool

of economic warfare that could be used to preserve its traditional control over Iranian oil. To give the boycott more teeth than simply the threat of legal action by the AIOC, the British government, which owned a controlling share of the AIOC's stock, stationed naval vessels in the waters of the Persian Gulf to deter would-be buyers.[7] From the very beginning of the boycott, then, the AIOC and the British government worked hand in glove to ensure its success. The co-operation that marked their policy on the boycott, however, did not carry over to other areas, as officials of the British government maintained a generally critical posture toward the AIOC throughout the Iranian oil crisis. They were especially harsh in their condemnation of Sir William Fraser, the long-time chair of the company's board of directors. Government policymakers were convinced that Fraser's hard-line refusal to take account of Iranian demands had contributed mightily to the nationalization imbroglio, and this conviction ultimately pushed them to take a more active role in formulating company policy thereafter. With regard to the Iranian oil boycott, though, the two sides were in concord.[8]

The AIOC and the British government were counting on the realities of the international petroleum industry to make the boycott work, with one of those realities being the control that the large oil companies exerted over all facets of the industry's operations, from production to transportation. For example, British personnel in the employ of the AIOC had held the majority of high-ranking, technical jobs in Iran before nationalization, a galling reality for Iranians, who had made their exclusion from such positions one of their main complaints against the company during concession renegotiations in 1950. After the withdrawal of the British workers in the fall of 1951, the Iranians felt confident that they could easily hire non-British technicians to run the industry and then quickly train their own nationals to replace them. Unfortunately, this did not prove to be the case. The United States, Sweden, Belgium, the Netherlands, Pakistan, and Germany all refused to make their technicians available to the nationalized Iranian industry. Only Italy complied.[9] The lack of co-operation Iran received in its search for foreign technicians demonstrated that most industrialized countries supported Britain over Iran in the nationalization dispute and contributed to the boycott's ultimate success in bringing the Iranian oil industry to a virtual standstill. It also fueled Iranian accusations that the other nations were allied with Britain in an imperialistic effort to keep Iran weak and underdeveloped.

A second reality of the international petroleum industry that worked against Iran was the control the major petroleum companies exerted over the world's tanker fleet. At the time of Iran's nationalization, 30.5 percent of the world's tankers were controlled by the AIOC, and another 42.5 percent were controlled by the U.S. petroleum companies, for a total of 73 percent, or about three-quarters of the total tanker capacity of fifteen hundred T-2 equivalents.[10] Iran, conversely, in the words of one AIOC official, controlled "exactly none." With the majority of the tanker fleet controlled by the international oil companies, and with the owners of the independent tankers facing legal action by the AIOC if they transported Iranian oil, Iran found it difficult to locate shippers willing to move its oil to market.[11] This fact proved to be especially important later on in the oil crisis, when Iran was able to sign contracts for oil sales but was unable to actually make good on them because the oil could not be delivered.

Finally, as the preceding discussion suggests, the AIOC's boycott was further strengthened by the fraternal relationship that had historically existed among the world's largest oil companies—Standard Oil of New Jersey (Exxon), Standard Oil of New York (Mobil), Standard Oil of California (Socal), the Texas Company (Texaco), the Gulf Oil Company, Royal Dutch Shell, and British Petroleum (as the AIOC was renamed in 1954). These companies were tied together by a series of interlocking directorates; they engaged in what amounted to production restrictions and price fixing in their international operations; and they operated under a code of behavior that stressed mutual aid and cooperation. They really were, in a phrase first popularized by Italian oil magnate Victor Mattei, like "seven sisters" linked by familial ties and operating almost without outside regulation or interference. The sisters looked out for each other, not so much from affection as self-interest. And their self-interest in the case of the AIOC's boycott called for compliance and support, which was precisely what Royal Dutch Shell and the U.S. majors delivered.[12]

This support had not been evident during the early days of the oil dispute, as the U.S. majors were unrestrained in their criticism of the AIOC's response to Iranian requests to renegotiate the Supplemental Agreement of 1949.[13] In a September 1950 meeting with officials from the State Department, U.S. oil executives expressed their belief that the AIOC and the British government had to accede to Iranian calls for better terms. Dealing generously with the Iranians, the assembled executives maintained, would be "a sound commercial proposition." Failure to be generous, they went on, could lead to disaster, not only for the AIOC but potentially for all of the majors. As commercial operations dependent on the goodwill of host governments, the oil giants could not afford to become targets of opposition and hatred throughout the oil-producing world.

And as far as the U.S. majors were concerned, the best way to earn and maintain that goodwill was through fair and even generous dealings with host governments. This sort of thinking motivated the U.S. oil giants to negotiate fifty-fifty profit-sharing deals with Venezuela and Saudi Arabia, and U.S. oil officials believed that the AIOC should follow this sort of strategy in Iran. The AIOC's defiant stubbornness with the Iranians was hardly likely to win friends and influence people, and indeed it had earned for the AIOC instead the condemnation of its fellow oil giants and the hatred of the Iranian people. The difficulties the AIOC experienced in Iran, the U.S. oil executives were initially convinced, were largely of its own making.[14]

After Iran nationalized the AIOC's Iranian operations in the spring of 1951, however, the companies changed their position considerably. In discussions with the State Department in mid-May, the executives acknowledged that Iran's campaign against the AIOC called into question the country's likelihood of honoring any future oil agreement and made dealing with it an unattractive proposition. They also expressed alarm at the way Iran had moved against the AIOC, and they assured department policymakers that no responsible firm would consider supplanting the AIOC in Iran. This kind of "concession jumping" would threaten the entire structure of the international oil industry by inducing countries to forfeit contracts with one company in favor of more lucrative arrangements with another and would thus amount to "cutting the industry's own throat." Loath to abet what they considered to be the unfair treatment of one of their brethren, the U.S. firms acquiesced completely

Mosaddeq and Acheson *(left and right),* conferring in Washington in October 1951. National Archives and Records Administration.

in the AIOC's boycott of Iranian oil and steadfastly refused to purchase nationalized oil. As a result, tankers bypassed Abadan for other producers, Iranian
storage tanks soon filled to capacity, and by the autumn of 1951 Iranian production seemed likely to stop altogether. The U.S. majors clearly understood
the importance of maintaining solidarity with the AIOC and joined the boycott willingly. Allowing Iran to profit from its action against the AIOC would
send a dangerous message to other producers that the oil companies could be
pushed around. It would thus damage the worldwide prestige of the U.S. companies and the U.S. government and lead to serious threats against "all American investment overseas and the [very] concept of the sanctity of contractual
relations." Weighty and important principles were at stake in Iran, the U.S.
companies maintained, and a united front in defense of those principles was absolutely essential.[15]

On perhaps a more practical level, the U.S. companies had no real reason to
purchase Iranian oil. Throughout the oil dispute, the world oil industry experienced "a buyer's market" in which, as one U.S. oil executive exclaimed, it was
often difficult to "find a home for oil." Despite increased consumption in the
decade immediately following World War II, production grew remarkably, as
did the number of large oil fields discovered in the Middle East, what the industry refers to as "elephants." And the discovery of these new fields in turn fueled a furious scramble among the majors for concession agreements with
producer countries. Given the AIOC's monopoly control in Iran, the U.S. majors made agreements with other countries, notably Kuwait and Saudi Arabia.
Buying oil from Iran in the absence of a dramatic increase in total worldwide
demand would force production cutbacks in those countries, ultimately decrease the royalties that they received from their oil operations, and potentially
imperil the U.S. majors' concessions by leading to nationalization efforts elsewhere. Purchasing Iranian oil at the substantial discounts at which it was being
offered might also upset the delicate price structure of the Middle Eastern petroleum industry, something to which the U.S. companies were strongly opposed. With no real need to purchase Iranian oil and every apparent reason not
to, the U.S. majors were more than happy to support the AIOC's boycott.[16]

The majors' support of the AIOC's boycott pleased George C. McGhee,
assistant secretary of state for Near Eastern, South Asian, and African Affairs,
whose responsibilities placed him at the center of the Iranian nationalization
imbroglio. A Texas oilman who had originally been unrestrained in his criticism of the AIOC, McGhee believed that the major oil companies, by virtue of
their immense economic power and special relationship with host govern-

ments, could "be made powerful instruments" in efforts "to develop the economic resources of the Middle East." But in order to do so, companies had to heed the rising tide of nationalism and ensure that their conduct was "beyond reproach," for once they had "become the subject of criticism," as the AIOC had become in Iran, it was "extremely difficult . . . to recover the initiative." [17] Like the oil company executives, though, McGhee changed his line after the Iranian nationalization, an action he considered dangerous and potentially disastrous, as it might lead to a communist takeover in Iran and the loss of its valuable oil holdings to the Soviet bloc.

McGhee's departmental colleagues shared his sentiments, and the official State Department position on the boycott was to support the U.S. majors in their refusal to traffic in Iranian oil. As the department expressed its position, "The U.S. Government should not make the nationalization of Iranian oil a success for others to emulate." In addition to its determination to prevent other nations from following Iran's lead and nationalizing their natural resources, the department had several other reasons for its stance. On one level, it wished to avoid costly lawsuits against U.S. firms that might try to purchase Iranian oil, a very real fear since the AIOC had threatened legal action against all purchasers. On another, it surely recognized the harm that would come to Anglo-American relations should U.S. companies appear to be moving in on the AIOC's territory. And on yet another level it believed that the Mosaddeq government might be more willing to compromise in negotiations with the AIOC if it understood that U.S. firms would not market nationalized oil or operate a nationalized industry.[18] For all of these reasons, the State Department stood firmly behind the majors' decision to back the British boycott.

The response of the smaller U.S. oil companies to the boycott was less straightforward than that of the majors but ended up ultimately in much the same place. Not party to the secret compacts and interconnections that bound the majors together, the smaller U.S. oil companies did not feel the same sort of affinity for the AIOC. They had no foreign concessions to safeguard and instead lived almost hand-to-mouth, purchasing oil when and where they could and always searching for the best deals. Under these circumstances, Iranian oil would have been very attractive to them, especially offered as it was at significant discounts over prevailing prices. A number of important factors, however, prevented them from purchasing that oil. First off, the smaller companies lacked their own tanker fleets and would have had to contract with independent shippers to transport any oil they purchased from Iran. But with the seven sisters (which, as we have seen, were steadfast in their support of the AIOC's boycott) controlling almost three-quarters of the world's tankers, such arrange-ments were unlikely. A second factor working against independent support for Iranian nationalization, whether in the form of technical assistance or of oil purchases, was active discouragement of such activities by the U.S. govern-ment. Several U.S. independents considered providing technicians and other specialists to Iran during the early months of the oil dispute, but their plans were scotched by strong government opposition. The Truman administration took the same stance when it came to independent purchases of Iranian oil, re-minding the smaller companies that official U.S. policy was to support the boy-cott and warning them that they would be on their own if the AIOC prosecuted them for attempting to break the boycott. Although the smaller companies made sporadic efforts throughout the oil dispute to send personnel to Iran and to purchase Iranian oil, the firm opposition of the U.S. government and the almost complete control the majors exerted on the international oil in-dustry rendered such efforts ineffectual. In the end, the smaller companies were forced to acquiesce in the AIOC's boycott, although their acquiescence was often involuntary.[19]

If the U.S. oil companies and the U.S. government collectively worked to back the British boycott of Iranian oil, they were also determined to do what they could to minimize the damage they experienced as a result of the collapse of the Iranian oil industry. In July 1951 the U.S. Petroleum Administration for Defense (PAD), the agency responsible for managing U.S. oil supplies during the Korean War, organized representatives of nineteen of the nation's oil com-panies into the Foreign Petroleum Supply Committee. The committee quickly formulated what became known as Plan of Action No. 1, the heart of which was a call for cooperation by the nineteen companies in an effort to replace the 660,000 barrels of oil per day formerly supplied by Iran. This amounted to one-third of total Middle Eastern production and one-quarter of all refined products outside the Western Hemisphere. To offset the loss of this oil, which was vital to the U.S. war effort in Korea, the parties to Plan of Action No. 1 in-creased production and refining in other countries, realigned imports and ex-ports, and allocated markets. Under other circumstances these activities might have been construed as illegal restraints of trade. But because industry cooper-ation to maintain the highest possible production of oil was considered vital for national security purposes, the companies involved were granted immunity from antitrust prosecution under Section 708 of the Defense Production Act of 1950. It was clear that the Truman administration placed a higher priority on the military effort in Korea than on traditional U.S. concerns about antitrust

activity.[20] It also became clear over time that Plan of Action No. 1, which remained in effect until early July 1952, served its purpose admirably. According
to PAD head Oscar L. Chapman, the plan helped to avoid "desperate supply
dislocations" and increased free world petroleum production by 750,000 barrels per day, a gain of 90,000 barrels per day over the lost Iranian production.[21]

The PAD and its Foreign Petroleum Supply Committee demonstrated the
pattern of corporatist collaboration that had developed between the U.S. government and the U.S. oil companies. Industry officials provided the State Department and other agencies with invaluable assistance in dealing with the
worldwide shortages caused by the Korean War. They were also instrumental
in advising the government on how best to deal with the concurrent loss of
Iranian oil that resulted from the AIOC's boycott. And by finding alternatives
to Iranian oil they assisted Anglo-American efforts to convince Mosaddeq that
his country's resources were not irreplaceable. In this way, the U.S. oil companies were accomplices in what amounted to Anglo-American economic sanctions against Iran: by ensuring that the consequences of the Iranian shutdown
ran only one way, against Iran, the British and the Americans were trying to in-
duce Mosaddeq to adopt what they would consider a more reasonable posture.[22] U.S. officials, public and private alike, came together in supporting the
AIOC's boycott against Iran and in the process affirmed the traditionally close
relationship that had existed between the federal government and the U.S. petroleum majors.

As this account suggests, the U.S. government was wholeheartedly behind
the British effort to prompt Iranian concessions in the oil negotiations through
economic pressure. It supported the U.S. majors in their acquiescence in the
British boycott, discouraged U.S. independents from purchasing Iranian oil or
providing the nationalized Iranian industry with technical personnel, and
worked with the U.S. oil companies, large and small, to deal with the shortages
that resulted from the shutdown of the Iranian oil industry. Early on in the oil
dispute, the U.S. government came down squarely on the side of the British,
despite its claims of impartiality and its declared intention to act as an honest
broker in a settlement that met the demands of both sides.[23] Backing Britain
against Iran served U.S. interests and hinted at the ever closer Anglo-American
cooperation that would develop throughout the oil dispute. U.S. officials saw
the British boycott as a way to extract concessions from Mosaddeq that might
make possible a settlement that allowed the British to remain in Iran. After such
hopes faded in the wake of Mosaddeq's continued refusal to give in, they also
came around to the British conviction that the sort of economic warfare char-

acterized by the boycott could weaken Mosaddeq's government so severely that it would collapse, with the end result being the appointment of a new prime minister who was more amenable to an oil settlement that favored British— and, by extension, Western—interests.[24] Anglo–American officials, in fact, discussed repeatedly the sort of oil deal and financial assistance they would provide to Mosaddeq's successor. It is significant that they steadfastly refused to make concessions or offer aid to Mosaddeq.[25]

Dealing with the Domestic Consequences of the Boycott

Mosaddeq was surprised at the difficulties of producing and marketing nationalized oil, and particularly surprised that the U.S. government did not rush immediately to Iran's assistance.[26] Although he advocated true international independence for Iran and wanted no country to exert undue influence on its affairs, Mosaddeq also recognized that Iran's weak economic position vis-à-vis Great Britain placed it at a distinct disadvantage in the oil dispute. Iran's weakness, of course, became even more obvious after the AIOC's boycott shut down the Iranian oil industry, thereby depriving Mosaddeq's government of important revenue and foreign exchange and creating serious domestic challenges. Given Iran's rich petroleum reserves and its key geographical location astride the Soviet Union, the prime minister had believed, mistakenly, as it turned out, that the U.S. fear of a communist takeover would push Washington to purchase Iranian oil and help run the nationalized industry.[27] In the absence of those actions, he at least expected U.S. financial assistance to support Iran's national budget and help to offset the loss of foreign exchange that accompanied the AIOC's boycott.[28] None of these hopes panned out. The Truman administration supported the boycott, discouraged oil company assistance to the nationalized industry, and refused to provide budgetary assistance in the absence of an oil settlement. The Eisenhower administration continued these policies when it assumed office in January 1953. In late May of that year Mosaddeq warned the new administration of the precarious state of Iran's economy and lamented that the United States had thus far done nothing to provide his government with economic assistance. He referred several times to the "serious consequences" that would result from a failure to provide Iran with "prompt and effective" aid, apparently in an effort to exploit U.S. fears of a communist coup that would deliver Iran and its rich oil fields to the Soviet bloc. Eisenhower did not accept Mosaddeq's bait. Although he admitted that conditions in Iran were not good, he refused to commit to economic assistance for Mosaddeq's government and instead hoped that the government would "take such steps as are in its power to prevent further deterioration of the situation . . . before it is too late."[29] When word of Eisenhower's refusal to provide Iran with economic assistance was made public in Tehran, it constituted a humiliating blow for Mosaddeq, who had led the Iranian people to believe that U.S. aid would be forthcoming.[30]

Iran's efforts to attract assistance in running the oil industry were no more successful with other countries. Early on in the dispute, Mosaddeq had sarcastically derided the "supernatural" British who had dominated Iran's oil industry for so long, and he expressed confidence that foreign technicians would run the nationalized industry until Iranians could be trained to take over. When these technicians failed to appear, Iran found it impossible to maintain refining operations at Abadan. The government also proved unable to sell crude oil, even at substantial discounts over then-prevailing Persian Gulf prices and even though it promised that the Iran Insurance Company would protect purchasers and shippers from legal action by the AIOC. The solidarity with which the international petroleum industry approached the Iranian crisis was a serious blow to Iran's nationalization effort. It required the Mosaddeq government to take a variety of measures to deal with the unexpected effects of the AIOC's boycott and to create what amounted to an oil-less economy.[31]

The AIOC's boycott created several difficulties for Mosaddeq's government. One problem was budgetary: the AIOC's oil royalties and indirect contributions to the Iranian treasury, such as income taxes on company workers and customs receipts on nonexempt goods the company imported into Iran, were no longer coming in. To make up for the lost revenue, the government floated a series of public bonds, increased income taxes on urban wage earners and customs duties on nonessential imports, and raised the price of the government-controlled monopolies on sugar, tobacco, opium, and tea. Mosaddeq hoped that these measures would at once improve the condition of the national treasury and demonstrate to the world Iran's ability to survive, at least in the short term, without its oil industry. The government also had to deal with the sudden loss of foreign exchange previously generated by the sale of oil, a reality that would seriously hurt Iran's efforts to maintain normal trading relations with other countries. To conserve badly needed foreign exchange, Mosaddeq's government imposed strict limits on imports, going so far as to prohibit the importation of goods that were available domestically or that could be exported for profit. Among the goods on the prohibited list were meat, poultry, military items, and rubber products. To otherwise improve the nation's balance-of-payments position, the government worked tirelessly to encourage non-oil exports, such as agricultural products and textiles. By FY 1953–54, the latter had become an especially important component of Iran's non-oil exports, amounting in that year to one-half of the country's total. Increasing production of agricultural products and textiles required little capital outlay but promised large dividends in foreign exchange receipts. Emphasizing the profitability of such exports, particularly textiles, also hearkened back to Iran's glorious past and demonstrated that it had much more to offer the world than simply rich oil reserves. In taking these various measures, the prime minister demonstrated his conviction that Iran had to deal realistically with the consequences of the oil boycott. Simply waiting for a resolution to the dispute with the AIOC while the nation's economy deteriorated, he clearly understood, was not an option.[32]

Contemporary evidence and decades of hindsight demonstrate that some of the measures taken by the government actually did prove to be successful. Although scholars are divided over the effectiveness of Mosaddeq's efforts to meet the economic crisis, most are of the opinion that the government performed better than expected. As the data in table 1 make clear, for example, the government's efforts to limit imports while increasing non-oil exports were largely successful, leading by the last two years of Mosaddeq's premiership to a fairly decent trade surplus. This surplus stood in stark contrast to the trade situation during the immediate post-Mosaddeq period, when imports far exceeded exports. The government also managed to keep its budget deficits to a

TABLE I

The Non-oil Balance of Trade, 1948–1953

(in Millions of Rials)

Year	Exports (Excluding Oil)	Imports	Balance
1948	1,867	5,480	–3,613
1949	1,785	9,320	–7,535
1950	3,563	7,109	–3,546
1951	4,391	7,405	–3,014
1952	5,832	5,206	626
1953	8,426	5,756	2,670
1954	10,288	8,024	2,264
1955	8,034	10,896	–2,862
1956	7,931	26,202	–18,271

Source: Bharier, *Economic Development in Iran* (London: Oxford Univ. Press, 1971) 105–6, 112.

minimum despite the decrease in direct and indirect revenues from the oil industry and the increased expenditures of continuing to pay the now-idle workers formerly employed by the AIOC.[33] Although the government's fortunes
rose and fell over the course of its tenure, at the end of Mosaddeq's premiership
the government treasury had a net balance of 1.1 billion rials, a fact that gave lie
to Anglo-American assertions that the government was bankrupt.[34] It also succeeded in minimizing the impact of the "abrupt and severe" loss of foreign exchange that resulted from the British boycott of Iranian oil sales, sales that had
previously generated a large portion of Iran's foreign exchange earnings. According to Patrick Clawson and Cyrus Sassanpour, who have studied the foreign exchange consequences of the boycott in detail, at no point during the oil
dispute did Iran's foreign exchange reserves ever fall to "a critically low level."[35]
Finally, as table 2 indicates, the Mosaddeq government was able to keep domestic inflation to very manageable levels, performing in this area better even
than its successor, which did not face the domestic constraints of the British
boycott. All things considered, the government dealt appropriately with the
economic consequences of the boycott and did its best to avoid serious domestic dislocation.[36]

Still, the AIOC's boycott proved to be a persistent thorn in the side of the
Mosaddeq government, denying it the benefits of its primary policy initiative—the nationalization of the oil industry—and creating serious economic
difficulties that necessitated sacrifices on the part of the domestic population.
Most Iranians accepted these burdens as the necessary price for the nation's
chance to control its own oil.[37] The nation was not wracked by the bread riots
that had occurred during the Second World War, a significant indication that
the government's policies had support from the bulk of the Iranian population.[38] Yet, the government did come in for its share of criticism, mostly from

TABLE 2

Changes in Various Price Indices, 1951–1955

(in Percentages)

	Wholesale	*Home-prod. Goods*	*Cost of Living*
1951–52	12.7	6.0	4.5
1952–53	4.5	7.9	8.6
1953–54	20.4	13.7	5.9
1954–55	18.7	23.1	16.8

Source: Katouzian, *Struggle for Power,* 154.

conservatives traditionally allied with Great Britain and from members of the upper class, who resented the government's restrictions on nonessential imports, opposed the higher customs duties that were part of the government's effort to formulate an oil-less economy, and refused to support the government by purchasing government bonds issued in an effort to raise revenue.[39] The government was also forced to curtail implementation of the $650 million Seven Year Plan for economic development, which was to depend heavily on oil royalties for its funding. Begun in 1949, the Seven Year Plan was expected to accomplish "social development through economic improvement." It had been drawn up by a team of U.S. development experts and was a pet project of the shah, who saw it as a way of bringing Iran into the twentieth century. Mosaddeq considered the plan an expensive luxury at a time of serious economic duress, and as the British oil boycott intensified, government funding for the plan was drastically curtailed. As a result, in the words of economic historian Julian Bharier, "what had started out as a 'big push' to attain economic self-sufficiency thus ended as a feeble puff."[40]

In addition to generating no small amount of domestic discontent, the various measures taken by the government to deal with the boycott were all ultimately very short term. The only permanent solution to the nation's economic woes was a settlement of the oil dispute that resulted in significant economic benefits for Iran. Mosaddeq knew this all too well, despite his repeated exclamations that the nation's oil was better left in the ground than controlled by foreign influences such as the AIOC. The prime minister was practical enough to seek ways of circumventing the problems caused by the boycott, but he was also realistic enough to work at the same time toward finding purchasers of Iranian oil, and the history of the oil dispute is replete with evidence that Mosaddeq was prepared to find those purchasers wherever he could.

Seeking Buyers for Nationalized Oil

As early as December 1951, Mosaddeq tried to circumvent the AIOC's boycott by offering Iranian oil to all buyers, even those from communist countries. Because the AIOC's former customers had acquiesced in the firm's boycott of Iranian oil sales, he maintained that oil would now be available to any firm or nation that wished to purchase it. Mosaddeq's offer was not likely to generate many contracts, since few, if any, Iron Curtain countries had the wherewithal to purchase and ship large quantities of Iranian oil, let alone the need. It was probably merely a bargaining chip designed to prod the U.S. government into providing Iran with economic assistance or purchasing Iranian oil.[41] The prime minister's threats led to neither of these eventualities, although they did promise serious consequences for Iran, namely the possibility of triggering the Battle Act of October 1951, which prohibited recipients of U.S. aid from shipping raw materials, including oil, to countries behind the Iron Curtain. Sales of Iranian oil to the communist bloc could bring a halt to the work of the U.S. military missions then attached to the Iranian army and gendarmerie and block funds from Truman's Point IV program, scheduled to begin in 1952, from reaching Iran.[42] Despite the warnings of U.S. ambassador Loy Henderson, Mosaddeq at first refused to allow U.S. law to restrict his freedom to sell oil to whomever he wished. He also blanched at requirements in the U.S. Mutual Security Act that called on recipients of U.S. military aid to declare their allegiance to the West. Ultimately, Mosaddeq's oil sales offers came to naught and did not really pose a threat to the Western position in the global battle for control of strategic raw materials. And in the spring of 1952 Mosaddeq modified his position on an oath of allegiance and affirmed Iran's support for "the principles of the charter of the U.N.," an affirmation that satisfied U.S. officials and allowed U.S. military aid to continue to flow into Iran.[43] The fact that Mosaddeq was able to impose conditions on U.S. military aid allowed him to claim a victory over the United States, one that boosted his domestic standing with the Iranian people at a critical phase in the oil crisis.

A few months later, while the International Court of Justice (ICJ) in The Hague was deliberating its jurisdiction over the Anglo-Iranian dispute and after months of stalled efforts to reach a settlement that would restart the Iranian oil industry, Mosaddeq moved dramatically to break the British-led boycott of Iranian oil sales. In mid-June, the *Rose Mary*, a 632-ton freighter, "owned by a Panamanian company, flying the Honduran flag, chartered to a Swiss company, [and] commanded by an Italian," had loaded one thousand tons of Iranian crude at the Persian Gulf port of Bandar Mashur on behalf of the Ente Petrolifero Italia Medio-oriente (EPIM), a private Italian company.[44] This "experimental voyage" was designed to test the strength of the AIOC's boycott. If it succeeded, the EPIM planned to send larger tankers to Iran to purchase twenty million tons of Iranian oil over the next ten years. The *Rose Mary*, Mosaddeq declared elatedly, was only the first of many ships that would soon transport Iranian oil, and the British could do nothing to stop them. As the chairman of Iran's Commission for Oil Exports had earlier asserted, "If one shipment [is] made, then the deadlock [will] be broken and Iran [will] have no difficulty in selling its oil."[45] The *Rose Mary* seemed to be the ship that would break the boycott and lead to Iran's economic salvation.

Iranian hopes for the saving power of the *Rose Mary* were misplaced. On June 17, British naval vessels forced the ship into British Aden, where local authorities promptly impounded its cargo. The AIOC then instituted legal proceedings against everyone associated with the tanker's activities—its owners, captain, charterer, and the EPIM. Although the dispute over the true ownership of the *Rose Mary*'s cargo dragged on for months, the stopping of the ship in a British territory foretold the outcome. In January 1953 the *Rose Mary* case ended in a triumph for the British when the courts they controlled in Aden upheld the legality of the AIOC's claims to Iranian oil. It also contributed to the deterioration of Anglo-Iranian relations, further widening the gap between the two nations and delaying settlement of the oil question.[46]

Meanwhile, on July 22, 1952, the ICJ ruled that it had no competence to consider the Anglo-Iranian dispute and withdrew an injunction it had issued early on in the oil imbroglio prohibiting both the British and the Iranians from interfering with Iranian oil operations. Iran, it seemed, was now free to seek purchasers of its oil on the open market. Although the Iranian people considered the ICJ decision a great victory for their nation and expected that it would deal a deathblow to the British-led boycott, such was not the case. The decision did prompt a number of oil producers to send tankers to Abadan to pick up previously purchased oil, and the Iranian people declared a public holiday to celebrate their victory. But the decision had no effect on the British, who did not relax their boycott and in fact became even less inclined to compromise than they had been previously. They considered the ICJ decision simply a recognition that the court could not decide the dispute, not a ruling that the AIOC's claims against the Iranians were invalid. The boycott, which the British termed an effort "to support . . . the A.I.O.C. in its attempts to secure satisfaction for the wrong it has suffered," would continue as before.[47]

To be sure, Iran did succeed in making some small dents in the British boycott. In early 1953, Supor, an Italian firm, loaded forty-six hundred tons of Iranian oil onto the tanker *Miriella*. By mid-February the *Miriella* had reached Venice, where the Italian courts rejected British claims that the tanker's cargo constituted stolen oil. Subsequent purchases of Iranian oil by Supor were successful, as were those by the Japanese firm Idemitsu Kosan, whose first shipment left Iran aboard the *Nissho Maru* in April. These sales, though, and others that would follow, were minuscule compared to Iran's exports under the AIOC. Total oil exports during 1952 and the first six months of 1953 amounted to only 118,000 tons, compared to total oil exports in 1950, the last full year of the AIOC's Iranian operations, of 31 million tons. To put these figures in a slightly different perspective, Iran's total oil sales during this period were roughly equivalent to one day's production under the AIOC.[48] Table 3, which details Iranian oil exports after nationalization, demonstrates how insignificant those exports really were—and by extension how successful the boycott proved to be.

Mosaddeq blamed the United States for allowing the boycott, and by extension Iran's economic troubles, to continue, and he threatened to "treat the United States Government as [he] had treated Her Majesty's Government" unless U.S. officials changed their ways. The prime minister could not understand why the Truman administration had not shown enough concern about Iran's economic and political position. Although U.S. officials had continuously paid lip service to the importance of Iran's strategic location and rich oil supplies for Western security, they had not coupled their rhetoric with economic assistance. Instead, they had sided with the British and supported the boycott, leaving Iran in serious economic straits and fueling Mosaddeq's ire at what he saw as an Anglo-American plan to destroy his government, turn back nationalization, and keep Iran weak and under the thumb of the rapacious West.[49]

As Mosaddeq was soon to learn, the change in administrations in Washington that came in January 1953 did not result in a change in U.S. policy. Mosaddeq's effort that spring to convince the U.S. government to purchase Iranian oil was roundly rebuffed. When asked how the United States could justify such purchases in the absence of an Iranian settlement with Great Britain, Mosaddeq

TABLE 3

Exports of Iranian Oil by NIOC after Nationalization (to May 1, 1953)

Country of Destination	Name of Company	Name of Tanker	Date of Shipping	Weight in Tons
Italy	EPIM	*Rose Mary*	May 20, 1952	crude 786
Italy	Supor	*Miriella*	Jan. 20, 1953	crude 4,600
Italy	Supor	*Miriella*	Mar. 15, 1953	crude 4,900
Italy	Supor	*Alba*	Mar. 15, 1953	crude 11,500
Italy	EPIM	*Pax*	Apr. 1953	crude 4,500
Japan	Idemitsu	*Nissho Maru*	Apr. 15, 1953	ref 18,000
Italy	Supor	*Alba*	May 1, 1953	crude 11,500
Italy	Supor	*Bertza*	May 1, 1953	crude 11,500

Source: Robert M. Carr (counsellor for economic affairs, U.S. embassy, Tehran) "Exports of Oil from Iran by the National Iranian Oil Company," May 13, 1953, dispatch no. 940, RG 59, 888.2553/5–1353.

played the cold war card by saying that the purchases would help "to prevent Iran from becoming Communist." If the U.S. government refused to buy Iranian oil, according to the prime minister, he would have to sell it at any price to all buyers—even to countries behind the Iron Curtain. In truth, the prime minister had no intention of selling oil to Soviet bloc nations. But threats to do so had worked to good advantage in the past. They had pushed the Truman administration into waiving restrictions regarding the dispersal of U.S. military aid in early 1952, and the prime minister had every reason to believe that they would work again. What he did not realize, however, was that the Eisenhower administration approached the Anglo-Iranian oil dispute from a different perspective than its predecessor and that, by the time of his final search for U.S. oil purchases, the British and American governments were already plotting to overthrow him. Although the Eisenhower administration continued to search for an oil settlement throughout the spring of 1953, it had already abandoned hope of reaching any settlement with Mosaddeq and was determined to join the British in a plot to topple his government.[50]

The Boycott's Contribution to the 28 Mordad Coup

By the spring of 1953, as plans for Mosaddeq's removal took shape, Anglo-American officials had come to believe that Iran's economic troubles were considerable, and they used this belief as one justification to remove Mosaddeq from office. To be sure, the Iranian government had negotiated oil sales with Italian and Japanese firms, and these sales had been upheld in courts in Venice and Tokyo. But the Iranians failed to break the international boycott by generating long-term contracts. Moreover, with world oil output now outstripping demand, extended contracts were unlikely in the near future, even though Iran by the spring of 1953 was offering its oil at less than half the world price. By April, according to the U.S. embassy in Tehran, Iran had "psychologically entered a new economic era, characterized by general acceptance of the fact that no oil settlement is in prospect." If Iranians accepted this fact intellectually, however, U.S. officials believed that they were not reconciled to the hardships that would accompany the deterioration of their economy. As they saw the situation, labor unrest, crippling strikes, and eventual economic collapse were likely unless the government did something quickly to improve the standard of living and stabilize domestic prices.[51] And in their estimation, those sorts of developments could only come about if a new government settled the oil dispute with the AIOC and thereby allowed Iranian oil once more to reach world markets.

U.S. officials throughout the oil dispute took a gloom-and-doom view of the effect of the oil boycott on Iran's economy. They warned repeatedly that Mosaddeq's government could not make up the lost revenues resulting from the boycott, the country's economy was near collapse, and collapse would be followed by a communist takeover. Typical of these warnings was the sentiment expressed in a December 1952 meeting with oil company executives that the Iranians were not likely to "use their heads in the situation" and that through "irrational acts" and "panic" the Mosaddeq government would allow "uncontrollable civil disturbances within the country, followed by a take-over by the Tudeh party."[52] What such claims revealed was a complete misunderstanding on the part of U.S. officials regarding the nature of the Iranian economy. U.S. policymakers attributed far more importance to oil revenues as a percentage of the Iranian national budget than was really the case. In 1950, for example, the AIOC's last full year of operation before nationalization, oil royalties amounted to only 12 percent of government revenue and a mere 4 percent of national income.[53] The bulk of Iran's income was obviously coming from non-oil sources. Yet, U.S. officials continually insisted that Iran was heavily dependent on oil revenue for its day-to-day expenses. They mistakenly saw Iranian economic conditions through the lens of an industrialized nation. And they either refused or failed to see that the economy was adjusting fairly well to the loss of oil revenues.

By contributing to the U.S. belief that Mosaddeq's government was about to collapse and that its collapse would be followed by a communist takeover of Iran, the AIOC's boycott of Iranian oil was thus an indirect but nevertheless important cause of the coup that ousted Mosaddeq in the summer of 1953. Objective evidence, both at the time and from the benefit of hindsight, points out the government's impressive success in meeting the numerous problems generated by the boycott. Although the government's austerity measures and other coping mechanisms did generate some domestic opposition, most Iranians viewed the hardships as the short-term price they had to pay for the long-term right to control their own natural resources. But rather than seeing the nation's economic conditions objectively, U.S. officials always insisted that Iran was close to collapse and that with its inevitable economic collapse would come a communist takeover of the country. They therefore believed the propaganda circulated by Mosaddeq's domestic opponents that the government was on its last legs and that the communists would soon take over the country. Because they placed the Iranian oil crisis within a larger cold war context, they were primarily concerned with how particular developments or eventualities might benefit the Soviet bloc or the domestic communist party, the Tudeh.[54]

Bolstering U.S. misinterpretation of the actual state of Iran's economy was the accepted Western wisdom at the time that Iran (or any other oil-producing country, for that matter) could not survive without oil revenues. To consider such a possibility would have severely damaged the international oil industry and dealt a serious blow to the Western world, which was heavily dependent on oil for its very survival. Iran had to be made to see not only that oil sales were the only thing that could save its economy but also that those sales could only be made within the framework of the international oil industry. Mosaddeq himself contributed to this belief by coupling his efforts to create an oil-less economy with repeated efforts to break the British boycott by selling oil. Although he publicly declared on numerous occasions that the best place for Iran's oil was in the ground, the very fact that he tried to sell that oil belied such assertions and fed the Western belief that oil-producing nations needed to sell their oil in order to survive.

In the end, the AIOC's boycott was precisely the political weapon the company and the British government had hoped it would be. By helping to provide the impression that Mosaddeq's government was near bankruptcy and by fueling U.S. fears that Iran's bankruptcy would lead to massive public demonstrations, increased popular support for the Tudeh Party, and ultimate victory for the Soviet bloc, the boycott served its intended purpose of removing Mosaddeq from office, replacing him with a more malleable, pro-Western prime minister, and effecting an oil settlement that once again allowed for Western control of Iran's oil. To be sure, the AIOC's boycott did not directly cause Mosaddeq's overthrow. As the essays in this volume by Fakhreddin Azimi, Mark J. Gasiorowski, and Wm. Roger Louis suggest, the government's domestic opponents were highly successful in weakening public support for the Mosaddeq government for reasons that had little to do with the AIOC's boycott.[55] Still, because the boycott did provide one justification for moving against the prime minister, it proved to be a most successful policy in the British—and by extension, American—arsenal.

The AIOC's boycott of Iranian oil sales also illustrated how public and private interests could collude to formulate and implement a foreign policy that benefited both. Success of the boycott depended on support from the U.S. majors, which were all too willing to back the British refusal to traffic in Iranian oil. Buying nationalized oil from Iran or helping to run the nationalized industry would have hurt the interests of the U.S. companies. It would also have run counter to official U.S. policy, which was to refuse economic aid to the Mosaddeq government in the absence of a settlement with the AIOC. Stopping Iranian oil sales served both public and private U.S. interests, with the alliance of the U.S. companies with the Truman and Eisenhower administrations and the AIOC and the British government constituting the main reason that the boycott succeeded. Had the U.S. majors broken ranks with the boycott and worked to help Iran rather than to isolate it, the boycott would have collapsed from ineffectiveness. That did not happen, of course, as the companies saw the boycott as a way of furthering their own interests and protecting their own concessions in other countries. Their support for the boycott doomed Iran's hopes of selling its nationalized oil and illustrates quite clearly how effective powerful private interests can be in helping to implement official policy.

6

The Road to Intervention

Factors Influencing U.S. Policy Toward Iran, 1945–1953

Malcolm Byrne

O n June 26, 1950, the day after North Korean forces attacked South Korea and opened a bleak new chapter in the cold war, President Harry S. Truman told an aide that in spite of the heightened communist threat to the Far East, he was actually more disturbed about the Middle East. Studying a globe, Truman put his finger on Iran and said: "Here is where they will start trouble if we aren't careful. . . . [I]f we stand up to them like we did in Greece three years ago, they won't take any next steps. But if we just stand by, they'll move into Iran and they'll take over the whole Middle East. There's no telling what they'll do if we don't put up a fight now."[1]

Truman's remarks reflect several relevant points. First, Iran had become a significant focus of U.S. strategic thinking after World War II, not only in its own right but because of how closely U.S. officials tied its fate to the rest of the Middle East. Second, cold war conceptions of the communist menace had by this time—thanks largely to the Korean invasion—taken on truly global proportions, enabling Truman to make the easy leap from the Far East to the Persian Gulf in gauging the USSR's probable "next steps." Third, Truman's determination to "put up a fight" was characteristic of his pugnacious approach to confronting communism, a trait that is sometimes overlooked when comparing his policies with those of his successor, Dwight D. Eisenhower.

I would like to thank Mark J. Gasiorowski, James G. Hershberg, William Burr, and Vladislav Zubok for their comments on earlier drafts of this essay.

Throughout his presidency, Truman and his advisers grew increasingly certain of Iran's strategic significance and of the need to take firm action to anchor the country in the Western camp. Yet Truman never seriously contemplated going so far as to mount a coup to achieve his ends, the way Eisenhower did. Instead, he steadfastly pursued a negotiated settlement between Iran and Great Britain as the best solution to the lengthening oil nationalization crisis. Eisenhower, too, tried to work out a compromise agreement between the British and Iranian governments during his first weeks in office. There are even indications that he wished he had the political freedom to extend to Iran the economic aid it needed to help it out of the crisis. But in the end he decided the United States had no choice but to remove Prime Minister Mohammad Mosaddeq in order to protect perceived American interests in the region.

What caused U.S. strategists to shift Iran from its location on the periphery of American vital interests to its status as a crucial component of Western security? And what explains the apparent change in U.S. policy from supporting Iran's exercise of national sovereignty to carrying out a covert intervention against its elected leader? The evidence suggests a variety of factors, extending beyond the differences in outlook that existed between the two presidents. This chapter examines those underlying factors, centering on the crucial element of the cold war, which formed the backdrop for every major foreign policy decision during those years. The chapter does not, however, attempt to recount the evolution of U.S.-Iran relations, a topic that far exceeds the scope of a single essay.[2] Nor does it describe the details of the coup itself, which is the subject of another chapter in this volume.

The Truman Worldview

Well before World War II drew to a close, U.S. officials began to articulate a conception of the postwar world and the place of the United States in it. Following the armistice, the Truman administration battled national feelings of war-weariness and isolationism in support of the view that, as the predominant world power, America's interests now stretched around the globe.[3] From this point forward, ensuring the nation's security would require maintaining a level not just of military superiority over its rivals but of economic "preponderance" as well, which in turn entailed a guarantee of unfettered access to natural resources, skilled labor, and markets, as well as military facilities, on a global scale. American officials did not see themselves as pursuing interests that were aggressive or acquisitive in a traditional colonial sense. Nor did the White House consciously seek to establish outright hegemony in international affairs. Instead, the new vision the administration embraced was the lofty one of ensuring the conditions necessary for peace and economic prosperity for all nations—conditions that were tightly linked, and seen as fully consistent, with furthering the economic and national security interests of the United States.[4]

For U.S. strategists, the USSR and Soviet-supported communism quickly crystallized into the principal source of threat to this conception of a peaceful world order. Germany and Japan had been vanquished, but the Soviet Union, despite horrific losses, continued to deploy armed forces on a large scale and retained the economic and industrial potential to develop into a dominant Eurasian power. Moscow's rush to seize control of territories from Central Europe and the Baltics to the Kurile Islands, and the ruthless tactics Soviet forces employed were taken as warning signs by U.S. officials that Kremlin ambitions went beyond just providing for their own security. For the time being, facing the monumental task of recovering from the war and having no means of mounting a serious military threat against the United States, the Soviet Union seemed to pose little immediate hazard to American vital interests. However, a series of events beginning even before the end of the war combined to harden the Truman administration's views of Kremlin intentions.

Early Crises: 1945–1948

The West had been concerned about Soviet aims for years, particularly since the signing of the 1939 Nazi-Soviet pact, which had led to attacks on Finland and the occupation of eastern Poland and the Baltics. By the time the Allied leaders met at Yalta in February 1945, the Red Army's brutal sweep across much of Eastern Europe in the wake of Germany's retreat had magnified Western worries over the region's postwar future. Yalta produced a loose agreement that each side ultimately interpreted its own way; the accord did little to quell those fears.

By the beginning of 1946, several developments had convinced President Truman of the need to take a harder line. In early January, ever attuned to public opinion and growing Republican criticism that Secretary of State James Byrnes had been following too soft a course with Moscow, Truman wrote to Byrnes: "Unless Russia is faced with an iron fist and strong language another war is in the making. . . . I'm tired of babying the Soviets."[5] One month later, on February 9, Stalin delivered a speech that sounded to many American observers like a renunciation of the wartime alliance, a reassertion of Marxist-

Leninist dogma indicting the imperialist West, and a warning to the Soviet population to steel themselves for eventual future conflict. In hindsight, the speech, which mainly targeted a domestic audience, now seems mild by comparison, but at the time it struck a nerve. Supreme Court justice William O. Douglas, for example, called it "a Declaration of World War III." [6] Two weeks later, U.S. diplomat George F. Kennan wired his "Long Telegram" to Washington depicting the Soviet leadership as driven by historical insecurity covered with the "fig leaf" of Marxism. Their ideology in turn, he wrote, led them to see the world as divided into two camps and committed them to fight for the socialist cause while undermining the capitalist side. From Moscow's perspective, he concluded, peaceful coexistence was impossible. [7] In early March, Winston Churchill's "Iron Curtain" speech in Fulton, Missouri, encouraged the president in his view that Kremlin aims were corrupt and had to be confronted with absolute resolve.

One of the earliest episodes that contributed to this stiffening of attitudes was the crisis in the northern Iranian province of Azerbaijan. Since August 1941, Soviet and British forces had occupied the northern and southern segments of Iran, respectively, in order to deny the country to Germany, to set up a much-needed military supply route to the USSR, and, in the longer term, to lay claim to Iran's oil reserves. In January 1942, by agreement with the 22-year-old shah, Mohammad Reza Pahlavi, who had been installed by the occupying powers in place of his father the year before, the Soviets and British pledged to withdraw their forces within six months after the end of hostilities. When the March 2, 1946, deadline arrived, the British complied, but Moscow balked, citing threats to Soviet security. [8] During the intervening three years, Stalin had begun to expand Soviet political influence in Azerbaijan (and Kurdistan), working through the communist leadership of the Soviet republic of Azerbaijan, Mir Jafaar Bagirov, to develop nationalist forces across the Iranian border and to exert pressure on the central government in Tehran. On December 12, 1945, after weeks of violent clashes between Marxist and nationalist proponents of autonomy on the one hand and government forces on the other, the Soviet-backed Democratic Republic of Azerbaijan was founded. [9] Red Army units blocked access to the province to government troops sent to reestablish control. As the target date for Soviet withdrawal came and went, British and American alarm peaked. Iran, with Washington's encouragement, took the issue to the newly founded United Nations while Tehran's prime minister, Ahmad Qavam, traveled to Moscow to strike a deal directly with the Kremlin. By early May, Stalin finally decided to remove his forces from Azerbaijan. Although his reasons are still debated, the entire saga led the Truman administration to draw very definite conclusions about Soviet conduct, generally and in relation to Iran.

For Truman personally, the Azerbaijan crisis constituted proof that Moscow harbored aggressive intentions toward its neighbors, particularly Iran. He concluded that Stalin's conduct in Azerbaijan and Kurdistan, coming on the heels of Soviet suppression of Eastern Europe, could only be seen as hostile to Western interests and confirmation that the Kremlin could not be trusted to honor its international commitments. The U.S. perception of a Soviet threat to the region's crucial oil resources added urgency to the situation.[10] To senior officials such as Undersecretary of State Dean Acheson, Azerbaijan was also an object lesson in Soviet tactics, confirming U.S. intelligence assessments that Moscow was unlikely to risk open war under current conditions but instead would rely on infiltration, cooptation, and subversion in Iran and elsewhere on the "periphery."[11] The Tudeh Party played a key role in this regard, a fact that would weigh on the minds of U.S. officials in coming years.[12] On a more positive note for Washington, Stalin's decision to pull out without serious protest backed up the administration's conviction that an "iron fist and strong language" could keep Moscow in check.[13]

The Azerbaijan crisis also underscored Iran's importance in the burgeoning East-West struggle. Aside from possessing oil reserves of its own, the country was an important buffer between the USSR and the Persian Gulf and Indian subcontinent. U.S. officials took it on faith that the Russians had coveted a port on the "warm waters" of the gulf since Peter the Great. If Moscow gained that access, Western strategists were afraid that it would place the even larger oil fields of the Saudi peninsula, and beyond them British military and commercial interests from Suez to India, under direct threat. Neither Washington nor London was prepared to let that happen.

Truman's concerns about Iran and the region were reinforced the following year by crises in Turkey and Greece. Along with Iran, these two countries constituted the Northern Tier in U.S. strategy—a first line of defense against communism stretching from the Mediterranean to South Asia. In August 1946, the Soviets demanded military rights to the Dardanelles with Turkey. Coming on the heels of so many other apparently provocative steps, the Kremlin's proposal for joint defense of the straits with Turkey was interpreted in Washington as a hostile move that would not only give the Soviet navy direct access to the Mediterranean through the Black Sea but would also, as Truman later wrote, "in the natural course of events, result in Greece and the whole

Near and Middle East falling under Soviet control."[14] The Soviet threat to Turkey, along with the Azerbaijan crisis, led many administration officials for the first time to see a very real possibility of war with the USSR, and prompted intensified military planning to meet that contingency.[15]

In Greece, the civil war had flared up again by late November 1946. Even though there was no evidence of direct Soviet involvement, U.S. officials quickly drew parallels to the ongoing crisis in Iran, particularly to the presence of an active communist party and attempts to encourage a separatist movement in the north.[16] The Truman administration understood that Greece's problems arose mainly out of the war and the repressive nature of the regime, but it still focused on forestalling the communist threat as the immediate priority. Otherwise, the administration worried that it might be impossible to check the spillover into neighboring countries. As Dean Acheson warned members of Congress the following February: "Like apples in a barrel infected by one rotten one, the corruption of Greece would infect Iran and all to the east. It would also carry infection to Africa through Asia Minor and Egypt, and to Europe through Italy and France." It was a sentiment to which the president himself heartily subscribed.[17]

During the immediate postwar period, by mutual agreement with the United States, primary responsibility for defense of the Middle East rested with Britain.[18] This reflected a recognition of long-standing British economic and security interests as much as an awareness of the limitations on the U.S. military's global reach. But Britain's own economic picture was bleak as the crippling effects of the war, compounded by successive harsh winters, forced a reevaluation of the country's ability to manage its far-flung assets. In February 1947, the Foreign Office secretly told the State Department that London would soon be unable to uphold its military and economic commitments to Greece and Turkey.[19] The news jolted the Truman administration, which had concluded that defense of the Northern Tier was critical, even as a newly elected Republican Congress began pressing for a return to isolationism at home.

Ever since the outbreak of the Turkish crisis the previous August, the White House had become more and more determined to take vigorous action to block Soviet moves across the Northern Tier. As the sense of urgency heightened in the fall of 1946, the views of the president and his advisers became more rigid. In late September, a particularly influential study known as the Clifford-Elsey report crossed Truman's desk. It synthesized the consensus of several senior experts, depicting Soviet international behavior in heavily ideological terms and warning of the need to be prepared to confront the Soviets "vigorously," using, if necessary, the "language of military power . . . the only language which disciples of power politics understand."[20] In the Near East, as in other parts of the world, the Kremlin had been able to "flow into the political vacuum" of the region "because no other nation was both willing and able to prevent it." Soviet leaders fed on easy success, the authors declared. "They are now preparing to take over new areas in the same way." Having commissioned the report in the wake of the Azerbaijan crisis that spring, when he had first shaken his fist at Moscow, the president was predisposed to embrace the message.

However, only after the British, who had already agreed to withdraw from Burma, Palestine, and India, admitted they could no longer shore up Turkey and Greece did the administration decide the time was right to take its case to Congress. The enunciation of the Truman Doctrine on March 12 was not itself a turning point in U.S. thinking—the key decisions had been taken months earlier—but with its broad statement of intent "to support free peoples who are resisting attempted subjugation by armed minorities or outside pressures," it was an unmistakable sign that British influence, on the decline in the Near East, was about to give way to American activism.[21]

Despite the seemingly broad scope of the president's address, the Truman Doctrine reflected the more constrained "strongpoints" strategy as described by Kennan and already in use by the United States at the time. Originally, the concept of containing the Soviet Union had entailed reacting to Kremlin aggression anywhere it appeared.[22] But U.S. strategists and politicians realized that a "perimeter" defense was both militarily and economically unfeasible. Not even the United States had the resources for an undertaking of that scope, and the domestic political mood so soon after the war militated against expanding obligations overseas. Instead, certain areas of the world were identified as being crucial to American interests and deserving of the commitments needed to keep them in the Western camp. For postwar planners, Europe and Japan were the most critical areas because of their enormous industrial and economic potential. They were therefore the focus of the most extensive economic and military restructuring schemes of the period, including the Marshall Plan, expounded in June 1947. Other areas of the world that were mainly rich in strategic resources such as oil, and likely to be targets of the Soviets, formed a second tier of importance. This category included the Near East, which comprised not only Greece and Turkey but the Persian Gulf states and the rest of the Middle East as well.

Thus, U.S. policymakers in the late 1940s considered Iran to be "vital to the security of the United States" but not critical enough to warrant the highest levels of U.S. support.[23] After Soviet forces withdrew from northern Iran and the autonomy movements disintegrated, the Truman administration at least temporarily reverted to a more hands-off approach, including rebuffing Iran's repeated requests for substantial military and financial aid.[24] Yet, the significance of the Truman Doctrine was that it brought the United States a major step closer toward assuming the lead role in defending Western interests in the region.

Soviet Objectives Toward Iran after World War II

Given the growing rigidity of American attitudes toward the Soviet Union, it is worth asking how accurate those views were. The opening of portions of the archival record from the former Soviet bloc makes it possible to glean at least a few clues into Soviet thinking. Perhaps not surprisingly, these glimpses tend both to confirm and contradict earlier Western-based analyses. Generally speaking, Stalin seems not to have had a consistent postwar strategy. Beyond pursuing certain cherished security aims such as establishing Soviet-dominated regimes in Eastern Europe,[25] he responded to each situation on a case-by-case basis, bringing to bear a mix of motivations deriving from historical Russian objectives, revolutionary ideology, security concerns, economic or material imperatives, power politics, domestic factors, and even personal impulses. All of these strands together formed a pattern of steady, probing expansionism that was opportunistic in the extreme but that also stopped short of deliberately provoking a military confrontation with the West.

By war's end, Stalin seemed reasonably satisfied with Soviet territorial gains. Surveying a map of the USSR's new borders at his dacha in the summer of 1945, he reportedly traced his pipe over the Baltics and Finland and pronounced, "Everything is all right to the north."

"It's okay to the west," he added, while to the east, "everything is in order." "But," he declared, tapping at the area below the Caucasus, "I don't like our border right here!"[26]

Since at least the eighteenth century, the tsars had eyed Persia both as a gateway to the gulf and south Asia and as a barrier to outside, mainly British, interference.[27] The experience of World War II reinforced this assortment of defensive and offensive motives, especially as oil became a critical resource. Even before the war, Moscow had shown a long-term interest in the gulf. Soviet foreign minister Vyacheslav Molotov had insisted in November 1940 that a secret protocol with Germany on postwar spheres of influence specify "that the area south of Batum and Baku in the general direction of the Persian Gulf is recognized as the center of the aspirations of the Soviet Union."[28]

After the Soviet-German alliance collapsed, Stalin concluded the January 1942 Tripartite Treaty of Alliance with Britain and Iran, expelling German diplomats and intelligence agents from Iran and gaining the coveted foothold for the USSR in the northern part of the country. As the war wound down, the Soviets seemed to take for granted that they would keep hold of the region as partial compensation for their extraordinary wartime sacrifices. Roosevelt and Churchill could not easily quarrel since they still needed the Red Army in Europe and, ultimately, in Japan. Both leaders also had their own countries' spheres of influence to consider. Churchill's "percentages" agreement on the Balkans with Stalin in October 1944, and his seeming endorsement in Tehran of Moscow's drive toward warm-water ports, only validated the Soviets' conception of what would be acceptable.[29]

Moscow's thinking on Iran also depended on a variety of additional factors. Security considerations played a central part. In December 1945, Stalin told British foreign secretary Ernest Bevin that the Red Army was needed in Azerbaijan to prevent hostile Iranian forces from sabotaging the petroleum industry centered in Baku.[30] Although Bevin wondered how Iran's paltry forces could possibly threaten the USSR, the underlying sense of vulnerability was genuine. Early in the war, the Soviets had uncovered German plans targeting that very region. Even the CIA acknowledged that Moscow had an interest in protecting "its vital Baku oil fields" from outside attack.[31] With its new global stature, Kremlin ambitions expanded correspondingly, broadening in turn the definition of what constituted a threat to Soviet national interests. At a certain point, the distinctions between defensive and expansionist aims necessarily blurred.

Ideology was another factor shaping Soviet behavior. Not unlike the United States, the Soviet Union saw itself as the champion of a political system and way of life that had universal appeal. In fact, Stalin's approach combined elements of ideology and pragmatism and could be modified as circumstances dictated.

On the one hand, Stalin was "a child of the Russian revolution," who ingeniously tied the success of communist victory to the defense and strengthening of the Soviet Union.[32] In effect, what was good for the USSR was good for international communism. Furthermore, he never completely abandoned the notion of inevitable conflict between the capitalist and socialist camps, nor the possibility of clashes erupting within the capitalist world itself. In early

1947, he sought a military alliance with London to try to exacerbate the West's "internal contradictions."[33] Only after declaration of the Truman Doctrine, the Marshall Plan and, finally, the creation of the North Atlantic Treaty Organization (NATO) did his expectations in that regard finally fade.

On the other hand, nearly obsessed with bolstering Soviet security, Stalin was fully prepared to subordinate the interests of world communism to those of the Soviet state. He was ready, for example, to cooperate with the British or Americans at the expense of promoting revolutions, at least in the short term, if it would strengthen Soviet security. His willingness to sacrifice the Democratic Party of Azerbaijan in 1946 in order to guarantee an oil agreement with Tehran and a presence in the country's north was an example.[34]

Reinforcing the Soviets' sense of ideological exceptionalism was Stalin's determination that the USSR be accorded equal status with the other Allied powers. For all the devastation of the war, the Soviet Union had emerged as a world power, and the Russians, as confirmed by a recent Russian study, generally felt entitled to their " 'fair share' of the war spoils." Those claims consisted of "new territories, trusteeships, an expanded sphere of influence and some strong points in the areas stretching beyond that sphere."[35]

In Iran, the Soviets were intent on retaining a sphere of influence in the north, a process that culminated in the proclamation of democratic republics in Azerbaijan and Kurdistan in December 1945. Stalin proceeded cautiously at first. As early as 1941, he personally authorized the gradual build-up of local nationalist sentiments and pro-Moscow sympathies, particularly in Azerbaijan.[36] Even though his implicit goal at this stage was to contain Western influence, he made sure to do nothing to provoke his former allies.[37] In 1944, an oil shortage and a poor showing in local parliamentary elections prompted the Soviets to focus more keenly on Azerbaijan. Lavrentii Beria, Stalin's secret-police chief and a key influence on the Soviet leader's attitude toward Iran, urged Stalin to press the Iranians to grant Moscow an oil concession or risk losing the advantage to the Americans or the British.[38] Finally, in mid-1945 Stalin decided that it was time to significantly augment Moscow's standing in the province. Moving with remarkable speed and efficiency, the Soviets managed to create a fully fledged autonomous Azeri government, including a national administration and parliament, within just six months.[39]

Yet, Stalin was never able to realize even his basic political goals in Azerbaijan, much less to establish full control over the province. Still dependent on the more powerful Western governments and their wartime agreements (especially Yalta) to advance Soviet international interests, he agreed in April 1946 to pull the Red Army out of Iran in return for several considerations: the creation of a joint Soviet-Iranian oil company, a guarantee of stability in the northern provinces, and a "friendly" attitude on Tehran's part toward Moscow. Each of these points, according to Russian historian Natalia Yegorova, was closely tied to both traditional imperial aims and more immediate security concerns.[40] In the end, however, Moscow was left virtually empty handed because the Iranian parliament, the Majles, never ratified the agreement. According to new evidence, the Soviets may have dropped the ball by failing to make sure that the Majles acted before the seven-month deadline for ratification expired on October 24.[41]

The recent archival revelations and scholarship coming out of the former Soviet bloc offer a number of important insights. Interestingly, they show that Moscow's outlook during and after the war mirrored Washington's perceptions in several fundamental ways. Both sides defined broad roles for themselves in the postwar order that included staking out expanded security interests. Each power typically saw the other in the most negative light and operated on the assumption that it posed direct, even imminent, threats to those interests.[42]

In general, Soviet bloc records show that early U.S. intelligence assessments of Kremlin intentions were essentially on target. The basic assumptions in George Kennan's February 1946 "Long Telegram" stand up well, for example, as do other analyses that recognized the mixture of ideological and practical considerations that underlay Stalin's hostility toward the West and drove Soviet attempts, in Molotov's words, "to expand the borders of our Fatherland" as far as possible.[43] As for the Near East, a typical report from July 1946 states, accurately: "The Soviet Union desires to include Greece, Turkey, and Iran in its security zone through the establishment of 'friendly' governments in those countries." The same report goes on to note that Moscow recognized the "danger of provoking Great Britain and the United States" and that in peripheral areas the Kremlin "will prove grasping and opportunistic, but flexible in proportion to the degree and nature of the resistance encountered."[44]

The president and his top advisers undoubtedly read intelligence analyses of this sort,[45] but they also tended, under the sway of the cold war and domestic politics,[46] to focus on the potential threat from Moscow without weighing the constraints on Soviet actions. The Clifford-Elsey report, for example, gave inordinate emphasis to the ideological component of Soviet thinking while discounting the USSR's many weaknesses and Stalin's corresponding concern not to provoke the West. The Truman Doctrine speech and the landmark policy document NSC 68 (see below) were just as stark in their warnings about

Moscow's intentions, without accounting for the factors that combined to limit the Soviets' ability to reach those goals. Aside from focusing on the Kremlin's most aggressive inclinations, U.S. policy-makers—and indeed strategists on all sides throughout the cold war—too often equated capabilities with intentions and then tended to exaggerate those capacities, as American analysts did in assessing the Soviet and Tudeh threat in the early 1950s. In the end, however, most of the blame for any American overreaction to Moscow's international forays has to fall to Stalin himself; Stalin's behavior, particularly in the Near East, did little to assuage Western concerns about the real nature and limits of Kremlin objectives. Years afterward, even Molotov would confide to an acquaintance that in pressing Soviet ambitions in both Turkey and Iran after the war, "we admittedly went a bit too far." [47]

The Cold War Intensifies: 1949–1953

By early 1950, international events and developments inside Iran had led U.S. officials to undertake fundamental policy reassessments. Mao Zedong's establishment of the People's Republic of China in October 1949 confirmed the "loss of China" and opened up new threats to the rest of Asia. If Japan were to fall to the Communist bloc or even to turn toward neutralism, American strategists worried that it might give the Soviets the capability of "significantly altering the balance of world power." [48] Even more dangerous for U.S. security was Moscow's acquisition of nuclear weapons. In August 1949, the Soviets successfully tested an atomic bomb, several years earlier than U.S. experts had anticipated. The realization that Moscow would soon be able to launch nuclear strikes directly against American targets, either in a surprise attack or to deter a U.S. nuclear response to Soviet conventional aggression, shook the assumptions of U.S. strategy.

In January 1950, President Truman instructed the State Department to reevaluate basic U.S. national security policy. The response, produced the following April, was NSC 68. [49] Long considered one of the basic statements of U.S. cold war policy, the new study articulated a conception, far broader than in previous documents, of the threat facing the United States from Soviet-backed communism. "The assault on free institutions is worldwide now," the document read, "and in the context of the present polarization of power a defeat of free institutions anywhere is a defeat everywhere." As with the Truman Doctrine, the authors of NSC 68 framed their arguments in harsh terms in order to ensure support within the government and Congress for their drastic policy proposals. In this case, the call was for a shift from the "strongpoints" defense to a "perimeter" approach that would focus not just on key regions of special security interest but on virtually *any* point where the communist threat surfaced.[50]

North Korea's attack on South Korea seemed to confirm NSC 68's darkest predictions about the global nature of the communist threat, specifically about Moscow's readiness to use military force rather than to rely solely on infiltration and subversion. Ironically, Stalin probably expected that the United States would not see Korea as in its sphere of interest and would decline to respond in kind. But to the Joint Chiefs of Staff the attack represented "one of the greatest dangers in history," and NSC 68's thesis that no place on earth was safe from communist aggression took firm root.

President Truman immediately applied the lesson of Korea to Iran. For the time being, the distinction between "vital" and "peripheral" interests disappeared, just as Iran was about to be plunged into crisis under its new premier, Mohammad Mosaddeq.

The Regional and Iranian Context

As with every area of "vital" interest to the United States, the burgeoning cold war had the effect of amplifying the importance of events in the Middle East. As the East-West rivalry intensified and U.S. apprehensions over Soviet intentions grew, so too did the tendency to evaluate virtually any development in the Persian Gulf or Northern Tier countries of Greece and Turkey from the point of view of its effect on the balance of forces there. A number of these regional factors are worth identifying separately.

The Near East had been a target for American oil companies since before World War II. However, one effect of the war was to focus U.S. official attention on the vital strategic, not just commercial, value of petroleum. The State Department advised Truman at the time of the Potsdam Conference that Saudi oil represented "a stupendous source of strategic power, and one of the greatest material prizes in world history."[51] In the event of another war, it would behoove the West to have access to this vital resource and, at the same time, to deny it to the Russians.[52] After the war, oil was also desperately needed to ensure the economic recovery and reconstruction of Western Europe and Japan. As much as 70 percent of that oil came from the Near East.[53] Defense of Western access to the region's oil, therefore, was a top priority for Washington, higher than the defense of Iran itself, and as such it heavily influenced U.S. decision making on Iran during this period.[54] So important was the question of who controlled the region's petroleum that beginning in September 1948 the Truman administration drew up contingency plans to deny enemy access to it by destroying vital components of refineries and plugging the wells in the event of a Soviet attack in Iran or elsewhere in the Persian Gulf.[55]

The Near East's importance extended beyond oil. Western military, economic, and political stakes in the region were high. Numerous allied military facilities, including the major British base at Suez, and significant trade and transportation interests dating back to colonial times dotted the area. As noted above, the Northern Tier countries of Greece, Turkey, and Iran also constituted a "first line of defense" for the Mediterranean to the west, and eastward for the rest of Asia. If Iran were to fall under Soviet "domination," it would give the USSR advance bases bordering on Turkey, Iraq, the Persian Gulf, Afghanistan, and Pakistan, and allow it much closer proximity to vital U.S. and British military facilities in the region.[56] Even if Iran's loss did not produce an immediate and direct military threat, U.S. officials were unwilling to risk the likely damage to American prestige.

Since the Americans and British conceived of the Middle East in time of war as a region "of importance second only to Western Europe," it was natural that they would create a security organization to maintain Western control of the area. By mid-1950, the United States had signed a Mutual Defense Assistance Agreement with Iran providing for an infusion of $23 million in military aid through 1956.[57] In the summer of 1951, the U.S. and British governments, along with France and Turkey, elaborated a multilateral agreement for a Middle East Command (MECOM) centered around Egypt. But Egypt was experiencing the same anti-British mood as Iran, and the Cairo government dismissed the proposal out of hand in October 1951.[58] Allied strategists soon began to reshape the idea and by the following summer had worked out a basic accord involving the United States, Britain, Turkey, and four other sponsors to establish a security network, called the Middle East Defense Organization (MEDO), with a mission that now extended beyond the earlier Suez focus to the entire Middle East, including protection of the oil fields of the Persian Gulf.[59]

In May 1953, Secretary of State John Foster Dulles pursued the concept during a tour of the region. Egypt rebuffed the idea again, after which Dulles visited Turkey and Pakistan. On the strength of that experience he came away convinced that the Northern Tier countries, strategically located and mostly friendly to the West, did indeed form a natural defensive belt against Soviet aggression. The implications for Iran and its place in U.S. strategic thinking were now all the more critical. Dulles saw the country as "the obvious weak spot" in the new arrangement. Therefore, if MEDO was to succeed, as the Eisenhower administration was determined it would, it was even more important than ever to "save Iran."[60]

As the cold war intensified, U.S. officials kept an eye on events unfolding inside Iran. Worries about instability momentarily eased in the late 1940s after the crushing of the autonomy movements in the north and the concomitant decline of the Tudeh Party, but the administration took advantage of the opportunity to expand the American presence in the country. Existing army, air force, and gendarmerie missions were extended and the size of the embassy swelled, including the addition of a CIA station.[61] But the quiet spell did not last long. General unrest began to build, in part because of inflexibility by the Anglo-Iranian Oil Company (AIOC), which helped spawn the formation of the opposition National Front. In February 1949, an assassination attempt against the shah resulted in the banning of the Tudeh.

Beginning in 1950, the trend toward worsening internal conditions accelerated significantly, exacerbated by a poor harvest and a serious economic depression. The Tudeh began to build in strength, despite its illegal status. So did the National Front. A senior State Department official visiting Iran in March 1950 warned that the situation had become "dangerous and explosive." Others in the department began calling quietly for pressure on the shah to replace the current, largely ineffective, government.[62]

By far the most significant internal Iranian development at this time was the crisis surrounding the nationalization of the country's oil industry. After the Iranian government's takeover of the AIOC in late April 1951, the United States stepped in to act as an intermediary between Iran and Great Britain, thus drawing the country ever deeper into Iran's affairs. As the crisis continued through 1952, there were increasing calls from within the Truman administration to go further by supplanting the British as principal guardian of Western interests in Iran. By the summer of that year, defense secretary Robert Lovett was arguing that the United States brooked unacceptable risks by allowing the British to continue on their current track. The Joint Chiefs of Staff agreed, and by late November official (classified) U.S. policy declared: "It is clear that the United Kingdom no longer possesses the capability unilaterally to assure stability in the area."[63]

Interestingly, even as Iran's domestic crisis steadily worsened from May 1951 on, the Truman administration continued to press doggedly for an oil agreement they thought would be equitable to both Great Britain and Iran, rather than consider overt intervention. Warnings about the deteriorating state of affairs and the spreading communist menace flowed regularly from the U.S. embassy in Tehran to Washington,[64] however, and as policymakers became more agitated over the lack of a solution to the impasse, they took steps to anticipate the worst-case scenarios of a communist coup or even a Soviet invasion.

Since the late 1940s, the United States had begun carrying out a series of covert actions aimed mainly at undermining Moscow's position in Iran. Run by the newly created Central Intelligence Agency, the operations included anti-Soviet and anti-Tudeh activities inside Iran, crossborder intelligence and destabilization campaigns in the USSR, and preparations in the event of a conflict with Soviet forces.[65] American fears of an invasion of Iran were genuine; foreign service officers posted in the northern provinces, for example, were warned by local Iranian officials to be ready to evacuate on just a half hour's notice. Anxious to anticipate any Soviet move, diplomats and CIA officers, much as they did in Western and Eastern Europe at this time, marked out escape and evasion routes, complete with buried caches of weapons and gold, and worked out "stay-behind" plans with local tribes in southern Iran.[66]

Fear of Soviet-backed subversion of Iran also ran high. The communist coup d'état in Czechoslovakia in February 1948 added to the expectation that the real threat from Moscow would not come from open conflict but through Kremlin efforts "to extend its influence and control by political, economic, and psychological methods"—not just in Europe but throughout "the Near and Middle East."[67] The Czechoslovak crisis also highlighted the danger of tolerating any degree of communist participation in a coalition government. As part of the reaction to the coup, U.S. officials began to focus more intently on developing a covert political action capability to counter Soviet subversive tactics.[68]

The CIA, formed in 1947, already had vague authority to "perform . . . other functions and duties related to intelligence affecting the national security," which could be interpreted as authorization to carry out psychological or other clandestine activities. But in June 1948, in response to the Prague coup and the Berlin blockade, President Truman signed NSC 10/2, a directive that greatly expanded the U.S. government's covert operations capability, now defined broadly to include "propaganda; . . . sabotage, anti-sabotage, demolition, and evacuation measures; . . . subversion . . . including assistance to underground resistance movements, guerrillas and refugee liberation groups, and support of indigenous anti-communist elements in threatened countries of the free world."[69]

Directly in line with NSC 10/2's mandate to counter the "vicious covert activities of the USSR," the CIA in the late 1940s set up Operation TPBEDAMN, a wide-ranging program to undermine communist influence in Iran.[70] Well funded at $1 million per year, TPBEDAMN had several elements. They included planting articles and cartoons in local newspapers targeting the Tudeh, paying off right-wing nationalist organizations as well as religious figures, provoking violent acts and blaming them on the communists, and hiring thugs to break up Tudeh rallies. Two Iranians, Ali Jalali and Faruq Kayvani, coordinated these activities locally. Code named Nerren and Cilley by the CIA, they would go on to play important parts in the anti-Mosaddeq coup d'état.

By late 1952, near the end of Truman's term, U.S. alarm about Iran's vulnerability to subversion had escalated to a point where the president was persuaded to sign a new Iran policy statement authorizing a series of aggressive military, political, "special," and other operations "in the event of either an attempted or an actual communist seizure of power." In the case of a successful Tudeh coup, one of the goals would be, "if possible, to bring about the overthrow of the communist government." If the Soviets themselves launched a direct attack on the country, the United States could then "decide in the light of the circumstances existing at the time" whether to treat such a move as a "*casus belli*."[71]

This willingness to use force and even to consider going to war over Iran represented a significant shift in the Truman administration's thinking.[72] But it is important to note that the new directive, known as NSC 136/1, assumed that U.S. action would follow a major overt act of communist aggression—either a coup or an invasion. At no point in the crisis, not even in mid- and late 1952, when British operatives proposed a joint coup with Washington,[73] did the Truman White House embrace overthrowing a noncommunist government or consider taking any of the drastic steps in NSC 136/1 without the trigger of a prior hostile act by the Tudeh or Moscow. The notion of a preemptive strike was an Eisenhower administration innovation.

The U.S. Tilt Toward the British

Washington's prosecution of the cold war placed great reliance on the cooperation of Great Britain. As a wartime ally of the United States and a nation with whom Americans shared wide-ranging political and cultural values (one of "the English-speaking peoples," in Churchill's formulation), the British were natural partners. Despite the war's effects, Britain had the world's third largest economy and retained many of its possessions and interests abroad. Washington counted on London's support to fulfill global strategies from European defense and economic integration to fighting the war in Korea. For its part, Britain was desperate to prolong its influence over former colonies, protect important economic assets such as the AIOC refinery at Abadan, and at all costs to retain U.S. economic, political, and, if need be, military support.

Of course, this did not mean there were no serious differences between Washington and London. The two sides disagreed over questions ranging from sharing nuclear weapons technology to deploying armed forces in Asia. During the war, Washington had been highly critical of London's "blunt, uncompromising attitude" toward Iran and its propensity for interfering in the country's political affairs.[74] After the war, the Americans tried, mostly unsuccessfully, to convince the British that failing to address legitimate nationalist aspirations in former imperial realms risked driving local populations into the Soviet camp. U.S. officials in the immediate postwar period, including Truman and Acheson, had always been more sympathetic toward the concept of nationalism in the Third World than most of their British colleagues, an attitude that extended to supporting the principle of nationalization of foreign-owned industries, albeit with proper compensation by the host government. With the advent of the Eisenhower administration, the feelings of affinity and common interest only grew with respect to Iran.[75] Churchill's unwillingness to cooperate more closely on such priorities as joining in the economic and military integration of Europe irked Eisenhower, but the United Kingdom was still important in the battle to keep the Middle East communist-free, and despite continuing mutual strains in some areas the fact remained that, in the view of the new president and his top aides, the United States shared a far broader range of interests and needs with Great Britain than it did with Iran.[76]

The U.S. Domestic Context

While the cold war was being contested overseas, it was also being played out in the United States. In fact, the two fronts were closely connected. As America's involvement abroad expanded, international developments inevitably had a greater impact on domestic political discourse, while the growing "Red Scare" beginning in the late 1940s became a significant influence on at least the tone, and sometimes the direction, of U.S. policy abroad. From 1946 to 1951, a series of espionage-related events contributed to this unhealthy environment. A Canadian nuclear spy ring was uncovered, followed by Whittaker Chambers' accusations against Alger Hiss, the arrest of Klaus Fuchs and the Rosenbergs, and the flight of Donald MacLean and Guy Burgess to Moscow. In early 1950, Sen. Joseph McCarthy (R–WI) created headlines with charges that Acheson's State Department harbored security risks, thus beginning a four-year campaign of haranguing both the Truman and the Eisenhower administrations for allegedly coddling foreign and domestic communists.

The stirring of anticommunist hysteria made conducting a restrained foreign policy more difficult for the Truman White House. Episodes such as Gen. Douglas MacArthur's public criticisms of how the administration was handling the "limited war" in Korea, which led Truman to relieve him of command in April 1951 and which in turn sparked a string of conservative attacks on Truman, added to the pressure.[77] Secretary of State Acheson came in for some of the most virulent attacks, for the crisis in Korea as well as for supposedly protecting hundreds of communists within his own department. Truman and Acheson, both personally disgusted with the attacks, felt obliged to make concessions. They made a number of personnel changes in key State Department posts, including asking Republican John Foster Dulles to oversee the process of preparing a peace treaty with Japan.[78] Truman appointed Eisenhower's former chief of staff during the war, Gen. Walter Bedell Smith—"about as right-wing as a professional army officer was likely to get," according to Eisenhower's biographer—to head the CIA, which McCarthy had indicated was his next target after finishing with the State Department.[79] The president also instituted a loyalty regime for civil servants to prove his determination to fight internal subversion.

The tense political atmosphere of the time had an undeniable chilling effect on the foreign policy process. As George Kennan later wrote: "[T]here would not be a president who would not stand in a certain terror of the anticommunist right wing . . . and would not temper his actions with a view to placating it and averting its possible hostility."[80] Intense public pressure, agitated by the McCarthy hearings and by the revelations of the Rosenberg, Hiss, and Fuchs cases, fed a tendency to blur subtleties in the public's eye on such issues as the distinction between independent nationalism and Kremlin cronyism in the emerging Third World. During the early Eisenhower years, this tendency became more pronounced. John Foster Dulles later acknowledged deliberately exaggerating the dangers of anticommunism, admitting that fanning the flames served important purposes, including preserving allied unity abroad and garnering support for tough policies at home.[81] The national media regularly added to the hyperbole. As Iran prepared to take over the AIOC from Britain,

Time magazine caricatured the country's nationalist movement as "one of the worst calamities to the anti–Communist world since the Red conquest of China." [82]

Ironically, Truman's stark depictions of the communist menace abroad helped to arouse these same concerns, even as domestic political pressures stiffened his own approach. [83] The main goal of his March 12, 1947, declaration on Greece and Turkey was precisely to stir up public and congressional alarm. Inside the government, NSC 68 had the same purpose. The president was also plainly aware of the hazards of going too far, however. In September 1946, he ordered that all twenty copies of the Clifford-Elsey report be collected and stored in a White House safe to keep the report's explosive conclusions from being leaked to the public. [84]

While U.S. officials understood their own ability to sway popular attitudes, they were highly susceptible to the pressures of public opinion themselves. After being criticized for his soft treatment of Moscow, Secretary of State Byrnes in early 1946 made a point of pressing the Azerbaijan issue in the United Nations Security Council and dramatically stepped up his rhetoric. By March of that year, memories of Munich, widely revived in the press, helped convince the White House that any policy smacking of "appeasement" of the Kremlin carried far too many political risks at home. [85]

An important example of the exaggerated fear of the communist threat can be found in official U.S. assessments of the Tudeh Party in Iran. The Tudeh was the most organized communist party in the region by the early 1950s and clearly took inspiration, if not always direction, from Moscow. But recent research in Iranian and former Soviet materials, as well as recollections of CIA operatives, raise doubts about the common perception that the Tudeh was prepared to take control of the country during this period. Splits existed within the Tudeh leadership over strategy, tactics, and even personalities, including the question of whether to support or oppose Mosaddeq and the National Front. [86] Internal Tudeh files captured after the coup showed that the party had decided not to interfere because theoretical precepts coming out of the Soviet Union indicated that the country was not yet "ripe" for action. A CIA analyst who followed Iran's communists at the time said that in his view the Tudeh was "politically not ready" and did not want to "contend" with Mosaddeq and the National Front who were "really too much for them." He speculated that the clandestine branch of the agency had tried to create a "false impression" about the Tudeh's strength in order to influence the American and British governments to move ahead with a coup. He acknowledged that the CIA knew little about the nature and extent of Tudeh connections with Moscow or about Kremlin intentions toward Iran.[87]

Deliberately or not, officials elsewhere in the U.S. government magnified the scale and immediacy of the Tudeh threat to a degree that made inaction unacceptable—at least to the incoming Eisenhower administration. Still, this sort of hyperbolic perspective was entirely in keeping with the ideological atmosphere of the times.

The impact of the anticommunist mood in America showed even more clearly during the 1952 presidential election campaign. The Republicans challenging Truman's record played heavily on the charge that he had not been firm enough against the communist threat either at home or abroad. While vice presidential candidate Richard Nixon reprised his role on the House Un-American Activities Committee, future secretary of state Dulles assailed the Democrats' foreign policy program, even criticizing the White House for letting Iran become "a second China."[88] Eisenhower, too, felt at pains to identify himself with these sentiments, even though he had played a key role in implementing both Roosevelt's and Truman's policies. He publicly insisted that he was as determined as anyone that "any kind of Communistic, subversive or pinkish influence be uprooted from responsible places in our government." In a campaign speech in Denver, he declared: "If we had been less trusting, if we had been less soft and weak, there would probably have been no war in Korea!"[89] As president, Eisenhower stepped back from the heat of the elections, but in the public mind he and his more uncompromising aides had already set clear expectations for a hard-hitting campaign against international communism. By the time he assumed the presidency, Iran had been a growing flashpoint in that struggle for almost two years.

Eisenhower Versus Truman

Presidents Truman and Eisenhower shared a number of basic conceptions on international affairs. Despite the rhetoric that publicly divided the two, they fundamentally agreed on the global nature and scope of American interests, the threat posed by Soviet-backed communism, and the need for the United States to play an active role on the world stage. Their general views also coincided on Iran. Both leaders were prepared to act vigorously to preserve stability, a Western political orientation, and the uninterrupted flow of oil from the country. Their differences lay mainly in how they assessed Iran's internal political situation and whether Mosaddeq was part of the solution or the problem.

Truman and Mosaddeq *(left and right),* during Mosaddeq's October 1951 visit to Washington. National Archives and Records Administration. Courtesy of the Harry S. Truman Library. National Park Service Photograph.

Truman, the record shows, never veered from his hope for a negotiated oil settlement between Great Britain and Iran. The Truman-Acheson approach presupposed that both sides, while deserving of criticism, had legitimate positions that should and could be reconciled.[90] The fact that the two men had invested considerable effort and prestige in the mediation process, and had developed a personal rapport with Mosaddeq during his October 1951 visit to the United States, contributed to their attitude. Eisenhower and his senior advisers never sought the same kind of relationship with Mosaddeq.

To be sure, frustration with Mosaddeq built up over time. Hopes for a resolution almost disappeared during critical points of the crisis, such as the expulsion of AIOC technicians (September 1951), the 30 Tir 1331 (July 1952) riots, which brought Mosaddeq back to power, and the closing of the British embassy (October 1952). After 30 Tir, Ambassador Loy Henderson became progressively more pessimistic about Mosaddeq, even questioning his mental stability.[91] Other advisers shared his pessimism and pressed for more drastic action. Truman and Acheson were not immune to these views. During a post-election transition briefing for Eisenhower in late November 1952, Acheson, with Truman present, warned that the "wholly unreasonable" attitudes of both the Iranians and the British could "bring the country to a state of chaos." He told the president-elect that it was time to consider "what the United States alone might do to solve this problem." [92] Two days later, Truman signed off on NSC 136/1, his most assertive strategy to date for dealing with potential communist aggression in Iran.

Yet, Truman and Acheson's concept of a more assertive, unilateral tack did not go beyond certain limits. Acting alone did not imply undermining Mosaddeq but bypassing Britain, largely by giving financial support to the Iranian government or by helping to open markets for oil through American companies. Any greater aggressiveness on Washington's part would be aimed at bolstering the government, not bringing it down. [93] This was the key point. To the very end of Truman's presidency there was no confidence at the top levels that a reasonable alternative to Mosaddeq existed. [94] As defense secretary Robert Lovett warned Acheson in October 1952, Mosaddeq's departure, either through resignation or "find[ing] himself overthrown by the Majles," would "most probably result in . . . the ultimate absorption of Iran in the Soviet system." [95] This was exactly the outcome the United States wanted to avoid, and it was largely for that reason that the Truman administration put off the British proposal in November 1952 to topple Mosaddeq.

Why, then, did the Eisenhower group opt for a coup d'état? Several factors came into play. The new president and his top advisers fully endorsed Iran's crucial strategic importance. The Republicans entered office in January 1953 partly on the strength of campaign promises to roll back communism across the board, and although Eisenhower himself quickly showed an aversion to confronting Moscow in Central Europe, [96] especially after the Soviet hydrogen bomb test in August 1953, he was not nearly as reluctant to act forcefully to block potential Soviet advances in the Third World. [97]

Covert action would be a vital weapon in this campaign. Based on his wartime experiences, Eisenhower was convinced of its value as a means for accomplishing sensitive missions at relatively low cost in military, political, and economic terms. Furthermore, he wholly subscribed to the views of the Doolittle Commission on clandestine operations, which he convened after the coup, and which concluded: "It is now clear that we are facing an implacable enemy whose avowed objective is world domination by whatever means and at whatever cost. There are no rules in such a game. Hitherto acceptable norms of human conduct do not apply. If the United States is to survive, long-standing American concepts of 'fair play' must be reconsidered. We must . . . learn to subvert, sabotage and destroy our enemies by more clever, more sophisticated, and more effective methods than those used against us." [98]

Eisenhower was bolstered in these views by several high-level advisers who had served under Truman. Although Truman had created the CIA, vested it with authority to carry out covert operations, and then authorized a stream of highly risky ventures behind Soviet lines—much more hazardous than Eisenhower ever permitted—he eventually scaled back on his support for clandestine activities. Most of these sensitive operations had ended in catastrophe, and particularly after the Soviets acquired nuclear weapons he was anxious to avoid sparking a conflict with Moscow. One result of that decision was to alienate a number of senior intelligence officers who began to look to a new president to succeed Truman who would reinvigorate covert operations. These "crossovers" included Allen W. Dulles, who was promoted from deputy to director of the CIA, Walter Bedell Smith, the former CIA chief who was named undersecretary of state, and Frank Wisner, who became head of the agency's clandestine services division. [99] All three later supported the coup d'état against Mosaddeq. [100]

Eisenhower's greater readiness to use covert action did not mean that he had made up his mind immediately to overthrow Mosaddeq. If anything, his

A proponent of aggressive anti-Soviet policies, CIA director Allen Dulles gave early encouragement to the idea of a coup against Mosaddeq. Courtesy of the Princeton University Library.

natural cautiousness led him to explore other avenues for settling the crisis. Ambassador Henderson, one of the administration's most trusted Iran experts, discussed negotiating proposals with Mosaddeq at least until early March 1953, and he continued to back negotiations for another two months after that.[101] Eisenhower, and even Dulles, brought up other ideas for keeping Mosaddeq afloat. In early spring, the president mused to his advisers, "If I had $500,000,000 of money to spend in secret, I would get $100,000,000 of it to Iran right now."[102] Foreign Secretary Anthony Eden noted that Eisenhower continually sought "some imaginative way of making some new approach to the Persian problem which would prevent the country being taken into the Soviet orbit. . . . The President kept repeating that we could not do nothing."[103] Eisenhower was probably so insistent because the final option (already under consideration) was so extreme, and he may have wanted to satisfy himself, and others afterward, that he had ruled out every alternative.

The factor that finally tipped the scales for Eisenhower was the belief that Mosaddeq was likely to be the vehicle for communism's accession to power in Iran instead of an obstacle to that eventuality. Unlike Truman and Acheson, Eisenhower's top advisers maintained that Mosaddeq, because of his perceived character flaws and growing political isolation, would have to be replaced. A turning point in official thinking on this point came in February 1953 when the bulk of Mosaddeq's remaining allies in the National Front formally severed ties with him, leaving the Tudeh Party as his only visible source of organized support.[104] By early March, the State Department reached the "very gloomy" assessment that Mosaddeq could not keep himself in power, that the shah was "hopeless," the army unreliable, and the acceptable alternatives scarce.[105] After the prime minister turned down yet another oil proposal on March 20, the president and his closest advisers were ready seriously to consider a different path.

The overarching goals of the late Truman and early Eisenhower administrations toward Iran were identical—to prevent the country's loss to the Soviet camp. Only their prescriptions differed. But given Truman's steady evolution in attitude throughout his term, it is still an open question how he might have dealt with Iran had he stayed in office beyond January 1953 and perhaps come to the difficult conclusion that his diplomatic approach had failed. After all, by late 1952 he had made the groundbreaking determination that keeping Iran out of the Soviet sphere might be worth the risk of global war, thus raising the level of U.S. military commitment to the region. At the same time, he had authorized planning for expanded special operations (utilizing the TPBEDAMN network as the designers of the August coup later would) along with other interventionist steps, indicating that he was willing in principle to intervene depending on the circumstances. And although the policy changes he implemented still envisioned reacting to a communist takeover or attempted seizure of power, rather than initiating action, it is entirely possible that events such as the February 1953 rift within the National Front would have progressively eroded his confidence in Mosaddeq's ability to hold off the communist threat. In the face of a continuing downward spiral inside Iran, and against the backdrop of rising cold war tensions, Truman may well have reached the same conclusion as Eisenhower—that it would be more dangerous to wait for a communist first strike than to steal the march with a preemptive coup.

7

The 1953 Coup d'État Against Mosaddeq

Mark J. Gasiorowski

In November 1952, Christopher Montague Woodhouse of Britain's Secret Intelligence Service and Sam Falle of Britain's Foreign Office met with officials of the U.S. Central Intelligence Agency in Washington. Their ostensible purpose was to discuss covert operations the two countries were undertaking in Iran to prepare for a possible war with the Soviet Union. After these discussions, they proposed that the United States and Britain jointly carry out a coup d'état against Iranian prime minister Mohammad Mosaddeq. The British had been trying to overthrow Mosaddeq since he was named prime minister in April 1951 after leading a movement to nationalize Iran's British-controlled oil industry. Their latest effort, undertaken in collaboration with retired general Fazlollah Zahedi, had collapsed in October 1952, resulting in the arrest of several of Zahedi's collaborators and leading Mosaddeq to break diplomatic relations with Britain. Having failed repeatedly to overthrow Mosaddeq, and no longer having an embassy to work from in Iran, the British hoped the Americans now would take up the task.[1]

The CIA officials who participated in this initial meeting were surprised by the British proposal and said only that they would study it. Woodhouse and Falle then met with Assistant Secretary of State Henry Byroade and other State Department officials, who were unenthusiastic about the proposal but also agreed to study it. They also met with CIA deputy director Allen Dulles, who was slated to become CIA director under president-elect Dwight Eisenhower, and with Frank Wisner, the head of CIA covert operations. Dulles and Wisner expressed interest in the proposal and said Eisenhower and Allen Dulles's brother, secretary of state-designate John Foster Dulles, might agree to it after the new administration was inaugurated in January. Woodhouse and Falle had brought with them the names of fifteen Iranians the British considered appropriate candidates to replace Mosaddeq, although Fazlollah Zahedi was their first choice. They discussed these names with CIA officials, who agreed that Zahedi was the best candidate. At about the same time, British officials in London proposed a joint coup to Kermit Roosevelt, the thirty-six-year-old grandson of Theodore Roosevelt and head of CIA covert operations in the Middle East, who was returning home from a trip to the region. Roosevelt expressed interest and said he had already been thinking about the idea himself.[2]

These discussions eventually led to the joint CIA–SIS coup against Mosaddeq that occurred on August 19, 1953. This chapter gives a detailed account of the coup, focusing first on the decision making and preparations that preceded it and then on the execution of the coup itself. This account is based on my interviews with many of the American and British participants, a CIA history of the coup that was leaked to the *New York Times* and published on its Web site in April 2000, the memoirs of several participants, and documents from U.S. and British historical archives.[3] My interviews clarified the broad outlines of these

Kermit Roosevelt, grandson of Theodore Roosevelt, was thirty-six years old when he took charge of the coup operation in August 1953. This formal portrait was taken shortly afterward, in the mid-1950s. Courtesy of Chase Photography, Bethesda, Maryland.

events and many crucial details, including some that are not covered in the CIA history. The CIA history confirms most of what I learned in my interviews and adds a wealth of additional detail. The memoirs and the U.S. and British archival material contain further detail, especially about events preceding the coup. These sources together provide a thorough account of the coup, although a few important issues remain unclear. Since almost all of the key participants in these events have passed away and most CIA documents on the coup have been destroyed, these issues may never be clarified.[4]

The U.S. Decision to Undertake the Coup

Since the beginning of the cold war, the United States had considered Iran a vital Western ally because of its strategic location between the Soviet Union and the Persian Gulf oil fields. After the 1945–46 Azerbaijan crisis, when Soviet-backed separatists tried to create "autonomous republics" in two of Iran's northern provinces, the main concern U.S. officials had about Iran was that political instability might emerge there, creating conditions that could be exploited by the communist Tudeh (Mass) Party. The Tudeh Party was closely aligned with the Soviet Union and was quietly expanding its cadres and infiltrating key institutions during this period, with the goal of eventually seizing power. U.S. officials believed that the Tudeh was pursuing a popular-front strategy that involved building alliances with progressive noncommunist forces. They were deeply concerned that it would try to subvert the National Front (*Jebheh-ye Melli*), a coalition of political parties and prominent individuals established by Mosaddeq in 1949 to promote democracy and nationalization of the oil industry. After Mosaddeq became prime minister, U.S. officials feared that the dispute with Britain over oil nationalization would create political unrest that would strengthen the Tudeh and make Mosaddeq increasingly dependent on it, perhaps enabling the Tudeh to seize power and bring Iran into the Soviet camp. With memories of the Azerbaijan crisis and the 1948 Soviet-backed coup in Czechoslovakia still fresh, and with a bitter war against Soviet-backed forces raging in Korea, these fears were very real.[5]

The Truman administration knew that Mosaddeq was very wary of the Tudeh and the Soviet Union and believed that his popularity could make him an effective bulwark against Tudeh influence. As a result, U.S. officials initially developed a positive relationship with Mosaddeq, making a series of proposals to settle the oil dispute, persuading Britain not to invade Iran in May 1951 and again in September 1951, and hosting Mosaddeq in Washington in October

1951. However, when Mosaddeq resigned in July 1952 and was swept back into office in a tumultuous popular uprising, U.S. officials became deeply concerned that political instability would grow in Iran, perhaps giving the Tudeh an opportunity to seize power. They therefore conducted a thorough review of the situation in Iran, considering all possible means of preventing further deterioration, including a coup. However, they soon concluded that Mosaddeq was "the only and uncertain chance of preventing the rapid spread of chaos," and they decided to continue supporting him and not to back a coup against him.[6]

Soon after the July 1952 uprising, Mosaddeq persuaded Parliament to grant him expanded powers so he could circumvent the obstructionist activity of his British-backed opponents. However, in the following months several key allies left Mosaddeq's coalition and began to work against him. The most important was Ayatollah Abolqasem Kashani, a prominent clergyman and political activist, who was a leading member of Mosaddeq's coalition and had played a key role in organizing the July uprising. Kashani was elected Speaker of Parliament in August. He then met several times with Fazlollah Zahedi, who had been approached by the British as a possible candidate for anti-Mosaddeq activity, and encouraged Zahedi to work against Mosaddeq. U.S. officials received reports in this period that Kashani also met with Tudeh leaders, who agreed to help him replace Mosaddeq and work against U.S. influence in Iran. Several other key members of the coalition also turned against Mosaddeq, including Hossein Makki, Abolhasan Ha'erizadeh, and Mozaffar Baqa'i, who headed the prolabor, anticommunist Toilers (*Zahmatkeshan)* Party. U.S. officials were very alarmed by these events, viewing them as evidence that Mosaddeq was losing control over the situation. They were especially concerned about the growing strength and independence of Kashani, who they believed was hostile to Western interests and more willing than Mosaddeq to tolerate the Tudeh.[7]

In light of these trends, Iran analysts in the CIA and other U.S. government agencies undertook a comprehensive review of conditions in Iran, producing a National Intelligence Estimate (NIE) on Iran in mid-November 1952. The NIE did not foresee severe political instability or a Tudeh seizure of power in the near future, stating, "It appears probable that a National Front government will remain in power through 1953." It also stated that Mosaddeq "almost certainly desires to keep US support as a counterweight to the USSR." However, the NIE warned that "if present trends in Iran continue unchecked beyond the end of 1953, rising internal tensions and continued [economic] deterioration . . . might lead to a breakdown of government authority and open the way for at least a gradual assumption of control by [the] Tudeh." The National Security Council revised its statement of U.S. policy toward Iran in mid-November, concluding that "the Iranian situation contains very great elements of instability" and "failure to arrest present trends in Iran involves a serious risk to the national security of the United States."[8]

U.S. officials promised Woodhouse and Falle in November 1952 that they would study the British proposal for a coup. In early January 1953, Iran analysts reexamined the situation and produced an updated version of the NIE. The updated NIE was almost identical to the original version, implying that its authors believed no substantial changes had occurred in Iran since early November. The State Department's Office of Intelligence Research also carried out a major study of Iran at this time that drew similar conclusions.[9]

Almost all U.S. officials working on Iran at the time shared the view that a Tudeh takeover was not imminent but might occur if conditions did not improve. However, they differed considerably about what approach the United States should take to prevent a Tudeh takeover. Secretary of State Dean Acheson continued to oppose a coup and still hoped to forestall a Tudeh takeover by resolving the oil dispute. Accordingly, in November 1952 he instructed U.S. ambassador to Iran Loy Henderson to make another attempt to settle the dispute. Outgoing president Harry Truman presumably shared this view. Assistant Secretary of State Byroade and Ambassador Henderson also opposed a coup and preferred diplomatic efforts to resolve the crisis, although both later changed their minds. Henderson's deputy in the Tehran embassy, Gordon Mattison, also opposed a coup, as did CIA chief of station Roger Goiran, who reportedly viewed the idea as "putting U.S. support behind Anglo-French colonialism." Goiran loyally participated in some of the planning sessions for the coup and helped prepare for it in Tehran, and he may eventually have come to support it. However, he inexplicably stepped down as station chief two weeks before the coup began. Several CIA Iran specialists in Washington also opposed the coup.[10]

However, top officials in the incoming Eisenhower administration favored a more aggressive approach toward the Soviet Union and its allies, both globally and in Iran. During the 1952 election campaign, at the height of the cold war and the "Red Scare" in Washington, John Foster Dulles and other Republicans had called for a "rollback of the Iron Curtain" and accused Truman of letting Iran become "a second China." Although their enthusiasm for "rollback" later waned, Dulles, his brother Allen, and other officials slated for top positions in the new administration were eager to take a more aggressive posture toward the

Soviets. They also were more eager than their predecessors to use the CIA's covert political action capabilities. The Dulles brothers discussed the British proposal for a coup frequently in the weeks before Eisenhower was inaugurated on January 20, 1953. Another important advocate was Walter Bedell Smith, who was CIA director under Truman and became Dulles's undersecretary of state. Frank Wisner and Kermit Roosevelt of the CIA strongly favored a coup as well, as did John Waller, who had just returned to CIA headquarters after serving in Iran since 1946.[11]

Soon after Eisenhower was inaugurated, Woodhouse and a British Foreign Office official traveled to Washington and had a series of meetings with U.S. officials to discuss the coup proposal. In a meeting they had with the Dulles brothers, Roosevelt, and Smith, John Foster Dulles informally approved their proposal and agreed that Zahedi should replace Mosaddeq. He also named Roosevelt to lead the operation, which was given the code name TPAJAX. Eisenhower still hoped that political stability could be restored in Iran by resolving the oil dispute. In a March 4 National Security Council meeting, he stated that the United States should consider disassociating itself from the British position and make a $100 million loan to Iran. However, a week later, after Mosaddeq broke off the last round of oil negotiations and British foreign secretary Anthony Eden implored Dulles not to assist Iran, Eisenhower changed his position and declared that a unilateral U.S. initiative of this sort almost certainly would not work. The CIA was authorized to begin planning a coup at some point in March, and Henderson and Goiran were then informed of the decision. On April 4, $1 million was given to the Tehran CIA station for use "in any way that would bring about the fall of Mosaddeq," subject to the approval of Goiran and Henderson.[12]

Conditions continued to deteriorate in Iran during the winter and spring of 1953. Henderson's attempt to resolve the oil dispute foundered and was conclusively rejected by Mosaddeq on March 9. Kashani, Baqa'i, and other prominent figures moved increasingly into the anti-Mosaddeq camp, especially after Mosaddeq won a bitter struggle to renew his expanded powers in early January. Zahedi and his allies created an incident that led Iran's monarch, Shah Mohammad Reza Pahlavi, to threaten to leave Iran in late February. Kashani and other opposition leaders then organized large crowds that attacked Mosaddeq's home and clashed violently with his supporters, in what Fakhreddin Azimi calls a "proto-coup." Zahedi and other retired military officers were arrested briefly in connection with these events. Although the Tudeh Party was not actively involved, the U.S. embassy received reports afterward that it was drawing closer to Mosaddeq. In late April, close associates of Zahedi and Baqa'i kidnapped and murdered Mosaddeq's police chief, Gen. Mahmud Afshartus, in what was widely considered another coup attempt. In addition, Soviet leader Joseph Stalin died suddenly in March, creating uncertainty about the future course of Soviet foreign policy.[13]

These events led U.S. officials to become increasingly concerned about Iran during this period. They continued to believe that a Tudeh takeover was not imminent. However, the defections of Kashani and other National Front leaders had weakened Mosaddeq by reducing his ability to organize crowds in the streets. As a result, U.S. officials believed that Mosaddeq would have to rely increasingly on the Tudeh, which could mobilize crowds on his behalf. Moreover, Mosaddeq's rejection of the proposed oil agreement meant Iran's economy would continue to deteriorate, increasing popular unrest and playing into the hands of the Tudeh and its popular-front strategy. These adverse trends reinforced the conviction of U.S. officials who already favored a coup and led some key U.S. officials who had opposed the idea earlier—Byroade, Henderson, and perhaps Goiran—to change their minds. However, a few U.S. officials remained resolutely opposed to a coup.[14]

The Coup Plan

CIA specialists on Iran began to prepare for the coup after they were authorized to do so in March. They studied the situation and completed a preliminary report on April 16 that concluded that a CIA-backed coup was feasible and Zahedi was the best candidate to replace Mosaddeq. The CIA favored Zahedi because he was courageous, well respected, pro-American, and the only person openly vying for the premiership. U.S. officials then formally decided that the CIA should carry out the operation jointly with the SIS. They arranged to have CIA consultant Donald Wilber and SIS officer Norman Darbyshire meet in Nicosia, Cyprus, in mid-May to draw up the initial draft of a plan for the coup. Wilber was an architect and archaeologist who had worked extensively in Iran and other Middle Eastern countries in the 1930s and served in Iran during World War II in the CIA's predecessor, the Office of Strategic Services (OSS). After the war he earned a doctorate at Princeton and worked part-time for the CIA, specializing in psychological warfare operations in the Middle East and South Asia. In this capacity he traveled frequently to Iran and was stationed there from January to July 1952, running the CIA station's main political action operation. Darbyshire had served in Iran for many years, eventually running

Donald Wilber, Princeton-
educated scholar of Middle
Eastern architecture, principal
planner for TPAJAX, and author
of an internal CIA history of the
coup. Courtesy of V. Peggy
Wilber.

the main SIS political action operation. He now headed the SIS's Iran station, which had been moved to Nicosia after Mosaddeq broke diplomatic relations with Britain.[15]

Wilber and Darbyshire worked on the initial draft from May 13 until May 30, maintaining contact with CIA headquarters and the Tehran CIA station through a special three-way communications channel that had been set up for this purpose. Darbyshire and other British officials were very deferential in these and subsequent meetings, allowing the CIA to take the lead in planning the coup. Wilber and Darbyshire began by reviewing the most prominent Iranian political figures of the day to determine whether Zahedi really was the best candidate to replace Mosaddeq and who else might be enlisted into the operation. They quickly agreed that Zahedi was the only candidate with the necessary "vigor and courage," although U.S. and British officials in the past had described him as "unscrupulous" and an "opportunist." They also agreed that every effort should be made to obtain the shah's cooperation, which would be crucial in persuading Iranian military officers and civilians to back the coup. Recognizing that the shah's indecisive personality and "pathological fear of British intrigues" might make this difficult, they concluded that forceful efforts would be needed to persuade him to support the plot.[16]

The coup planners then discussed how the operation would be carried out. Darbyshire described to Wilber the main SIS political action network in Iran, which was run by the three Rashidian brothers. The Rashidians had been working for the British since World War II and had built up a network of contacts and operational agents that encompassed much of Iran's political elite, including members of Parliament and other politicians, members of the royal court, military officers, businessmen, newspaper editors, clergymen, mob leaders, and apparently even a "British" wing of the Tudeh Party. After Iran nationalized its oil industry in April 1951, the main task of this network was to destabilize Mosaddeq's government. The Rashidians did this by planting anti-Mosaddeq articles in the press, organizing anti-Mosaddeq street mobs, trying to persuade influential people to oppose Mosaddeq, and carrying out other such activities. The British gave them a monthly stipend of ten thousand pounds (approximately $28,000), which was a large amount of money in Iran at the time. The Rashidians began plotting with Zahedi against Mosaddeq in July 1952 and were among those arrested when Zahedi's British-backed plot was broken up in October. The British then developed a preliminary plan for a coup under which the Rashidians would use their network to seize control of Tehran and arrest Mosaddeq and his ministers. This was the plan Woodhouse and Falle proposed to U.S. officials in November 1952, and Darbyshire presumably brought it with him to Nicosia.[17]

Wilber told Darbyshire about the CIA's main political action network in Iran, which had first been created in the late 1940s for an anti-Soviet operation code-named TPBEDAMN. TPBEDAMN was created to counter the Soviet Union's extensive overt and covert political activity in Iran, most of which was carried out through the Tudeh Party, which had an elaborate propaganda apparatus and held frequent rallies and demonstrations. Under TPBEDAMN, Wilber and other CIA psychological warfare experts prepared newspaper articles, cartoons, leaflets, and books and had them translated into Persian by Iranians working under TPBEDAMN. CIA officers in Tehran then disseminated this material through Iranian newspapers and other outlets in ways that disguised ("gray" propaganda) or deliberately misrepresented ("black" propaganda) their real source. Most of this propaganda consisted of newspaper articles that portrayed the Soviet Union and the Tudeh as anti-Iranian or anti-

Islamic, described the harsh reality of life in the Soviet Union, or explained the Tudeh's close relationship with the Soviets and its popular-front strategy. CIA officers also funded anticommunist organizations such as the Pan-Iranist Party, the SOMKA (*Socialist-e Melli-ye Kargaran-e Iran,* or National Socialist Workers of Iran) Party, and the Toilers Party through TPBEDAMN and paid these organizations and mob organizers like Sha'ban "the brainless" Ja'fari to attack Tudeh rallies. They even gave money to Iranian clergymen to denounce the Soviet Union and the Tudeh. These activities were carried out through Iranian agents working under TPBEDAMN, so the newspaper editors, party leaders, clergymen, and other people involved generally did not know they were being manipulated by the CIA. Britain and the Soviet Union were, of course, carrying out similar activities in Iran as well.[18]

In late 1950 or early 1951, two Iranians named Ali Jalali and Faruq Kayvani approached the U.S. embassy and offered to work on behalf of the United States to weaken Soviet influence in Iran and strengthen the monarchy. CIA station chief Goiran determined that Jalali and Kayvani had a network of their own and a good understanding of intelligence "tradecraft," which he assumed they had learned from the British or German intelligence services. Goiran arranged to have them travel to the United States, where Roosevelt and other CIA officers evaluated them and concluded that they could be very useful. They demonstrated their effectiveness in July 1951 by having agents provocateurs organize a "black" demonstration ostensibly by the Tudeh against U.S. envoy Averell Harriman, who was in Tehran trying to resolve the oil dispute. The CIA decided to hire Jalali and Kayvani at about this time, giving them the code names Nerren and Cilley. Wilber went to Tehran in January 1952 on a six-month assignment to work with Jalali and Kayvani and learn more about their network and capabilities, and they soon became the principal agents in TPBEDAMN. By the time Wilber and Darbyshire met in Nicosia, Jalali and Kayvani had over one hundred subagents in their network, and TPBEDAMN apparently had a budget in the range of $500,000 to $1 million per year— roughly 1 percent of the CIA's entire $82 million budget for covert operations. Wilber described their network to Darbyshire but did not reveal their names, telling him the names of two other Iranian agents instead.[19]

After Wilber and Darbyshire revealed the assets each country would contribute, they began to develop a plan for the coup. Their initial plan had six steps. First, the Tehran CIA station would immediately begin to destabilize Mosaddeq's government with propaganda. This destabilization campaign would be expanded sharply just before the coup to bring anti–Mosaddeq sentiment to a "fever pitch." Second, Zahedi would immediately begin to organize a network of army officers to carry out the military side of the coup, using sixty thousand dollars from the CIA and SIS. To assist him, the CIA station would, if necessary, try to "subsidize" key officers. Third, Ambassador Henderson and an unnamed U.S. envoy would try to secure the shah's cooperation and "maneuver" him into appointing Zahedi. Fourth, the Rashidians would "purchase" the cooperation of enough members of Iran's Parliament to permit a "quasi-legal" vote to dismiss Mosaddeq from office. Fifth, on the morning of "coup day," Jalali and Kayvani, the Rashidians, and unnamed religious and bazaar leaders would organize thousands of demonstrators to take sanctuary (*bast*) in the parliament compound and denounce Mosaddeq for being "anti-religious" and leading Iran toward collapse. This would trigger the quasi-legal vote in Parliament to dismiss Mosaddeq. At the same time, Zahedi's military network would take steps to stop the expected reaction by the Tudeh Party and pro-Mosaddeq Qashqa'i tribal forces. Finally, if this quasi-legal effort failed, Zahedi's military network would forcibly seize power.[20]

Wilber and Darbyshire completed this version of the plan on May 30 and sent copies to Washington and London, where CIA and SIS officers reviewed it. On May 29 CIA paramilitary warfare expert George Carroll arrived in Nicosia to begin planning the military side of the coup. Wilber, Roosevelt, Goiran, and Carroll then met in Beirut June 10–13 to work further on the plan. They decided that it would not be necessary to take action against Qashqa'i tribal forces, greatly simplifying the military planning. Goiran, who continued to oppose the coup, suggested that they develop an alternative plan that would involve backing a plot of some sort then being developed by one or two of the Amini brothers and the Qashqa'i tribal *khans* (chiefs). Goiran's colleagues agreed to keep this option alive, but they did not pursue it further. Wilber and Roosevelt then traveled to London on June 15 and met with SIS officials, who added a few minor comments on the plan but continued to defer to the Americans. They then returned to Washington on June 17 and wrote up the final version of the plan, incorporating the revisions made in Beirut and London.[21]

The final coup plan consisted of the six steps outlined in the Nicosia plan but provided more detail on how these steps would be financed and carried out. A sum of $150,000 was budgeted for the precoup destabilization campaign, whose goal was to "create, extend, and enhance public hostility and distrust and fear of Mosaddeq and his government." This campaign was to include a "massive" gray and black propaganda effort immediately before the coup, whose main themes would be that Mosaddeq was pro-Tudeh and anti-Islamic; he was deliberately destroying army morale and promoting economic collapse; he was fostering regional separatism to facilitate a Soviet invasion; and he had been corrupted by power and was being manipulated by unscrupulous advisers. One part of this propaganda effort called for the dissemination of falsified black documents detailing a secret agreement under which the Tudeh would use all of its resources to support Mosaddeq against religious leaders and the army and police. The destabilization campaign also was to include anti-Mosaddeq political activity by Islamic leaders and bazaar merchants. The plan stated that the CIA team in Iran had "firm contacts" with prominent Islamic leaders, whose "pro-Zahedi capabilities . . . are very great." These contacts almost certainly were arranged through the Rashidians. The Islamic leaders were expected to make speeches opposing Mosaddeq and supporting the shah, tell the shah privately that they supported him, and organize anti-Mosaddeq demonstrations. An Islamic "terrorist gang"—almost certainly the Fada'iyan-e Islam (Warriors of Islam)—would threaten pro-Mosaddeq officials. Bazaaris also would organize demonstrations and spread rumors against Mosaddeq. The Rashidians, Jalali, and Kayvani presumably would use their networks to assist these activities.[22]

Zahedi had already begun to receive the sixty thousand dollars allocated under the Nicosia plan for his efforts to organize a military network. Under the final plan, the CIA budgeted another seventy-five thousand dollars to enable Zahedi "to win additional friends and . . . influence key people." The final plan called for Zahedi to appoint a military secretariat headed by an officer acceptable to the United States and Britain. The CIA team carrying out the coup would brief this secretariat on the military aspects of the plan, which called for army units to arrest Mosaddeq, his chief associates, and over one hundred leading Tudeh activists; take control of Tehran's streets; and seize targets such as the army's general staff headquarters, the police and gendarmerie headquarters, the army radio station, Radio Tehran, the telephone exchange, post and telegraph offices, the parliament, the national bank, and Mosaddeq's home. The military secretariat then would recruit appropriate officers to carry out these tasks. The plan also called for Zahedi to appoint a director of press and propaganda, who would be subject to U.S. and British approval. After the coup, this individual would be responsible for running Radio Tehran and overseeing a propaganda effort aimed at promoting political stability, presumably with help from the CIA team and the TPBEDAMN network.[23]

The final plan called for an elaborate effort to persuade the shah to support the coup. It described the shah as "a creature of indecision, beset by formless doubts and fears, [who] must be induced to play his role." Ambassador Henderson had been called back to Washington by this time and would remain away from Iran until after the coup as part of a "war of nerves" against Mosaddeq, so he could no longer participate in this effort. In his place, the final plan proposed that the shah's twin sister, Princess Ashraf, be recruited to oversee an effort to persuade the shah to support the coup and back Zahedi. Asadollah Rashidian, a frequent guest at the shah's palace, would also participate in this effort, as would retired U.S. Army general Norman Schwarzkopf, who had gained the shah's confidence when he commanded Iran's gendarmerie during 1942–48. Princess Ashraf, Rashidian, and Schwarzkopf would visit the shah repeatedly and try to persuade him to sign royal decrees (*farmans*) naming Zahedi army chief of staff and calling on the army to accept Zahedi's orders, as well as signing an open letter ordering army officers to support Zahedi. Since the shah would soon "brood and . . . doubt," he would then be "removed from the capital" until after the coup, apparently to prevent him from rescinding these actions. Note that the plan did not call for the shah to sign decrees dismissing Mosaddeq and appointing Zahedi, presumably because the planners feared he might refuse to do so. The plan states that the coup would be carried out "without the shah's active cooperation," if necessary.[24]

The final plan also explained in more detail how the quasi-legal overthrow of Mosaddeq would be accomplished. It would begin with "staged attacks . . . against respected religious leaders," presumably carried out by the mob leaders in the Rashidian and TPBEDAMN networks. Other religious leaders would blame these attacks on Mosaddeq and issue statements denouncing him. They would then take sanctuary in the parliament compound and call on their followers to do the same in mosques and other public buildings throughout Tehran. The Rashidians, Jalali, and Kayvani would organize crowds to participate in this effort. At the same time, bazaar leaders would close the Tehran bazaar to dramatize the situation. Zahedi would then take over as chief of staff, arrest Mosaddeq, and carry out the other military measures described above. The members of Parliament who had been "purchased" would vote to dismiss Mosaddeq and appoint Zahedi prime minister. Zahedi would assume office, "with or without . . . a royal decree." Only then would the shah return to Tehran and, presumably, ratify the Parliament's actions. The plan also called for the latter phases of this process to be implemented if Mosaddeq offered his resignation or tried to force the shah into exile in a bid to outmaneuver his adversaries. If this quasi-legal effort failed, Zahedi's military forces would simply seize power by implementing the military aspects of the plan.[25]

Of the $285,000 budgeted for the coup under the final plan, $147,500 was to be provided by the United States and $137,500 by Britain. It is not clear whether these funds were part of the $1 million that had been given to the Tehran CIA station in April. In addition to this $1 million, $11,000 per week was allocated to the Tehran station beginning on May 20 to "purchase" members of Parliament.[26]

As the coup plan was being developed, a small group of State Department officials began examining the diplomatic aspects of the matter. They decided in early June that the United States should be prepared to make a large aid package available immediately to Mosaddeq's successor and that Britain should give assurances that it would show an appropriate measure of flexibility in resolving the oil dispute after the coup. The Foreign Office finally gave such assurances on July 23.[27]

With a detailed plan for the coup now ready, Secretary of State Dulles called a meeting of top State Department and CIA officials on June 25. The group unanimously endorsed the plan, although Kermit Roosevelt believed that at least three senior State Department officials who participated in the meeting quietly opposed the coup. This decision was communicated to London, where Prime Minister Winston Churchill and Foreign Secretary Anthony Eden gave their approval on July 1. President Eisenhower and Secretary Dulles gave their final approval on July 11.[28]

Anticipating that the operation would be approved, the CIA on June 22 created two teams in Washington to prepare for the coup. John Waller was put in charge of these teams and reported directly to deputy CIA director Frank Wisner, bypassing the CIA's Iran desk. One team, headed by Carroll, prepared a detailed plan for the military side of the coup, which Carroll then would present to Zahedi and his military secretariat. The other team, headed by Wilber, was responsible for preparing psychological warfare material to be used in the precoup destabilization campaign, including anti-Mosaddeq newspaper articles, cartoons, broadsheets, and wall posters. Roosevelt, who was to lead the coup, traveled to Iran in mid-July, arriving on July 19. Carroll, who was to oversee the military aspects of the operation, arrived in Iran on July 21. Goiran left Iran on August 2 and was replaced as station chief by Joe Goodwin, a former journalist who had covered the Azerbaijan crisis and had served in the CIA station since September 1952. CIA officer John Leavitt was sent to Nicosia to maintain liaison with the SIS Iran station and oversee the Tehran-Nicosia-Washington communications channel. The Tehran CIA station arranged to maintain covert liaison with Zahedi, who was in hiding at this time, through his son Ardeshir; and it established direct contact with the Rashidians in late June.[29]

The Military Network

Carroll's military planning team began its activities by trying to determine which senior officers in the Iranian armed forces might be willing to participate in the coup. They quickly realized that neither the CIA nor U.S. military intelligence sources had much information about Iran's officer corps. They therefore asked the Tehran CIA station to find out which officers Zahedi was planning to work with and to gather information on its own about the officer corps and the organizational structure of the armed forces. The Tehran station soon reported back that most senior officers were loyal to Mosaddeq, including army chief of staff Gen. Taqi Riahi and the commanders of at least three of the five army brigades based in Tehran. Carroll also sought information from the SIS, which reported that a Colonel Ashrafi, who was military governor of Tehran and commander of Tehran's Third Mountain Brigade, was willing to participate in the coup. Carroll's team therefore developed an initial plan that called for the Third Mountain Brigade to arrest Riahi and his staff and neutralize all other military forces in Tehran, which consisted of two additional infantry brigades and two armored brigades. They also enlisted the cooperation of Col. Abbas Farzanegan, an Iranian military attaché in Washington who was working for the CIA as a translator in the TPBEDAMN operation. Farzanegan was given special training and a lie detector test in Washington and sent to Tehran in early July.[30]

Carroll traveled to London on July 15 to work more on the military plan with SIS officials. They finalized lists of Iranian civilians, military personnel, and Tudeh members who would be arrested during the coup. They also developed a list of targets in Tehran that would be neutralized, including Riahi's office, the military communications network, the Ministry of Post and Telegraph, and a machine gun factory. While Carroll was in London, Zahedi finally told the Tehran CIA station which officers he planned to work with. He did not have reliable contacts in any of the five Tehran brigades. Instead, he planned to work with the shah's Imperial Guard, a unit consisting of seven hundred handpicked soldiers, which was commanded by Col. Ne'matallah Nasiri; with the army garrison at Kermanshah (525 kilometers west of Tehran), which was commanded by Col. Teimur Bakhtiar; and with units from the army's transportation branch, the police, and the border guard. Zahedi had failed to appoint a military secretariat, as called for in the coup plan. This information was passed on to Carroll, who concluded that Zahedi's assets were inadequate for carrying out the coup and that the shah might realize this and refuse to support the plot. It was clear to the CIA team that "it would be necessary for CIA to seize the initiative and to furnish [Zahedi] with a military plan and military forces." [31]

Carroll arrived in Tehran on July 21 and made contact with Farzanegan, who had been renewing his contacts in the officer corps. Farzanegan reported that his old friends Gen. Nader Batmanqelich and Col. Hassan Akhavi might be useful. Carroll told Farzanegan to determine what assets Akhavi had. After a long delay Akhavi reported that he was in touch with three colonels who might be useful. He also reported that Colonel Ashrafi could not be trusted and that Batmanqelich lacked courage but might be willing to participate if he was appointed chief of staff after the coup. Akhavi introduced Carroll to a Colonel Zand-Karimi, deputy commander of the Second Mountain Brigade, who claimed to have a variety of useful contacts. Carroll, Farzanegan, and Akhavi then met repeatedly with Zand-Karimi on August 6–8 and, based on his contacts, developed a list of some forty officers who held command positions in the five Tehran brigades and the police and might be useful in carrying out the coup. These officers became the military network for the coup. Farzanegan, Akhavi, and Zand-Karimi became the military secretariat and helped Carroll develop the final version of the military plan. [32]

On August 9 or 10, Colonel Akhavi met with the shah and described the military network to him. The shah told Akhavi he wanted the armed forces' support if he decided to back the coup. This statement helped the military secretariat recruit officers into the military network. The shah also asked Akhavi to meet with Zahedi, who did not know Akhavi or Zand-Karimi. On August 11 Akhavi met with Zahedi, who agreed to appoint Batmanqelich chief of staff. Zahedi then met with Farzanegan and asked him to head his military bureau and serve as his liaison with the CIA team. A retired general named Guilanshah, who was a long-standing ally of Zahedi, also joined the military network. Zahedi also met with Batmanqelich and with Zand-Karimi, who explained the military plan to him. On August 13 Carroll, Batmanqelich, and the military secretariat met and decided that the military network could be mobilized for action within forty-eight hours of the shah's decision to support the coup. They also decided to have Colonel Nasiri of the Imperial Guard deliver the shah's decree dismissing Mosaddeq. [33]

The Precoup Destabilization Campaign

The plan for TPAJAX called for the Tehran CIA station to use the TPBE-DAMN and Rashidian networks to destabilize Mosaddeq's government with propaganda and other covert means in the months prior to the coup.

Although TPBEDAMN was initially authorized as an anti-Soviet and anti-Tudeh operation, the Tehran CIA station had been carrying out covert activities against Mosaddeq and the National Front under its auspices at least since the summer of 1952. As discussed above, the Truman administration continued to support Mosaddeq during this period. However, Roosevelt and other top CIA officials had concluded by this time that Mosaddeq's refusal to settle the oil dispute on terms acceptable to the British was creating political instability in Iran, making a Tudeh takeover increasingly likely. Accordingly, despite Truman's policy of supporting Mosaddeq, by the summer of 1952 CIA leaders had instructed Wilber and the other CIA officers working on TPBEDAMN to carry out covert activities aimed at undermining Mosaddeq and the National Front.[34]

The main goals of this activity seem to have been to discredit Mosaddeq and other National Front leaders and create splits within the National Front. Much of this was aimed at Ayatollah Kashani, whom U.S. officials considered an anti-American, populist demagogue and a likely target of Tudeh overtures. CIA officers disseminated propaganda that attacked Kashani and tried to create friction between him and Mosaddeq. In an effort to build a clerical alternative to Kashani and drive pious Iranians away from the National Front, they gave money indirectly to a clergyman named Mohammad Taqi Falsafi, and possibly to other clergymen as well. Ironically, CIA officers also tried unsuccessfully to establish direct contact with Kashani in this period, and they indirectly gave him money. In addition, CIA officers tried to turn the Toilers and Pan-Iranist Parties against Mosaddeq and provoke tension between pro-Mosaddeq and anti-Mosaddeq factions within these parties. In one case, a CIA contract officer approached Toilers' leader Baqa'i in the fall of 1952 and encouraged him to break with Mosaddeq, and the CIA gave Baqa'i money. The CIA also approached National Front leader Hossein Makki and Ayatollah Mohammad Behbahani, a well-known cleric, and may have given them money as well. The CIA's financial support for Falsafi, Kashani, and most or all of these other figures was provided through Iranians working under TPBEDAMN, so the recipients generally did not know the real source of this money. The Rashidians were carrying out similar activities on behalf of the British at this time.[35]

It is not clear how much of an impact these activities or the parallel activities carried out by the Rashidians had in undermining Mosaddeq. Kashani, Baqa'i, Makki, and other National Front leaders had begun to turn against Mosaddeq by the fall of 1952, and they had conclusively broken with him by early 1953. Moreover, the Toilers and Pan-Iranist Parties both split into pro-Mosaddeq and anti-Mosaddeq factions in late 1952. This was precisely the time in which these activities were being carried out. However, these individuals were very ambitious and opportunistic and clearly had their own motives for breaking with Mosaddeq. Although new sources of financial support and hostile articles in the press may have contributed to their decisions to turn against Mosaddeq, it seems unlikely that they were as important in this regard as the personal motives of these individuals. Moreover, the CIA officers who carried out these activities disagreed among themselves about their impact: one believed they were "important" in turning Kashani and Baqa'i against Mosaddeq, but another believed their effect was "limited." [36] While it is impossible now to judge how much of an impact these activities actually had, it seems best to conclude that they played only a minor role in undermining Mosaddeq at this time.

Whatever their earlier impact may have been, the scope of these anti-Mosaddeq activities increased sharply after the May 1953 Nicosia meetings. One such set of activities may have been an effort by the CIA team to "purchase" members of Parliament with the eleven thousand dollars per week allocated for this purpose on May 20. Parliament had only seventy-nine members at the time, so this would have been a large amount of money for this purpose. Severe tension had existed for several months between Mosaddeq and his opponents in Parliament, who were now led by Kashani and Baqa'i. Although Mosaddeq's opponents often could not muster a majority to vote against him, they effectively paralyzed Parliament by preventing a quorum from forming. These tensions continued after late May. Although pro-Mosaddeq members managed to oust Kashani as Speaker by a 41–31 vote on July 1, they were not able to prevent a vote several days later appointing Hossein Makki to supervise the government's monetary policy. With Makki in this powerful position and with Parliament effectively paralyzed, Mosaddeq called on his supporters in Parliament to resign. Although many members did resign, Parliament remained open. Mosaddeq then staged a referendum on August 4 in which Iranians voted overwhelmingly to dissolve Parliament. There were separate polling stations for yes and no votes, producing sharp criticism of Mosaddeq. Mosaddeq blamed the deadlock in Parliament on "agents of foreigners" and justified the referendum by saying that almost half of the members of Parliament were on the British payroll, which may well have been true. Mosaddeq's government also closed down an opposition newspaper in early August. [37]

Another set of anti-Mosaddeq activities the CIA carried out after the Nicosia meetings was an "all-out" propaganda campaign. Wilber's psychological warfare team prepared a large amount of propaganda material at CIA headquarters and sent it by courier to Tehran on July 19. The CIA station then began to distribute this material on July 22 through the TPBEDAMN and Rashidian networks, who placed it in some twenty newspapers. Most of this material was distributed in Tehran, although some was used in Azerbaijan. One aspect of the propaganda campaign was an effort to turn clerical leaders against Mosaddec by issuing black propaganda in the name of the Tudeh that threatened these leaders with "savage punishment" if they opposed Mosaddeq. Another was an effort to discredit Mosaddeq by claiming he was Jewish. The CIA team also "relentlessly" attacked Mosaddeq for the conduct of the August 4 referendum. The CIA history states, "There can be no doubt whatsoever that this [propaganda] campaign . . . reached a very large audience and . . . directly influenced their thinking in a most positive way." CIA officials in Washington also tried to generate support for the coup by planting articles hostile to Mosaddeq in the U.S. press, including one in the August 10 issue of *Newsweek* that was titled "Iran: Reds. . . . Taking Over." [38]

The CIA team also used more aggressive means to undermine Mosaddeq in the weeks prior to the coup. Its Iranian agents made threatening "black" phone calls to clerical leaders in the name of the Tudeh and carried out a "sham bombing" at the home of one of these clerical leaders. They also had a "stink bomb" thrown into a Tehran mosque, and they may have arranged other attacks on mosques. As with the black propaganda, the goal of these activities was to turn clerical leaders against Mosaddeq. As part of its "war of nerves" against Mosaddeq, the CIA team persuaded the heads of the U.S. economic and military assistance groups in Iran to reduce their contact with pro-Mosaddeq officials. British officials developed plans to shut down Tehran's central telephone exchange. CIA officers also took steps to neutralize the Qashqa'i-Amini "plot" mentioned above and prevent Qashqa'i tribal forces from assisting Mosaddeq. Henderson's deputy, Gordon Mattison, apparently met with leaders of the Qashqa'i-Amini group and tried to "divert [their] attention . . . from the real purpose of TPAJAX." CIA officers were in regular contact with the Qashqa'i *khans* during this period, and CIA station chief Goodwin traveled to southern Iran while the coup plot was underway to discourage the Qashqa'i from helping Mosaddeq. British officials offered to use their contacts to foment tribal revolts in the Qashqa'i region, although this does not seem to have occurred. [39]

In addition to these covert activities, the United States also used overt diplomatic means to undermine Mosaddeq. Secretary of State Dulles deliberately snubbed Mosaddeq by skipping Iran when he visited Pakistan, Saudi Arabia, Iraq, and Turkey in May 1953. In late May, Mosaddeq sent a secret letter to Eisenhower asking for U.S. economic aid and hinting that communist influence in Iran might increase if it was not forthcoming. Eisenhower did not reply for a month and then sent a letter to Mosaddeq bluntly turning down his request. The U.S. embassy spread rumors in Iran about Eisenhower's letter, and the State Department then released both letters on July 9, deeply embarrassing Mosaddeq. CIA officials in Washington persuaded Secretary Dulles on July 28 to state publicly that growing Tudeh activity in Iran was of concern to the United States, putting further pressure on Mosaddeq. Finally, Ambassador Henderson conspicuously remained out of Iran for more than two months prior to the coup as part of the "war of nerves" against Mosaddeq.[40]

Although these various destabilization activities were much more extensive than those carried out earlier under TPBEDAMN and the Rashidians, it remains difficult to judge how much of an effect they had. As we have seen, Mosaddeq himself blamed "agents of foreigners" for the deadlock in Parliament; and the CIA history states that the CIA team's influence in Parliament was "at least partially responsible" for Mosaddeq's decision to hold what it considered a fraudulent referendum.[41] However, the Rashidians undoubtedly had been engaged in similar activities before this time, and parliamentary opposition to Mosaddeq does not seem to have increased much after the CIA team was authorized to "purchase" members of Parliament in late May. Therefore, while the CIA team's efforts to manipulate Parliament in this period may not have had much additional effect, it seems likely that these efforts, together with the Rashidians' earlier efforts, undermined Mosaddeq by stiffening parliamentary opposition to him, thus encouraging him to undertake the referendum. The CIA's propaganda campaign and other destabilization activities probably played some role in turning the clergy and other elements against Mosaddeq, although Kashani, most other leading clergymen, and most Iranians in general had already chosen sides by this time. Similarly, U.S. influence may have helped discourage the Qashqa'i from acting on Mosaddeq's behalf, although it is doubtful that they could have acted quickly enough to help him. Consequently, while these activities probably helped undermine Mosaddeq in the weeks prior to the coup, they seem mainly to have exacerbated trends that were already underway.

Obtaining the Shah's Support

The architects of TPAJAX believed that it was important to obtain the shah's support for the coup, both because he could confer the legitimacy of the monarchy upon it and because his approval was necessary to dismiss Mosaddeq and appoint Zahedi legally. However, there were two major obstacles to obtaining the shah's support. First, he was extremely indecisive. Second, he had repeatedly told Ambassador Henderson and Henderson's predecessor that he opposed Zahedi as prime minister.[42] The architects of TPAJAX therefore developed plans to persuade the shah to support the coup. Moreover, the CIA team intended to keep him out of Tehran while the coup was taking place so he would not change his mind; and the team was prepared to carry out the coup without his support, if necessary.

The first version of the coup plan developed in late May had called for Henderson to approach the shah about supporting the coup. Accordingly, Henderson met with the shah on May 30 and asked what he thought about Zahedi as prime minister. The shah replied that while Zahedi was not an "intellectual giant," he would be acceptable if he had broad support, came to power legally, and was given "massive economic aid" by the United States or Britain. The shah also told Henderson that he believed Mosaddeq was more capable of resolving the oil dispute and that Zahedi would not succeed if he came to power through a military coup.[43] Although these statements were more positive than the shah's previous statements about Zahedi, they certainly were not what U.S. officials had hoped for. These statements may have led the architects of TPAJAX to develop the more elaborate approach to the shah featured in the final version of the plan.

The final plan called for Princess Ashraf to lead an effort to persuade the shah to support the coup. Ashraf was in France at the time, so the CIA team asked Darbyshire and Col. Stephen Meade of the U.S. Army to go there and seek her help. Darbyshire and Meade arrived in France on July 10 and eventually located Ashraf on the Riviera on July 16, with the help of Asadollah Rashidian. Ashraf was reluctant to approach her brother about the plot. She apparently agreed to do so only after Darbyshire gave her a large sum of money and Meade made an unauthorized promise to her that the United States would support the shah in the style to which he was accustomed if the coup failed. Ashraf then arrived in Iran on July 25, producing a sharp outcry from Mosaddeq's supporters. The shah initially refused to see her, so she sent him a letter through Soleiman Behbudi, the head of the royal household (and a British agent), saying General Schwarzkopf would soon visit him. She then had a brief, stormy meeting with her brother on July 29 and returned to France. Within days Mosaddeq had learned the true purpose of Ashraf's visit.[44]

Asadollah Rashidian then visited the shah on July 30 and 31. To prove to the shah that he was speaking on behalf of the British, he arranged to have a phrase chosen by the shah broadcast over BBC radio. The shah accepted Rashidian's connection to the British but told Rashidian he needed more time to consider the situation.[45]

General Schwarzkopf agreed to approach the shah. He left the United States on July 21 under the pretext of touring the region. His main objective was to persuade the shah to support the coup and sign a royal decree naming Zahedi chief of staff. Schwarzkopf arrived several days later in Tehran, where his visit was denounced in the pro-Mosaddeq press as a "nefarious plot." He then met with the shah on August 1. The shah refused to sign the decree, saying he was not fully confident of the army's loyalty; and he asked for more time to assess the situation.[46]

During the following days, Kermit Roosevelt and Asadollah Rashidian both visited the shah several times and tried to persuade him to sign the decree and support the coup. The shah vacillated, at times agreeing to back the coup, but then changing his mind. Roosevelt threatened to leave the country and warned the shah that the United States might act without him if he refused to cooperate, but he continued to vacillate. On August 9 or 10 Colonel Akhavi met with the shah and described the military network to him, but still he refused to act. Rashidian then met with the shah and told him Roosevelt would leave the country if he did not cooperate. The shah finally agreed to sign the decree and meet with Zahedi the following day, but Rashidian failed to draw up the decree on time. The shah then went to the royal resort at Ramsar, on the Caspian Sea. Roosevelt and Rashidian decided to ask him to sign two decrees, one dismissing Mosaddeq and the other appointing Zahedi. Rashidian and another British agent drew up the decrees. On the evening of August 12, Colonel Nasiri flew the decrees to Ramsar, where the shah signed them. Nasiri returned with the decrees to Tehran on the following evening, and the shah remained at Ramsar.[47]

The Initial Coup Attempt

Mosaddeq's decision to close Parliament in early August made it impossible for Parliament to dismiss him and appoint Zahedi. Moreover, although the Rashidians had assured the CIA team that the clerical leaders included in the coup plan "would take whatever action was required of them," these leaders refused to cooperate.[48] Consequently, the quasi-legal effort to overthrow Mosaddeq was no longer feasible. The CIA team therefore improvised a new quasi-legal effort that focused on having the shah, rather than Parliament, dismiss Mosaddeq. The crucial step in this new effort was to persuade the shah to sign the decrees dismissing Mosaddeq and appointing Zahedi. After these decrees were signed, the military network would arrest Mosaddeq and his colleagues and seize control of Tehran, as envisioned in the coup plan.

Once the shah signed the decrees, the CIA team made plans for Nasiri to deliver the first decree and arrest Mosaddeq during the night of August 14–15. However, this action was inexplicably delayed until the following night, apparently by Zahedi and the military secretariat. The CIA team temporarily lost contact with Zahedi and the secretariat, so they did not learn about the delay until the night of August 14. Mosaddeq's government learned about the coup attempt on August 14 or 15, apparently through a variety of channels, and took steps to stop it. The decision to delay the arrest of Mosaddeq by one night was responsible for this breakdown in security, which led to the failure of the initial coup attempt.[49]

On the evening of August 15, Nasiri went to the Imperial Guard base in western Tehran to assemble forces to arrest Mosaddeq. Other members of the military network began to implement their parts of the coup plan as well at this time, arresting several of Mosaddeq's cabinet ministers and certain loyalist military officers, occupying (but not shutting down) the central telephone exchange, and cutting telephone lines at certain locations. As these actions were occurring, Riahi contacted the commanders of the five Tehran brigades and had them deploy troops throughout the city. Pro-Mosaddeq forces arrested Nasiri when he tried to arrest Mosaddeq at his home. Other loyalist units seized army headquarters and other strategic locations and disarmed the Imperial Guard. The military network then began to collapse, with many officers refusing to carry out their assigned tasks. The Mosaddeq allies who had been arrested were released. By 2:30 A.M. the anti-Mosaddeq forces had given up. General Batmanqelich "lost heart and went into hiding." Farzanegan fled to the U.S. embassy compound. At dawn, Radio Tehran broadcast the news that a coup attempt had been stopped.[50]

On the morning of August 16, pro-Mosaddeq army units were deployed throughout Tehran and they established control over the city. They began to arrest people suspected of participating in the coup attempt, eventually arresting Batmanqelich, Zand-Karimi, several other high-ranking officers in the military network, Baqa'i, Behbudi, Minister of Court Abolqasem Amini, the shah's confidant Ernest Perron, and scores of other suspected plotters. They also began an intense search for General Zahedi. The Tudeh published details of the coup attempt in its newspaper and held demonstrations, as did Mosaddeq sup-

porters. Foreign Minister Hossein Fatemi, who had been arrested and then released during the night, addressed a large pro-Mosaddeq demonstration near
the parliament and made a series of radio broadcasts, denouncing the shah and
calling him a traitor. Fatemi's newspaper described the royal court as a
"brothel" and said the Iranian people wanted the shah hanged. The shah fled
the country in panic without telling Zahedi or the CIA team, flying to Baghdad and later to Rome, with London apparently his eventual destination. News
that the shah had fled was broadcast that evening, and Fatemi and other Mosaddeq supporters made speeches demanding that he abdicate. On the following
day the pro-Mosaddeq press declared that the United States was involved in the
coup attempt, and Radio Tehran called for Zahedi to surrender. On August 18
the Tudeh called for a popular front of "anti-colonial organizations," abolition
of the monarchy, creation of a "democratic republic," and the expulsion of U.S.
officials from Iran. Some pro-Mosaddeq newspapers announced that the shah's
dynasty had come to an end.[51]

On the morning of August 16, the CIA team got in touch with General
Zahedi and his colleagues and took steps to prevent them from being arrested,
hiding Zahedi in the house of one of the CIA officers and hiding his son, the
Rashidians, Farzanegan, and Guilanshah in the U.S. embassy compound and
other secure locations. They also sent a series of cables to CIA headquarters explaining what had happened. Roosevelt sent the commander of the U.S. military assistance mission, Gen. Robert McClure, to see Riahi, who told him that
the shah's decree was a forgery and the army would support Mosaddeq. Mc-
Clure then suggested to Roosevelt that they support Riahi in the hope that he
might eventually try to overthrow Mosaddeq. Mattison and Melbourne told
the CIA team that they thought there was no longer any hope of success. Jalali
and Kayvani apparently wanted to end their participation in the plot but
changed their minds after Roosevelt threatened to kill them if they did so.[52]

On August 17, a message arrived from CIA headquarters advising Roosevelt to leave Iran as soon as possible. Roosevelt made contingency plans to
evacuate himself, General Zahedi, and a few other participants in a U.S. military attaché's airplane. On the following day he asked headquarters for help in
arranging the clandestine evacuation of up to fifteen people, and headquarters
told him to give up the coup attempt. In Baghdad, the shah met with the U.S.
ambassador to Iraq, telling him that "he would be looking for work shortly as
he has a large family and very small means outside of Iran," and that he hoped
eventually to move to the United States. In Rome, he told a reporter, "I hope
to go back [to Iran]. Everyone lives on hope."[53]

From Failure to Success

Despite these setbacks, neither the CIA team nor Zahedi and his colleagues were ready to give up. On the morning of August 16, soon after the initial coup attempt failed, Roosevelt drove to Zahedi's hiding place to discuss the situation. Zahedi and his son Ardeshir believed there was still some chance of success. They suggested that the plotters try to rally the army and public opinion to their side by publicizing the fact that the shah had legally dismissed Mosaddeq and appointed Zahedi.[54]

Accordingly, the CIA team made a series of efforts to publicize the shah's actions. Roosevelt sent a message through CIA headquarters to the New York office of the Associated Press explaining what the shah had done. The Associated Press then disseminated this information, and it was later picked up by Iranian newspapers. Jalali and Kayvani made copies of the shah's decrees dismissing Mosaddeq and appointing Zahedi and disseminated them through the Iranian press. They also disseminated a broadsheet stating that the coup attempt that had occurred was aimed at overthrowing the shah; and they fabricated a favorable interview with Zahedi and had it published the following day. Members of the CIA team also made copies of the shah's decrees, using a duplicating machine in the home of one of the CIA officers. The CIA team contacted Kennett Love, a reporter for the *New York Times,* and invited him to a meeting with Ardeshir Zahedi at this CIA officer's home. Ardeshir told Love about the shah's decrees and gave him copies, which he then distributed to other reporters. On the afternoon of August 16, the CIA team and Ardeshir Zahedi prepared a public statement by General Zahedi about the coup and had it disseminated. These press-related efforts continued during the following days. However, pro-Mosaddeq police units were soon posted at all Tehran print shops, making these efforts more difficult.[55]

After the CIA team learned that the shah had fled the country, it tried to have him make a favorable radio broadcast from Baghdad. CIA officers wrote statements for the shah to make and sent them to CIA headquarters to be relayed to Baghdad. The State Department opposed a U.S. effort to contact the shah, however, and suggested that the British do it. The British SIS station in Nicosia endorsed this idea and made preparations to send Darbyshire and Leavitt to Baghdad, but London opposed this effort. The shah met secretly with the U.S. ambassador in Baghdad and asked for advice on whether he should publicly oppose Mosaddeq; he posed the same question to the British ambassador through an intermediary. Acting on his own initiative, the U.S. ambassador ad-

vised the shah to make a statement emphasizing that he had acted constitutionally in dismissing Mosaddeq and that Mosaddeq's resistance constituted a coup
against him. The shah then broadcast a statement along these lines, adding that
he had not abdicated. CIA headquarters sent propaganda guidance concerning
the situation in Iran to the CIA stations in Karachi, New Delhi, Cairo, Damas-
cus, Istanbul, and Beirut. It also directed a CIA officer in France to ask the
Agha Khan, a prominent Islamic leader, to contact the shah and offer moral
support. The Agha Khan refused to do so.[56]

The CIA team also made efforts to generate support for Zahedi in the
Iranian armed forces. Either the CIA team or Zahedi's group drew up and circulated a declaration calling for the armed forces to support the shah. The U.S.
military advisory mission in Iran apparently distributed blankets, boots, uni-
forms, electric generators, and medical supplies to the Iranian armed forces on
an emergency basis "to create an atmosphere in which they could support the
shah."[57]

The CIA team also took more active steps to organize political activity
against Mosaddeq. On the evening of August 16, one of the CIA officers gave
Jalali and Kayvani fifty thousand dollars to finance their anti–Mosaddeq activities. Jalali and Kayvani then had agents provocateurs organize a raucous black
crowd to march into central Tehran on the following morning, pretending to
be a Tudeh mob. Genuine Tudeh members, who did not realize this was a
CIA-financed provocation, also came out into the streets, as did other Iranians.
These crowds created chaos in Tehran, tearing down statues of the shah and his
father, Reza Shah, attacking Reza Shah's mausoleum, and throwing stones at
mosques. The shah's picture was removed from most homes, restaurants, offices, and government ministries in Tehran. These activities continued on the
following day, with black Tudeh mobs looting and vandalizing shops, smashing
windows in mosques, clashing with Mosaddeq supporters, ransacking the
headquarters of the pro-Mosaddeq Pan-Iranist Party, and calling for the expulsion of American diplomats. Several Americans were assaulted during these
events. The Tudeh leadership responded to what they thought was a spontaneous popular uprising by calling for the abolition of the monarchy and the establishment of a democratic republic. The Rashidians may have carried out
similar black activities during this period, and the Pan-Iranists and other pro-
Mosaddeq organizations were also active in the streets. Statues of the shah were
also torn down in Tabriz and Shiraz; and pro-Mosaddeq or anti-shah activity
occurred in Kermanshah, Kerman, Babolsar, and probably other cities. With
the exception of a small demonstration in Tehran on August 18, no anti-
Mosaddeq or pro-shah street activity occurred during this period.[58]

These black activities helped undermine Mosaddeq in several ways. First, together with the informational activities described above, they contributed to the increasingly tense climate in Tehran, which led many Iranians to believe that Mosaddeq was losing control of the situation. As a result, many civilians and members of the armed forces either failed to back Mosaddeq or joined his opponents during the decisive events of August 19. Second, Ambassador Henderson, who suddenly returned to Iran on August 17, told Mosaddeq on August 18 that the mobs had been assaulting Americans and said he would recommend that all Americans leave Iran if the security forces could not provide better protection. In a fateful decision, Mosaddeq then telephoned the chief of police and ordered him to break up the mobs. The security forces, which had been confined to their barracks on the morning of August 17, attacked the "Tudeh" mobs in a "frenzy." They reappeared in the streets the following day, and some of them joined the crowds that brought down Mosaddeq. Mosaddeq also told National Front leaders not to hold demonstrations and issued an order forbidding demonstrations and calling for offenders to be arrested, blaming "agitators" for the unrest. Mosaddeq's supporters therefore were not in the streets on August 19. Finally, when the security forces attacked the "Tudeh" mobs, the Tudeh leadership ordered its cadres to withdraw. Tudeh forces therefore also were not in the streets on August 19.[59]

On the evening of August 17, Roosevelt had a long meeting with the Zahedis, Farzanegan, Guilanshah, and the Rashidians. In this meeting they decided to try to launch an uprising against Mosaddeq on August 19, based on three sets of activities. First, they decided to contact Ayatollah Behbahani and ask him to persuade Iran's leading Shi'i clergyman, Ayatollah Mohammad Hossein Borujerdi, to issue a religious decree (fatwa) calling for a holy war against communism. It is not clear whether these contacts were made, but Borujerdi did not issue such a decree. Second, they decided to seek support from army garrisons outside Tehran. Toward this end, they sent Ardeshir Zahedi and George Carroll to Isfahan and Farzanegan and another CIA agent to Kermanshah, using forged identification papers and travel documents provided earlier by CIA headquarters. The Isfahan garrison commander refused to cooperate. However, the Kermanshah commander, Colonel Bakhtiar, agreed to help and led a column of tanks and armored cars toward Tehran. They stopped in Hamedan to suppress a Tudeh demonstration but arrived in Tehran too late to play a direct role in the overthrow of Mosaddeq, although news that they were marching encouraged the participants in the coup. Third, Roosevelt and his colleagues decided to organize large anti-Mosaddeq demonstrations on August

254 | Mark J. Gasiorowski

19, based on the theme that "it was time for loyal army officers and soldiers and the people to rally to the support of religion and the throne." [60]

The CIA team worked through several channels to organize these demonstrations. The Rashidians suggested that they seek help from Ayatollah Kashani and said he could be contacted through their ally Ahmad Aramesh. In the early morning of August 19, two CIA officers therefore went to Aramesh's home and gave him ten thousand dollars to give to Kashani to organize demonstrations. It is not clear whether Kashani received this money and, if so, whether he used it for this purpose. Ayatollah Behbahani apparently played a key role in organizing the demonstrations of August 19. He also allegedly wrote lurid black letters in the name of the Tudeh Party to other clergymen, threatening to hang them in the streets. Although the CIA team may have facilitated these activities, it seems unlikely that Kashani and Behbahani knowingly cooperated with the CIA. The Rashidians almost certainly helped organize these demonstrations, although it is not clear how they did so. The notorious mob organizer Sha'ban Ja'fari also likely played a role. Ja'fari apparently was a subagent in the TPBEDAMN network under Jalali and Kayvani, so he may have received money from them to organize anti-Mosaddeq demonstrations. In addition, the SOMKA Party and a pro-shah wing of the Pan-Iranist Party, which CIA officers had often hired through TPBEDAMN to stage demonstrations and attack Tudeh rallies, were active in these demonstrations. [61]

On the morning of August 19, crowds began to form in the bazaar area in south Tehran. It is not clear how these crowds formed, although it seems likely that some of their members were organized by the CIA team's contacts and others joined spontaneously. The CIA history states that Jalali and Kayvani were in the bazaar area in connection with their propaganda activities and began to lead these crowds, working with their subagent Mansur Afshar and two others named Majidi and Rezali. Jalali led one crowd to the parliament building, stopping along the way to set fire to the office of Foreign Minister Fatemi's newspaper, *Bakhtar-e Emruz*. Afshar led another crowd to sack the offices of the Tudeh newspapers *Shahbaz, Besui-ye Ayandeh,* and *Javanan-e Demokrat*. These or other crowds also sacked the headquarters of the pro-Mosaddeq Iran Party and burned the Tudeh-sponsored Saadi Theater. Jalali led a crowd to the military police headquarters and secured the release of Colonel Nasiri and General Batmanqelich from prison. The crowds shouted pro-shah slogans and forced passing motorists to put on their headlights and display pictures of the shah to make it difficult for Mosaddeq's supporters to identify one another, apparently on instructions from the CIA team. [62]

When the CIA team learned that these crowds were marching, it instructed the Rashidians and Jalali and Kayvani to encourage the crowds to seize Radio Tehran and to try to persuade the security forces to join the crowds. Army units commanded by members of the military network began to join the crowds, and by 10:15 A.M. pro-shah forces controlled all of the main squares in Tehran. More crowds came from the bazaar area into central Tehran and were joined by onlookers who feared a return of the "Tudeh" mobs of the previous days or had become disillusioned with Mosaddeq for other reasons. Five tanks and twenty trucks filled with soldiers joined the crowds. Trucks and buses loaded with Bakhtiari tribesmen and other civilians arrived in Tehran from outlying areas, presumably funded by the CIA team's contacts. By noon, anti-Mosaddeq army and police officers had largely taken over leadership of the crowds. These crowds did not encounter resistance from substantial pro-Mosaddeq or Tudeh crowds, presumably because of the chaos and confusion of the previous days and the decisions by Mosaddeq and the Tudeh leaders to keep their supporters off the streets.[63]

The combined military and civilian crowds began to clash with pro-Mosaddeq military units and take over key locations in the early afternoon. They seized the central telegraph office and the Ministry of Press and Propaganda, enabling their leaders to send messages to other cities encouraging uprisings against Mosaddeq. Other crowds attacked police headquarters, army headquarters, and the Ministry of Foreign Affairs, where bloody fighting continued until late in the afternoon. Two thousand people backed by a tank staged a noisy demonstration at the Soviet embassy. Trucks and buses brought civilians and army personnel to the facilities of Radio Tehran, north of the city, and seized the station just after 2 P.M., after a brief clash that left three people dead. Various speakers then began to broadcast statements encouraging Iranians to support the coup, including some who apparently had been assigned this task under the coup plan.[64]

General Zahedi had been hiding for two days in the home of one of the CIA officers. At about 4 P.M., Roosevelt drove to Zahedi's hideout to arrange for him to broadcast a statement over Radio Tehran. Soon after, Guilanshah, who had been hiding in another CIA officer's home, arrived at Zahedi's hideout in a tank and brought him to Radio Tehran. Zahedi then broadcast a statement at 5:25 P.M. explaining that he was the legal prime minister and that his forces were now largely in control of the city.[65]

The decisive battle between pro- and anti-Mosaddeq forces occurred at Mosaddeq's home, which had been heavily fortified by loyalist troops. Early in the afternoon of August 19, a General Nakhi, who was apparently an agent of the CIA station, assembled members of the Imperial Guard and attacked Mosaddeq's home, which was defended by pro-Mosaddeq army units backed by three tanks. Bloody fighting ensued. Six tanks that had been involved in the seizure of Radio Tehran drove to Mosaddeq's home and joined the fighting. The two groups of tanks exchanged fire for two hours, using armor-piercing shells, and the three defending tanks were destroyed. The anti-Mosaddeq forces then destroyed the walls surrounding Mosaddeq's home and attacked the house itself. The defenders were eventually overwhelmed, in a fierce battle that reportedly took two hundred lives. One hundred other people were killed in fighting elsewhere in Tehran that day. Mosaddeq escaped over the roof of his house, but surrendered to Zahedi's forces the following day. Looters dragged Mosaddeq's possessions into the street and sold them to passersby, and his house was set on fire. The shah, still in Rome, shook violently when he heard that Mosaddeq had been overthrown and asked a reporter, "Can it be true?" [66]

Anti-Mosaddeq forces also triumphed outside of Tehran. In Tabriz, Mohammad Deyhim, the head of a small organization called Fadakaran-e Azerbaijan (Devotees of Azerbaijan) and apparently a subagent in the TPBEDAMN network, led forces that seized Radio Tabriz in the late afternoon. In Isfahan, anti-Mosaddeq forces seized the radio station; and clergymen, military officers, and followers of Baqa'i then broadcast statements in support of the shah. In Mashad, pro-shah forces looted the shops of Tudeh sympathizers and searched for Tudeh members. Other cities and towns soon fell to anti-Mosaddeq forces as well. [67]

The Aftermath of the Coup

In the days after the coup, Zahedi's forces mopped up the remaining pockets of resistance. Zahedi declared a curfew in Tehran and deployed troops and tanks throughout the city. He closed Iran's borders to prevent fugitives from fleeing. Army and police units broke up scattered pro-Mosaddeq demonstrations in Tehran and elsewhere, and pro-shah forces held demonstrations. The security forces hunted down Mosaddeq's colleagues and Tudeh Party members, arresting many. Pro-Mosaddeq newspapers were harassed or closed down. Zahedi made a speech promising to raise wages, reduce the cost of living, provide free medical care, pave roads, mechanize agriculture, permit political freedom, and hold new elections. The shah flew back to Iran on August 22 with an Iraqi fighter escort, unsure of the loyalty of his own air force. Sha'ban Ja'fari organized crowds to welcome him. An honor guard met the shah at the airport but was kept fifty yards away to prevent an assassination attempt.[68]

In the following months, Zahedi gradually eliminated all major sources of opposition. He crushed occasional National Front and Tudeh demonstrations and carried out a wave of arrests, jailing some twenty-one hundred people by the end of 1953. These arrests severely weakened the National Front and the Tudeh, and the surviving members went underground. Mosaddeq was tried in November 1953 and given a three-year prison sentence, after which he lived under house arrest until his death in 1967. Hossein Fatemi remained in hiding for many months but was eventually arrested, summarily tried, and executed. Several other top National Front leaders were given long prison terms. Pro-Mosaddeq Qashqa'i tribal forces staged an uprising near Shiraz in September but were surrounded and disarmed by army units, leaving them powerless; their leaders were then sent into exile. Some three thousand alleged Tudeh members were dismissed from government service in the months after the coup. The armed forces were purged and some eighteen hundred pro-Zahedi officers were promoted. The parliamentary elections of early 1954 were thoroughly rigged, preventing a significant opposition presence from emerging in this body. In September 1954, the secret police dismantled a large Tudeh network in the armed forces, breaking the back of the Tudeh Party. Zahedi even turned on Kashani and Baqa'i, restricting their activities and eventually banishing Baqa'i to a remote part of Iran for several months. By the time the shah dismissed him in April 1955, Zahedi had created the foundations of an authoritarian regime that remained in place until the 1978–79 revolution.[69]

The United States played a key role in facilitating the creation of this authoritarian regime. The CIA station gave Zahedi roughly one million dollars in cash immediately after the coup. Within three weeks the U.S. government gave Iran an additional $68 million in emergency aid, accounting for one-third of the estimated $200 million in oil revenue the country had lost since May 1951. During the next decade the United States gave Iran an additional $1.2 billion in aid. CIA officers helped put down the September 1953 Qashqa'i uprising and a November 1953 National Front demonstration in Tehran. They used TPBE-DAMN to support the Zahedi government and helped Zahedi's chief of propaganda, Esfandiar Bozorgmehr, who had worked in the TPBEDAMN network, carry out similar activities. The CIA station also gave Zahedi intelligence on the Tudeh and played a minor role in rigging the 1954 parliamentary elections. In September 1953 Colonel Meade was sent to Iran under cover as a military attaché to organize, train, and command a new intelligence unit, which later evolved into the shah's dreaded security agency SAVAK. It was this unit that broke up the Tudeh military network in September 1954. After Meade left Iran in early 1955, CIA personnel continued to work closely with this organization until the early 1960s, when relations became more distant. The United States also played a key role in arranging the October 1954 agreement under which Iran resumed its oil exports, giving the Iranian government a rapidly increasing source of revenue that helped defuse popular unrest in the following years.[70]

Most key participants in the 1953 coup were rewarded handsomely for their efforts. Batmanqelich was named army chief of staff and later served as minister of interior. Farzanegan was named minister of post and telegraph. Bakhtiar was promoted to general and appointed martial law governor of Tehran. Meade's intelligence unit was set up within Bakhtiar's martial law administration, and Bakhtiar later became the first head of SAVAK. Nasiri also was promoted to general, and he later headed SAVAK as well. Ardeshir Zahedi served in a series of top government positions and was later Iran's ambassador to the United States for many years; he also married (and divorced) the shah's daughter. The Rashidians became very wealthy in business, profiting from their close ties to the shah. Kermit Roosevelt traveled to London a few days after the coup, where Churchill told him, "If I had been but a few years younger, I would have loved nothing better than to have served under your command." The Dulles brothers asked Roosevelt to lead coups in Guatemala, Egypt, and other countries in the following years, but he refused, saying conditions in those countries were not favorable. He retired from the CIA in 1958 and was given the National Security medal. He then held a top position in the Gulf Oil Company and later established a successful consulting business, taking advantage of his close connections with the shah and other Middle Eastern leaders. Most of the other American participants in TPAJAX went on to have very successful careers in the CIA. Most of the British participants were very successful as well.[71]

Perhaps the most striking aspect of the coup is the dramatic change of fortune that occurred between the first coup attempt on the night of August 15–16 and the second, successful attempt on August 19. The key change that occurred is that anti-Mosaddeq crowds somehow formed on the morning of August 19 and were soon joined by army and police units and additional civilians. The combined crowds clashed with pro-Mosaddeq army units and seized key locations, establishing control over Tehran and overthrowing Mosaddeq's government by the end of the day.

Several key issues bearing on these events remain unclear. First, it is not clear exactly who organized the crowds that emerged on August 19 and, in particular, how much of a role the CIA team played in organizing them. Second, once these crowds had been organized, it is not clear how many Iranians spontaneously joined them and thus to what extent the events of August 19 reflected genuine popular discontent. Finally, it is not clear how important the CIA team's actions during the previous days—such as the precoup destabilization campaign and the black Tudeh mobs—contributed to the discontent that fueled these events. While it seems certain that the CIA team played a crucial role in the events of August 19, we have no way to determine the extent to which Iranian actors—such as Kashani, Behbahani, and the people who spontaneously joined these crowds—independently contributed to them. Since almost all of the key participants in these events have passed away and much of the existing documentary record has already been examined, these issues probably never will be fully clarified.[72]

Nevertheless, we can draw several conclusions about why the second coup attempt succeeded. First, despite the premature failure of the coup plan, it is clear that the CIA team's meticulous preparations for the coup were crucial to its success. The CIA's prior development of the TPBEDAMN network and Britain's development of the Rashidian network gave the CIA team invaluable assets for implementing the coup. The CIA sent several energetic, resourceful officers to Iran to carry out the coup. The military network developed by the CIA team provided much of the leadership for the army units that acted on August 19. The CIA team's precoup destabilization campaign and its efforts to gain the shah's cooperation undoubtedly very much influenced the events of August 16–19. Finally, the safe houses and other facilities of the Tehran CIA station and the money, forged travel documents, and other items the CIA sent to Iran in advance were essential for carrying out key aspects of the coup.

Second, after the initial coup attempt collapsed, the resourcefulness and determination of the CIA coup team were crucial to the success of the second attempt. The CIA team made various efforts to publicize the shah's dismissal of Mosaddeq and appointment of Zahedi. It took steps to generate support for Zahedi in the armed forces and persuade the garrison commanders in Isfahan and Kermanshah to cooperate. Working through Jalali and Kayvani, it organized black Tudeh mobs that helped create the chaos that emerged on August 17 and 18. Ambassador Henderson apparently played a crucial role in persuading Mosaddeq to bring the security forces back into the streets on August 18. The CIA team and its Iranian agents made various efforts first to organize the crowds that emerged on August 19 and then to steer and coordinate the crowds as they moved through Tehran. The members of the CIA team undertook these actions in an atmosphere of considerable danger, and after they had been ordered to stop the operation and leave the country. By all accounts, Kermit Roosevelt was the mastermind behind these activities and displayed considerable ingenuity and bravery. He clearly deserves much of the credit—and blame—for overthrowing Mosaddeq. Of the Iranian participants, Jalali and Kayvani, the Rashidians, and Ardeshir Zahedi seem to have been the most resourceful and courageous.

Third, it seems clear that both Mosaddeq and his colleagues and the Tudeh Party made crucial tactical mistakes during August 16–19 that contributed very much to the success of the second coup attempt. After August 16 the Mosaddeqists did not organize large demonstrations to rally their supporters and intimidate their opponents, and Mosaddeq banned all demonstrations. On August 17 Mosaddeq failed to deploy the security forces to stop the "Tudeh" mobs that were beginning to create chaos in Tehran. He also failed to restrain Foreign Minister Fatemi and others who denounced the shah and called for the abolition of the monarchy, fueling the growing chaos. Mosaddeq then changed course on August 18 and had the security forces attack the mobs, adding further to the chaos and enabling elements of the security forces to join the anti-Mosaddeq crowds the following day. Tudeh leaders pulled their cadres off the streets when the security forces attacked the mobs, leaving them unavailable to confront the anti-Mosaddeq crowds on August 19. The passivity of the Mosaddeqists and the Tudeh toward the events of August 16–19 stands in marked contrast to their actions during earlier confrontations and undoubtedly contributed to Mosaddeq's downfall.

Finally, it must be added that Mosaddeq's opponents enjoyed a great deal of luck during the fateful days of August 16–19. After the initial coup attempt failed, there was not much reason for optimism, and, indeed, many members of the coup team gave up hope. The change of fortune that occurred during these days resulted from the confluence of many disparate events whose occurrence and timing were crucial to the success of the coup. If any of these events had turned out differently, Mosaddeq might not have been overthrown.

Conclusion

Why Did Mosaddeq Fall?

Mark J. Gasiorowski

The U.S.-instigated coup d'état of August 19, 1953, against Prime Minister Mohammad Mosaddeq was a crucial turning point both in Iran's modern history and in U.S.-Iran relations. As discussed in Katouzian's chapter of this book, the coup ended Mosaddeq's tentative steps toward democracy and initiated the reestablishment of arbitrary rule under Shah Mohammad Reza Pahlavi. During the next decade the shah gradually eliminated his various rivals and alienated those elements of society that had once supported him, leaving him without a social base of support and thus setting the stage for Iran's 1978–79 revolution. Many Iranians blamed this on the United States, arguing that the 1953 coup and the extensive U.S. support for the shah in subsequent years were largely responsible for the shah's arbitrary rule. As a result, the revolution had a deeply anti-American character, and U.S.-Iran relations have remained tense ever since. Indeed, the coup has had such a powerful impact on Iran's political consciousness that many Iranians today still believe that the United States is working covertly to undermine or overthrow their government.

Although much has been written about how the coup occurred, this issue remains very controversial, both among scholars and in the popular imagination. Supporters of Mosaddeq generally blame foreign actors for his downfall, arguing that the British government and the international oil companies first undermined Mosaddeq by boycotting Iranian oil and by continually plotting against him and that the United States then finished him off with the coup. Mosaddeq's opponents usually deny that a coup really occurred or that foreign actors played an important role, arguing instead that Mosaddeq was overthrown in a national uprising (*qiyam-e melli*) by the Iranian people against a leader who had squandered his popularity by refusing to settle the oil dispute and adopting dictatorial methods. A third explanation, given by many U.S. and British officials, is that foreign actors did, indeed, instigate the coup, but their essential contribution was merely to encourage and assist certain Iranian actors, who really were the main agents of Mosaddeq's downfall.

The central goal of this book has been to resolve this controversy, to the extent possible, by presenting a balanced, comprehensive account of how and why Mosaddeq fell. Each chapter has examined the contributions made by one particular actor or group of actors to Mosaddeq's downfall. For a comprehensive account we must bring these separate strands of the story together and evaluate the relative importance of each actor in bringing down Mosaddeq. That is the focus of this concluding chapter.

Narrowly speaking, it was the coup of August 19, 1953, that brought down Mosaddeq. However, as the preceding chapters make clear, the coup was a complex event shaped by a variety of circumstances. At one level, the coup occurred because certain domestic and foreign actors took certain actions in the period leading up to August 19. However, at a higher level, the actions of these actors were shaped by the changing configuration of political forces in Iran at the time and by certain broader conditions prevailing in Iran and in the world. A comprehensive account of Mosaddeq's downfall therefore requires that we identify the immediate circumstances responsible for the coup's success, the changing domestic political forces that contributed to the coup, and the broader domestic and international conditions involved. In this concluding chapter I first examine these three sets of factors. Based on this discussion, I then consider the relative importance of the various actors involved in overthrowing Mosaddeq. Although I draw heavily on the work of the other contributors to this book, the interpretations I present are strictly my own.

Why the Coup Succeeded

In the most immediate sense, Mosaddeq was overthrown because hostile army and police units and crowds of civilians seized strategic locations in Tehran on August 19 and arrested many of his associates; Mosaddeq himself went into hiding but surrendered to his opponents the following day. Although the army was commanded by Mosaddeq supporters, only a few loyalist units came to his defense on August 19. Similarly, neither the National Front nor the Tudeh Party organized crowds to confront Mosaddeq's opponents on that day, and no large crowds emerged spontaneously to defend him. Consequently, to understand why the coup succeeded, we must explain why forces hostile to Mosaddeq emerged and acted so decisively and why Mosaddeq's supporters did not come to his defense. The answers to these questions lie partly in the actions of certain key actors in the period leading up to August 19.

It is clear that the U.S. government played a crucial role in organizing and leading the hostile forces that overthrew Mosaddeq. As chapter 7 shows, the CIA planned, financed, and led the coup, with limited help from Britain. U.S. officials, in consultation with their British counterparts, chose Fazlollah Zahedi as the nominal coup leader and persuaded the shah to accept Zahedi and support the coup. The CIA station in Tehran undertook an extensive propaganda and political action campaign against Mosaddeq and, apparently, a major effort to buy off members of Parliament. In the weeks before the coup, the CIA worked through its own network of Iranian agents, led by Ali Jalali and Faruq Kayvani, and through a British network, led by the Rashidian brothers. These events culminated in the initial coup attempt, carried out on the night of August 15–16. Although this initial coup attempt failed, the CIA coup team remained in Tehran and still had a variety of useful assets, which it used to organize a second coup attempt.

During the next few days, the CIA team worked to undermine Mosaddeq and foment another coup by publicizing the shah's dismissal of Mosaddeq and appointment of Zahedi, having agents provocateurs organize black Tudeh Party crowds and create an atmosphere of chaos in Tehran, and trying to build support for the coup in the armed forces. The U.S. ambassador met with Mosaddeq and persuaded him to deploy the security forces, which had been confined to their barracks, compounding the chaos that had already emerged. On the morning of August 19, Jalali and Kayvani, and probably also the Rashidians and other Iranian opponents of Mosaddeq, organized anti-Mosaddeq crowds, which marched throughout the city. These crowds were joined by onlookers who were alarmed by the chaos that had emerged and by Mosaddeq's refusal to accept the shah's order dismissing him. Emboldened by these events, army units commanded by officers who had backed the initial coup attempt then began to seize strategic locations in Tehran and arrest Mosaddeq's associates. These units were joined by other army and police units, and they faced only scattered resistance from pro-Mosaddeq forces. By the end of the day they had taken over Tehran and driven Mosaddeq from power. The coup clearly would not have occurred at the time and in the manner it did without this extensive U.S. involvement.

The British government played a relatively minor role in the coup itself. Although the British initially proposed the coup, U.S. officials already had considered undertaking one; and the Eisenhower administration's enthusiasm for the coup suggests that it probably would have undertaken one without British encouragement. The British helped plan and finance the coup, but their role was fairly small, and the CIA team abandoned the plan when the initial coup attempt failed. The main British contribution to the coup itself lay in the actions of the Rashidians, who worked closely with the CIA team in carrying out the coup and apparently helped organize the crowds that emerged on August 19. However, the Rashidians' role in the coup does not seem to have been more important than that of Jalali and Kayvani, and they were, in any case, acting under American rather than British leadership at this time. The British contribution to the coup itself therefore does not seem to have been essential, although Britain had exerted considerable effort to undermine Mosaddeq prior to the coup.

Various Iranian actors also contributed to the success of the coup. Zahedi and his immediate collaborators were the most directly involved. However, as is shown in chapter 7, their role in the coup was limited. Zahedi had been trying unsuccessfully to overthrow Mosaddeq since July 1952, and by the summer of 1953 he had no real organization and an arrest warrant had forced him into hiding. The CIA gave Zahedi a large sum of money to recruit a secretariat and military network, but he failed to do so. The CIA team therefore appointed the secretariat, which included several officers Zahedi had never even met, and assembled the military network. Their main Iranian collaborator in these activities was not Zahedi but Col. Abbas Farzanegan, who was on the CIA payroll. Zahedi and his associates apparently delayed the initial coup attempt by one night, enabling Mosaddeq to discover it. When Mosaddeq's forces intercepted the initial coup attempt, many members of the military network refused to carry out their assigned tasks. The CIA team then hid Zahedi and his key collaborators in the U.S. embassy compound and the homes of CIA officers, where most of them remained until the coup had succeeded. Zahedi did participate in some of the CIA team's planning sessions, and members of the military network led some of the army units that seized power on August 19. Although these were important contributions, it seems doubtful that Zahedi and his collaborators would have undertaken them without the CIA team's leadership.

Another important Iranian contributor was the shah, who issued decrees dismissing Mosaddeq and appointing Zahedi and then abruptly fled the country on August 16. These actions probably were crucial in catalyzing the forces that overthrew Mosaddeq on August 19. However, U.S. officials had worked doggedly for several weeks to persuade the shah to take these actions. Moreover, most accounts of these events maintain that the shah fled the country in panic rather than in an effort to catalyze opposition to Mosaddeq, and his statements and actions in the following days are entirely consistent with this view. Consequently, while the shah's contribution to the coup probably was essential to its success, it seems clear that he too would not have acted without U.S. leadership.

The CIA's principal Iranian agents, Jalali and Kayvani, and their network of subagents played essential roles in the coup by implementing the CIA's precoup propaganda and political action campaign, using agents provocateurs to create chaos in Tehran after the initial coup attempt failed, helping to publicize the shah's dismissal of Mosaddeq and appointment of Zahedi, and helping to organize the anti-Mosaddeq crowds on August 19. However, Jalali and Kayvani were working under U.S. leadership and almost certainly would not have taken these actions on their own. Indeed, they apparently wanted to end their involvement after the initial coup attempt failed and continued to cooperate only after the head of the CIA team threatened to kill them.

Chapter 7 mentions that Ayatollahs Kashani and Behbehani may have helped organize the anti-Mosaddeq crowds of August 19, although if they did so they probably did not know they were working with the CIA. Kashani, Behbahani, and other religious figures had been working against Mosaddeq for some time, so it is certainly possible that they were involved. While the coup plan called for certain prominent religious figures to denounce Mosaddeq and organize demonstrations against him, these figures declined to do so. Similarly, after the initial coup attempt failed, the CIA team tried unsuccessfully to have Ayatollah Borujerdi call for a holy war against communism in order to undermine Mosaddeq. The available evidence therefore suggests that while many religious figures opposed Mosaddeq, they refused to become involved in the CIA's plot against him, at least until August 19. Although Kashani and Behbehani may have contributed to the fateful events of that day, this is not certain. And if they were involved, there is no way to judge how essential their contributions were.

Finally, Mosaddeq, his National Front colleagues, and the Tudeh Party made a series of glaring tactical mistakes in the days leading up to August 19 that facilitated the coup. Mosaddeq's decision to conduct a controversial referendum to close Parliament gave the CIA's precoup propaganda campaign an easy target, probably helped persuade the shah to support the coup, and undoubtedly turned some Iranians against Mosaddeq. After August 16, Mosaddeq and his colleagues failed to organize demonstrations to display their strength, and Mosaddeq banned all demonstrations. When CIA-backed agents provocateurs began to create chaos on August 17, Mosaddeq did not deploy the security forces to stop them. He also failed to restrain those who denounced the shah and called for an end to the monarchy. He then abruptly reversed himself the following day and brought the security forces into the streets, compounding the chaos and enabling army and police units to join the anti-Mosaddeq crowds that emerged on August 19. When the security forces attacked black and genuine Tudeh demonstrators, Tudeh leaders ordered their cadres off the streets, making them unavailable to confront Mosaddeq's opponents on August 19. Although it is impossible to say what would have happened if these mistakes had not been made, it seems clear that the events of August 19 might have turned out very differently.

Domestic Political Forces

The chapters by Azimi, Behrooz, and Katouzian examine the changing configuration of political forces in Iran during the Mosaddeq era and how these forces contributed to Mosaddeq's downfall. Following Azimi, we can distinguish four key groups of Iranian actors during this period. The first consists of royalists, Anglophiles, and religious rightists who opposed Mosaddeq throughout his tenure in office. The second consists of several key National Front leaders who initially supported Mosaddeq but then defected and turned against him after the July 1952 uprising. The third is the Tudeh Party, which opposed Mosaddeq on ideological grounds but increasingly supported him for strategic reasons after July 1952. The fourth group consists of loyal National Front members and common Iranians who continued to support Mosaddeq throughout his tenure.

As discussed by Azimi in chapter 2, Iranian royalists and Anglophiles intrigued unceasingly against Mosaddeq from his first days in office. Their efforts clearly weakened Mosaddeq by helping to turn some military officers and civilians against him, encouraging Britain and the United States to oppose him, and leading him to seek expanded powers, which dismayed many of his supporters and led some to turn against him. However, the royalists and Anglophiles manifestly had failed in their efforts to overthrow Mosaddeq throughout 1951 and 1952, despite British support; and when Zahedi, the National Front defectors, and the United States began their relentless attacks on Mosaddeq in late 1952 and early 1953, the only royalists or Anglophiles who were deeply involved were the Rashidians. Moreover, while opposition from the royalists and Anglophiles weakened Mosaddeq, it also inadvertently helped him by increasing his popularity among intellectuals and the middle class. Therefore, apart from the Rashidians, who were acting on behalf of Britain and later the United States, the royalists and Anglophiles do not seem to have played a crucial role in Mosaddeq's downfall.

Azimi shows that the shah was wary of Mosaddeq's popularity and therefore refused to confront him openly prior to the coup, although he did work quietly against Mosaddeq by tacitly endorsing oppositional activity by members of the court and other royalists. The shah's refusal to work actively against Mosaddeq before August 1953 frustrated the royalists, the Anglophiles, and the British, who found it difficult to act decisively without his active cooperation. By inadvertently restraining Mosaddeq's most persistent opponents in this way, the shah may have helped Mosaddeq as much as he hurt him prior to August 1953.

Religious rightists such as Ayatollah Behbahani, the cleric Mohammad Taqi Falsafi, and members of the Feda'iyan-e Islam also actively opposed Mosaddeq from his first days in office, weakening him by turning members of the urban middle and lower classes against him and intimidating the Mosaddeqists with threats, street mob activity, and violence. However, like the royalists and Anglophiles, the religious right made little headway against Mosaddeq in 1951 and 1952; and they inadvertently helped him by alienating intellectuals and the middle class. The religious right was hampered in its efforts to undermine Mosaddeq by Grand Ayatollah Borujerdi's refusal to oppose him and by Ayatollah Kashani's collaboration with him until the fall of 1952. When Kashani defected and began to work actively against Mosaddeq in early 1953, Behbehani and street mobs connected to the religious right played an important role in undermining Mosaddeq, most notably during the crisis of February 1953 and the events of August 19.

As Azimi shows, Kashani and the other National Front defectors played a more important role in undermining Mosaddeq than the royalists, Anglophiles, and religious rightists. After they broke with Mosaddeq in late 1952 and early 1953, the National Front defectors frequently attacked him and led the parliamentary opposition, forming a de facto coalition with royalist and Anglophile deputies that often was large enough to command a majority. By early 1953 Kashani and the other defectors had begun to collaborate with Zahedi. The most important such instance of collaboration prior to the coup came in February 1953, when Kashani and Behbehani organized violent demonstrations in conjunction with disturbances fomented by allies of Zahedi. These events almost toppled Mosaddeq and revealed his weaknesses very clearly, presaging the August 19 coup. Kashani also gave Zahedi sanctuary in parliament, enabling him to avoid arrest. Mozaffar Baqa'i, another National Front defector, collaborated with allies of Zahedi in the murder of General Afshartus, a key Mosaddeq ally.

These actions by the National Front defectors undermined Mosaddeq in crucial ways. Most importantly, by breaking ranks with Mosaddeq and harshly attacking him, the defectors created the appearance—whether true or false—that his popularity and grip on power were declining. This emboldened Mosaddeq's domestic opponents, raised doubts among Iranians who were neutral toward him, and helped persuade U.S. officials that a coup was necessary to prevent a descent into chaos or a Tudeh takeover. In addition, Kashani and to a lesser extent Baqa'i controlled powerful networks of street thugs and other activists who had demonstrated their potency during the July 1952 uprising. The only other actor with street networks as powerful as these was the Tudeh Party, which had a very ambivalent relationship with Mosaddeq. Therefore, by withholding these networks from Mosaddeq and using them on behalf of his opponents, Kashani and Baqa'i sharply undermined Mosaddeq's ability to control the streets, as became evident in February 1953 and, of course, on August 19.

As discussed by Behrooz in chapter 3, the Tudeh Party was very hostile toward Mosaddeq and the National Front before July 1952. Its harsh rhetoric and menacing presence in the streets during this period alarmed many Iranians and U.S. and British officials, leaving them increasingly doubtful of Mosaddeq's ability to maintain order. The Tudeh's participation in the July 1952 uprising increased these concerns and helped persuade some U.S. officials that Mosaddeq should be removed from office. The Tudeh's moderate faction gradually gained control over the party after July 1952 and led it to adopt a united popular front strategy, which involved supporting Mosaddeq by reducing its criticism of him and joining the National Front in rallies and demonstrations. The Tudeh's growing support for Mosaddeq in this period further alarmed U.S. and British officials, pushing them toward undertaking a coup. Ironically, as Behrooz shows, the Tudeh's support for Mosaddeq was fairly superficial: it did not stockpile weapons or mobilize its powerful military organization or large crowds to stop the coup, and it deactivated the vanguard cells it had created earlier to defend Mosaddeq. Consequently, despite the Tudeh's growing support for Mosaddeq, the net effect of its actions, both before and after July 1952, was to undermine Mosaddeq quite severely by producing growing fears that it might seize power. Indeed, in this way the Tudeh may have done more to undermine Mosaddeq than the royalists, Anglophiles, and religious rightists.

Finally, in addition to the tactical mistakes they made during the days leading up to the coup, Mosaddeq and his National Front colleagues earlier had made several crucial strategic mistakes that helped make the coup possible. First, as discussed by Azimi, the leaders of the National Front failed to create an organization that could effectively mobilize support for their movement. Their lack of organization, together with Mosaddeq's refusal to manipulate the electoral process, prevented them from obtaining a solid majority in the parliamentary elections of 1951. As a result, the Parliament served as a source of persistent opposition to Mosaddeq, leading him to circumvent it in ways that helped his opponents. The Mosaddeqist wing of the National Front also failed to develop the capability to mobilize popular support in the streets, enabling Kashani, Baqa'i, the Tudeh Party, and unscrupulous mob organizers to dominate this crucial political arena in the year preceding the coup.

Second, Mosaddeq failed to act forcefully toward the Rashidians, Zahedi, Kashani, Baqa'i, and others who were clearly plotting against him, despite the illegal nature of their activities. He also failed to act forcefully toward the Tudeh Party, which was illegal and posed an obvious threat both to the existing order and to Mosaddeq's own goals.

A third crucial strategic mistake was Mosaddeq's failure to settle the oil dispute with Britain, which led directly to the U.S. decision to carry out the coup. Although the British were extremely obstinate in the negotiations, they were willing to concede the crucial point of nationalization and agree to a division of profits along the lines then accepted by other oil-exporting countries. Moreover, the United States was prepared to offer Iran considerable financial aid and other assistance if an agreement could be reached. Mosaddeq certainly would have been attacked from all sides for almost any kind of settlement he might have reached with Britain, and he might well have been forced out of office. However, with a carefully designed campaign to sell an oil agreement to the Iranian public, he might have been able to succeed. Although settling the dispute carried obvious risks, it is hard to imagine an outcome worse for Mosaddeq's movement than the disaster it suffered as a result of the coup.

Mosaddeq's strategic and tactical mistakes are, of course, much easier to see in retrospect than they were at the time. Moreover, conditions in Iran sharply limited Mosaddeq's options, especially his ability to settle the oil dispute. Nevertheless, it seems clear that the fate of Mosaddeq's regime—and, indeed, Iran's subsequent history—might have been very different if he had acted more pragmatically and carefully.

Broader Conditions

Both the occurrence of the coup itself and the domestic political forces that contributed to it were shaped by a variety of broader conditions that prevailed in Iran and in the world at the time.

Three sets of domestic conditions were especially important. First, as a result of its growing contact with the Western world since the mid-nineteenth century, Iran had experienced profound economic, social, and cultural changes that, in turn, dramatically affected its social structure. Most importantly, these changes created a small but growing educated middle class, which, as Azimi shows, provided the main social base for Mosaddeq's movement and much of the Tudeh Party's leadership. These changes also created both an industrial working class, whose political loyalties were divided among the Tudeh, Baqa'i's Toilers Party, and pro-shah and pro-British trade unions, and an urban underclass, which was largely the domain of populist demagogues like Kashani and unscrupulous mob organizers. The emergence of these new classes had begun to transform Iranian politics by the early 1950s, with organizations like the National Front and the Tudeh in effect challenging the dominance of the shah and the traditional upper class, whose interests were defended by royalist and Anglophile politicians and the religious right. However, these new classes were still rather small, so the balance of power between the challengers and defenders was relatively even. Moreover, the interests and loyalties of these new classes were fairly heterogeneous, so the political movements challenging the status quo at this time were beset by powerful centrifugal forces.

In practical terms, this meant that while the National Front was initially quite powerful and had a realistic chance of bringing about far-reaching change, the defection of Kashani, Baqa'i, and others left the Mosaddeqist wing of the National Front with only a narrow social base, consisting mainly of the educated middle class. This problem was compounded by the failure of the Mosaddeqists to broaden their social base beyond this class and by the Tudeh's posture toward the Mosaddeqists, which was, at best, ambivalent. Although Mosaddeq undoubtedly was still quite popular by the summer of 1953, the Mosaddeqists' failure to develop strong ties to the industrial working class and urban underclass left them unable to organize large crowds on his behalf to stop the coup. If Mosaddeq's movement had developed a broader social base, or if it had emerged a generation later, when the educated middle class was much larger, it might well have been more successful.

Second, as discussed by Azimi, Iran's political institutions in the early 1950s were very weak, hindering Mosaddeq's ability to govern and facilitating his opponents' efforts to undermine him. The Mosaddeqists were poorly organized, which prevented them from triumphing in the 1951 parliamentary elections and developing a broader social base. The only well-organized political party in this period was the Tudeh, whose influence was limited by the narrow appeal of its ideology and its illegal status. The absence of effective political parties meant, in turn, that Iranian politics was very personalistic and that Parliament was undisciplined and easily manipulated by outside forces. The press also was undisciplined and permeated with political influence, both domestic and foreign. The shah's strong constitutional prerogatives and ability to use patronage seriously weakened the office of prime minister. Law enforcement and electoral oversight were very weak, enabling Mosaddeq's opponents to plot unceasingly against him and use blatantly illegal methods, including murder. These problems were compounded by Mosaddeq's commitment to democratic practices and the rule of law, which gave his less-principled opponents a distinct advantage.

A third set of broad domestic conditions that facilitated the coup was the political culture that prevailed in Iran at the time. Due partly to the limited size of its educated middle class and the weakness of its political institutions, the spirit of trust, compromise, fair play, and civic duty that is essential to democratic practice was not widespread in Iran. Rather, most Iranian elites were self-interested and relished intrigue; and common Iranians generally were unsophisticated and easily manipulated. Thus, Mosaddeq's opponents plotted continuously against him; key allies deserted him; foreign influence was pervasive; popular support was ephemeral; and Mosaddeq himself increasingly sought to concentrate power in his own hands. These political-cultural traits were more conducive to the cycles of arbitrary rule and chaos described in Katouzian's chapter than to stable democracy.

In addition to these domestic conditions, several broad international conditions prevailing at the time contributed to Mosaddeq's downfall. One was the oil boycott and other economic sanctions levied against Iran. As discussed in the chapters by Heiss and Louis, the British government and the Anglo-Iranian Oil Company (AIOC) began a boycott of Iranian oil exports soon after Iran nationalized the AIOC's Iranian assets in 1951. The other major international oil companies then joined the boycott. Although smaller oil companies tried to circumvent the boycott, Britain and the major companies prevented them from purchasing significant amounts of Iranian oil. The U.S. government supported the boycott and took steps to minimize its effect on U.S. consumers, and the United States and most other British allies facilitated the boycott by preventing their citizens from working as oil technicians in Iran. The British also implemented a variety of minor unilateral economic sanctions against Iran during this period.

As Heiss shows, the oil boycott and these other actions hurt Iran's economy but did not devastate it. Although these measures undoubtedly aggravated domestic unrest, they did not produce bread riots, strikes, or other direct manifestations of economic distress, as had occurred in Iran during World War II. Indeed, while they may have undermined Mosaddeq by aggravating unrest, they also inadvertently helped him by creating a foreign threat he could use to rally public support. As Heiss argues, these economic sanctions contributed to Mosaddeq's downfall primarily by persuading U.S. officials that a coup was necessary to prevent economic collapse and political chaos, not by undermining his popularity.

As discussed in Louis's chapter, the British tried to undermine Mosaddeq in other ways as well. British diplomats and intelligence officers, working mainly through the Rashidians, began to carry out covert political operations against Mosaddeq soon after he first took office. The British also backed a series of candidates to replace Mosaddeq as prime minister, culminating in a nascent plot with Zahedi that collapsed when Mosaddeq broke diplomatic relations with Britain in October 1952. These activities contributed very much to the chaos that was growing in Iran during this period. However, after eighteen months of concerted effort, the British had failed to bring Mosaddeq down by the time Mosaddeq broke relations with them. Lacking a direct presence in Iran, the British then were forced to seek help from the United States against Mosaddeq. Indeed, when U.S. officials reacted coolly to the initial British proposal for a coup, the British reduced their funding for the Rashidians' covert operations, presumably because they thought these activities were not having much effect. Moreover, as with the oil embargo, British intrigue against Mosaddeq inadvertently helped him by creating a foreign threat he could use to rally public support. Consequently, while the British efforts to undermine Mosaddeq contributed to the general deterioration that occurred during this period and in this way helped persuade U.S. officials and some Iranians to back a coup, these efforts themselves did not gravely weaken Mosaddeq.

As discussed in chapters 6 and 7, the United States under the Truman administration supported Mosaddeq and took a number of steps that strengthened him. Most importantly, U.S. officials persuaded the British not to invade Iran in the late summer of 1951 and pressed them persistently to moderate their position in the oil negotiations. The Truman administration also made a series of innovative proposals to settle the oil dispute, gave Iran significant amounts of economic aid, hosted Mosaddeq in Washington, and made frequent statements expressing support for him. Their actions strengthened Mosaddeq domestically by suggesting that the United States approved of his policies and by creating optimism that the oil dispute soon would be settled. Although the United States supported the British oil boycott and the CIA carried out covert operations that undermined Mosaddeq in minor ways, the net effect of U.S. policy under Truman seems to have been beneficial for Mosaddeq.

The inauguration of the Eisenhower administration in January 1953 produced a dramatic change in U.S. policy toward Iran. U.S. officials continued to seek a settlement of the oil dispute until Mosaddeq rejected Ambassador Henderson's final initiative in March 1953. However, they also quickly began to prepare for the coup, approving the general idea within a month of Eisenhower's inauguration, authorizing the CIA to begin planning a coup during the following month, and allocating $1 million for precoup covert operations against Mosaddeq in early April. As discussed above, the CIA then planned, financed, and led the coup, with limited help from Britain and from certain Iranians. The Eisenhower administration also took a series of diplomatic actions during this period that helped undermine Mosaddeq.

What broader conditions were responsible for this fateful change in U.S. policy toward Iran? It is tempting simply to blame the Eisenhower administration's more aggressive approach toward containing Soviet influence. However, many U.S. officials who had worked on Iran under the Truman administration, from the assistant secretary of state for Near Eastern affairs and top CIA officials in Washington to State Department and CIA officers stationed in Tehran, had concluded by the summer of 1953 that growing chaos and perhaps a communist takeover were likely in Iran and that Mosaddeq therefore had to be overthrown to prevent Iran from falling into Soviet hands. Although it is impossible to say with any certainty, this suggests that the United States might well have carried out a coup against Mosaddeq eventually, even if Eisenhower had not been elected president. The advent of the Eisenhower administration led the United States to act more rapidly than it otherwise might have, but Iran's continuing political deterioration, in the prevailing geostrategic context, made it almost inevitable that the United States would undertake a coup.

As discussed in chapter 6, two broad geostrategic conditions led the United States to take this fateful step. First, the climate of intense cold war rivalry between the superpowers, together with Iran's strategically vital location between the Soviet Union and the Persian Gulf oil fields, led U.S. officials to believe that they had to take whatever steps were necessary to prevent Iran from falling into Soviet hands. These concerns seem vastly overblown today, especially in light of the weakness of the Tudeh Party described in chapter 3. However, after the 1945–46 Azerbaijan crisis, the consolidation of Soviet control in Eastern Europe, the communist triumph in China, and the Korean War—and with the Red Scare at its height in the United States—U.S. officials simply could not risk allowing the Tudeh Party to gain power in Iran.

Second, U.S. officials believed that resolving the oil dispute was essential for restoring stability in Iran, and after March 1953 it appeared that the dispute could be resolved only at the expense either of Britain or of Mosaddeq. Britain was the closest ally of the United States, and the two countries were working as partners on a wide range of vitally important matters throughout the world at this time. Preserving this close relationship was more important to U.S. officials than saving Mosaddeq's tottering regime. Faced with an apparent choice between Britain and Mosaddeq, U.S. officials therefore chose Britain, although they did so in many cases with considerable reluctance.

Consequently, it was geostrategic considerations, rather than a desire to destroy Mosaddeq's movement, to establish a dictatorship in Iran, or to gain control over Iran's oil, that persuaded U.S. officials to undertake the coup. As had occurred repeatedly during the first half of the twentieth century, Iran's strategic location once again led foreign powers to intervene decisively in its domestic politics.

Who Overthrew Mosaddeq?

Each of the three broad explanations of Mosaddeq's downfall mentioned at the beginning of this chapter clearly has some merit.

There is no doubt that foreign actors played a crucial role in the overthrow of Mosaddeq, as emphasized by many of his supporters. The coup against Mosaddeq clearly would not have occurred when and how it did without extensive U.S. involvement. The British government and the major international oil companies also made essential contributions to the coup, mainly by creating conditions that led the United States to act. Many Iranians today, including many who disdain Mosaddeq, still are very angry with the U.S. and British governments for their involvement in the coup. This anger certainly is justified.

Although foreign actors therefore were crucial to Mosaddeq's downfall, their role generally has been overemphasized, while the role of Iranian actors in these events has been underemphasized. The single most important Iranian participant was the shah. Although the shah was reluctant to become involved and fled at the first sign of trouble, and while the CIA planned to carry out the coup without his support, if necessary, the army and police units and civilian crowds that overthrew Mosaddeq probably would not have acted as they did without the shah's tacit approval. Zahedi and his colleagues obviously were involved in the coup, but their contributions were relatively minor. Jalali and Kayvani and the Rashidians were deeply involved in undermining Mosaddeq and carrying out the coup, but they were working as agents for the U.S. and British intelligence services and almost certainly would not have acted on their own.

The Tudeh greatly undermined Mosaddeq by acting in ways that led U.S. and British officials to fear that it might eventually seize power and by failing to use its considerable political resources to stop the coup. Kashani and the other National Front defectors also played a key role in Mosaddeq's downfall by created the appearance that he had lost considerable support, denying him the support of their street networks, and possibly using these networks against him on August 19. Various royalists, Anglophiles, and religious rightists worked against Mosaddeq as well, although none seem to have made essential contributions to his downfall.

In addition to the shah, the Tudeh, and the National Front defectors, two other groups of Iranians acted in ways that were crucial to Mosaddeq's downfall. First, Mosaddeq and his colleagues made a number of key strategic and tactical mistakes. Most importantly, they failed to create an organization capable of mobilizing broad support for their movement; they refused to take the difficult steps necessary to settle the oil dispute; and they did not act forcefully against their various opponents, either before the coup or while it was underway. In light of the social, institutional, political-cultural, and geostrategic conditions that prevailed in Iran at the time, these mistakes contributed substantially to the occurrence of the coup and to its success. Mosaddeq's goals of increasing Iran's independence and promoting democracy were important and widely supported; and he was popular, bold, and brave. However, Mosaddeq also made crucial mistakes, mistakes that contributed not only to his demise as a politician but also to his failure to achieve these important goals.

Second, while the CIA coup team made various efforts to mobilize the army and police units and civilian crowds that emerged on August 19, the Iranians who participated in these events chose to do so, and some participated spontaneously. Moreover, no large crowds emerged to defend Mosaddeq, indicating that his supporters were less organized and perhaps less committed to him than they had been during earlier confrontations. There are no reliable estimates of the size of the anti-Mosaddeq crowds that emerged that day, but they probably numbered in the upper thousands. Although this is far from the "national uprising" that Mosaddeq's opponents claim was responsible for his downfall, it does indicate that Mosaddeq had deeply alienated a significant number of Iranians by this time, especially middle- and lower-ranking army and police personnel. Consequently, in addition to the shah, the Tudeh, and the National Front defectors, a relatively small but significant number of common Iranians also contributed to Mosaddeq's downfall.

Finally, what are we to make of the claim by many U.S. and British officials that, while foreign actors instigated the coup, their main role was to encourage and assist certain Iranian actors who were the main agents of Mosaddeq's downfall? More generally, what was the relative importance of foreign and domestic actors in bringing down Mosaddeq?

The foregoing discussion demonstrates that both foreign and domestic actors were crucial to Mosaddeq's downfall. Beyond this, there is no clear way to establish whether one set of actors was more important than the other and, if so, how much more important it was; any attempt to do so would involve mere speculation. However, the main Iranians directly involved in the coup—Zahedi and his colleagues, Jalali and Kayvani, and the Rashidians—were selected for their roles by U.S. and British officials and acted largely under U.S. leadership. The shah's contribution was probably crucial, but U.S. officials had to make extensive efforts to persuade him to act. A relatively small but significant number of army and police personnel and civilians participated spontaneously in the coup, but they were responding in part to conditions that had been created by the CIA team. Consequently, the claim that foreign actors merely encouraged and assisted Iranian actors to carry out the coup attributes more initiative and determination to these Iranians than seems warranted. While it is impossible to say what would have happened if the CIA had not instigated the coup, there is no reason to think that these Iranians—or any others, for that matter—would have overthrown Mosaddeq any time soon.

Nevertheless, the coup cannot be blamed solely on foreign actors or, more specifically, solely on the United States. The actions of the Tudeh Party and the National Front defectors during the preceding year were crucial in persuading U.S. officials to undertake the coup. Mosaddeq and his colleagues made strategic and tactical mistakes that very much facilitated it. The shah and common Iranians made essential contributions. Consequently, while the United States delivered the final blow to Mosaddeq's regime, Iranian actors—together with the British and the major international oil companies—played crucial roles as well.

Notes

Selected Bibliography

Index

Notes

Abbreviations

CIG   Central Intelligence Group
FO   Foreign Office
FRUS   Foreign Relations of the United States
NIE   National Intelligence Estimate
NA   National Archives
ORE   Office of Reports and Estimates
PRO   Public Records Office

Introduction

1. *New York Times,* Mar. 18, 2000.

2. Mohsen Rezai, also former head of the Revolutionary Guard Corps, is quoted in *RFE/RL Iran Report* 3, no. 13 (Mar. 27, 2000); for the Khamenei quote, see Associated Press, "Iran's Top Leader Slams U.S. Gesture as Deceitful," Mar. 25, 2000.

3. A particularly noteworthy volume to which several of the current authors contributed is James A. Bill and Wm. Roger Louis, eds., *Musaddiq, Iranian Nationalism, and Oil* (Austin: Univ. of Texas Press 1988).

4. Another useful CIA source that was recently declassified and made available to the National Security Archive, albeit in highly excised form, is Scott A. Koch, *"Zendebad, Shah!": The Central Intelligence Agency and the Fall of Iranian Prime Minister Mohammad Mosaddeq, August 1953* (History Staff, Central Intelligence Agency, June 1998).

5. *New York Times* reporter James Risen obtained the history from a former CIA officer and wrote major stories to cover each stage of the document's release in the paper's editions of April 16 and June 18, 2000.

6. The *Foreign Relations of the United States: Diplomatic Papers* series (hereinafter cited as FRUS) was originally published by year and subsequently by administration. The volume covering the Mosaddeq years is *FRUS, 1952–1954,* vol. 10, *Iran: 1951–1954* (Washington, D.C.: Government Printing Office, 1989). The series description appears in State Department histo-

rian William Z. Slany's preface on page iii. The CIA's refusal to part with relevant historical records created a scandal and led the chairman of the State Department's historical advisory committee of independent scholars, Warren I. Cohen, to resign in protest in February 1990. See *Washington Post,* Apr. 16, 1990, A13; and Bruce R. Kuniholm, "Perspectives," *American Historical Association Newsletter* 28, no. 5 (May/June 1990): 1, 11–12.

7. The sentence, which appears on page 64 of the Wilber history, reads: "Headquarters spent a day featured by depression and despair." The CIA's rationale for releasing it was that it "was previously disclosed in a publication." See "Declaration by William N. McNair, Information Review Officer, Directorate of Operations, United States Central Intelligence Agency," in *National Security Archive v. United States Central Intelligence Agency,* Civil Action 99–1160 (CKK), United States District Court for the District of Columbia, 3.

1. Mosaddeq's Government in Iranian History: Arbitrary Rule, Democracy, and the 1953 Coup

1. See Homa Katouzian, *Musaddiq and the Struggle for Power in Iran* (1990; 2d paperback ed., London and New York: I. B. Tauris, 1999); and id., *The Political Economy of Modern Iran,* part 3 (London and New York: Macmillan and New York Univ. Press, 1981).

2. See Homa Katouzian, *State and Society in Iran: The Eclipse of the Qajars and the Rise of the Pahlavis* (London and New York: I. B. Tauris, 2000), esp. chaps. 1–3; id., *Iranian History and Politics: The Dialectic of State and Society in Iran* (London: Routledge Curzon, 2003); id., "Liberty and Licence in the Constitutional Revolution of Iran," *Journal of the Royal Asiatic Society* 8, no. 2 (1998): 159–80; id., "Towards a General Theory of Iranian Revolutions," *Journal of Iranian Research and Analysis* 15, no. 2 (Nov. 1999): 145–62; and id., "European Liberalisms and Modern Concepts of Liberty in Iran," *Journal of Iranian Research and Analysis* 16, no. 2 (Nov. 2000): 9–29. See also Janet Afary, *The Iranian Constitutional Revolution, 1905–1911: Grassroots Democracy, Social Democracy, and the Origins of Feminism* (New York: Columbia Univ. Press, 1996); Vanessa Martin, *Islam and Modernism: The Iranian Revolution of 1906* (London and New York: I. B. Tauris, 1989); and Mangol Bayat, *Iran's First Revolution: Shi'ism and the Constitutional Revolution of 1905–1909* (New York: Oxford Univ. Press, 1991).

3. See Katouzian, *State and Society,* esp. chaps. 8–11. See further Abbasqoli Golsha'iyan, "Yaddashtha-ye Golsha'iyan," in *Yaddashtha-ye Doktor Qasem Ghani,* ed. Cyrus Ghani, vol. 11 (London: Ghani, 1984); and Hossein Makki, *Tarikh-e Bist saleh-ye Iran* (Tehran: Elmi, 1995).

4. See Fakhreddin Azimi, *Iran: The Crisis of Democracy, 1941–1953* (London and New York: I. B. Tauris and St. Martin's Press, 1989); and Katouzian, *Musaddiq and the Struggle.*

5. There now are many sources on this. For a very recent study of the southern revolt that also discusses the revolts in Azerbaijan and Kurdistan, see Reza Jafari, "Centre-Periphery Relations in Iran: The Case of the Southern Rebellion in 1946," D.Phil. thesis, Faculty of Oriental Studies, Univ. of Oxford, 2000.

6. See Amir Esma'ili, *Jan bar Sar-e Qalam* (Tehran: Esma'ili, 1987). This source includes a photocopy of the front-page article as well as a signed statement in the publisher-editor's handwriting (authenticated by a notary public) affirming his offer of the bounty for Qavam's life.

7. For Mosaddeq's political biography, see Katouzian, *Musaddiq and the Struggle;* Moham-

mad Musaddiq, *Musaddiq's Memoirs,* ed. Homa Katouzian, trans. S. H. Amin and H. Katouzian (London: JEBHEH, 1988); and Farhad Diba, *Mohammad Musaddiq, a Political Biography* (London: Croom Helm, 1986).

8. See documents cited in note 12 below. For example, in the meeting of Francis Shepherd, the British ambassador, with the shah, the shah said that it would be difficult to dismiss Mosaddeq's government unless his failure became apparent. He therefore suggested that the mere halting of oil exports would not be sufficient and that it might be necessary to close down the Abadan refinery as well. Besides, he said, there was need for radio and press propaganda against Mosaddeq to reduce his popularity. See Shepherd to FO, July 12, 1951, FO 248/1514. All documents cited herein as "FO" documents are held at the Public Record Office, London.

The deputy minister of the royal court told Oriental counsellor L. F. L. Pyman that any substantial payment to Mosaddeq's government for settling the oil dispute would be wrong and totally useless. See Pyman's report of the meeting, July 14, 1951, FO 248/1514. A leading conservative politician and Majles deputy told Pyman that all the tankers in Abadan must remain anchored, Mosaddeq's request for British technicians to remain there must be turned down, and he must not be allowed to employ other foreign technicians. See British embassy to FO, July 10, 1951, FO 248/1514 IV. An influential journalist told Pyman that he and his associates were mobilizing all their resources to discredit Mosaddeq. See Pyman, embassy circular, July 7, 1951, FO 248/1512. Sayyed Hasan Taqizadeh, chairman of the Senate, told the British ambassador, in a meeting held at the ambassador's request, that the ambassador should stop seeing the shah and leading politicians in a bid to bring down Mosaddeq's government, but the ambassador rejected his advice. See Shepherd to FO, Sept. 22, 1951, FO 248/1514 V.

9. See the chapters by Wm. Roger Louis and Mary Ann Heiss in this volume, as well as the sources cited by them; Mohammad Naser Qashqa'i, *Salha-ye Bohran,* ed. Nasrollah Haddadi (Tehran: Rasa, 1987); and Homa Katouzian, "Barkhi az Salha-ye Bohran dar Yeki az Qarnha-ye Bohran," in *Estebdad, Demokrasi ve Nehzat-e Melli,* 3d ed. (Tehran: Nashr-e Markaz, 2002). See also Azimi, *Crisis of Democracy.*

10. The chapter by Heiss in this volume gives a detailed account of the various aspects of the oil boycott and its consequences. See further the references therein.

11. The literature on the oil dispute and proposals for its resolution is quite extensive. See, for example, Katouzian, *Musaddiq and the Struggle;* id., *Musaddiq's Memoirs;* id., "Oil Boycott and the Political Economy, Musaddiq and the Strategy of Non-oil Economics," in Bill and Louis; Ronald W. Ferrier, "The Anglo-Iranian Oil Dispute, a Triangular Relationship," in Bill and Louis; George C. McGhee, "Recollections of Dr. Musaddiq," in Bill and Louis; Kamran M. Dadkhah, "Iran's Economic Policy during the Mosaddeq Era," *Journal of Iranian Research and Analysis* 16, no. 2 (Nov. 2000); id., "The Oil Nationalisation Movement, the British Boycott and the Iranian Economy, 1951–1953," in *Essays on the Economic History of the Middle East,* ed. Elie Kedourie and Sylvia G. Haim (London: Frank Cass, 1988); M. G. Majd, "The 1951–53 Oil Nationalization Dispute and the Iranian Economy, a Rejoinder," *Middle Eastern Studies,* 31, no. 3 (1995): 449; Mostafa Elm, *Oil, Power, and Principle: Iran's Oil Nationalization and Its Aftermath* (Syracuse: Syracuse Univ. Press, 1992); Azimi, *Crisis of Democracy;* Mary Ann Heiss, *Empire and Nationhood: The United States, Great Britain, and Iranian Oil, 1950–1954* (New York: Columbia Univ. Press, 1997); George C. McGhee, *Envoy to the Middle World: Adventures in Diplomacy* (New York: Harper and Row, 1983); Mostafa Fateh, *Panjah Sal Naft-e Iran* (Tehran: Chehr, 1956); and

Fo'ad Ruhani, *Tarikh-e Melli Shodan-e San'at-e Naft-e Iran* (Tehran: Jibi, 1974). For a detailed discussion and appraisal of the World Bank proposal and the Iranian government's responses to it, see Homa Katouzian, "Mosaddeq va Pishnahad-e Bank-e Jahani," *Mehregan* (spring 1992), reprinted in *Estebdad, Demokrasi.*

12. See Louis in this volume. For a detailed documentation of the efforts of the British embassy in Tehran, between May and September 1951, to bring down Mosaddeq's government through the shah and the Majles, see Katouzian, "Koosheshha-ye Sefarat-e Inglis bara-ye Ta'in-e Nakhost Vazir-e Iran az Melli Shodan-e Naft ta Khal'-e yad," in *Estebdad, Demokrasi.* For the documents in question, see L. A. C. Fry, minutes on paper by G. Keating, Jan. 30, 1951, FO 371/91452; Francis Shepherd (British ambassador in Tehran) to FO, Jan. 19, 1951, FO 371/91452; Shepherd to FO, Mar. 7, 1951, FO 248/1518; L. F. L. Pyman, report on meeting with Sayyed Zia, Aug. 9, 1951, FO 248/1518; Shepherd to FO, report of lunch with the shah, Mar. 7, 1951, FO 248/1518; Shepherd to Bowker (in the Foreign Office), Mar. 12, 1951, FO 371/91452; Shepherd, memo on meeting with Asadollah Alam, Mar. 21, 1951, FO 248/1518; Shepherd to FO, Mar. 21, 1951, FO 371/91454; Oliver Frank to FO, Mar. 27, 1951, FO 371/9154; and Shepherd, memo on meeting with Henry Grady (American ambassador in Tehran), Apr. 1, 1951, FO 248/1518. Also, Shepherd to FO, June 22, 1951; Shepherd, report on meeting with the shah, July 1, 1951; Pyman, memo, July 7, 1951; Pyman, report of meeting with Dr. Ahmad Human, deputy minister of the royal court, July 14, 1951; Shepherd, report of meeting with the shah, July 12, 1951; Pyman, report of meeting with Dr. Taheri Yazdi, July 10, 1951; George Middleton, report of meeting with Mr. Daliri (Ahmad Qavam's envoy), Sept. 18, 1951; Pyman, report of meeting with Sayyed Zia, Sept. 22, 1951; and Shepherd to FO, report of meeting with Taqizadeh, Sept. 22, 1951; all of the aforementioned documents are found in FO 248/1514.

13. For example, Sir Samuel Falle, Oriental secretary in the British embassy in Tehran, 1952, and Sir Denis Wright, British chargé d'affaires, 1954, who reopened the embassy and negotiated the Consortium Oil Agreement and became British ambassador in the 1960s, expressed this view in a conference, "Mohammad Mosaddeq and the 1953 Coup in Iran," at St. Antony's College, Oxford, June 8–10, 2002.

14. This happened so unexpectedly that the British were taken by surprise and were not able to organize support for Qavam through the Rashidian network (see Louis in this volume). But the strategy of replacing Mosaddeq by Qavam had been actively canvassed by them.

15. That Mosaddeq had intended to resign primarily in anticipation of failure at the World Court has emerged from a recent study. See Homa Katouzian, "Dalil-e Asli-ye Est'fa-ye Mosaddeq dar Vaqe'h-ye Si-ye Tir," in *Estebdad, Demokrasi;* id., *Musaddiq and the Struggle;* and *Musaddiq's Memoirs,* vol. 2, chap. 9.

16. See, for example, Katouzian, *Musaddiq and the Struggle, Estebdad, Demokrasi,* and *Musaddiq's Memoirs;* Azimi, *Crisis of Democracy;* Ervand Abrahamian, *Iran Between Two Revolutions* (Princeton, N.J.: Princeton Univ. Press, 1982); Nikki Keddie, *Roots of Revolution* (New Haven, Conn., and London: Yale Univ. Press, 1981); and Elm, *Oil, Power, and Principle.*

17. See Fakhreddin Azimi's chapter in this volume; and Katouzian, *Musaddiq and the Struggle,* chap. 12.

18. See sources in note 13 above; and Katouzian, introduction to Khalil Maleki, *Khaterat-e Siasi,* 2d ed., ed. Homa Katouzian (Tehran: Enteshar, 1989).

19. Report by Sir Samuel Falle at conference "Mohammad Mosaddeq and the 1953 Coup in Iran," St. Antony's College, Oxford, June 8–10, 2002.

20. The above brief is based on Katouzian, *Musaddiq and the Struggle.* See also Azimi's chapter in this book and his *Crisis of Democracy;* Keddie; and Abrahamian, *Iran Between Two Revolutions.*

21. See, for example, Katouzian, *Musaddiq and the Struggle;* id., "Statement of April 1953," in *Musaddiq's Memoirs,* vol. 2, chaps. 2, 7; Mohammad Reza Shah Pahlavi, *Mission for My Country* (New York: McGraw-Hill, 1961); and Azimi, *Crisis of Democracy.*

22. See, for example, Katouzian, *Musaddiq and the Struggle;* Azimi, *Crisis of Democracy;* and Mohammad Torkaman, *Tote'eh-ye Robudan va Qatl-e Afshartus* (Tehran: Rasa, 1984). This Khatibi must not be confused with the late Dr. Hossein Khatibi, the professor of Persian literature who later headed Iran's equivalent of the Red Cross.

23. See further Homa Katouzian, "The CIA Documents and the 1953 Coup in Iran," in *The CIA Documents on the 1953 Coup,* ed. Gholamreza Vatandoust (Tehran: Rasa, 2000) (published in English and Persian).

24. Henderson to the secretary of state, May 4, 1953, 788.00/5–453/4311.

25. Henderson to the secretary of state, May 5, 1953, 788.00/5–553/4324.

26. Minutes of a meeting of Henderson and some American embassy staff with the shah's trusted envoy on May 17, 1953, 788.00/5–1953/975.

27. See in particular Col. G. Mosavvar-Rahmani, *Khaterat-e Siasi: Bist-va-panj sal dar Niru-ye Hava'i Iran* (Tehran: Ravaq, 1984), who insists that Riahi's appointment had been a mistake and that they had recommended Amini for the post. Rahmani was a leading member and organizer of the pro-Mosaddeq army officers.

28. See, for example, Henderson to the secretary of state, May 20, 1953, 788.00/5–2053/982. See further Babak Amir-Khosravi, *Nazari az Darun beh Naqsh-e Hezb-e Tudeh-ye Iran* (Tehran: Ettela'at, 1996/1375).

29. See Mark Gasiorowski's chapter on the 1953 coup in this volume, and the references therein.

30. John Waller, a retired CIA officer who was closely involved in the coup operations from the headquarters in Washington, firmly believes that no such moneys were paid and that if they were, it must have been done by the British agents. Homa Katouzian interview with John Waller, Oxford, June 11, 2002. The CIA history, on the other hand, says that this was planned in the initial joint American and British plan, "The London Draft," in Donald N. Wilber, *Overthrow of Premier Mosaddeq of Iran, November 1952-August 1953,* app. B, "London Draft of the TPAJAX Operational Plan" (1954),

31. See Gasiorowski's chapter on the coup; Katouzian, "The CIA Documents"; and Ervand Abrahamian, "The 1953 Coup in Iran," *Science and Society* 65, no. 2 (2001), 182–213.

32. See, for example, Homa Katouzian, "Problems of Democracy and the Public Sphere in Iran," *Comparative Studies of South Asia, Africa, and the Middle East* 18, no. 2 (1998); and id., *Iranian History and Politics.*

33. A look at almost any issue of *Sobh-e Vesal,* for example, would show the point. This was a newspaper created just for the purpose, but some others already in existence before Mosaddeq's premiership, for example, *Atesh,* were not different in that respect.

34. See further Katouzian, *Musaddiq and the Struggle;* id., introduction to *Musaddiq's Memoirs;* and id., introduction to *Khaterat-e Siasi.*

35. On the shah's land reform policy see, for example, Katouzian, *Political Economy;* id., "Oil Versus Agriculture, a Case of Dual Resource Depletion in Iran," *Journal of Peasant Studies* 5, no. 3 (1978): 348–68; and id., "Land Reform in Iran, a Case Study in the Political Economy of Social Engineering," *Journal of Peasant Studies* 1, no. 2 (1974): 220–39.

36. See further Katouzian, *Political Economy;* id., *Musaddiq;* Abrahamian, *Iran Between Two Revolutions;* and H. E. Chehabi, *Iranian Politics and Islamic Modernism: The Liberation Movement of Iran under the Shah and Khomeini* (New York: Cornell Univ. Press, 1990).

37. Quoted in Martin F. Herz, *A View from Tehran: A Diplomatist Looks at the Shah's Regime in June 1964* (Washington, D.C.: Institute for the Study of Diplomacy, Georgetown Univ., 1979).

38. On the history and sociology of state-society relations in Iran, see Katouzian, *Iranian History and Politics.*

39. See Katouzian, *Political Economy.*

40. Ibid.

41. See further Katouzian, *State and Society,* chap. 2.

42. The above analysis has been more widely presented and discussed in several of my works, including "Towards a General Theory"; "The Pahlavi Regime in Iran," in *Sultanistic Regimes,* ed. H. E. Chehabi and J. Linz (Baltimore, Md.: Johns Hopkins Univ. Press, 1997); "Arbitrary Rule"; and *Political Economy,* chaps. 17, 18. For other studies of the subject, see, for example, John Foran, ed., *Theorising Revolutions* (London and New York: Routledge, 1997); and id., *A Century of Revolution* (Minneapolis: Univ. of Minnesota Press, 1994); Chehabi, *Iranian Politics and Islamic Modernism;* Valentine Moghadam, "Populist Revolution and the Islamic State in Iran," in *Revolution in the World System,* ed. Terry Boswell (New York and London: Greenwood, 1989), and id., "Iran: Development, Revolution, and the Problem of Analysis," *Review of Radical Political Economics* 16, no. 3-4 (summer-fall 1984): 227-40; Said Amir Arjomand, *The Turban for the Crown* (Oxford and New York: Oxford Univ. Press, 1988); Mansoor Moaddel, *Class, Politics, and Ideology in the Iranian Revolution* (New York: Columbia Univ. Press, 1993); Abrahamian, *Iran Between Two Revolutions,* chap. 11; and Keddie, *Roots of Revolution,* chap. 7.

43. For a more elaborate explanation of the reasons behind this great change of agenda between the two revolutions and, therefore, the differences between the relative power and importance of different ideologies and their upholders, see Katouzian, *Political Economy,* especially chaps. 4, 10, 17, 18, and "Towards a General Theory."

44. See Katouzian, *State and Society,* chaps. 4–10.

45. See statement by Committee for the Defence and Promotion of Human Rights in Iran, London, Nov. 12, 1979, which condemned the hostage taking, explaining that it was not justified by grievances against the United States, including the 1953 coup. This is reprinted in League for the Defence of Human Rights in Iran, *Human Rights* 52 (spring 1981): 95–96.

2. Unseating Mosaddeq: The Configuration and Role of Domestic Forces

1. In the fall of 1998, Abdollah Nuri, a reformist and former Khatami minister accused of a host of offenses, was tried by the Special Clerical Court and sentenced to five years' imprisonment. One of the charges against Nuri was that of supporting Mosaddeq and the National Front in his newspaper, *Khordad,* which in one issue had defended Mosaddeq against the "baseless"

charge of apostasy, maintaining that "no noble Iranian could be opposed to Mosaddeq." The article had listed Mosaddeq's enemies as "British, American, and Russian colonialists, the deposed shah, Ashraf and her hangers-on, Sayyed Zia, Qavam, and their mercenaries,. . . . the likes of Baqa'i, Ha'erizadeh, Mir-Ashrafi, Amidi-Nuri, Jamal Emami, and their protégés, who are still active" *Khordad,* Feb. 1, 1999; see also Nuri's defense in court, *Shokaran-e Eslah* (Tehran: Tarh-e Nou, 1999), 163–69, 296–98.

2. Minute by Jackson, Feb. 20, 1952, FO 248/1531.

3. Middleton to Eden, Apr. 28, 1952, FO 371/98599; for the text of Kharrazi's report, see *Journal de Tehran,* Apr. 24, 1952.

4. Donald N. Wilber, *Overthrow of Premier Mosaddeq of Iran, November 1952-August 1953* (1954), 27.

5. Henderson to Department of State, Feb. 22, 1953, telegram 3334, 788.00/2–2253.

6. Azimi, *Crisis of Democracy,* 157–58.

7. The pro-Mosaddeq Qashqa'i chieftain, former senator Mohammad Naser Qashqa'i, congratulated Mosaddeq on defeating the military stage of the coup. He also chastised Zahedi for letting himself be used as a catalyst *(muhallel)* by Mosaddeq's enemies. Nasrollah Haddadi, *Salha-ye Bohran: Khaterat-e Ruzaneh-ye Mohammad Naser Solat Qashqa'i* (Tehran: Rasa, 1987/1366), 396–402. In the aftermath of the coup, in view of the Qashqa'i support for Mosaddeq there was for some time a danger of military confrontation between the Qashqa'is and the Zahedi government.

8. Mohammad Reza Pahlavi to his mother, Taj al-Moluk, Nov. 12, 1952/21 Aban 1331, text in *Tarikh-e Mo'aser-e Iran* 4 (1992/1371): 253.

9. Abbasqoli Golsha'iyan, *Gozashtehha va Andisheha-ye Zendegi, ya Khaterat-e Man* (Tehran: Einstein, 1998/1377), 1:880–84, 1:926–27.

10. Henderson to Department of State, Sept. 30, 1951, telegram 1215, 888.2553/9–3051.

11. Mohammad Mosaddeq, speech in the Majles, *Mozakerat-e Majles,* May 25, 1950/4 Khordad 1329.

12. Qavam's open letter, Mar. 17, 1950/26 Esfand 1328, text in *Bakhtar-e Emruz,* Apr. 8, 1950/19 Farvardin 1329. Also in Hossein Makki, *Vaqaye'e Si-ye Tir 1331* (Tehran: Bongah-e Tarjomeh va Nashr-e Ketab, 1981/1360), 157–60.

13. Soon after the coup, when the shah's disregard of constitutional provisions began to become too glaring, a host of politicians vented their complaints to the British and American ambassadors, expecting them to exert a restraining influence over him. Few would, however, publicly voice any direct criticism of the royal conduct, and many continued to invoke contingent factors, such as the impossibility or dangers of real constitutionalism in the prevailing circumstances, to condone the shah's behavior and justify their own role in bolstering him.

14. Hossein Makki, interview, *Tarikh-e Mo'aser-e Iran* 1, no. 1 (spring 1997/1376): 179–216, esp. 195. For a critique of this interview's content, see Aryan Nouzari's article in *Tarikh-e Mo'aser-e Iran* 1, no. 3 (fall 1997/1376): 313–25.

15. Mosaddeq's speech in the Majles, *Mozakerat-e Majles,* May 25, 1950/4 Khordad 1329.

16. Henderson to Department of State, Sept. 27, 1951, telegram 1180, 888.2553/9–2751.

17. Middleton to Bowker, Dec. 17, 1951, FO 371/98595. Mosaddeq's complaints against the queen mother and his threat to resign also reached the press: see *Iran-e Ma,* Dec. 21, 1951/29 Azar 1330.

18. Further on Perron, see Daniela Meier, "Between Court Jester and Spy: The Career of a Swiss Gardener at the Royal Court in Iran. A Footnote to Modern Iranian History," *Critique,* no. 16 (spring 2000): 75–88.

19. Minute by Middleton, Dec. 20, 1951, FO 248/1531.

20. Minute by Middleton, Apr. 18, 1952, FO 248/1531.

21. Minute by Berthoud, June 15, 1951, FO 371/91548.

22. Minute by Zaehner, May 15, 1952, FO 248/1531.

23. Minute by Middleton, June 4, 1952, FO 248/1531.

24. Minute by Middleton, Dec. 20, 1951, FO 248/1531.

25. Wilber, *Overthrow,* 23.

26. Alinaqi Alikhani, *Yaddashtha-ye Alam* (Bethesda, Md.: Iranbooks, 1995), 3:118–19.

27. In his diaries, Alam recounts how, while in exile, he arranged for the kidnapping in Mahshad of a pro-Mosaddeq newspaper proprietor who had "insulted" his wife. The gruesome treatment the man received while being taken to Birjand necessitated prolonged medical treatment. Alikhani, 2:229.

28. Wright to MacMillan, Aug. 3, 1955, FO 371/114811. He later described Alam as "the Shah's pet." Minute by Wright, July 16, 1957, FO 371/127075.

29. Minute by Stevens, July 5, 1955, FO 248/1556; minute by Wright, July 14, 1955, FO 248/1556; minute by Wright, July 29, 1955, FO 248/1556.

30. Henderson to Department of State, May 30, 1952, telegram 4573, 788.11/5–3053.

31. The shah reportedly told Deputy Hadi Taheri that "Musaddiq's reputation should be totally destroyed before he fell." Minute by Pyman, Apr. 17, 1952, FO 248/1531.

32. Wilber, *Overthrow,* 33.

33. Ibid., 23.

34. Fakhreddin Azimi interview with Norman Darbyshire, London, April 1984; Stephen Dorril, *MI6: Fifty Years of Special Operations* (London: Fourth Estate, 2000), 588.

35. Wilber, *Overthrow,* 22–36.

36. Mohammad Mosaddeq, speech in the Majles, *Mozakerat-e Majles,* Apr. 11, 1951/22 Farvardin 1330. In August 1955, Ala told the British chargé d'affaires, Denis Wright, that in his opposition to the AIOC's exploitation, Mosaddeq "had the whole nation behind him"; Mosaddeq "had even induced the Majles to pass his bills, whereas previously they had refused to pass the budget bill." Mosaddeq, Ala added, "had made two mistakes: he had encouraged the Tudeh as a weapon against Britain and the United States, and he had tried to diminish the position of the Shah, an action contrary to the beliefs of the whole nation." Minute by Wright, Aug. 2, 1955, FO 248/1556.

37. Minute by Middleton, July 4, 1952, FO 248/1531; minute by Falle, June 28, 1952, FO 248/1531.

38. Ala to Taqizadeh, Oct. 23, 1947/1 Aban 1326, text in *Ayandeh* 16, nos. 9–12 (Nov. 1990-Mar. 1991/Azar-Esfand 1369): 796–97.

39. Ala's daily reports to the shah, text in *Tarikh-e Mo'aser-e Iran* 1, no. 2 (summer 1997/1376): 130–74; see esp. report of Aug. 24, 1953/2 Shahrivar 1332, 134–36.

40. See, for instance, Ashraf to Ala, Dec. 27, 1953/6 Day 1332, text in Jalal Andarmanizadeh and Mokhtar Hadidi, eds., *Pahlaviha* (Tehran: Nasar, 1999/1378), 2:319.

41. Ala's report to the shah, Aug. 24, 1953, *Tarikh-e Mo'aser-e Iran* 1, no. 2 (summer

1997/1376):134–36. These politicians were, incidentally, among the most intractable enemies of Mosaddeq.

42. Henderson to Department of State, May 24, 1952, telegram 4540, 788.11/5–2452.

43. Henderson to Department of State, June 13, 1952, telegram 4837, 788.13/6–1352.

44. Henderson to Department of State, Mar. 31, 1953, telegram 3853, 788.00/3–3153.

45. Henderson to Department of State, Apr. 15, 1953, telegram 4027, 788.00/4–1553.

46. Quoted in Javad Shaikh al-Islami, *Sima-ye Ahmad Shah Qajar* (Tehran: Goftar, 1989/1368) 1:172.

47. Cyrus Ghani, ed., *Yaddashtha-ye Doktor Qasem Ghani* (London: Ithaca, 1984), 9:28, 9:151, 9:229–32; see also, Mohammad Reza Abbasi and Behruz Tayarani, *Khaterat-e Nasrollah Entezam* (Tehran: Iranian National Archives, 1992/1371), 189.

48. A typical example of Anglophile propaganda can be found in the pro-Sayyed Zia newspaper *Eradeh-ye Azerbaijan;* in its Apr. 12, 1952/23 Farvardin 1331 issue, the paper denounced Mosaddeq as a "reactionary" whose aim was to perpetuate the power of his own landowning class. It further argued that British intervention in Iran was needed in order to counterbalance Soviet influence. Copies of this article were provided by the Foreign Office to a number of British newspapers to use in their coverage of Iran.

49. Mohammad Mosaddeq, speech in the Majles, *Mozakerat-e Majles,* Sept. 8, 1951/17 Shahrivar 1330.

50. See, for instance, C. M. Woodhouse, *The New Concert of Nations* (London: Bodley Head, 1946). Woodhouse wrote, "What is particularly striking is the way in which the emotion can be tapped not only to excite hostility against foreigners but also for internecine purposes amounting virtually to civil war" (37); for a similar view of nationalism, see Elie Kedourie, *Nationalism* (London: Hutchinson, 1960).

51. Shepherd to FO, Sept. 4, 1951, FO 371/91463; Shepherd, "A Comparison Between Persian and Asian Nationalism," Oct. 11, 1951, FO 371/91464; Wheeler's letter, Oct. 1951, FO 371/91464; minute by Sarell, Feb. 13, 1952, FO 371/98596. Relying on Lambton, Sarell provided a characterization of Iranian nationalism more nuanced than Shepherd's. See Wm. Roger Louis's essay in the present collection.

52. For the dilemmas facing the British government, the nuances of the British position, and the role of key individuals involved, see Wm. Roger Louis, *The British Empire in the Middle East, 1945–1951* (Oxford: Oxford Univ. Press, 1984); id., "Musaddiq and the Dilemmas of British Imperialism," in Bill and Louis, 228–60; and Louis's chapter in the present collection.

53. Shepherd to FO, Sept. 19, 1951, FO 371/91433.

54. Azimi's interview with Darbyshire, April 1984. According to Darbyshire, the cost of the coup was seven hundred thousand pounds sterling; this was the sum that he himself spent.

55. Wilber, *Overthrow,* 7.

56. Alkhani, 3:57, 3:73, 3:98, 3:110.

57. Falle's letter, Feb. 28, 1957, FO 371/127074. Falle wrote: "We cannot afford to neglect those who over a long period of time have proved their loyalty to us."

58. See C. M. Woodhouse, *Something Ventured* (London: Granada Publishing, 1982), 104–35. Hasan Alavi, a physician and deputy for Bushehr in the Sixteenth Majles, is one of the contacts he names. A known Anglophile, Alavi acted as an informer rather than as an active opponent of Mosaddeq. Among those who assisted Woodhouse were Shapour Reporter, who ini-

tially worked for MI6 but when diplomatic relations with Britain were severed went to work for the American embassy. With the resumption of Anglo-Iranian diplomatic relations, Reporter resumed his work with MI6, for some time posing as a correspondent for the *Times* of London. He would later acquire considerable influence, mainly as a political and business broker. Woodhouse also mentions a "Director-general of an important department" in Mosaddeq's government who provided him with "intimate details, from within the Iranian administration" and whom Woodhouse refers to as "Omar" (112–13). The identity of "Omar" is still not known for certain; among the most likely candidates is Abdolhossein Meftah, the deputy foreign minister. He was married to an English woman and was the son of Sir Dawood Meftah, a diplomat with close links with Britain who was created Knight Commander of the Order of St. Michael and St. George (KCMG) by the king of England in 1905. Abdolhossein Meftah also reportedly provided information to the American embassy. See Makki, *Kudeta-ye 28 Mordad 1332* (Tehran: Elmi, 1999/1378), 303–4. Meftah retained his position at the foreign ministry following the coup.

59. Azimi's interview with Darbyshire.

60. Shepherd to FO, May 1, 1951, FO 371/91456; minute by Hillier-Fry, May 3, 1951, FO 248/1514. Mostafa Fateh, a former employee of the AIOC, fairly regularly sent his "diaries" or observations on the Iranian political scene to the company's headquarters in England, invariably predicting the imminent collapse of the Mosaddeq government. The company passed these diaries on to the Foreign Office.

61. Minute by Zaehner, May 3, 1952, FO 248/1531.

62. Minute by Pyman, July 11, 1951, FO 248/1514; minute by Pyman, Sept. 13, 1951, id.

63. Minute by Hillier-Fry, July 12, 1951, FO 248/1514; minute by Pyman, Sept. 13, 1951, id.; minute by Pyman, Aug. 28, 1951, id.; minute by Pyman, Aug. 30, 1951, id.; FO minute, Aug. 29, 1951, FO 371/91462; minute by Pyman, Aug. 29, 1951, FO 248/1514; minute by Pyman, Sept. 5, 1951, id.; minute by Pyman, Aug. 30, 1951, id.; minute by Pyman, Dec. 19, 1951, id.

64. Minute by Pyman, Sept. 8, 1951, FO 248/1514; minute by Jackson, Dec. 13, 1951, id.

65. Minute by Zaehner, May 1, 1952, FO 248/1531.

66. Shepherd to Morrison, July 16, 1951, FO 371/91462; Shepherd to FO, Sept. 15, 1951, FO 371/91463. Hillier-Fry of the British embassy had maintained that the "strong-arm or rough-neck side of the party should be organized as soon as possible." Minute by Hillier-Fry, July 12, 1951, FO 248/1514. In addition, the party headquarters was a center of intelligence gathering. Minute by Jackson, Feb. 13, 1952, FO 248/1531.

67. Minutes by Pyman, Sept. 15, 17, 1951, FO 248/1415; minute by Middleton, Sept. 18, 1951, id.

68. Minute by Rothnie, Sept. 5, 1951, FO 248/1415; Baker to Attlee, Sept. 2, 1951, FO 371/91463.

69. Henderson to Department of State, Sept. 27, 1951, telegram 1180, 888.2553/9–2751; rather than insisting on his own appointment as prime minister, Sayyed Zia concentrated on pressing the shah to accept that the time had come to replace Mosaddeq.

70. Minute by Pyman, Sept. 1951, FO 248/1514. The shah told Sayyed Zia that he could not tell the people that he had appointed him prime minister "because London wanted it."

71. For Qavam's open letter and Hakimi's response, see *Bakhtar-e Emruz,* Apr. 8, 1950/19 Farvardin 1329. See also Qavam's response, id., July 3, 1950/12 Tir 1329.

72. Minute by Pyman, Nov. 5, 1951, FO 248/1514; Middleton to FO, Nov. 16, 1951, FO 371/91465; see further Fakhreddin Azimi, "Qavam va Soda-ye Chirehgar-e Qodrat," in *Haftad Maqaleh,* ed. Iraj Afshar and Yahya Mahdavi (Tehran: Asatir, 1369/1990), 1:242–69.

73. Grady to Department of State, May 7, 1951, telegram 2692, 788.005–751.

74. See for instance, Alikhani, 1:390–91.

75. Taqizadeh to Qavam, Nov. 29, 1942/8 Azar 1321, in Iraj Afshar, *Namehha-ye Landan* (Tehran: Farzan, 1996/1375), 7–17.

76. Taqizadeh to Nasrollah Entezam, Feb. 15, 1945/26 Bahman 1323, in Afshar, *Namehha-ye Landan,* 153–87.

77. Taqizadeh, speech in the Majles, *Mozakerat-e Majles,* Jan. 27, 1949/7 Bahman 1327.

78. Fakhreddin Azimi's interview with Iraj Afshar, Tehran, July 2000.

79. Minute by Shepherd, Sept. 22, 1951, FO 248/1514.

80. Iraj Afshar, ed., *Zendegi-ye Tufani: Khaterat-e Sayyed Hasan Taqizadeh* (Tehran: Elmi, 1993/1372) 366–72.

81. For the names of these deputies and journalists, see *Shahed,* Dec. 12, 1951/20 Azar 1330.

82. *Bakhtar-e Emruz,* Dec. 11, 1951/19 Azar 1330.

83. Middleton to Bowker, Dec. 17, 1951, FO 371/98595.

84. Minute by Pyman, Jan. 2, 1952, FO 248/1531; minute by Pyman, Jan. 27, 1952, id.; minute by Pyman, Apr. 22, 1952, id.; minute by Zaehner, May 3, 1952, id.

85. Minute by Pyman, Jan. 7, 1952, FO 248/1531.

86. According to Richard Cottam, the army, prompted by the shah, engineered the election of Mehdi Mir-Ashrafi, the "thoroughly corrupt and opportunistic editor of *Atesh,*" as deputy for Meshkinshahr, a district that was part of "military zones under direct control of the Army." Richard Cottam, *Nationalism in Iran* (Pittsburgh, Pa.: Univ. of Pittsburgh Press, 1979), 276.

87. Middleton to Eden, May 5, 1952, FO 371/98599.

88. Mosaddeq to the Majles, *Bakhtar-e Emruz,* Apr. 30, 1952/10 Ordibehesht 1331. See also Makki, *Vaqe'h-ye Si-ye Tir 1331,* 62–67.

89. Minute by Zaehner, May 15, 1952, FO 248/1531.

90. Ibid.

91. Minutes by Falle, June 14, June 21, 1952, FO 248/1531.

92. Minute by Falle, July 13, 1952, FO 248/1531.

93. Henderson to Department of State, June 13, 1952, telegram 4837, 788.13/6–1352. Henderson urged the shah to show the same "decisiveness" he had shown in 1946 regarding the Azerbaijan crisis, and warned him that if he allowed Iran to "continue [the] drift towards ruin," confidence in the throne might "dangerously ebb."

94. Minute by Zaehner, June 11, 1952, FO 248/1531.

95. Henderson to Department of State, July 7, 1952, telegram 98.1, 788.13/7–752.

96. Minute by Falle, July 9, 1952, FO 248/1531.

97. Middleton to Eden, July 28, 1952, FO 371/98602. Julian Amery, a Conservative mem-

ber of the House of Commons, had also worked hard on Qavam's behalf, but, according to Darbyshire, he "failed miserably." Azimi's interview with Darbyshire.

98. Woodhouse, *Something Ventured,* 116–17.

99. Henderson to Department of State, July 7, 1952, telegram 98.1, 788.13/7–752.

100. Minute by Zaehner, Mar. 18, 1952, FO 248/1531; minute by Zaehner, May 17, 1952, id.

101. Minute by Pyman, Jan. 2, 1952, FO 248/1531; minute by Pyman, Jan. 23, 1952, id.

102. Henderson to Department of State, June 27, 1952, telegram 5047, 788.00/6–2752.

103. Middleton to Eden, July 28, 1952, FO 371/98602. The fall of Qavam, for which the shah was primarily blamed, provoked considerable British anger against the shah and plans for his denunciation. A. D. M. Ross of the Foreign Office noted, "I think as far as our influence goes we should try to call off the denigration of the Shah. It can not do us any good now." Minute by Ross, July 22, 1952, FO 371/98603.

104. Mohammad Mosaddeq, *Khaterat va Ta'allomat,* ed. Iraj Afshar (Tehran: Elmi, 1986/1365), 260. Mosaddeq pledged to the shah that he was not opposed to constitutional monarchy nor did he intend to change the regime or become president.

105. Minute by Zaehner, May 15, 1952, FO 248/1531.

106. Mohammad Ali Movahhed, *Khab-e Ashofteh-ye Naft: Doktor Mosaddeq va Nehzat-e Melli-ye Iran* (Tehran: Karnameh, 1999/1378), 2:776.

107. According to the British embassy, Kashani's sons, Abulma'ali and Mostafa, started a lucrative business assisting "merchants to clear from customs goods on the prohibited [government] list." Minute by Jackson, Feb. 20, 1952, FO 248/1531. With three wives, Kashani sired no fewer than twenty-six children, including twelve sons. According to Shams Qanatabadi, his one-time protégé and the leader of the pro-Kashani group Association of Muslim Warriors, "among his sons in those days only Mostafa was good and worthy." Qanatabadi uses derogatory terms to describe Kashani's eldest son, Mohammad. Shams Qanatabadi, *Sayri dar Nehzat-e Melli Shodan-e Naft: Khaterat-e Shams Qanatabadi* (Tehran: Markaz-e Barrasi-ye Asnad-ye Tarikhi. 1998/1377), 271–76. Mostafa Kashani, actively involved in the anti-Mosaddeq campaign, won a seat in the Eighteenth Majles. Similarly, Qanatabadi, who collaborated in the coup, was rewarded with a seat in the Majles; soon after, he abandoned his turban and other pretenses in favor of close links with the royal court.

108. Henderson to Department of State, June 27, 1952, telegram 5047, 788.00/6–2752.

109. See further Azimi, *Crisis of Democracy,* 291ff.

110. Mosaddeq to Kashani, July 28, 1952/6 Mordad 1331, text in Mohammad Torkaman, *Namehha-ye Doktor Mosaddeq* (Tehran 1998/1377), 1:216.

111. *Bakhtar-e Emruz,* Sept. 23, 1952/1 Mehr 1331, Sept. 27, 1952/5 Mehr 1331. According to Middleton, a large number of deputies congregated in Kashani's house, where pro-Kashani deputies such as Qanatabadi and Karimi attacked the government. Middleton to Eden, Sept. 30, 1952, FO 371/98604.

112. Mohammad Dehnovi, *Majmu'eh'i az Maktubat, Sokhanraniha va Payamha-ye Ayatollah Kashani* (Tehran: Ashna, 1982–85/1361–64), 3:206–8.

113. Ibid., 205, 213. See also Kashani's letter to Mosaddeq, ibid., 210–12.

114. Kazem Hasibi, unpublished diaries, entry for Feb. 20, 1953/1 Esfand 1331, quoted in Movahhed, *Khab-e Ashofteh-ye Naft,* 2:775–76.

115. CIA memorandum prepared for the president, Mar. 1, 1953, S/P-NSC files, lot 61D167, *FRUS, 1952–1954,* 10:689–91. Qanatabadi, however, describes Kashani as a "true royalist" who used to say, "My considered opinion is that for Moslems a monarchical regime and a monarch *(soltan)* is better and more appropriate than all other regimes." *Sayri dar Nehzat-e Melli Shodan-e Naft,* 271–72.

116. *Keyhan,* Mar. 1, 1953/10 Esfand 1331; Dehnovi, 3:272. One Foreign Office official noted, "If in the end Musaddiq succeeds in reasserting his control of events, Kashani will have suffered his most serious setback to date." Minute by Rothnie, Mar. 2, 1953, FO 371/104563.

117. On parliamentary factions, see *Jebheh-ye Azadi,* Apr. 21, 1953/1 Ordibehesht 1332.

118. Minute by Rothnie, May 11, 1953, FO 371/104565.

119. CIA memorandum, Mar. 1, 1953. The British concurred; minute by Rothnie, FO 371/104565.

120. Henderson to Department of State, Aug. 11, 1952, telegram 624, 788.00/8–1152. See also Taher Ahmadzadeh, "Tahlili az Nehzat-e Melli-ye Iran," in Bahram Afrasiabi, *Mosaddeq va Tarikh* (Tehran: Nilufar, 1981/1360), 257–339, esp. 324–26.

121. See, for instance, Kashani's statement of July 6, 1953/15 Tir 1332 in Dehnovi, 3:395–98.

122. For a cogent Mosaddeqist assessment and critique of Kashani's political conduct, see Farhang Rehman, "Kashani va Mosaddeq," *Jebheh-ye Azadi,* May 1–27, 1953/16 Ordibehesht–6 Khordad 1332.

123. Gholam Reza Nejati, ed., *Shast Sal Khedmat va Moqavemat: Khaterat-e Mohandes Mehdi Bazargan* (Tehran: Rasa, 1998/1377), 1:291.

124. Minute by Middleton, Sept. 22, 1951, FO 248/1531.

125. Nejati, *Shast Sal Khedmat.* Bazargan asserts that "on all issues, Makki considered himself entitled to order others around."

126. According to a U.S. report of early April quoting Ala, Kashani and Makki, while supporting Zahedi, "hesitated to go all out" and appeared "to maintain a position which would allow them to plead non-involvement should the attempt to overthrow Musaddiq by peaceful or other means fail." Top secret memorandum, Apr. 7, 1953, FO 371/104564.

127. *Bakhtar-e Emruz,* June 7, 1953/17 Khordad 1332. See also Mohammad Ali Safari, *Qalam va Siasat* (Tehran: Namak, 1992/1371), 1:787–88.

128. Most of Makki's books, although useful as documentary sources, are compilations, interspersed with comments aimed at underlining his own crucial role and impeccable record. See, for instance, Makki, *Vaqay'-e Si-ye Tir;* id., *Khaterat-e Siasi-ye Hossein Makki* (Tehran: Elmi, 1989/1368); and id., *Kudeta-ye 28 Mordad 1332.* See also Hossein Makki, *Ketab-e Siah* (Tehran: Bongah-e Tarjomeh va Nashr-e Ketab/Elmi, 1981–98/1360–77).

129. Karim Sanjabi, *Omidha va Naomidiha* (London: Jebheh, 1989/1368), 125.

130. FO to New York, Nov. 19, 1952, FO 371/98606.

131. Minute by Rothnie for Director of Military Intelligence, Jan. 17, 1953, FO 371/104561.

132. Minute by Rothnie, Feb. 7, 1953, FO 371/104562.

133. On July 16, 1952, the very day of Mosaddeq's resignation, Sepahbodi wrote a letter urging Baqa'i to make continuation of Toilers Party support for Mosaddeq conditional upon obtaining tangible concessions and radical changes in Mosaddeq's policies. Sepahbodi to Qavam,

July 16, 1952/25 Tir 1331, text in Hossein Abadian, *Zendeginameh-ye Siasi-ye Doktor Mozaffar Baqa'i* (Tehran: Institute of Political Studies and Research, 1998/1377), 142–44

134. Baqa'i's loyalists, constituting a small minority, could only accomplish this and occupy the party headquarters with support provided by Qanatabadi. Qanatabadi, *Sayri dar Nehzat-e Melli Shodan-e Naft*, 322–25. For a revealing indictment of Baqa'i by a Maleki loyalist, see Jalal Al-e Ahmad's letter to Baqa'i, published in *Niru-ye Sevvom*, Oct. 18, 1952/26 Mehr 1331, reprinted in Ali Dehbashi, ed., *Namehha-ye Jalal Al-e Ahmad* (Tehran: Bozorgmehr, 1988/1367), 43–49.

135. Fakhreddin Azimi's interview with Mozaffar Baqa'i, Tehran, Sept. 1979. Maleki's steady support for Mosaddeq added to Baqa'i's bitterness; in the interview he asserted that "Mosaddeq purchased Maleki in order to use him against us."

136. Abadian, 170.

137. Middleton to Ross, Oct. 13, 1952, FO 371/98605.

138. In January 1952, the shah called Jahangir Tafazolli, editor of *Iran-e Ma*, and "reproached him bitterly" for his attacks against Baqa'i and the Toilers Party. Middleton to Ross, Jan. 28, 1952, FO 248/1531. In 1955 Hasan Emami told an employee of the British embassy that Baqa'i had connections with the shah before the July 1952 uprising and was still in league with him. According to Emami, "The Shah uses him [Baqa'i] as a dog to attack others, but does not realize that the dog might attack his master if necessary." Minute by S. M. Sajjadi, Apr. 16, 1955, FO 248/1555. The shah also reportedly referred to Baqa'i as the "dog of Naziabad" (a district in Tehran), which attacks his master as well as strangers. Makki, *Khaterat*, 605.

139. See Mozaffar Baqa'i, *Doktor Mozaffar Baqa'i Kermani dar Pishgah-e Tarikh* (Kerman: Param, 1979/1358).

140. Azimi's interview with Baqa'i.

141. See *Shahed*, especially April 1953 onward. The newspaper concentrated on the theme of "the terrible specter of communism" haunting the country. *Shahed*, Apr. 9, 1953/20 Farvardin 1332. *Shahed* helped to spread rumors damaging to Mosaddeq; in the Aug. 3, 1953/12 Mordad 1332 issue it announced that Ayatollah Borujerdi intended to leave Iran in protest against Mosaddeq's policies; on Aug. 18, 1953/27 Mordad 1332, while publishing the royal decree appointing Zahedi as prime minister, its editorial announced, "Hitler Burnt the Reichstag: Mosaddeq Fakes a Coup."

142. *Bakhtar-e Emruz*, Mar. 1, 1953/10 Esfand 1332.

143. Not surprisingly, Makki lavishes praise on Ha'erizadeh as a man unrivaled in "courage, tenacity of purpose, veracity, nobility of spirit, love of mankind, love of liberty, and candor; more significantly, he has no peers in friendship, sincerity, and lack of hypocrisy." Makki, *Khaterat*, 521–22.

144. Ha'erizadeh, speeches in the Majles, *Mozakerat-e Majles*, May 19, 20, 1953/29, 30 Ordibehesht 1332.

145. Henderson to Department of State, Mar. 31, 1953, telegram 3853, 788.00/3–3153. According to British sources, he was pressed by Ayatollah Behbahani to refuse. Minute by Rothnie, Apr. 2, 1953, FO 371/104564. This offer had apparently been made to him by Fatemi. *Bakhtar-e Emruz*, Mar. 30, 1953/10 Farvardin 1332. Ha'erizadeh was eventually appointed to this position by Zahedi, as well as being given a seat in the Eighteenth Majles; he was the only prominent defector thus rewarded.

146. Ardeshir Zahedi, "Five Decisive Days, August 14–16, 1953," mimeograph, 3.

147. Ahmadzadeh, "Tahlili az Nehzat-e Melli-ye Iran," 313.

148. Threats from the Feda'iyan accounted for Shams al-Din Amir Ala'i's relinquishing his position as minister of justice. Middleton to Ross, Feb. 11, 1952, FO 371/98596; see also Hasibi, diary entry for Feb. 17, 1952/27 Bahman 1330, text in Movahhed, *Khab-e Ashofteh-ye Naft,* 1:443.

149. Two weeks later, Sayyed Zia told Zaehner that Fatemi had initiated a plan for the elimination of five opponents, including Sayyed Zia, Jamal Emami, Abolhasan Amidi-Nuri, and Mehdi Piraseh. Minute by Zaehner, Mar. 1, 1952, FO 248/1531. Further on Fatemi, see Bahram Afrasiabi, *Khaterat va Mobarezat-e Doktor Hossein Fatemi* (Tehran: Sokhan, 1987/1366); Mohammad Torkaman, *Beh Yad-e Shaheed Doktor Hossein Fatemi* (Tehran: Hazaran, 1995/1374); see also Azimi, *Encyclopaedia Iranica,* s.v. "Fatemi, Hosyn."

150. Minute by Zaehner, Feb. 16, 1952, FO 248/1531.

151. The government continued to prosecute Razmara's assassin, Tahmasebi, for illegal possession of weapons. In an interview Tahmasebi had, however, regretted the assassination attempt on Fatemi, maintaining that foreigners had indirectly used and manipulated the Feda'iyan. *Bakhtar-e Emruz,* Aug. 10, 1952/19 Mordad 1331.

152. Ahmadzadeh, "Tahlili az Nehzat-e Melli-ye Iran," 314. In *Nagoftehha* (Tehran: Rasa, 1991/1371) Mehdi Eraqi attributes the defection to disagreements with Vahedi. The index indicates that Sayyed Zia's name is mentioned on page 122, where the defection is discussed, but it does not in fact appear on that page. Hajji Ebrahim Sarrafan, an associate of Sayyed Zia, is alleged to have financially supported the Feda'iyan and to have exerted influence over its leader. It is claimed that, in the hope of appealing to the group, Sayyed Zia had pledged to restore the veil *(hejab).* The court also apparently had tried to infiltrate and use the Feda'iyan through Bahram Shahrokh, a Zoroastrian and former Persian broadcaster for the Nazi regime's overseas radio service in Berlin. See further Mohammad Torkaman, *Tashannojat, Dargiriha-ye Khiabani va Tote'ehha dar Doran-e Hokumat-e Doktor Mohammad Mosaddeq* (Tehran: Rasa, 1980/1359), esp. 101–8.

153. The CIA and SIS intended to use the Feda'iyan, which they referred to as a "terrorist gang," "to threaten that they [were] ready to take direct action against pro-Mosaddeq deputies and members of Mosaddeq's entourage and government." Wilber, *Overthrow,* app. B, 21.

154. In late May 1952, for instance, a cleric named Abolhasan Sharif al-Ulama told the British embassy not to neglect spending money to provoke the clergy against Mosaddeq, adding that whereas a few months before half a million toman had been needed, now one hundred thousand would suffice. Minute by Jackson, May 28, 1952, FO 248/1531.

155. Minute by Jackson, May 21, 1951, FO 248/1531; see further Azimi, *Crisis of Democracy,* 391 n. 161.

156. *Azad Mard: Shaheed Tayyeb Haj Reza'i beh Revayat-e Asnad-e Savak* (Tehran: Markaz-e Barrasi-ye Asnad-e Tarikhi, 1999/1378), 33–39.

157. Minute by Jackson, May 24, 1952, FO 248/1531.

158. Ali Davani et al., eds., *Khaterat va Mobarezat-e Hojjat al-Islam Falsafi* (Tehran: Documentation Center, Islamic Revolution, 1997/1376), 138.

159. Fyman to Ross, Mar. 3, 1952, FO 371/98596.

160. Minute by Jackson, June 6, 1952, FO 248/1531.

161. Davani, *Khaterat va Mobarezat-e Hojjat al-Islam Falsafi,* 112–17.

162. Ibid., 133.

163. Ibid., 136.

164. Ibid., 141.

165. Sayyed Nureddin and his followers attacked the pro-government Iran Party, as well as the office of the American Point IV program. Fereydun Tavallali alleges police and local authority complicity with Sayyed Nureddin's mobs. See Tavallali, letter in *Niru-ye Sevvom,* Apr. 18, 1953/29 Farvardin 1332. See also *Ettela'at,* Apr. 18, 1953. Similarly, in Mashhad the clerics collected funds, prepared a pro-shah petition, and intended to resort to anti-Tudeh activities. Minute by Rothnie, May 13, 1953, FO 371/104566.

166. Such figures in Tehran included Sayyed Reza Firuzabadi, Sayyed Reza Zanjani, Sayyed Mahmud Taleqani, Sayyed Ja'afar Gharavi, and Sayyed Zia al-Din Javadi.

167. Fakhreddin Azimi's interview with Professor Mehdi Ha'eri Yazdi, Oxford, Sept. 1985. Ha'eri liaised between Mosaddeq and Borujerdi.

168. *Keyhan,* Apr. 28, 1953/8 Ordibehesht 1332.

169. See Davari, *Khaterat va Mobarezat-e Hojjat al-Islam Falsafi,* 134.

170. According to a confidential report by the Reuters correspondent in Baghdad quoting the Iraqi ambassador in Tehran, soon after the coup of August 1953 the shah and Zahedi paid Kashani a visit, kissing his hand and "thanking him for his spiritual and open cooperation to restore [the] monarchy in the country." Reuters correspondent, Baghdad, to chief news editor, diplomatic desk, Sept. 1, 1953, FO 371/104571.

171. Wilber, *Overthrow,* 57.

172. Ibid., app. A, 4–5.

173. See, for instance, *Shahed,* Aug. 3, 1953/12 Mordad 1332.

174. The party newspaper denounced Mosaddeq and the National Front as having gained power with American backing and as being dedicated to enhancing American influence in Iran. *Razm,* July 15, 1951/23 Tir 1330; *Mardom,* July 21, 1951/29 Tir 1330; *Mardom,* Aug. 6, 1951/14 Mordad 1330.

175. *Mardom,* Aug. 22, 1951/30 Mordad 1330.

176. *Mardom,* Aug. 11, 18, Sept. 1, 1951/19, 26 Mordad, 9 Shahrivar 1330.

177. *Nameh-ye No (Beh Su-ye Ayandeh),* Oct. 15, 1952/23 Mehr 1331.

178. In the post-July 1952 uprising period, for instance, the party organized three major labor strikes in Tehran; see [Arsalan Puriya], *Karnameh-ye Mosaddeq va Hezb-e Tudeh* (Florence: Mazdak, n.d.), 2:401ff. See further Abdollah Borhan, *Karnameh-ye Hezb-e Tudeh va Raz-e Soqut-e Mosaddeq* (Tehran: Elm, 2000/1379); see also Maziar Behrooz's chapter in this volume and his *Rebels with a Cause: The Failure of the Left in Iran* (London: I. B. Tauris, 1999).

179. According to the British embassy, by the end of 1951, out of seventeen anti-government demonstrations, at least fourteen had been organized by the Tudeh Party. Minute by Pyman, Dec. 23, 1951, FO 248/1531.

180. Nureddin Kianuri, a prominent party leader, unconvincingly claims that the demonstrations had nothing to do with Harriman's arrival (Kianuri, *Khaterat-e Nureddin Kianuri* [Tehran: Ettela'at, 1992/1371], 220–21). The ensuing clashes with the police and anti-Tudeh groups resulted in more than twenty deaths and over two hundred injured. This episode also involved elements other than the Tudeh Party. According to one account, intending to demonstrate their effectiveness and impress the CIA, which was considering their recruitment, Ali Jalali

and Faruq Kayvani played a role in planting agents provocateurs among the demonstrators. See Gasiorowski's essay in this collection.

181. See, for instance, Emami's parliamentary speeches, *Mozakerat-e Majles,* July 15, Nov. 1, Nov. 28, 1951/23 Tir, 9 Aban, 6 Azar 1330.

182. Minute by Logan, Apr. 9, 1951, FO 371/91467. Bozorg Alavi, a former Tudeh leader, concurs with Shepherd's estimate. Fakhreddin Azimi's interview with Bozorg Alavi, Oxford, May 1983.

183. *Beh Su-ye Ayandeh,* Feb. 12, 13, 1952/22, 23 Bahman 1330.

184. *Shahbaz,* Jan. 11, 1953/21 Day 1331; see also *Beh Su-ye Ayandeh,* Jan. 15, 20, 21, 1953/25, 30 Day, 1 Bahman 1331. This newspaper described Mosaddeq as a "despot" bent on trampling underfoot the rights of the Iranian people in the interests of "American imperialists"; it later characterized Mosaddeq's attitude as "doubt-ridden, indecisive and compromising." Feb. 2, 1953/11 Esfand 1331.

185. The Tudeh Party did advocate the formation of an anti-imperialist front, particularly when Mosaddeq's government was facing right-wing challenges. *Beh Su-ye Ayandeh,* Feb. 29, 1953/9 Esfand 1331. Such calls were dismissed by Mosaddeqists who maintained that the firmly pro-Soviet Tudeh Party "played no role in the anti-imperialist struggles of the Iranian people." *Jebheh-ye Azadi,* June 17, 1953/27 Khordad 1332.

186. Mohammad Mosaddeq, *Khaterat va Ta'allomat,* 272.

187. Ibid., 237–38.

188. Hossein Khoshniyat, *Sayyed Mojtaba Navab Safavi* (Tehran: Manshur-e Baradari, 1981/1360), 112.

189. Wilber, *Overthrow,* 37.

190. This is more or less admitted by the Tudeh activists. See, for instance, Mohammad Ali Amui, *Dord-e Zamaneh* (Tehran: Anzan, 1998/1377), 77.

191. Minute by Falle, July 28, 1952; FO248/1531.

192. On the oil issue, see further Movahhed, *Khab-e Ashofteh-ye Naft,* Elm, *Oil, Power, and Principle,,* and Heiss, *Empire and Nationhood,.*

193. Secretary of state to the secretary of defense (Lovett), Nov. 4, 1952; 888.2553/11–2452.

194. John Colville, *The Fringes of Power: 10 Downing Street Diaries, 1939–1955* (New York and London: Norton, 1986), 653–54. Colville adds, "But Anthony Eden, completing his honeymoon in Lisbon, is furious. It is not the substance but the method which displeases him: the stealing by Winston of his personal thunder."

195. Acting secretary of state to the embassy in the United Kingdom, Aug. 24, 1952, telegram 1310, 888.2553/8–2452.

196. Minute by Bowker, July 3, 1951, FO 371/91461; Bowker to Shepherd, July 5, 1951, id.

197. Shepherd to Strang, Sept. 11, 1951, FO 371/91463.

198. Minute by Middleton, Jan. 10, 1952, FO 248/1463; minute by Falle, May 24, 1952, id.

199. Embassy minute, July 26, 1952, FO 248/1513.

200. Minute by Ross, July 29, 1952, FO 248/1531.

201. Middleton to Bowker, July 28, 1952, FO 371/98602.

202. Henderson to Department of State, July 31, 1952, telegram 481, 788.13/7–3152.

203. Henderson to Department of State, Sept. 20, 1952, telegram 1220, 888.2553/9–2052.

204. Minute by Falle, July 22, 1952, FO 248/1531.

205. War Office to Military Attaché, Tehran, July 29, 1952, FO 371/98602.

206. Middleton to FO, Aug. 6, 1952, FO 371/98602.

207. Henderson to Department of State, Aug. 25, 1952, telegram 843, 888.2553/8–2552.

208. Minute by Falle, Aug. 7, 1952, FO 248/1531.

209. Id., July 28, 1952.

210. Amembassy, Tehran, to SecState, Washington, D.C.., Jan. 28, 1979, text in *Asnad-e Laneh-ye Jasusi,* vol. 27 (Tehran, n.d.).

211. Henderson to Department of State, Mar. 31, 1953, telegram 3853, 788.00/3–3153.

212. Middleton to FO, Oct. 22, 1952, FO 371/98605.

213. Henderson to Department of State, Feb. 22, 1953, telegram 3334, 788.00/2–2253.

214. Top secret memorandum, Apr. 7, 1953, FO 371/104564.

215. Minute by Falle, Aug. 7, 1952, FO 248/1531.

216. Middleton to Ross, Oct. 12, 1952, FO 371/98605.

217. *Bakhtar-e Emruz,* Oct. 13, 1952/21 Mehr 1331.

218. Zahedi's statement, *Dad,* Oct. 15, 1952/23 Mehr 1331; Zahedi, speech in the Senate, *Mozakerat-e Sena,* Oct. 15, 1952/23 Mehr 1331.

219. British consulates in Iranian provincial towns were closed down in January 1952. This development, the Fatemi-edited *Bakhtar-e Emruz* argued, should have been followed by Iranian demands for the recall of British diplomatic personnel such as Zaehner, Jackson, and Pyman, thereby putting an end to their "sabotaging activities." *Bakhtar-e Emruz,* Apr. 5, 1952/16 Farvardin 1331.

220. *Dad,* Oct. 15, 1952/23 Mehn 1331.

221. Henderson to Department of State, Jan. 17, 1953, telegram 2754, 888.2553/1–1753.

222. Ibid.

223. Henderson to Department of State, Feb. 14, 1953, telegram 3184, 888.2553/2–1453.

224. Henderson to Department of State, Feb. 22, 1953, telegram 3334, 788.00/2–2253.

225. Henderson to Department of State, Feb. 24, 1953, telegram 3358, 788.00/2–2453.

226. Henderson to Department of State, Feb. 25, 1953, telegram 3393, 788.11/2–2553.

227. Henderson to Department of State, Feb. 22, 1953, telegram, 3334, 788.00/2–2253.

228. Henderson to Department of State, Feb. 24, 1953, telegram 3358, 788.00/2–2453.

229. Minute by Rothnie, Feb. 24, 1953, FO 371/104562.

230. *Azad Mard,* 33–39.

231. Ja'fari later asserts that Kashani told him to do everything to prevent the shah's departure from the country, adding that "if the Shah should leave, our turbans will also be lost." Homa Sarshar, ed. *Sha'ban Ja'fari* (Los Angeles: Nab, 2002/1381), 82.

232. Haj Reza'i had been released earlier; Ja'fari was freed from jail on August 19/28 Mordad by anti-Mosaddeq forces and was able to participate in the pro-shah clamor. Ali Behzadi, *Shebh-e Khaterat* (Tehran: Zerrin, 1998/1375), 119: see also Sarshar, 159–71.

233. CIA memorandum for the president, Mar. 1, 1953, S/P-NSC files, lot 61D167.

234. Amini was Mosaddeq's preferred candidate for chief of staff, but on the very occasion of his presentation to the shah, he inexplicably did not turn up; therefore, Riahi was sent to the

shah to introduce himself as chief of staff. Fakhreddin Azimi's interview with Nosratollah Khazeni, Tehran, July 2000.

235. Gholam Reza Mosavvar-Rahmani, *Kohneh Sarbaz: Khaterat-e Siasi va Nezami* (Tehran: Rasa, 1988/1367), 207–28; Gholam Reza Nejati, *Mosaddeq, Salha-ye Mobarezeh va Moqavemat* (Tehran: Rasa, 1997/1376), 2:174–76. In early May 1953 Amini was appointed head of the gendarmerie (rural police).

236. Mohammad Mosaddeq, *Khaterat va Ta'allomat,* 267.

237. Henderson to Department of State, Feb. 28, 1953, telegram 3349, 788.11/2–2853.

238. CIA memorandum for the president, Mar. 1, 1953.

239. Gholam Hossein Mosaddeq, *Dar Kenar-e Pedaram* (Tehran: Rasa, 1990/1369), 65.

240. Henderson to Department of State, Mar. 4, 1953, telegram 3543, 888.00/3–453.

241. Henderson to Department of State, Jan. 4, 1952, telegram 2462, 888.2553/1–452.

242. Henderson to Department of State, May 28, 1952, telegram 4609, 788.00/5–2852.

243. Minute by Bowker, Mar. 4, 1953, FO 371/104633.

244. Mohammad Mosaddeq, *Khaterat va Ta'allomat,* 186, 262–66.

245. Henderson to Department of State, Mar. 4, 1953, telegram 3543, 888.00/3–453.

246. Henderson to Department of State, Mar. 10, 1953, telegram 3627, 788.00/3–1053.

247. Ibid; further on Henderson, see H. W. Brands, *Inside the Cold War: Loy Henderson and the Rise of the American Empire, 1918–1961* (New York: Oxford Univ. Press, 1991).

248. Azimi's interview with Darbyshire. According to Darbyshire, Ardeshir Zahedi, who was tirelessly active on behalf of his father, was also involved in the plot. Detailed documentary evidence verifying this, and several other assumptions regarding the murder of Afshartus, has yet to be unearthed.

249. See further Hosseinqoli Sarreshteh, *Khaterat-e Man* (Tehran 1988/1367), 37ff. For a critical assessment of Sarreshteh's account that sheds further light on the death of Afshartus and the coup of August 1953, see Abdollah Borhan, "Aya Qatelan-e Afshartus Shekanjeh Shodand?" *Negah-e No* 25 (Aug.-Sept. 1995/Mordad 1374): 48–87. See also Mohammad Torkaman, *Tote'eh-ye Robudan va Qatl-e Afshartus.*

250. Government statement, *Bakhtar-e Emruz,* May 2, 1953/12 Ordibehesht 1332; *Ettela'at,* May 2, 1953. See also *Bakhtar-e Emruz,* Apr. 28, 1953/8 Ordibehesht 1332.

251. Fatemi reportedly told Henderson that Baqa'i had asked Afshartus to mediate between him and Mosaddeq, and had several times met the chief of police at the house of Hossein Khatibi, Baqa'i's protégé. Fatemi also added that on the night of April 20, when Afshartus was seized, the car in which he was taken was driven by Mostafa Kashani. Minute by Rothnie, May 1, 1953, FO 371/104565.

252. See various issues of *Shahed* from April 1953 onward.

253. One tactic used by Mosaddeq's opponents was to blame Afshartus's elimination on the government itself. See, for instance, Qanatabadi, speech in the Majles, *Mozakerat-e Majles,* May 19, 1953/29 Ordibehesht 1332. Legal action against the culprits proceeded, but following the coup they were all exonerated of any wrongdoing.

254. Text in *Shahed,* July 2, 1953/12 Khordad 1332.

255. Wilber, *Overthrow,* 18–19.

256. Ibid., app. A, 4.

257. Ibid., 31.

258. *Bakhtar-e Emruz,* July 14, 1953/23 Tir 1332.

259. Wilber, *Overthrow;* see esp. app. B, "London Draft of the TPAJAX Operational Plan."

260. Henderson to Department of State, Mar. 6, 1953, telegram 3576, 788.00/3–635.

261. Henderson to Department of State, Apr. 15, 1953, telegram 4027, 788.00/4–1553.

262. Henderson to Department of State, May 30, 1953, telegram 4573, 788.11/5–3053.

263. Makins to FO, May 21, 1953, FO 371/104659.

264. Makins to FO, May 28, 1953, FO 371/104659; Makins to FO, June 2, 1953, id.

265. FO secret and Whitehall secret distribution (Aug. 1952), FO 371/98603.

266. Wilber, *Overthrow,* 89. The possibility of launching a coup without the shah's "active cooperation" had been considered. "London Draft," 10. The draft was, however, premised on the assumption that the Majles would be in existence and did not predict the referendum that dissolved it.

267. Wilber, *Overthrow,* 34.

268. Interview with Nosratollah Khazeni, Mahmud Torbati-Sanjabi, *Kudetasazan* (Tehran: Farhang-e Kavosh, 1997/1376), 45–91; Azimi's interviews with Khazeni, June 1997, July 1999.

269. Nejati, *Mosaddeq: Salha-ye Mobarezeh va Moqavemat,* 2:110; Mosavvar-Rahmani, *Kohneh Sarbaz,* 229–39. See also Sarreshteh, 85ff.

270. Wilber, *Overthrow,* app. E, Military Critique/TPAJAX, 3–4.

271. Wilber, *Overthrow,* app. D., 4–10.

272. Nejati, *Mosaddeq: Salha-ye Mobarezeh va Moqavemat,* 105. The CIA estimated that at least three out of the five brigade commanders in Tehran were completely under General Riahi's control. Wilber, *Overthrow,* app. D., 3. According to Colonel Sarreshteh, all of these brigades were loyal to Mosaddeq's government. Sarreshteh, 116.

273. Wilber, *Overthrow,* 27.

274. Wilber, *Overthrow,* app. D, 4.

275. Ibid.

276. Wilber, *Overthrow,* app. E, Military Critique/TPAJAX, 5.

277. Mansur Ali Atabaki and Ahmad Bani-Ahmad, *Panj Ruz Rastakhiz-e Mellat* (Tehran 1953/1332), 117–18.

278. See Gholam Hossein Sadiqi, "Ruz-e Kudeta," *Donya-ye Sokhan* 13, no. 75 (Aug.-Sept. 1997/Mordad-Shahrivar 1376): 32–39. See also *Rah-e Mosaddeq,* nos. 19, 20 (Oct. 26, 1955/4 Aban 1334).

279. Wilber, *Overthrow,* 58.

280. In the course of his trial, Riahi asserted that he assumed Mosaddeq's worries to have stemmed solely from the activities of left-wing parties and therefore gave orders for coercive measures against them. Jalil Bozorgmehr, ed. *Mosaddeq dar Mahkameh-ye Nezami* (Tehran: Tarikh-e Iran, 1984/1363), 2:573.

281. *Bakhtar-e Emruz,* Aug. 17, 18, 1953/26, 27 Mordad 1332.

282. Kazem Hasibi, diary entry for Aug. 18, 1953/27 Mordad 1332, text in Movahhed, *Khab-e Ashofteh-ye Naft,* 812–13.

283. Henderson to Department of State, Aug. 18, 1953, telegram 384, 788.00/8–1853.

284. Mohammad Mosaddeq, *Khaterat va Ta'allomat,* 290–91.

285. Wilber, *Overthrow,* 64.

286. Movahhed, *Khab-e Ashofteh-ye Naft,* 821.

287. Sadiqi.

288. Ahmad Zirakzadeh, the loyal Mosaddeqist deputy, asserts, "There is no doubt that on 19 August/28 Mordad the government of Dr. Mosaddeq could have easily defeated the plotters . . . but what about a month, two months or several months later?" Ahmad Zirakzadeh, *Porseshha-ye bi Pasokh dar Salha-ye Estesna'i: Khaterat Mohandes Ahmad Zirakzadeh* (Tehran: Nilufar, 1998/1376) 312.

289. The shah suspected that British agents were responsible for the failure of the initial stage of the coup. Henderson to Department of State, Aug. 23, 1953, telegram 466, 788.11/8–2353. Before his flight to Rome, in addition to meeting the British and American ambassadors in Baghdad, the shah also met and was much encouraged by the anti-Mosaddeq Ayatollah Shahrestani; the latter advised the shah to give interviews emphasizing his dismissal of Mosaddeq and appointment of Zahedi. The American ambassador failed, however, to persuade the shah to remain in Baghdad for a few more days. Bramly to Marquis of Salisbury, Aug. 19, 1953, FO 371/104570.

290. See, for instance, Manuchehr Riahi, *Sarab-e Zendegi* (Tehran: Tehran, 1992/1371), 561–84.

291. Wilber, *Overthrow,* 65–77; for the role of the mob leaders, see further Torbati-Sanjabi, *Kudetasazan,* 103–6.

292. Mohammad Mosaddeq, *Khaterat va Ta'allomat,* 250.

293. Ibid.

294. Mosaddeq primarily blamed the existing electoral laws for the outcome of the elections for the Seventeenth Majles. Mosaddeq to the Majles, *Bakhtar-e Emruz,* Apr. 30, 1952/10 Ordibehesht 1331.

295. Gen. Ahmad Vosuq, then commander of the gendarmerie, asserts that he did not receive any orders either from the shah or from Mosaddeq to exert influence over the course of the elections, but on his own initiative he summoned all the regional gendarmerie commanders and instructed them to prevent the election of "opponents of the regime, leftists, and those glaringly lacking in principles." Sepahbod Ahmad Vosuq, *Dastan-e Zendegi* (Tehran, n.d.), 97.

296. Hossein Fatemi, *Khaterat,* text in Afrasiabi, *Mosaddeq va Tarikh,* 352–71, esp. 369; Habib Ladjevardi, ed., *Khaterat-e Shapour Bakhtiar* (Cambridge, Mass.: Center for Middle Eastern Studies, Harvard Univ., 1996), 32.

297. Fatemi, *Khaterat.*

298. Makki, interview; also Fatemi, *Khaterat.* According to Middleton, Kashani's ceaseless interventions provoked the constant complaints of the newly appointed interior minister, Mohammad Ebrahim Amir-Teymur Kalali. The matter "was brought to a head" and Kalali resigned in protest over Kashani's efforts to secure the election of his protégé Qanatabadi to the seat for Shahrud. Middleton to Bowker, Jan. 7, 1952, FO 371/98595. Kalali was succeeded by Allahyar Saleh, who also resigned soon after his appointment. For further on elections in Iran see Fakhreddin Azimi, "Entekhabat Bedun-e Haqq-e Entekhab? Entekhabat-e Parlemani va Tadavom-e Farhang-e Siasi dar Iran," *Negah-e No,* no. 42 (fall 1999/1378): 13–47.

299. Fatemi, *Khaterat,* 367.

300. Movahhed, *Khab-e Ashofteh-ye Naft,* 886–90.

301. See further Fakhreddin Azimi, "On Shaky Ground: Concerning the Absence or Weakness of Political Parties in Iran," *Iranian Studies* 30, nos. 1–2 (winter-spring 1997–98): 53–75. See also Zirakzadeh, 338.

302. Mosaddeq maintains that in order to avoid provoking the suspicions of the shah, he did not attempt to unify civic nationalist parties. *Khaterat va Ta'allomat*, 238.

303. Azimi's interview with Khazeni, July 2000.

304. Hasibi, diary entry for 12 July 1953/21 Tir 1332, quoted in Movahhed, *Khab-e Ashofteh-ye Naft*, 847.

305. Movahhed, *Khab-e Ashofteh-ye Naft*, 848.

306. For Kashani's statement, see Dehnovi, 3:407–21.

307. Mosaddeq's Public Security Act of Aug. 11, 1952/20 Mordad 1331 was designed to counter such activities. See Mosaddeq to Majles Speaker, undated, text in Torkaman, *Namehha-ye Doktor Mosaddeq*, 1:218–20. It provoked considerable objections from opposition deputies such as Baqa'i, but in practice it did not prove particularly effective in countering antigovernment moves.

308. Wilber, *Overthrow*, 10. Fatemi left Iran for Europe at the end of May 1953, mainly to receive medical treatment; he returned on August 11, five days before the launching of the coup. Rashidian most probably obtained his exit visa while Fatemi was away and with the assistance of Meftah, Fatemi's deputy. See also above, note 58.

309. See, for instance, *Jebheh-ye Azadi*, Mar. 15, 1953/24 Esfand 1331; see also various issues of *Niru-ye Sevvom*.

310. Jalal Al-e Ahmad, *Dar Khedmat va Khianat-e Rowshanfekran* (Tehran: Kharazmi, 1978/1357), 2:210.

311. Khalil Maleki, "Sarnevesht-e Tarikhi-ye Liberalism dar Du Qarn-e Akhir," *Elm-o-Zendegi* 1, no. 7, (Aug.-Sept. 1952/Shahrivar 1331): 580–84, 652–67.

312. Sanjabi recounts that he was present, along with Mosaddeq and several other supporters, when Maleki strongly advocated curbing Tudeh activities and detaining the party's leading activists. Sanjabi, 138. For Maleki's own views see references in the following note.

313. Maleki, "Sarnevesht," 664; id., "Mobarezeh ba Bozorgtarin Khatari keh Nehzat-e Melli ra Tahdid Mikonad," *Elm-o-Zendegi* 2, no. 3 (May-June 1953/Khordad 1332): 203–6, 291–95, esp. 293. See also id., "Tahlil-e Mokhtasari az Gozashteh," *Nabard-e Zendegi* 1, no. 10 (April-May 1956/Ordibehesht 1335): 27–59. Maleki's major articles are collected in Abdollah Borhan, *Nehzat-e Melli-ye Iran va Edalat-e Ejtema'i* (Tehran: Markaz, 1999/1377). On Maleki's relations with Mosaddeq, see further Katouzian, *Struggle for Power*, esp. chap. 8.

314. *Bakhtar-e Emruz*, May 2, 3, 1951/11, 12 Ordibehesht 1330.

315. Wilber, *Overthrow*, 26.

316. See, for instance, *Ettela'at*, editorial, Aug. 18, 1953/27 Mordad 1332. Shaheedi was subsequently transferred from his post.

317. Wilber, *Overthrow*, 91–92.

318. Behzadi, 640.

319. Mosaddeq later wrote, "At no point [in Iranian history] was the press as free as during my term of office, . . .Those papers that were managed with foreign money and encouragement, wrote whatever they wished, were at no point prosecuted and had no impact on society." Mohammad Mosaddeq, *Khaterat va Ta'allomat*, 374; the impact of such propaganda was, however, more damaging than Mosaddeq assumed.

320. In April 1953 Mosaddeq wrote to Shayegan, "Physically I am not too bad, but my sprits are very low and I am deeply depressed; in view of the prevailing moral degeneracy I do not

know how this country is going to fare." Mosaddeq to Ali Shayegan, Apr. 15, 1953/26 Farvardin 1332, text in Torkaman, *Namehha-ye Doktor Mosaddeq,* 2:160–61.

321. Mosaddeq to Shayegan, May 15, 1953/25 Ordibehesht 1332; text in Torkaman, *Name-hha-ye Doktor Mosaddeq,* 163; Hasibi, diary entry for June 8, 1952/18 Khordad 1331, text in Movahhed, *Khab-e Ashofteh-ye Naft,* 418.

322. He even favorably considered the payment of compensation of some $800 million over twenty years. Hasibi, diary entry for July 29, 1953/7 Mordad 1332, quoted in Movahhed, *Khab-e Ashofteh-ye Naft,* 844–45. See also Mohammad Mosaddeq, *Khaterat va Ta'allomat,* 268. The compensation the AIOC eventually received has been calculated at nearly $1.5 billion. Movahhed, *Khab-e Ashofteh-ye Naft,* 869.

323. According to Darbyshire, the oil negotiations of 1952 were, as far as the British were concerned, 'essentially face saving." Azimi's interview with Darbyshire. Blaming his domestic opponents, Mosaddeq maintained that if the idea of a speedy resolution of the oil dispute by a successor government had not been constantly impressed upon his foreign antagonists, he would have been able to resolve the issue in the country's best interest. *Ettela'at,* Feb. 24, 1953/5 Esfand 1331.

324. Makki contends that within a month and a half of the coup, in Tehran alone the military governor's office had imprisoned thirteen thousand people. *Khaterat-e Siasi,* 546. This figure appears to be exaggerated, but a large number of people were indeed arrested or imprisoned.

325. See Bozorgmehr, *Mosaddeq dar Mahkameh-ye Nezami;* and id., *Mosaddeq dar Dadgah-e Tajdid-e Nazar-e Nezami* (Tehran: Enteshar 1986/1365).

3. The 1953 Coup in Iran and the Legacy of the Tudeh

1. Wilber, *Overthrow.* Wilber's report and its related appendixes first appeared on the *New York Times* Web site (www.nytimes.org) in installments posted in April and June 2000. The full text of the new material may be found on the following Web sites: www.nytimes.com/library/world/mideast/041600iran-cia-index.html; www.nsarchive.org; and www.cryptome.org/cia-iran-all.htm.

2. See Wilber, *Overthrow,* 1, app. A, 2; app. B, 5–6.

3. Bizhan Jazani, *Tarh-e Jame'eh Shenasi va Mabani-ye Esteratezhi-ye Junbesh-e Enqelabi-ye Khalq-e Iran* (Tehran: Maziar, 1979), 45.

4. Kianuri, 281–82.

5. U.S. embassy to the State Department, "The Tudeh Party Today," declassified documents, 308D, as cited in Abrahamian, *Iran Between Two Revolutions,* 320.

6. National Intelligence Estimate (hereafter NIE) 6, Apr. 5, 1951, 4; NIE 46, Feb. 4, 1952, 2; NIE 75, Nov. 13, 1952, 5.

7. Mark Gasiorowski interview with Anthony Cuomo, Rome, Jan. 5, 1985. Cuomo was an embassy officer who specialized in the Tudeh. I would like to thank Professor Gasiorowski for providing me with a transcript of this interview.

8. See note 5 in Mark Gasiorowski's chapter in this volume; and "Political Trends Between March 1952 and the Fall of the First Mosaddeq Government," Sept. 15, 1952, U.S. National Archives, Washington, D.C. (hereafter USNA), Record Group (hereafter RG) 84, Box 29.

9. For various versions of the TPMO's history see Ruhallah Abbasi, *Khaterat-e Yek Afsar-e*

Tudeh'i 1330–1335 (Montreal: Farhang, 1989); Amui; Mohammad Hosein Khosrow-panah, *Sazman-e Afsaran-e Hezb-e Tudeh-ye Iran 1323–1333* (Tehran: Shirazeh, 1999); id., "Tarikhcheh-ye Zohur va Soqut-e Sazman-e afsaran-e hezb-e Tudeh-ye Iran" *Negah-e No* (Tehran), no. 33 (summer 1997); for a version of the organization's activities written under the shah, and information produced after its discovery, see *Ketab-e Siah* (Tehran: Matbu'at, 1955).

10. Fereidun Azarnur, *Rah-e Azadi,* no. 24, 15.

11. Ibid., 13–17.

12. Kianuri, *Khaterat,* 288.

13. Ibid., 297.

14. Ibid., 285–86.

15. Abrahamian gives ample evidence that many American and British officials were aware that the Tudeh was not a real danger and that the party was used as a smokescreen. See Abrahamian, "The 1953 Coup in Iran," 204–5.

16. Abrahamian, *Iran Between Two Revolutions,* 338.

17. Amui, 72–73; Azarnur, 13–17.

18. Other chapters in this book cover this subject in more detail. I have previously written on it as well. Here, a concise version will be presented. See Behrooz, *Rebels with a Cause,* 5–10, 22–26.

19. James A. Bill, *The Eagle and the Lion: The Tragedy of American-Iranian Relations* (New Haven, Conn.: Yale Univ. Press, 1988), 75.

20. The analysis appeared in *Beh Su-ye Ayandeh,* Sept. 1950. See *Gozashteh Cheragh-e Rah-e Ayandeh* (n.p., n.d.), 523–24.

21. Ibid., 527.

22. Ibid., 530.

23. Ibid., 534–37.

24. For example, see the Tudeh publication *Dezh,* July 18, 1952, as quoted in *Gozashteh,* 573.

25. Ibid., 574.

26. In fact it is not clear exactly what the TPMO did during this period. In all probability it remained inactive as it would not have taken a step without orders from above. See Khosrow-panah, *Sazman-e Afsaran-e Hezb-e Tudeh-ye Iran,* 156–57.

27. See Babak Amir-Khosravi, *Nazari az Darun beh Naqsh-e Hezb-e Tudeh-ye Iran* (Tehran: Didgah Institute, 1996), 339–69; and *Gozashteh,* 574–78. Tudeh's historic Fourth Plenum held in the Soviet Union in 1957 makes a mention of the policy change. It suggests that the party's policy toward Mosaddeq until July 1952 was in error and that it was only partially corrected thereafter. The document views the party's policy as having been corrected only after March 1953. For the plenum's official proceedings, see Khosrow Shakeri, *Tarikh-e Moaser-e Iran,* 1:365; also see id., *Asnad va didgahha* (Tehran: Tudeh, 1979), 361–83. The complete text of the Fourth Plenum was never published. The version in *Tarikh-e Moaser-e Iran* was published by an independent researcher, while *Asnad va Didgahha* was published by the party after the 1979 revolution. There is a major discrepancy between the two in that the one published by the Tudeh includes a number of paragraphs that support Kianuri's position on his role during the 1953 coup and exonerate him of any major wrongdoing. According to Babak Amir-Khosravi, a Tudeh Central Committee member and a leading party figure until 1983, the paragraphs were added by Kianuri, under whose supervision the proceedings of the Fourth Plenum appeared in print in 1979. See *Adineh* (Tehran), no. 83 (Sept. 1993): 19.

28. For a more extensive discussion of Tudeh factionalism, see Behrooz, *Rebels with a Cause,* 16–26; and id., "Tudeh Factionalism and the 1953 Coup in Iran," *International Journal of Middle East Studies* 33, no. 3 (August 2001): 363–82.

29. *Seyr-e Komonizm dar Iran* (Tehran: Kayhan, 1957), 417–34.

30. Kianuri, who belonged to the opposing faction, suggests, "In my opinion our principal mistake was that we became followers of Mosaddeq and National Front policies, and as a result we sank with them." Kianuri, *Khaterat,* 303.

31. Ibid., 278.

32. *Seyr-e Komonizm dar Iran,* 425–30.

33. The correspondence was first published in Europe, then republished in Kianuri, *Khaterat,* 307–35; and *Rah-e Azadi,* nos. 22, 23 (June, Aug. 1992).

34. Kianuri, *Khaterat,* 264–65.

35. For more on Kianuri and Qasemi, see Amir-Khosravi, 251–69.

36. For more on the Fourth Plenum and personal differences among party leaders, see Shakeri, *Tarikh-e Moaser-e Iran,* 367.

37. *Seyr-e Komonizm dar Iran,* 422–23.

38. Kianuri, *Khaterat,* 262; Shakeri, *Tarikh-e Moaser-e Iran,* 367.

39. Wilber, *Overthrow,* 28.

40. Ibid., 38.

41. At this point, the Tudeh was unaware of TPAJAX as it had not yet gone into effect. But the party, and the Mosaddeq government itself, did know that some military personnel were trying to topple the prime minister. Notable among these was Gen. Fazlollah Zahedi, who ultimately replaced Mosaddeq.

42. Arjui, 69–70.

43. Kianuri, *Khaterat,* 264.

44. Ibid., 278.

45. Khosrow-panah, *Sazman-e Afsaran-e Hezb-e Tudeh-ye Iran,* 164–73. Pulad-dezh appears on page 54 of *Overthrow.*

46. Kianuri's wife, Maryam Firuz, was an influential party figure in her own right and the head of the party's Women's Organization; she was also from the Qajar family and a cousin of Mosaddeq.

47. Kianuri, *Khaterat,* 264–65. For an analysis of the Tudeh telephone calls to Mosaddeq, see Amir-Khosravi, 675–78.

48. Mohammad Mosaddeq, *Khaterat va Ta'allomat,* 379–80.

49. Wilber, *Overthrow,* 41.

50. Kosrow-panah, "Tarikhcheh," 57.

51. For a discussion of Fatemi's views, see Amir-Khosravi, 578–81.

52. For more detail on the National Front and Tudeh slogans that appeared on August 16, see *Gozashteh,* 612–13.

53. Wilber, *Overthrow,* 63.

54. This information came from an interview by Maziar Behrooz (Tehran, June 9, 2000) with a member of the Tehran Provincial Committee, the heart of the Tudeh organization, who wishes to remain anonymous. Kianuri, who had close ties to the TPMO, has also stated flatly that he had no knowledge of "black" crowds. Kianuri, *Khaterat,* 267–70.

55. Interviews by Maziar Behrooz included the following: Jahangir Behrouz, journalist

member of the Tudeh, London, June 2001; Mansur Kalantari-nazari, member of the Tudeh Youth Organization, London, June 2001; anonymous member of the Tudeh who was in charge of the party's University of Tehran organization and south Tehran neighborhoods, Tehran, July 2001; Abdollah Nasr, member of the Tudeh, Tehran, June 2001; Akbar Shahabi, member of the Tudeh, telephone interview, Tehran, July 2001; and correspondence with Sarem al-Din Sadeq-vaziri, member of the Tudeh, July 2001.

56. Maziar Behrooz interview with anonymous member of the Tudeh's Tehran Provincial Committee.

57. For the Tudeh's declaration, see *Gozashteh,* 616. The high-ranking Tehran Provincial Committee member (interview cited in note 54 above) was the person who suggested the "republic" demand. He was surprised to see his proposal turned into an even more radical version. He opposed the "democratic republic" slogan because of its allusion to the East European regimes, but he was overruled. It is not clear to this former official how the party's executive committee made such a decision. When I asked him why had he proposed the "republic" slogan, as it also seemed radical, he said that the people in the streets had become radicalized, and he commented that the Tudeh, as the vanguard party, had to stay one step ahead. The same impression may have prompted the "democratic republic" proposal. When I suggested that at least some of the street crowds may have been CIA-generated mobs, he showed no awareness of this possibility whatsoever.

58. Kianuri, *Khaterat,* 268.

59. The document is a set of minutes of a meeting of the Tudeh front organization, the Society for Peace, held on August 17 in Tehran. The society was made up of Tudeh cadres, and the discussion between rank-and-file and mid-level party members covers the situation after August 16, the new slogan, and the possible reaction by Mosaddeq. Amir-Khosravi, 576–78.

60. As with other information on Tudeh communications with Mosaddeq, Kianuri is the person who claims he contacted the premier on behalf of the party (Kianuri, *Khaterat,* 276). Other party members have questioned his claim.

61. Kianuri, *Khaterat,* 307–35; *Rah-e Azadi,* nos. 22,23 (June, Aug. 1992).

62. My interview with the anonymous member of the Tehran Provincial Committee also suggests that, early in the day on August 19, the committee was instructed to prepare for resistance, but then an order came to cease all activity until further notice.

63. Kianuri is noted to have strongly objected to the proposal. Kianuri, *Khaterat,* 314–15.

64. Jazani, 66.

65. *Seyr-e Komonizm dar Iran,* 70; Makki, *Ketab-e siah,* 93; Kianuri, *Khaterat,* 295.

66. Shakeri, *Tarikh-e Moaser-e Iran,* 1:364.

67. Ibid.

68. Kianuri, *Khaterat,* 285.

69. In an interview, John W. Waller, who was in charge of coup operations in Washington, D.C., agreed with this conclusion and suggested that the cold war and the Soviet Union were the prime concern for the United States and not the Tudeh strength in the field. Maziar Behrooz interview with John W. Waller, London, June 10, 2001.

70. Behrooz, *Rebels with a Cause,* 26–31.

4. Britain and the Overthrow of the Mosaddeq Government

1. My own analysis of the subject was presented some twelve years ago in "Musaddiq and the Dilemmas of British Imperialism," in Bill and Louis, 228–60. For present purposes I have drawn from my earlier essay, but I have also reworked it extensively and have elaborated at length on the post-November 1952 part of the operation. For discussion and correspondence, I am indebted to four former British officials who were all involved in one way or another in the affairs of Iran 1951–1953: Sir Denis Wright, Lord Terrington (C. M. Woodhouse), Christopher Gandy, and Sir Sam Falle. They have enabled me to give the present essay a measure of detail and exactitude that would otherwise not have been possible. Woodhouse, alas, died February 13, 2001. There is a perceptive and useful obituary by Richard Clogg in the *Guardian,* Feb. 20, 2001.

2. *New York Times,* Apr. 16, 2000. As elaborated on in earlier notes, the title of the study is *Overthrow of Premier Mosaddeq of Iran: November 1952-August 1953.* According to a note at the beginning, the monograph was written in March 1954 by Donald N. Wilber, a Princeton University scholar who was a CIA consultant and who participated in the operation. Parts of the study were initially published by the *New York Times,* and the full version eventually became electronically accessible but with certain names excised. The names have, on the whole, been restored, but there are problems in dealing with an electronic document that continues to evolve. For purposes of accuracy, this essay deals with my own copy dated August 18, 2000. (There are several other CIA studies of the 1953 operation, but references to *"Overthrow"* in the text and footnotes are to Wilber's.) For Wilber's autobiographical account, see his *Adventures in the Middle East.*

3. This is true of the general subject as well, thanks mainly to Stephen Dorril's comprehensive work *MI6: Fifty Years of Special Operations,* esp. part 4.

4. The best book generally on the Labour government is Kenneth O. Morgan, *Labour in Power, 1945–1951* (Oxford: Oxford, Univ. Press, 1984); see also esp. Alan Bullock, *Ernest Bevin: Foreign Secretary* (London: Heinemann, 1983). Neither mentions the Secret Intelligence Service.

5. The relevant series for studying the views of the Oriental Counsellors is FO 248 (Embassy Archives, Tehran).

6. Woodhouse, *Something Ventured,* 107.

7. Wilber mistakenly identifies him as an officer "of the British Intelligence station in Tehran." Wilber, *Overthrow,* 1. Falle had entered the foreign service in 1948, although it is true that he easily moved between the realms of the Foreign Office and MI6. See Sam Falle, *My Lucky Life in War, Revolution, Peace, and Diplomacy* (Lewes, Sussex: Book Guild, 1996).

8. Falle, 84–85.

9. This was especially true of Sir Donald Ferguson, permanent undersecretary at the Ministry of Fuel and Power, who once wrote: "It was British enterprise, skill and effort which discovered oil under the soil of Persia, which has got the oil out, which has built the refinery, which has developed markets for Persian oil in 30 or 40 countries, with wharves, storage tanks and pumps, road and rail tanks and other distribution facilities, and also an immense fleet of tankers. This was done at a time when there was no easy outlet for Persian oil in competition with the vastly greater American oil industry. None of these things would or could have been done by the Persian government or the Persian people." Quoted in Louis, *British Empire in the Middle East,* 683–84.

10. See J. H. Bamberg, *The History of the British Petroleum Company,* vol. 2, *The Anglo-Iranian*

Years, 1928–1954 (Cambridge: Cambridge Univ. Press, 1994), part 3; Elm, *Oil, Power, and Principle*,; and Heiss, *Empire and Nationhood.*

11. Denis Wright, who led the mission to restore relations with Iran in December 1953, commented that Iranian assumptions about the British had to be taken seriously: "The situation is complicated by a continuing and widespread belief in our mystical and all-pervading powers." Wright to Eden, confidential, Feb. 13, 1954, FO 248/1543.

12. Quoted in Vernon A. Walters, *Silent Missions* (Garden City, N.Y.: Doubleday, 1978), 247.

13. For a slightly later example, see Nancy Lambton, "The Impact of the West on Persia," *International Affairs* 33, 1 (Jan. 1957).

14. *Times* (London), Mar. 22, 1951, in an anonymous article written by Lambton.

15. Furlonge to Shepherd, secret, July 21, 1951, FO 248/1528. Lambton herself, as if wary of future historians, rarely committed to writing her thoughts on covert operations. The quotations of her comments by various officials, however, are internally consistent and invariably reveal a hard-line attitude toward Mosaddeq. I have the impression from the minutes that the officials quoting her sometimes wanted to invoke her authority to lend credibility to their own views.

16. Minute by Eric Berthoud (assistant undersecretary supervising economic affairs), June 15, 1951, FO 371/91548.

17. Rather in the tradition of Aldous Huxley, Zaehner also experimented with drugs to increase his sensory perception of eternal verities. Received into the Roman Catholic Church in 1946, he was profoundly religious. His last book, *Zen, Drugs, and Mysticism* (London, 1972; 1974 Vintage Books reprint), is an attack on American drug cults. Zaehner believed that a mastery of the scriptures, not LSD, was a prerequisite to the quest for religious truth.

18. One result of Zaehner's Foreign Office appointment (rather than a regular MI6 assignment) is that the records in the archives of the British embassy in Tehran contain many of Zaehner's minutes that remain intact and thus provide a window left ajar that ordinarily, on the subject of covert activities, would have been closed. Zaehner wrote compulsively, and his minutes are omnipresent in the FO 248 series.

19. See especially Bernard Donoughue and G. W. Jones, *Herbert Morrison: Portrait of a Politician* (London: Weidenfeld and Nicolson, 1973), chap. 36.

20. Quoted in Wm. Roger Louis, *Imperialism at Bay* (Oxford: Oxford Univ. Press, 1977), 14.

21. See James Cable, *Intervention at Abadan: Plan Buccaneer* (New York: St. Martin's Press, 1991).

22. See Dorril, *MI6: Fifty Years,* 561.

23. See Louis, *British Empire in the Middle East,* 686–89.

24. Cabinet Minutes 60 (51), Sept. 27, 1951, CAB 128/20, Public Records Office, London (hereinafter cited as PRO).

25. Dean Acheson, *Present at the Creation* (New York: Norton, 1969), 508. For the British decision in the context of plans to unseat Mosaddeq, see Mark J. Gasiorowski, "The 1953 *Coup d'État* in Iran," *International Journal of Middle East Studies,* 19, no. 3 (Aug. 1987): 263–64. For a judgment on the decision in relation to the Suez crisis, see Cable, *Intervention at Abadan,* 118: "If we think of the drastic pressure Eisenhower applied against Anglo-French intervention at Port Said in 1956 and the British debacle that ensued, we must concede Attlee's prudence in 1951."

26. Herbert Morrison, *An Autobiography* (London: Oldhams Press, 1960), 281.

27. There is no evidence of the company's complicity. Bamberg independently confirms my own judgment that the company was not involved. Bamberg, *History of the British Petroleum Company,* 588–89 n. 115. It would be a mistake to assume, however, that there were no connections between individual members of the company and MI6. Two officials of the company, Archibald Chisholm and Geoffrey Keating, had both served in Iran and both were involved in the company's intelligence network, which was publicly known as the Central Information Bureau (CIB). The principal function of the CIB was propaganda, but it also included "intelligence-gathering [and] bribing officials." Dorril, *MI6: Fifty Years,* 564. Chisholm and Keating moved in the same circles as MI6 officers. Chisholm had represented the company in Kuwait. A hint of Keating's influence can be found in a letter written by an official in the British embassy in Washington to the Oriental Counsellor in Tehran: "Geoffrey Keating is in our midst and being helpful." N. W. H. Gaydon to Lance Pyman, secret and personal, July 11, 1951, FO 248/1528.

28. For example, Shepherd to Bowker, confidential, May 28, 1951, FO 248/1514: "The situation in Persia during the four weeks of Dr. Mosaddeq's premiership has been on the whole a good deal more lunatic than ever. Y."

29. Middleton to Bowker, personal and secret, Sept. 1, 1952, FO 371/98697.

30. See minute by M. R. Starkey, May 14, 1951, FO 371/91534.

31. May 20, 1951, news cutting, in FO 248/1514.

32. Bill, *The Eagle and the Lion,* 88–89.

33. See especially Shepherd to Furlonge, confidential, May 6, 1951, FO 371/91459.

34. I am grateful to Denis Wright for information about Sarell. For the article see the *Times* (London), Mar. 22, 1951.

35. R. F. G. Sarell, "Nationalism in Persia," Feb. 13, 1952, FO 371/98596. Sarell's estimate was a rejoinder to Shepherd's "A Comparison Between Persian and Asian Nationalism in General," for which see Louis, *British Empire in the Middle East,* 639–40. Shepherd had previously served in Indonesia (one of the bases of the "comparison") where the nationalist movement appeared to him to be much more fully developed.

36. Sarell, "Nationalism in Persia."

37. See minute by Berthoud, Oct. 13, 1952, FO 371/98701.

38. Bill, *The Eagle and the Lion,* 91.

39. Wilber, *Overthrow,* 24.

40. The source for the figure of ten thousand pounds is Woodhouse, *Something Ventured,* 118. This may seem in retrospect an extravagant amount, but the CIA yearly budget for Iran was $1 million.

41. Ibid.,7.

42. Minute by Zaehner, Jan. 5, 1952, FO 248/1531.

43. Wilber, *Overthrow,* vii, 22.

44. Manucher Farmanfarmaian and Roxane Farmanfarmaian, *Blood and Oil* (New York: Random House, 1997), 226. This is a book with many shrewd insights into the British presence in Iran.

45. Dorril, *MI6: Fifty Years,* 563.

46. Meier, 77.

47. Minute by Zaehner, Aug. 27, 1951, FO 248/1514.

48. There was another long-standing British contact in the palace, the head of the royal

household, Sulayman Behbudi. The evidence on this point is obscure, but apparently he came to the assistance of the Rashidians in the critical days of August 1953 by acting as intermediary between Princess Ashraf and the shah. See Wilber, *Overthrow,* 23–24.

49. Minute by L. F. L. Pyman (Oriental Counsellor), July 19, 1951, FO 248/1515.

50. Quoted in Azimi, *Crisis of Democracy,* 212.

51. Minute by Pyman, Sept. 22, 1951, FO 248/1515.

52. The British fascination with Sayyid Zia continued even after the overthrow of Mosaddeq. Denis Wright, following an analysis by John Fearnley of the embassy staff, wrote in 1955: "Sayyed Zia has strength of character, experience, an imaginative understanding of his country and his fellow-countrymen, a plan of action, and loyal supporters in many different walks of life and in influential positions." Wright to Macmillan, secret, Aug. 3, 1955, FO 371/114811.

53. Shepherd to Strong, confidential, Sept. 4, 1951, FO 248/2529.

54. I am grateful to Sir Sam Falle for clarification on this point and for much detailed information on the Rashidians. On matters where no written evidence exists, I have tried to verify factual detail with all four of the British officials mentioned in note 1, Falle, Wright, Gandy, and, before his death, Woodhouse.

55. Minute by Falle, July 28, 1952, FO 248/1531. On this occasion Asadollah Rashidian had in mind Zahedi as a leader who could be put forward as a patriot with an appeal to diverse groups in Iranian society.

56. Wilber, *Overthrow,* 7.

57. Minute by Zaehner, Nov. 10, 1951, FO 248/1514.

58. Ibid.

59. Minute by Falle, Apr. 28, 1952, FO 248/1531.

60. Minute by Falle, June 30, 1952, FO 248/1531.

61. Minute by Falle, July 2, 1952, FO 248/1531.

62. Quoted in Azimi, *Crisis of Democracy,* 285.

63. Woodhouse, *Something Ventured,* 115.

64. Minute by Middleton, July 22, 1952, FO 248/1531.

65. Ibid.

66. See Brian Lapping, *End of Empire* (New York: St. Martin's Press, 1985), 214.

67. See Falle, 79.

68. Transcript, "End of Empire: Iran," Rhodes House, Oxford. This is a transcript of the interviews that Brian Lapping used in the television series and later in the book *End of Empire.*

69. See for example Kingsley Martin (editor of *New Statesman*), "Conversation with Dr. Mosaddeq," *New Statesman,* Jan. 11, 1952:

> Dr. Mosaddeq received me in bed—a plain iron bed in which he bounced rather than lay. . . . I saw no signs of the over-excitement or hysteria that some journalists have written about; he did not weep, though he laughed shrilly, stretching out his hand in a claw-like gesture that made him look at times like a benevolent pterodactyl. Here was a man of much force and capacity. . . . He believed that it was not enough to get rid of a Company which had exploited his country, but that it was right to make sure that no other body or foreign Power would be in a position to exercise the influence in Iran that the Anglo-Iranian Company had possessed.

> Martin was sympathetic. This was a view that hardly corresponded with *Through*

the *Looking-Glass,* which had been recommended to him by Zaehner. Martin had been irritated by the suggestion. For another sympathetic British portrait of Mosaddeq, see L. P. Elwell-Sutton, *Persian Oil: A Study in Power Politics* (London: Lawrence and Wishart, 1955). In the 1975 edition Elwell-Sutton stated that he was content that the book "should reappear in its original form as a record of the struggle of a small Asian country for independence and international recognition."

70. Middleton to A. D. M. Ross, confidential, Feb. 11, 1952, FO 371/98618.

71. For Mosaddeq's economic views, see Katouzian, *Political Economy,* esp. chap. 9.

72. Middleton to R. J. Bowker, strictly personal and confidential, Jan. 4, 1952, FO 371/98618.

73. Middleton to Bowker, secret and personal, July 28, 1952, FO 371/98602. There is a persistent theme in British political reporting that Kashani was opportunistic and willing to be bribed.

74. See Alan W. Ford, *The Anglo-Iranian Oil Dispute of 1951–1952* (Berkeley: Univ. of California Press, 1954), part 2, sec. 6.

75. Middleton to Eden, confidential, July 28, 1952, FO 371/98602.

76. Middleton to Bowker, personal and secret, July 28, 1952, FO 371/96802.

77. Ibid.

78. Middleton to Eden, confidential, Sept. 23, 1952, FO 371/98604.

79. Ibid.

80. Middleton to Eden, Oct. 5, 1952, FO 371/98700.

81. Middleton to Ross, personal and confidential, Oct. 20, 1952, FO 371/98605.

82. See minute by Berthoud, Oct. 13, 1952, FO 371/98701.

83. Minute by Sarell, Jan. 22, 1952, FO 371/98608.

84. Middleton to Bowker, personal and secret, Sept. 1, 1952, FO 371/98697.

85. Burrows to Bowker, secret, July 30, 1952, FO 371/98603.

86. Ibid.

87. Article of July 30, 1952, enclosed in Burrows to Bowker, secret, July 30, 1952, FO 371/98603

88. Burrows to Bowker, July 30, 1952.

89. Minute by Makins, June 7, 1952, FO 371/98690.

90. Minute by Ramsbotham recording a FO meeting, Apr. 26, 1952, FO 371/98689.

91. Ibid.

92. Minute by Eden, May 4, 1952, FO 371/98689.

93. *The Memoirs of Anthony Eden: Full Circle* (Boston: Houghton Mifflin, 1960), 227.

94. Ibid., 242.

95. Fergusson to Makins, May 27, 1952, FO 371/98689.

96. Quoted in a minute by Ramsbotham, June 19, 1952, FO 371/98690.

97. As quoted in a minute by Bowker, Aug. 20, 1952, FO 371/98694.

98. Minute by Eden, July 18[?], 1952, FO 371/98690.

99. Sir Eric Drake in the *Times* (London), Apr. 3, 1970.

100. McGhee, *Envoy to the Middle World,* 341.

101. Minute by Gandy, Jan. 25, 1954, FO 371/100078.

102. Obituary in the *Times* (London), Apr. 2, 1970: "[In] 1954 . . . a new international con-

sortium was established in which the company held 40 per cent and was compensated for what it had relinquished. This scheme was devised by him and it was largely by his efforts that it was brought to a successful conclusion."

103. Minute by Makins, July 19, 1952, FO 371/98691.

104. Benjamin Shwadran, *The Middle East, Oil, and the Great Powers* (New York: John Wiley, 1959), 390.

105. "I have little doubt," wrote A. D. M. Ross of the Eastern Department, "that both from motives of proper pride and from patriotism the Company would, in fact bestir themselves to get into the Persian business again if they were asked to do so by Her Majesty's Government." Minute of July 1, 1953, FO 371/104616. Others were more skeptical.

106. See minute of July 23, 1953, FO 371/98691.

107. Minute by Makins, Aug. 9, 1952, FO 371/98692.

108. Franks to Eden, secret, Aug. 24, 1952, FO 371/98694.

109. Minute by Bowker, Aug. 23, 1952, FO 371/98694.

110. See Heiss, *Empire and Nationhood,* 141–50.

111. For a general synthesis of the cold war, see Dorril, *MI6: Fifty Years,* esp. chap. 28.

112. Minute by Dixon, Feb. 19, 1953, FO 371/104613.

113. Wilber, *Overthrow,* iii.

114. Ibid., 14.

115. Dorril, *MI6: Fifty Years,* 580.

116. Woodhouse, *Something Ventured,* 106.

117. Ibid., 114.

118. Ibid., 110. For Henderson, see Brands, *Inside the Cold War,* chaps. 15–17.

119. Dorril, *MI6: Fifty Years,* 584.

120. Ibid., 577.

121. George K. Young, *Masters of Indecision* (London: Methuen and Co., 1962), 15.

122. Dorril, *MI6: Fifty Years,* 494, quoting George Blake, the MI6 officer who provided the Soviet Union with vital intelligence secrets.

123. Like Zaehner, Wheeler held a Foreign Office appointment as counsellor but had close links with MI6, if indeed he was not an MI6 officer. He is identified as such by Dorril, *MI6: Fifty Years,* 562, 568.

124. See Falle, 72.

125. In his autobiography Woodhouse referred to Shepherd as "a dispirited bachelor dominated by his widowed sister." *Something Ventured,* 109. For a much more favorable assessment of Shepherd, see Cable, *Intervention at Abadan,* for example, 17, 81.

126. Woodhouse, *Something Ventured,* 115–16.

127. See ibid., 112–13. Omar's identity is still uncertain. It is possible that he may have been Abdolhossein Meftah, the deputy foreign minister who attended cabinet sessions in the absence of the foreign minister. I gained the impression from Woodhouse in the summer of 2001, however, that Omar might have been a composite figure constructed in recollection.

128. George Young wrote in retrospect: " 'Neys' did stand by us during the Mossadegh interlude." Young to Denis Wright, Feb. 22, 1981, Wright Papers, privately held.

129. Another of Zaehner's contacts found useful by Woodhouse was (Sir) Shapoor Reporter, who later gained prominence in British-Iranian defense contracts. Reporter was a

Zoroastrian (Parsee) whose family came from Bombay and who held dual British and Iranian citizenship. In 1953 he worked in the U.S. embassy in Tehran. It is possible that he helped to provide the radio link with the MI6 Iran station-in-exile in Cyprus.

130. Falle, 82.

131. Woodhouse, *Something Ventured*, 118.

132. See Wilber, *Overthrow*, 1.

133. Woodhouse, *Something Ventured*, 121.

134. See Kermit Roosevelt, *Countercoup: The Struggle for the Control of Iran* (New York: McGraw-Hill, 1979), a book to be used with caution but nevertheless a basic source.

135. Minute by Dixon, Dec. 5, 1952, FO 371/98703.

136. See Eden to Sir C. Steel, top secret guard, Dec. 4, 1952, FO 371/98703.

137. As reported in Makins to FO, top secret, Mar. 7, 1953, FO 371/104614.

138. For this round of the abortive talks see CAB 129/58 et seq.; and Eden, *Memoirs*, 232–35.

139. Minute by Dixon, Feb. 23, 1953, FO 371/104613.

140. Minute by Dixon, Nov. 30, 1952, FO 371/98703.

141. Minute by Dixon, Mar. 19, 1953, FO 371/104614.

142. See Woodhouse, *Something Ventured*, 123. Woodhouse does not, however, identify any of those involved in the decision except Eden.

143. Winston S. Churchill, *The World Crisis* (New York: Thornton Butterworth, 1923), 1:140.

144. Woodhouse, *Something Ventured*, 125.

145. Technically the American operation held the CIA classification of TPAJAX. The prefix TP designated the covert operation in Iran.

146. See Stephen E. Ambrose, *Eisenhower: The President* (New York: Simon and Schuster, 1984), 111.

147. For a balanced discussion of the plots on Naser's life, see Keith Kyle, *Suez* (London: Weidenfeld and Nicolson, 1991), 149–51.

148. These meetings are not mentioned in *Overthrow*, but see Dorril, *MI6: Fifty Years*, 580–83.

149. It is this point, April 1953, that *Overthrow* identifies as the critical juncture.

150. For the World War II arrest of Zahedi, see Fitzroy Maclean, *Eastern Approaches* (London, 1949; 1964 edition), 271–72: "He was . . . a really bad lot: a bitter enemy of the Allies, a man of unpleasant personal habits. . . . he found himself looking down the barrel of my Colt automatic. Without further ado, I invited the General to put his hands up and informed him that I had instructions to arrest him and that, if he made any noise or attempt at resistance, he would be shot" (271–79).

151. Minute by Falle, confidential, Aug. 2, 1952, FO 248/1531.

152. Wilber, *Overthrow*, 8.

153. Falle, 82. In Falle's judgment, Zahedi was "tough and clear headed"—an assessment more favorable than that of the local CIA officers, who found him "lacking in drive, energy, and concrete plans." Wilber, *Overthrow*, 27.

154. Falle, 82.

155. Wilber, *Overthrow*, app. B, 20–21.

156. Transcript, "End of Empire: Iran."

157. Darbyshire's second in command was (Sir) Dick Franks, who became head of the MI6 station in Tehran after relations were restored in December 1953. Franks rose to become chief of the service.

158. "Junior partner" is the phrase explicitly used in *Overthrow,* for example at 87.

159. Wilber, *Overthrow,* 6.

160. After the decision to launch the operation, Woodhouse withdrew into the background: "I thought it best to absent myself from the scene, since the tactical control was in reliable hands and I did not want to be tempted to interfere with it." Woodhouse, *Something Ventured,* 126.

161. Ibid., 14.

162. In the course of the discussions the British revealed the details of the Rashidian network, but the Americans remained silent about their own undercover organization, which was also based on a pair of brothers, Ali Jalali and Faruq Kayvani, who had the code names Nerren and Cilley. "To the best of our knowledge," concludes *Overthrow* on this point, the CIA agents in Iran "were not uncovered by the Rashidian brothers or any other SIS agents during the course of this operation" (8).

The names of Ali Jalali and Faruq Kayvani were not generally known until the late twentieth century; by contrast, the Rashidians were open about their connections with the British. Some further details help to make the contrast. Nerren and Cilley paid special attention to newspapers, although not necessarily the principal newspapers, and mob rousers. This concentrated effort to manipulate the press and control the street mirrored the CIA's aim in combating the Tudeh. The Rashidian network, by contrast, consisted largely of the elite and included members of the Majles, government officials, clerics, and businessmen, although there was certainly a gangster and mob dimension as well. The British themselves were principally interested in influencing prominent Iranians. The Rashidian organization in turn reflected that aim. Nerren and Cilley had a network of at least 130 agents who by Iranian standards were effective. Their budget of $1 million was larger than that of the Rashidians, but Nerren and Cilley were not independently wealthy and probably did not invest any of their own resources. All in all, the strength of the two organizations was probably about equal. They overlapped but nevertheless complemented each other.

163. Wilber, *Overthrow,* app. C, July 23, 1953.

164. Ibid., 17.

165. See Dorril, *MI6: Fifty Years,* 587.

166. Minute by Falle, confidential, Aug. 2, 1952, FO 248/1531.

167. Woodhouse, *Something Ventured,* 126.

168. Azimi, *Crisis of Democracy,* 333.

169. For Mosaddeq's reforms, which included health and accident insurance as well as women's suffrage, see Katouzian, *Struggle for Power,* chap. 10.

170. There is no evidence of direct British involvement in the murder, but one of the motives of the Rashidians may have been that Afshartus had knowledge of their wide-ranging subversive activities, to a far greater extent than Mosaddeq. There are contradictory accounts of the murder itself, but the most interesting one on the British side is Darbyshire's. He was closer than any other MI6 officer to the internal developments in Iran at this time, and he could be relied on

to relate the unvarnished truth as he saw it, although sometimes rather impulsively. According to Darbyshire, the Rashidians had helped certain Royalist army officers to abduct Afshartus, but then things got out of hand: Afshartus "was kidnapped and held in a cave. Feelings ran high and Afshartus was unwise enough to make derogatory remarks about the Shah. He was under guard by a young army officer and the young officer pulled out a gun and shot. That man was never part of the programme at all but that's how it happened." Dorril, *MI6: Fifty Years,* 585. Darbyshire's account glosses over the probability that the Rashidians may have had him murdered for their own reasons. Afshartus may have been about to move against them. By eliminating him, the Rashidians would have acted in self-interest while also attempting to destabilize the Mosaddeq government.

171. Wilber, *Overthrow,* 7.

172. Ibid., 7.

173. The CIA was particularly interested in the way Asadollah Rashidian managed to obtain an exit visa and reentry permit "from no less a supporter of Mosaddeq than Foreign Minister Hoseyn Fatemi." It seemed to confirm that Fatemi had links with MI6. Fatemi in any event "was certainly aware of Rashidian's agent status with the British." Wilber, *Overthrow,* 10. It is, however, highly improbable that Fatemi had MI6 connections. He was one of the most radical of Mosaddeq's ministers and the only one later to be executed.

174. Dorril, *MI6: Fifty Years,* 588.

175. Wilber attributes the BBC signal entirely to Darbyshire: "In London the necessary arrangements had been made by Darbyshire to send the phrase over the BBC." *Overthrow,* 24.

176. Wilber, *Overthrow,* 79–80.

177. The unpublished British documents unfortunately add little to well-known accounts. See, for example, "Tehran Situation Report Evening August 22 Secret," written by the official in charge of Iranian affairs, Christopher Gandy, FO 371/104570. Gandy knew of MI6 involvement. But he and his Foreign Office colleagues were careful to write all documents as if the change of government had been an entirely Iranian development. Thus, according to the account prepared by the Eastern Department: "Mosaddeq rose to power on a platform of nationalism and opposition to dictatorship. His collapse was due to his abandonment of the second of these principles and his increasingly dictatorial methods; and also to his failure as a nationalist, both by his inability to create a working oil industry of Persia's own and by his increasing reliance on a foreign-inspired organisation, the Tudeh (Communist) party." Memorandum, Aug. 24, 1953, FO 371/104570. This became the standard line within the government as well as the interpretation given to the public. The British were much more discreet than the Americans. Until the publication of Woodhouse's book, hints of MI6 involvement came mainly from American circles. In the first edition of *Countercoup*—the edition he was forced to withdraw—Roosevelt attempted to obscure the complicity of the British government by alleging, erroneously, that the conspiracy originated with the Anglo-Iranian Oil Company. See Thomas Powers, "A Book Held Hostage," *Nation,* Apr. 12, 1980.

178. *Saturday Evening Post,* Nov. 6, 1954, quoted in Woodhouse, *Something Ventured,* 129.

179. Dorril, *MI6: Fifty Years,* 592. This angle of vision on the events of August 1953 led later to a simplistic interpretation apparently endorsed by some MI6 officers: "Roosevelt really did little more than show up in Iran with CIA funds to encourage agents the British had organized and then released to American control." Wilbur Crane Eveland, *Ropes of Sand: America's Failure in the*

Middle East (New York: W. W. Norton, 1980), 109. See also Christopher Andrew, *Secret Service: The Making of the British Intelligence Community* (London: Heinemann, 1985), 494.

180. Wilber, *Overthrow,* 78.

181. Ibid., 80.

182. Ibid., 83.

183. Ibid., 80.

184. Ibid., 81.

185. As for example in Wilber, *Overthrow,* 34.

186. Ibid., 81.

5. The International Boycott of Iranian Oil and the Anti-Mosaddeq Coup of 1953

1. Foreign Office to Athens and to other posts, Sept. 5, 1951, telegram 344, FO 371/UES15327/27. For more on the AIOC's statement see Bamberg, *History of the British Petroleum Company,* 2:453; and Elm, *Oil, Power, and Principle,* 146.

2. For an extensive discussion of public-private cooperation in the oil industry, especially the coincidence between public and private goals, see David S. Painter, *Oil and the American Century: The Political Economy of U.S. Foreign Oil Policy, 1941–1954* (Baltimore, Md.: Johns Hopkins Univ. Press, 1986), 199–210.

3. The AIOC and the British government tried repeatedly to win international support for their view that Iranian nationalization was illegal, but to no avail. Their appeals to the United Nations Security Council and the International Court of Justice at The Hague were unsuccessful. See Heiss, *Empire and Nationhood,* 97–99, 129–34.

4. Sir Francis Shepherd (British ambassador, Tehran) to Kazimi (Iranian foreign minister), Sept. 11, 1951, FO 371/91487/EP1112/181. For more on British economic sanctions against Iran, see C.M.(51) 58th Conclusions, Sept. 4, 1951, Cabinet 58(51), Cabinet Minutes, Conclusions, and Memoranda, Record Class CAB 128/20, Public Record Office; FO to British embassy, Tehran, Sept. 8, 1951, telegram 1170, FO 371/91586/EP1531/1517; Elm, *Oil, Power, and Principle,*, *Oil, Power, and Principle,*, 270–71; and Heiss, *Empire and Nationhood,* 93–94.

5. Walter S. Gifford (U.S. ambassador, London) to State Department, Oct. 2, 1951, telegram 1607, General Records of the Department of State, RG 59, file 888.2553/10–251, USNA 2, College Park, Md. For these developments see also Fatemi, *Khaterat,* 346; Schwadran, "Anglo-Iranian Oil Dispute," 203; and Bamberg, *History of the British Petroleum Company,* 2:433. A colorful account may be found in Henry Longhurst, *Adventures in Oil: The Story of British Petroleum* (London: Sidgwick and Jackson, 1959), 143–44.

6. Robert Stobaugh, "The Evolution of Iranian Oil Policy, 1925–1975." In *Iran under the Pahlevis,* ed. George Lenczowski (Stanford: Hoover Institution Press), 206 n. 10; Schwadran, "Anglo-Iranian Oil Dispute," 225–26. The company presented its own case in AIOC, *The Anglo-Iranian Oil Company and Iran: A Description of the Company's Contributions to Iran's Revenue and National Economy and Its Welfare Activities for Employees in Iran* (London, July 1951). This booklet was distributed to AIOC stockholders later that fall.

7. See Stobaugh, 208–9; Fatemi, *Khaterat,* 350; and Homa Katouzian, "Oil Boycott and Political Economy: Musaddiq and the Strategy of Non-oil Economics," in Bill and Louis, 203–27.

For other measures taken by the company to protect its interests, see Elm, *Oil, Power, and Principle*, 146–49. For Mosaddeq's own claims that the boycott was designed to force Iran's acquiescence to continued AIOC control, see Arthur L. Richards (chargé, U.S. embassy, Tehran) to State Department, Sept. 25, 1951, telegram, in *FRUS, 1952–1954*, 10:164–67.

8. For relations between the AIOC and the British government, see Heiss, *Empire and Nationhood*.

9. See Bamberg, *History of the British Petroleum Company*, 2:435.

10. Tanker figures from Elm, *Oil, Power, and Principle*, 145.

11. See Stobaugh, 208.

12. The close relationship among the major oil companies may be followed in, among other sources, Anthony Sampson, *The Seven Sisters: The Great Oil Companies and the World They Shaped*, rev. 4th ed. (New York: Viking, 1991); Daniel Yergin, *The Prize: The Epic Quest for Oil, Money, and Power* (New York: Simon and Schuster, 1991); Robert Engler, *The Politics of Oil: Private Power and Democratic Directions* (Chicago: Univ. of Chicago Press, 1961); Painter; and John Blair, *The Control of Oil* (New York: Pantheon, 1976).

13. The Supplemental Agreement (or Gass-Golsha'iyan Agreement) was a revision of the 1933 concession agreement between the Iranian government and the AIOC. Although it provided for increased royalties and other benefits for Iran, it was unpopular with most Iranians and was ultimately rejected by the Iranian Majles. See, among other sources, Elm, *Oil, Power, and Principle*,, chaps. 3, 4; and Heiss, *Empire and Nationhood*, chaps. 1, 2.

14. Richard Funkhouser (Office of African and Near Eastern Affairs, State Department) memorandum for McGhee, "Summary—11 September Meeting with Oil Officials," Sept. 18, 1950, in Senate Committee on Foreign Relations, Subcommittee on Multinational Corporations, *Multinational Corporations and United States Foreign Policy*, part 8, 93d Cong., 2d sess., 1974, 99. See also McGhee, *Envoy to the Middle World*,, 321.

15. Funkhouser memorandum of conversation, "Discussion of AIOC Problem with U.S. Oil Companies Operating in the Middle East," May 14, 1951, RG 59, 888.2553/5–145; McGhee memorandum of conversation with Secretary of State Acheson, Eugene Holman (president, SOCNJ), R. G. Follis (chairman of the board, SOCAL), Sidney A. Swensrud (Gulf), Brewster E. Jennings (president, SOCONY-Vacuum), and W. S. Rodgers (chairman of the board, Texaco), "Iranian Oil Problem," Oct. 10, 1951, Papers of Dean Acheson, box 66, folder: Memoranda of Conversations, Oct. 1951, Harry S. Truman Library, Independence, Mo. See also Acheson to U.S. embassy, Tehran, 11 May 1951, telegram, *FRUS, 1952–1954*, 10:51–54; Bamberg, *History of the British Petroleum Company*, 2:459; Stobaugh, 210; and Katouzian, *Struggle for Power*, 145.

16. Memorandum of conversation with oil industry representatives (Jennings, Letches, Holman, Sheppard, Proctor, Drake, and Long) and members of the State Department (Acheson, Bruce, Byroade, Fisher, Nitze, Henderson, and Linder), Dec. 4, 1952, RG 59, 888.2553/12–453. See also Wilkinson memorandum, "Iran," Dec. 12, 1952, FO 371/98668/EP1532/431; unsigned memorandum, "The Oil Facts," Jan. 1, 1953, RG 59, 888.2553/1–153; and Yergin, *The Prize*, 499–500.

17. Sir Oliver Franks (British ambassador, Washington) to FO, Sept. 18, 1950, telegram 2498, FO 371/82375/EP1531/51.

18. McGhee memorandum for Acheson, "12:45 Meeting with Oil Industry Executives,"

Oct. 10, 1951, RG 59, 788.00/10–1051. See also Funkhouser memorandum of conversation, "Discussion of AIOC Problem with U.S. Oil Companies Operating in the Middle East," May 14, 1951, RG 59, 888.2553AIOC/5–1451; Acheson to U.S. embassy, Tehran, May 16, 1951, telegram 2119, Records of U.S. Foreign Service Posts, RG 84, Tehran Embassy, confidential file, 523.1 AIOC, USNA 2; and Shepherd to Foreign Office, Aug. 26, 1951, telegram 1234, FO 371/91582/EP1531/1429.

19. For one example of State Department discussion with U.S. independents, see David Robertson (NE) memorandum of conversation with Edward Miller (Time Oil Company), David Saunders (Time Oil Company), John D. Jernegan (NEA), and Arthur L. Richards (GTI), "Interest of Time Oil Company in Purchase of Iranian Oil," May 20, 1953, RG 59, 888.2553/5–2053.

20. See PAD press release no. 114, July 3, 1951, Records of the Office of Civil and Defense Mobilization, RG 304, Oil and Gas Staff Records, box 1, USNA; PAD press release no. 115, July 6, 1951, RG 304, box 1; PAD memorandum, "Supplying Petroleum to Free World Without Iran," July 12, 1951, and PAD 126, "Plan Approved for Joint Action to Offset Loss of Iranian Oil," Aug. 2, 1951, both in Oscar L. Chapman Papers, Misc. Records, box 99, folder: Petroleum Administration for Defense (1), Truman Library; PAD press release no. 132, "Special Efforts by United States Oil Industry Needed to Offset Iranian Losses, Brown Says," Aug. 7, 1951, Records of the Office of the Secretary of the Interior, RG 48, Press Releases for Various Defense Agencies, 1950–1953, Petroleum Administration for Defense, box 1, USNA; "Co-Operative Action Approved," *Petroleum Press Service* 18 (Sept. 1951): 310–11; Burton I. Kaufman, *The Oil Cartel Case: A Documentary Study of Antitrust Activity During the Cold War Era* (Westport, Conn.: Greenwood Press, 1978), 42–43; and Gerald D. Nash, *United States Oil Policy, 1880–1964: Business and Government in Twentieth-Century America* (Pittsburgh: Univ. of Pittsburgh Press, 1968), 195–96.

21. Oscar L. Chapman to James M. Mead (chair, Federal Trade Commission), July 8, 1952, Stephen J. Spingarn Papers, FTC File, box 35, folder: International Petroleum Cartel Report, Truman Library.

22. See Bruce K. Brown, *Oil Men in Washington: An Informal Account of the Organization and Activities of the Petroleum Administration for Defense During the Korean War, 1950–1952* (n.p.: Evanil Press, 1965), 149–65; Painter, 179–81; and Bamberg, *History of the British Petroleum Company,* 2:460.

23. For the Truman administration's early efforts to work as an honest broker in the Anglo-Iranian dispute, see Heiss, *Empire and Nationhood,* chaps. 3, 4.

24. See Fatemi, *Khaterat,* 353; and Schwadran, "Anglo-Iranian Oil Dispute," 230.

25. For two examples of these sorts of discussions, see Furlonge memorandum with attached Persia Working Party paper, "Approach to a New Persian Government," Sept. 7, 1951, FO 371/91590/EP1531/1604; and George H. Middleton (British embassy, Tehran) to Saner, Sept. 18, 1951, FO 371/91589/EP1531/1600.

26. Among other sources, see Fatemi, *Khaterat,* 381; Schwadran, "Anglo-Iranian Oil Dispute," 229; and Jack Anderson, *Fiasco* (New York, 1983), 9. On Mosaddeq's misplaced optimism see also Shepherd to R. J. Bowker (Foreign Office), July 23, 1951, FO 371/91572/EP1531/1217.

27. For the strategic importance that U.S. officials did place on Iran at the time, see Malcolm Byrne's essay in this volume. As Byrne makes clear, the key to understanding U.S. policy in

Iran is the cold war. Additional discussions of Iran's importance to the United States may be found in Bruce R. Kuniholm, *The Origins of the Cold War in the Middle East: Great Power Conflict and Diplomacy in Iran, Turkey, and Greece* (Princeton, N.J.: Princeton Univ. Press, 1980); and Mark Hamilton Lytle, *The Origins of the Iranian-American Alliance, 1941–1953* (New York: Holmes and Meier, 1987).

28. A good discussion of Mosaddeq's thinking about U.S. oil purchases may be found in Dadkhah, "Iran's Economic Policy," 43–44.

29. Mosaddeq to Eisenhower, May 28, 1953, Royal Institute of International Affairs, *Documents on International Affairs, 1953* (London: Royal Institute of International Affairs, 1954), 349–51; Dulles to U.S. embassy, Tehran, transmitting Eisenhower reply to Mosaddeq, June 30, 1953, telegram 3295, Ann Whitman File—International Series, box 29, folder: Iran, 1953 Through 1959, Dwight D. Eisenhower Library, Abilene, Kans. See also Loy Henderson (U.S. ambassador Tehran) to State Department, May 31, 1953, telegram 4292, RG 59, 888.2553/5–3153; and Henry A. Byroade (NEA) memorandum for Dulles, "Letter from Dr. Mosaddeq to President Eisenhower," June 5, 1953, *FRUS, 1952–1954,* 10:732.

30. See Carr, "Monthly Economic Survey, Iran, May 1953," June 11, 1953, dispatch 1069, RG 59, 888.00/6–1153; Gordon Mattison (counselor, U.S. embassy, Tehran) to State Department, July 13, 1953, telegram, *FRUS, 1952–1954,* 10:734–35; Robert B. Parke (acting commercial attaché, U.S. embassy, Tehran), "Monthly Economic Survey, Iran, July 1953," Aug. 14, 1953, dispatch 104, RG 59, 888.00/8–1453; and Azimi, *Crisis of Democracy,* 326.

31. Parke, "Commission for Oil Exports: Transmission of Memorandum of Conversation with Dr. Z. Abou-Zia, Chairman of the Iranian Government Commission for Oil Exports," Mar. 4, 1953, dispatch 975, RG 59, 888.2553/3–453. See also Katouzian, "Oil Boycott," 203.

32. The government's various efforts to deal with the boycott are considered in greater detail in Katouzian, "Oil Boycott"; Elm, *Oil, Power, and Principle,*, 267–75; and Patrick Clawson and Cyrus Sassanpour, "Adjustment to a Foreign Exchange Shock: Iran, 1951–1953," *International Journal of Middle East Studies* 19, no. 1 (Feb. 1987): 1–23.

33. See Clawson and Sassanpour, "Adjustment," 15–17.

34. Detailed economic discussion may be found in Katouzian, *Struggle for Power,* 153.

35. Clawson and Sassanpour, "Adjustment," 1, 8.

36. An exception to the generally positive assessment of Mosaddeq's handling of the economic crisis is Dadkhah, "Oil Nationalisation Movement," 104–31. Other pessimistic appraisals may be found in Edward Ashley Bayne, "Crisis of Confidence in Iran," *Foreign Affairs* 24 (July 1951): 578–90; and Dadkhah, "Iran's Economic Policy," 39–54.

37. For public acceptance of Mosaddeq's economic measures see Clawson and Sassanpour, "Adjustment," 17.

38. For wartime hardships see Azimi, *Crisis of Democracy,* 44.

39. For opposition to Mosaddeq's economic measures see Katouzian, "Oil Boycott," 208, 215, 222; id., *Struggle for Power,* 155; and Elm, *Oil, Power, and Principle,*, 273–75.

40. Julian Bharier, *Economic Development in Iran, 1900–1970* (London: Oxford Univ. Press, 1971), 90. See also Elm, *Oil, Power, and Principle,*, 273; Clawson and Sassanpour, "Adjustment," 13–15; and Katouzian, "Oil Boycott," 222.

41. Dadkhah, "Oil Nationalization Movement," 113.

42. For U.S. aid to Iran during this period see, for example, Mark J. Gasiorowski, *U.S. For-*

eign Policy and the Shah: Building a Client State in Iran (Ithaca, N.Y.: Cornell Univ. Press, 1991), 50–56.

43. Henderson to State Department, Apr. 19, 1952, telegram, *FRUS, 1952–1954,* 10:371–75. See also Henderson to State Department, Dec. 14, 1951, telegram, *FRUS, 1952–1954,* 10:291–95; Foreign Office minutes, Dec. 15, 1951, FO 371/91617/EP1531/2294; Franks to FO, Dec. 16, 1951, telegram 3877, FO 371/91617/EP1531/2308; Acheson to U.S. embassy, Tehran, Dec. 21, 1951, telegram, and Henderson to State Department, Dec. 26, 1951, telegram, *FRUS, 1952–1954,* 10:295–300; and Acheson to U.S. embassy, Tehran, Apr. 21, 1952, telegram, Henderson to State Department, Apr. 23, 1952, telegram, and Acheson to U.S. embassy, Tehran, Apr. 23, 1952, telegram, *FRUS, 1952–1954,* 10:375–79.

44. Acheson, 679.

45. Middleton to Anthony Eden (foreign secretary), July 7, 1952, telegram, FO 371/98661/EP1532/230. See also Carr, "Monthly Economic Report," 2 June 1952, dispatch 1265, RG 59, 888.00/6–252; Carr, "Monthly Economic Report," July 3, 1952, dispatch 7, RG 59, 888.00/7–352; and Acheson, 679.

46. Hickinbotham (Aden) to FO, June 21, 1952, telegram 156, FO 371/98660/EP1532/204.

47. FO to British embassy, Tehran, July 23, 1952, telegram 460, FO 371/98661/EP1532/247.

48. Iran's efforts to break the British boycott are detailed in, among other sources, Elm, *Oil, Power, and Principle,*, 267–70.

49. Logan memorandum, Nov. 13, 1952, FO 371/98666/EP1532/364.

50. Henderson to State Department, Mar. 5, 1953, telegram 3548, RG 59, 888.2553/3–553. See also FO to British embassy, Washington, Mar. 7, 1953, telegram 1088, FO 371/10461/EP1531/211; John Foster Dulles (secretary of state) to U.S. embassy, Tehran, Mar. 13, 1953, telegram, *FRUS, 1952–1954,* 10:714–15; Henderson to State Department, Mar. 14, 1953, telegram 3688, RG 59, 888.2553/3–1453; and Henderson to State Department, Mar. 18, 1953, telegram, *FRUS, 1952–1954,* 10:716–19. For excellent scholarly coverage of planning for the coup, see Gasiorowski, "1953 Coup d'État,"262–86, and Gasiorowski's essay in this volume.

51. Carr, "Monthly Economic Survey: Iran, April 1953," May 12, 1953, dispatch 933, RG 59, 888.00/5–1253. For claims that the economic difficulties generated by the boycott were exaggerated, see, for example, Katouzian, "Oil Boycott," 225; and Azimi, *Crisis of Democracy,* 281, 327.

52. Memorandum of conversation with oil industry representatives (Jennings, Letches, Holman, Sheppard, Proctor, Drake, and Long) and members of the State Department (Acheson, Bruce, Byroade, Fisher, Nitze, Henderson, and Linder), Dec. 4, 1952, RG 59, 888.2553/12–452.

53. Figures from Jahangir Amuzegar and M. Ali Fekrat, *Iran: Economic Development under Dualistic Conditions* (Chicago: Univ. of Chicago Press, 1971), 21. For a complete analysis of the role of oil royalties during the nationalization period, see 17–23.

54. For the prevalence and power of anti-Mosaddeq propaganda, see Katouzian, "Oil Boycott," 225; and Clawson and Sassanpour, 8.

55. See essays by Fakhreddin Azimi, Mark J. Gasiorowski, and Wm. Roger Louis in this volume.

6. The Road to Intervention: Factors Influencing
U.S. Policy Toward Iran, 1945–1953

1. "Subject: President Truman's conversations with George M. Elsey," June 26, 1950, G. M. E. notes of June 26, 1950. This document was obtained from the Truman Library Web site under the title "Summary of conversation with President Harry S. Truman regarding intentions of the Chinese communists vis a vis Korea. Papers of George M. Elsey."

2. Major book-length treatments of this subject include Bill's *The Eagle and the Lion;* James F. Goode, *The United States and Iran: In the Shadow of Musaddiq* (New York: St. Martin's Press, 1997); Lytle, and Barry Rubin, *Paved with Good Intentions* (New York: Oxford Univ. Press, 1980). Two of the most important books on the United States and Iran in the late 1940s are Kuniholm, *Origins of the Cold War,* and Louise L'Estrange Fawcett, *Iran and the Cold War: The Azerbaijan Crisis of 1946,* (New York: Cambridge Univ. Press, 1992).

3. Franklin Roosevelt gave an early indication of this broad reading of American interests in a letter to Joseph Stalin on October 4, 1944, relating to the question of southeastern Europe, where Washington had traditionally shown little concern: "You, naturally, understand that in this global war there is literally no question, political or military, in which the United States is not interested." Quoted in Charles E. Bohlen, *Witness to History, 1929–1969* (New York: W. W. Norton, 1973), 162.

4. For the most thorough study of the shaping of postwar American national security policy, see Melvyn P. Leffler, *A Preponderance of Power: National Security, the Truman Administration, and the Cold War* (Stanford, Calif.: Stanford Univ. Press, 1992). For an examination of the underlying links between economic and military strength, see Paul M. Kennedy, *The Rise and Fall of the Great Powers: Economic Change and Military Conflict from 1500 to 2000* (New York: Random House, 1987).

5. Truman to Byrnes, which Truman says he read to Byrnes in the Oval Office on Jan. 5, 1946 (although Byrnes denies it); reprinted in Harry S. Truman, *Year of Decisions* (Garden City, N.Y.: Doubleday, 1955), 551–52. This document is also cited on page 289 in John Lewis Gaddis, *The United States and the Origins of the Cold War, 1941–1947* (New York: Columbia Univ. Press, 1972). For an extended discussion of the impact of this crucial period on U.S. attitudes toward the Soviet Union, see ibid., 282–315.

6. See William Taubman, *Stalin's American Policy: From Entente to Détente to Cold War* (New York: W. W. Norton, 1982), 133–35; see also Arnold A. Offner, *Another Such Victory: President Truman and the Cold War, 1945–1953* (Stanford, Calif.: Stanford Univ. Press, 2002), 128.

7. Moscow embassy telegram no. 511, Feb. 22, 1946, in *FRUS, 1946,* 6:696–709; see also Gaddis, *United States and Origins,* 302–4.

8. U.S. ambassador to Moscow Averell Harriman reported on the substance of the Stalin-Bevin-Byrnes talks in Moscow in late December 1945, in ambassador in the Soviet Union (Harriman) to the acting secretary of state, Dec. 23, 1945, cable 4262, in *FRUS, 1945,* 8:510–11; and ambassador in the Soviet Union (Harriman) to the secretary of state, cable 4311, in *FRUS, 1945,* 8:517–19. Even earlier, senior U.S. officials worried about Iran's ability to stave off threats, implicitly from the Soviet Union, after the withdrawal of Allied forces. See memorandum by the secretary of state to the secretary of war (Stimson), Dec. 21, 1944, in *FRUS, 1944,* 5:442–43. See also Stimson's reply on 444.

9. The Tudeh Party, communist by doctrine and loyal to Moscow, constituted only one of the groups agitating for greater autonomy and other socioeconomic goals in Azerbaijan.

10. See, for example, Daniel Yergin, *Shattered Peace: The Origins of the Cold War and the National Security State* (Boston: Houghton-Mifflin, 1977), 179–81.

11. See, for example, Central Intelligence Group (CIG), Weekly Summary, "The Azerbaijan Settlement," June 14, 1946; CIG, "Soviet Foreign and Military Policy," ORE 1, July 23, 1946; CIA, Weekly Summary, "Iran," Mar. 18, 1949; and CIA, Special Evaluation no. 39, "Possibility of Soviet Aggression Against Iran," July 27, 1950. These reports are reprinted in Woodrow J. Kuhns, ed., *Assessing the Soviet Threat: The Early Cold War Years* (Washington, D.C.: Center for the Study of Intelligence, CIA, 1997), docs. 1, 4, 127, and 185, respectively.

12. Actually, the picture was more complex. The Tudeh Party initially resisted the creation of the Democratic Party of Azerbaijan (DPA) because its leadership rightly saw the new party as a rival with different policies on certain issues such as membership. According to Azeri scholar Jamil Hasanli, the Tudeh was forced to join the DPA at a Tabriz Provincial Committee conference of the party on September 6, 1945. Jamil Hasanli, "The Creation of the Democratic Party and the Idea of Autonomy," chapter in unpublished manuscript based largely on former Azeri Communist Party documents.

13. In his memoirs, Truman recalls ordering Byrnes to send a "blunt message" to Stalin, although no record of such a note has ever been found. Harry S. Truman, *Years of Trial and Hope* (Garden City, N.Y.: Doubleday, 1956), 95. It seems clear now that multiple factors came into play in determining Moscow's decision to withdraw, including but not solely a tough U.S. reaction (see the discussion of Soviet motives below).

14. Truman, *Years of Trial and Hope,* 97.

15. See the discussion in Eduard Mark, "The War Scare of 1946 and Its Consequences," in *Diplomatic History* 21, no. 3 (summer 1997): 383–415, esp. 387, 399–401.

16. See Kuniholm, *Origins of the Cold War,* 399–405.

17. Acheson, 219; Truman, *Years of Trial and Hope,* 101.

18. See U.S. Joint Chiefs of Staff, *Documents Resulting from Conversations with the British in Regard to the Eastern Mediterranean and the Middle East, JCS 1819,* Nov. 25, 1947, cited in Gasiorowski, "1953 Coup d'Etat," 267, 282 n. 32. This view continued to hold until the early 1950s: see "Editorial Note" attaching portions of joint conclusions reached by U.S. and British officials on the Middle East and Iran, including the comment, "The U.S. Joint Chiefs of Staff . . . consider the area to be a British Commonwealth responsibility." *FRUS, 1947,* 5:610.

19. See *FRUS, 1947,* 5:32–37.

20. "American Relations with the Soviet Union: A Report to the President by the Special Counsel to the President," Sept. 24, 1946, in Arthur Krock, *Memoirs: Sixty Years on the Firing Line* (New York: Funk and Wagnalls, 1968), 419–82. Truman commissioned the report, compiled by Special Counsel Clark Clifford and his assistant, George Elsey, in the summer of 1946, in the wake of the Azerbaijan crisis. See Gaddis, *United States and Origins,* 320–23.

21. For the most detailed treatment of the U.S.-Soviet confrontation in the region, see Kuniholm, *Origins of the Cold War.* The Truman Doctrine address is reprinted on 458–63. For the August 1946 decision and a discussion of Turkey's importance to U.S. strategic interests, see especially 359–65. For a different perspective on the evolution of the superpower rivalry in the early postwar era, see Leffler, *Preponderance of Power,* specifically on the Near East and Iran, 77–81, 121–27, 142–47, 237–39, 288–91, 419–26, 476–85.

22. The Clifford-Elsey report advocated this approach. Although not always as clearly as he intended, Kennan disagreed. His best-known analyses of Soviet behavior and prescriptions for U.S. policy were contained in the "Long Telegram," Moscow embassy telegram 511, Feb. 22, 1946, *FRUS, 1946,* 6:696–709; and id., "The Sources of Soviet Conduct," *Foreign Affairs* 25 (July 1947): 572–76, 580–82. See also the extended discussion in John Lewis Gaddis, *Strategies of Containment* (New York: Oxford Univ. Press, 1982), chaps. 2, 3, esp. 57–65.

23. "The American Paper," prepared circa late October 1947 as part of "The Pentagon Talks of 1947" with the United Kingdom. See *FRUS, 1947,* 5:575. A virtually identical policy statement appears two years later in "Report of the National Security Council on the Position of the United States with Respect to Iran," NSC 54, July 21, 1949. See the National Security Archive's microfiche collection, *Iran: The Making of U.S. Policy, 1977–1980* (Alexandria, Va.: Chadwyck-Healey, 1990), record no. 00211.

24. See the discussion in Gasiorowski, *U.S. Foreign Policy and the Shah,* 52–53.

25. New evidence from Russian and East European archives indicates that Stalin also had well-developed ideas in other selected areas, such as consolidating the positions of communist parties in Western Europe. See Eduard Mark, "Revolution by Degrees: Stalin's National-Front Strategy for Europe, 1941–1947," Cold War International History Project, Working Paper no. 31, Woodrow Wilson International Center for Scholars, Washington, D.C., Feb. 2001.

26. As recounted in Albert Resis, ed., *Molotov Remembers: Inside Kremlin Politics, Conversations with Felix Chuev* (Chicago: Ivan R. Dee, 1993), 8.

27. See Martin Sicker, *The Bear and the Lion: Soviet Imperialism and Iran* (New York: Praeger, 1988), 9–35; also, generally, Peter Hopkirk, *The Great Game: The Struggle for Empire in Central Asia* (New York Kodansha International, 1994).

28. Quoted in Raymond James Sontag and James Stuart Beddie, eds., *Nazi-Soviet Relations, 1939–1941: Documents from the Archives of the German Foreign Office* (Washington, D.C.: Department of State, 1948), 259. Raymond Garthoff makes the point that the Germans originally urged Moscow to focus its sights to the south in hopes of "setting up a collision course between Russian and British interests." See Raymond L. Garthoff, *Détente and Confrontation: American-Soviet Relations from Nixon to Reagan* (Washington, D.C.: Brookings Institution, 1994), 1050 n. 202. But after Foreign Minister Joachim von Ribbentropp initially proposed more general language about Soviet interests pointing "in the direction of the Indian Ocean," Molotov (after checking with Stalin) demanded that the focus be narrowed to the vicinity of the Persian Gulf.

29. For a discussion of the percentages agreement based on declassified British documents that give more detail and a different slant than Churchill's memoir account, see Albert Resis, "The Churchill-Stalin 'Percentages' Agreement on the Balkans, Moscow, October 1944," *American Historical Review* 83, no. 2 (Apr. 1978): 368–87. For Churchill's comment in Tehran, see Taubman, 82.

30. Ambassador in the Soviet Union (Harriman) to the acting secretary of state, Dec. 23, 1945, cable 4262, in *FRUS, 1945,* 8:510–11.

31. See memorandum for the president from CIA director Roscoe Hillenkoetter, untitled, July 27, 1950, file: Iran-U.S. Relations, Documents, 1950, National Security Archive.

32. Vladislav Zubok and Constantine Pleshakov, *Inside the Kremlin's Cold War: From Stalin to Khrushchev* (Cambridge, Mass.: Harvard Univ. Press, 1996), 12–13.

33. See the discussion in John Lewis Gaddis, *We Now Know: Rethinking Cold War History* (Oxford: Oxford Univ. Press, 1997), 42–43.

34. See Natalia I. Yegorova, "The 'Iran Crisis' of 1945–1946: A View from the Russian Archives," Cold War International History Project, Working Paper no. 15, May 1996, 20–21. See also Vladimir O. Pechatnov, "The Big Three after World War II: New Documents on Soviet Thinking about Post War Relations with the United States and Great Britain," Cold War International History Project Working Paper no. 13, July 1995, 3.

35. Pechatnov, "The Big Three," 21.

36. This discussion is based in part on a paper presented by Fernande Scheid at the conference "Iran and the Second World War" held in Tehran Sept. 25–27, 1999. Scheid did extensive research in Azeri and Russian archives for her paper. She later published an article entitled "Stalin and the Creation of the Azerbaijan Democratic Party in Iran, 1945," in *Cold War History* 2, no. 1 (Oct. 2001): 1–38. Azeri scholar Jamil Hasanli has reached a somewhat different conclusion, namely, that Stalin ultimately planned to annex Azerbaijan province to the Soviet Union. Hasanli, "Creation of the Democratic Party."

37. On this point see Vojtech Mastny, *The Cold War and Soviet Insecurity: The Stalin Years* (New York: Oxford Univ. Press, 1996), 191.

38. See Yegorova, " 'Iran Crisis' of 1945–1946," 3–4. The Soviets demanded a concession as soon as they moved into the country in August 1941. At the time, however, the Iranians indicated only that they would be willing to discuss the idea. See Kuniholm, *Origins of the Cold War,* 192.

39. See Scheid paper, Hasanli, "Creation of the Democratic Party."

40. Yegorova, " 'Iran Crisis' of 1945–1946," 18.

41. Stalin himself purportedly "uncovered" this lapse by the foreign ministry. Writing to the Politburo on September 30, 1946, he pointed out that elections for the new parliament had not even been scheduled, and the ratification deadline was less than a month away. Cited in Vladimir O. Pechatnov, " 'The Allies Are Pressing on You to Break Your Will': Foreign Policy Correspondence Between Stalin and Molotov and Other Politburo Members, September 1945-December 1946," Cold War International History Project, Working Paper no. 26, Sept. 1999, 20.

42. See, for example, Pechatnov, "The Allies," 8.

43. Resis, *Molotov Remembers,* 8. Rating their own success at enlarging Soviet territory, Molotov went on to say, "And it seems that Stalin and I coped with this task quite well."

44. Central Intelligence Group, "Soviet Foreign and Military Policy," ORE 1, July 23, 1946, reprinted in Kuhns, *Assessing the Soviet Threat,* 56–66.

45. See the essay on Truman's creation and use of the Central Intelligence Group, precursor to the CIA, in Kuhns, *Assessing the Soviet Threat,* 3–4.

46. Throughout his book *Another Such Victory,* Arnold Offner provides a raft of evidence to support his view that Truman was excessively influenced by these factors.

47. Reis, 8.

48. Dean Acheson cable to Amb. Oliver Franks, Dec. 24, 1949, quoted in Leffler, *Preponderance of Power,* 333–34.

49. NSC 68, "United States Objectives and Programs for National Security," Apr. 14, 1950, in *FRUS, 1950,* 1:237–92.

50. See the discussion in Gaddis, *Strategies of Containment,* chap. 4; also generally Ernest R. May, ed., *American Cold War Strategy: Interpreting NSC 68* (Boston: Bedford Books of St. Martin's Press, 1993).

51. See *FRUS, 1945,* 8:45–48.

52. See, for example, "Need for Middle East Oil Throughout a War," Mar. 21, 1951, RG 218, CCS 463.7 (9–6–45), USNA.

53. NIE 14, "Importance of Iranian and Middle East Oil to Western Europe under Peacetime Conditions," Jan. 8, 1951, in *FRUS, 1951,* 5:270–75.

54. Some analysts have argued that U.S. policy on Iran was influenced by pressure from major oil interests. See, for example, the discussion in Bill, *The Eagle and the Lion,* 80–83. American oil companies certainly tried a variety of avenues to push government policy in a favorable direction. Referring to a meeting Dean Acheson held with representatives of the five major U.S. firms on December 4, 1952, a British Foreign Office memorandum notes: "After he [Acheson] had again emphasized the grave danger of communism in Iran, and the necessity for an early settlement, he added that another reason for early settlement was the fact that the State Department was under considerable pressure from Congressmen as a result of 'lobbying' on the part of various oil brokers interested in getting into the Iranian picture!" See Wilkinson memorandum, "Iran," Dec. 12, 1952, in FO 371/98668/EP1532/431. But the evidence from the documentary record (including Wilkinson's memorandum) indicates that U.S. government concerns centered around strategic rather than purely commercial priorities. As the CIA's Donald Wilber wrote in his 1954 internal history of the coup: "Iran was in real danger of falling behind the Iron Curtain; if that happened it would mean a victory for the Soviets in the Cold War and a major setback for the West in the Middle East." Wilber, *Overthrow,* iii.

55. See, for example, NSC 26/1, "A Report to the National Security Council by the Secretary of State on SANACC 398/4," Nov. 10, 1948, on the subject of "Demolition and Abandonment of Oil Facilities and Fields in the Middle East." A version of the plan received Truman's approval in January 1949. At one point, U.S. officials briefly discussed using radiological weapons to make the area around targeted oil fields uninhabitable. Journalists Steve Everly and Charles R. T. Crumpley reported the first accounts of the oil denial plans in the *Kansas City Star* on February 25, 1995. I am grateful to Steve Everly for sharing his documents with me. A series of related materials is also available at the Dwight D. Eisenhower Library.

56. See, for example, NSC 54, "Report of the National Security Council on the Position of the United States With Respect to Iran," July 21, 1949; and NSC 107/2, "The Position of the United States with Respect to Iran," June 27, 1951. Copies are available at the National Security Archive, Washington, D.C.

57. Gasiorowski, *U.S. Foreign Policy and the Shah,* 56.

58. See generally *FRUS, 1951,* 5:1–267, esp. secretary of state to the embassy in Egypt, Oct. 16, 1951, cable 584 (including n. 2), 226–27; see also ambassador in Egypt (Caffery) to the Department of State, Oct. 9, 1951, cable 921, 392–95. U.S. ambassador Jefferson Caffery reported in the latter cable that after the Egyptian prime minister called on Parliament to denounce the Anglo-Egyptian Treaty of 1936, the week before rejection of the MECOM proposal, "bedlam broke out" as every opposition party clamored to support the government's action. In a tone reminiscent of the attitude of many British and Americans toward Iran, Caffery commented: "The emotions of the moment were as irrational as the actions which the Prime Minister recommended." See also John C. Campbell, *Defense of the Middle East: Problems of American Policy* (New York: Frederick A. Praeger, 1960), 39–48.

59. See, among other documents, Dean Acheson cable "Secto 24" to the Department of State, June 27, 1952, in *FRUS, 1952–1954,* vol. 9, part 1, 251–54.

60. See "Memorandum of Discussion at the 147th Meeting of the National Security Council, Monday, June 1, 1953," in *FRUS 1952–1954,* vol. 9, part 1, 379–86, esp. 384. See also Brands, *Inside the Cold War,* 276–77; and Leffler, *Preponderance of Power,* 481–82, 484–85.

61. See Bill, *The Eagle and the Lion,* 39; and Gasiorowski, *U.S. Foreign Policy and the Shah,* 52–54.

62. This passage is based on Gasiorowski, *U.S. Foreign Policy and the Shah,* 56.

63. Robert Lovett, memorandum to State (Bruce), Aug. 16, 1952, RG 330, box 16, CD 092 (Iran), USNA. For the Joint Chiefs' views, see Goode, 92. The official policy statement, "United States Policy Regarding the Present Situation in Iran," NSC 136/1, Nov. 20, 1952, was the Truman administration's last such formulation on Iran. RG 59, "Records Relating to State Department Participation in the Operations Coordinating Board and the National Security Council, 1947–1963," box 68, folder: NSC 136: U.S. Policy Regarding the Present Situation in Iran, USNA. It is also on file at the National Security Archive.

64. See, for example, the following representative cables in *FRUS, 1952–1954,* vol. 10: Henderson to State, Oct. 22, 1951, cable 1478, 236–40; Henderson to State, Jan. 15, 1952, cable 2640, 323–27; and Henderson to State, Nov. 5, 1952, cable 1850, 513–17. Henderson repeatedly discussed Mosaddeq's possible removal with the shah's minister of court, Hossein Ala, who the ambassador understood was acting as the shah's personal emissary at these meetings. Henderson made it clear that the United States wanted to be rid of the prime minister. See, for example, Henderson to State, Sept. 27, 1951, cable 1180, *FRUS, 1952–1954,* 10:174–77; Henderson to State, May 24, 1952, cable 4540, 10:381–83; Henderson to State, June 6, 1952, cable 4736, 10:389–92.

65. See Mark Gasiorowski's chapter in this volume. See also Gasiorowski, *U.S. Foreign Policy and the Shah,* 54, 69–71. Only a handful of documents on the subject have been declassified. See, for example, NSC progress report, "United States Policy Regarding the Present Situation in Iran (NSC 136/1)," Mar. 20, 1953, RG 59, "Records Relating to State Department Participation in the Operations Coordinating Board and the National Security Council, 1947–1963," box 68, folder: NSC 136: U.S. Policy Regarding the Present Situation in Iran, USNA (also on file at the National Security Archive).

66. Malcolm Byrne interview with former CIA official who requested anonymity, Washington, D.C., June 30, 2000. See also the progress report cited in the previous note, "United States Policy Regarding the Present Situation in Iran (NSC 136/1)," Mar. 20, 1953.

67. See "Review of the World Situation As It Relates to the Security of the United States," CIA, Office of Research and Estimates, Sept. 26, 1947, reprinted in Kuhns, Document no. 37. This document specifically refers to the Near and Middle East as an area of priority "from the point of view of containing the USSR."

68. For a discussion of the impact of the Czechoslovak coup on U.S. policy making, see Malcolm Byrne and Thomas Blanton, "U.S. Perspectives on the Coup in Czechoslovakia: New Evidence from U.S. Intelligence Files," paper presented at the conference "The Czechoslovak 'February,' 1948: Preconditions and Repercussions at Home and Abroad," Prague, Feb. 19–21, 1998.

69. NSC 10/2, "National Security Council Directive on Office of Special Projects," June 18, 1948, in Thomas H. Etzold and John Lewis Gaddis, *Containment: Documents in American Policy and Strategy, 1945–1950,* (New York: Columbia Univ. Press, 1978) 125–28. See also the discussion on

the origins of this document and the early expansion of U.S. covert capabilities in "Final Report of the Select Committees to Study Governmental Operations with respect to Intelligence Activities," U.S. Senate, report no. 94–755, book 4, *Supplementary Detailed Staff Reports on Foreign and Military Intelligence* (Washington, D.C.: Government Printing Office, 1976), 25–31.

70. See Mark Gasiorowski's chapter in this volume.

71. The quotes are from "United States Policy Regarding the Present Situation in Iran," NSC 136/1, Nov. 20, 1952.

72. Francis J. Gavin points out this change in "Politics, Power, and U.S. Policy in Iran, 1950–1953," *Journal of Cold War Studies* 1, no. 1 (winter 1999), esp. 78–79.

73. The British approach in mid-1952 is alluded to in Gasiorowski, "1953 Coup d'Etat," 267, 282 n. 37, as well as in "Anglo-U.S. Discussions on the Persian Situation, July 29, 1952, FO 371/98691. The November 1952 British-American conversation is described in Woodhouse, *Something Ventured,* 116–19.

74. See, for example, the influential memorandum by John D. Jernegan of the State Department's Division of Near Eastern Affairs, "American Policy in Iran," Jan. 23, 1943, reprinted in Yonah Alexander and Allan Nanes, eds., *The United States and Iran: A Documentary History* (Frederick, Md.: Univ. Press of America, 1980), 94–99.

75. See Louis, "Musaddiq and the Dilemmas of British Imperialism," in Bill and Louis, 249.

76. This point shows through clearly in top-level deliberations during Eisenhower's first months as president. See, for example, the memoranda of discussion at the 135th and 136th meetings of the National Security Council in Washington on March 4 and 11, 1953, in *FRUS, 1952–1954,* 10:694–95, 712–13.

77. In April 1951, Truman relieved MacArthur of his command of UN forces in South Korea, which led to more recriminations against the president for, among other things, refusing to show greater resolve by bombing Chinese bases in Manchuria. See the general description of the MacArthur episode in David McCullough, *Truman* (New York: Simon and Schuster, 1992), 830–56. See also Gaddis, *Strategies of Containment,* 118–20.

78. See Leffler, *Preponderance of Power,* 344.

79. Stephen E. Ambrose, *Ike's Spies: Eisenhower and the Espionage Establishment* (Garden City, N.Y.: 1981) 170–71.

80. George F. Kennan, *Memoirs, 1950–1963* (Boston: Little, Brown and Company, 1972), 2:227–28.

81. John Lewis Gaddis discusses these points in *Strategies of Containment,* 102–3, 143–45.

82. *Time,* Mar. 26, 1951, 31, quoted in Bill, *The Eagle and the Lion,* 80.

83. For an interesting and relevant analysis of the link between foreign policy rhetoric and domestic anti-communism, see Richard M. Freeland, *The Truman Doctrine and the Origins of Mc-Carthyism: Foreign Policy, Domestic Politics, and Internal Security, 1946–1948* (New York: Knopf, 1972).

84. See Kuniholm, *Origins of the Cold War,* 370–71.

85. For a discussion of Truman's sensitivity to public opinion, see generally Gaddis, *United States and Origins,* esp. 312–13.

86. See Maziar Behrooz's chapter in this volume. For a full-length treatment of the subject, see also Behrooz, *Rebels with a Cause.*

87. Byrne's interviews with anonymous retired CIA officer.

88. "The United States' Ideas of a Settlement of the Oil Dispute," Oct. 20, 1952, FO 371/98702. Eisenhower's campaign staff saw Iran as one of a handful of "targets of opportunity." See, for example, "Eisenhower for President Research Service," *Weekly Report,* no. 21 (Aug. 20, 1952), Sherman Adams Records, box 37, folder: Research, General (2), Dwight D. Eisenhower Library; and "Eisenhower/Nixon Research Service," *Weekly Report,* no. 24 (Sept. 10, 1952), Sherman Adams Records, box 37, folder: Research, General (1), Dwight D. Eisenhower Library.

89. Eisenhower's quotes appear in Stephen E. Ambrose, *Eisenhower: Soldier, General of the Army, President-Elect, 1890–1952* (New York: Simon and Schuster, 1983), 530, 531, 534. Ambrose characterizes Eisenhower's handling of instances such as these as "appeasement of the right" (546).

90. See, for example, Dean Acheson's comments to Eisenhower as recorded in "Memorandum by the Secretary of State of a Meeting at the White House Between the President and General Eisenhower," Nov. 18, 1952, in *FRUS, 1952–1954,* vol. 1, part 1, 22–29.

91. See Henderson to State Department, July 28, 1952, cable 422, in *FRUS, 1952–1954,* 10:416–21. Henderson writes: "I cld not but be discouraged at thought that person so lacking in stability and clearly dominated by emotions and prejudices shld represent only bulwark left between Iran and communism. As during several previous conversations, I had feeling at times that I was talking with someone not quite sane" (416–17). See also Henderson to State Department, Mar. 10, 1953, cable 3627, in *FRUS, 1952–1954,* 10:706–8, where he sardonically pleads "diffidence" on the embassy's part in trying to explain Mosaddeq's attitude because "attempts to analyze motives his various actions in light ordinary rules logic or on basis of reason might well lead one astray" (707).

92. "Memorandum by the Secretary of State of a Meeting at the White House Between the President and General Eisenhower," Nov. 18, 1952, in *FRUS, 1952–1954,* vol. 1, part 1, 22–29.

93. This applies to official administration policy, not to the personal views of individuals such as Henderson and various CIA officials who had long ago reached the limits of their patience with Mosaddeq.

94. See, for example, "U.S.-U.K. Approach to Dr. Mussadiq," July 31, 1952, FO 371/98691. It is interesting to speculate on what Truman would have done if he had found a suitable candidate to replace Mosaddeq.

95. Robert A. Lovett to Dean Acheson, Oct. 24, 1952, RG 59, General Records of the Department of State, General Records of the Executive Secretariat, 1948–1956, box 8, folder: Middle East 1951–1953, USNA (also on file at the National Security Archive).

96. In response to worker unrest in East Germany beginning on June 17, 1953, Eisenhower, citing the risk of a U.S.-Soviet conflict, rejected several aggressive schemes proposed by his advisers in favor of instituting a food delivery program to East Berlin. See Christian F. Ostermann, *Uprising in East Germany, 1953: The Cold War, the German Question, and the First Major Upheaval Behind the Iron Curtain* (Budapest: Central European Univ. Press, 2001), esp. part 3.

97. Malcolm Byrne's interview with Robert R. Bowie, Washington, D.C., Feb. 24, 2000. For a recent scholarly, inside account of Eisenhower's early foreign policy debates, see Robert R. Bowie and Richard H. Immerman, *Waging Peace: How Eisenhower Shaped an Enduring Cold War Strategy* (New York: Oxford Univ. Press, 1998).

98. Report of the Doolittle Committee, quoted in *"Final Report of the Select Committees to Study Governmental Operations with Respect to Intelligence Activities,* U.S. Senate, report no. 94–755, book 4, *Supplementary Detailed Staff Reports on Foreign and Military Intelligence,* 52–53 n. 9.

99. For two recent accounts of early U.S. covert operations against the USSR, see generally Gregory Mitrovich, *Undermining the Kremlin: America's Strategy to Subvert the Soviet Bloc, 1947–1956* (Ithaca, N.Y.: Cornell Univ. Press, 2000); and Peter Grose, *Operation Rollback: America's Secret War Behind the Iron Curtain* (New York: Houghton Mifflin Company, 2000).

100. See Mark Gasiorowski's chapter in this volume.

101. In early May, Henderson wrote to the State Department urging that the United States make "one more really energetic effort" to settle the oil crisis, otherwise, "history may be unkind to us." See Henderson to the State Department, May 7, 1953, cable 4348, RG 59, 888.2553/5–753, USNA.

102. "Memorandum of Discussion at the 135th Meeting of the National Security Council, Washington, March 4, 1953," in *FRUS, 1952–1954,* 10:698.

103. Makins (Washington) to FO, Mar. 7, 1953, telegram 487, FO 371/104613/ EP1531/197. It seems clear from the context that Eisenhower is not hinting at a coup here.

104. John Waller, a former CIA officer who served extensively in Iran beginning in the 1940s and then coordinated the coup's implementation from agency headquarters, made this point at the conference "Mohammad Mosaddeq and the 1953 Coup in Iran," St. Antony's College, Oxford, June 8–10, 2002.

105. Undersecretary of State Walter Bedell Smith showed the State Department's latest analysis to the new British ambassador to Washington, Sir Roger Makins, who relayed it to London. See Makins (Washington) to FO, Mar. 9, 1953, telegram 526, FO 371/104613/ EP1531/200.

7. The 1953 Coup d'État Against Mosaddeq

1. Wilber, *Overthrow*, 1; Woodhouse, *Something Ventured,* 117–20; Mark J. Gasiorowski interview with George Middleton (British chargé d'affaires in Iran in October 1952), London, Jan. 16, 1985. Wilber's *Overthrow* was leaked to the *New York Times* and published on its Internet site (www.nytimes.org) in April 2000, although the names of most of the Iranian participants in the coup were blanked out. Those names were subsequently obtained, and most were published on the Internet site cryptome.org, which is where I obtained them. It is not clear who leaked *Overthrow*. However, Wilber once cryptically suggested that he might release the unsanitized version of his memoir, which was heavily redacted by CIA censors, in the year 2000. See Wilber, *Adventures in the Middle East,* 158. See the Louis article in this book for a full account of Britain's efforts to overthrow Mosaddeq.

2. Wilber, *Overthrow*, 1; Woodhouse, *Something Ventured,* 117–20; Mark J. Gasiorowski interview with Henry Byroade, Potomac, Md., Aug. 7, 1984; Roosevelt, *Countercoup,* 117. Byroade and other State Department officials had discussed carrying out a coup against Mosaddeq with the British in July 1952, but they soon concluded that there was "no reasonable alternative" to Mosaddeq. See "Anglo-U.S. Discussions about the Persian Internal Situation and the Oil Question," July 29, 1952, PRO, FO 371/98691; and "U.S.-U.K. Approach to Dr. Mussadiq," July 31, 1952, PRO, FO 371/98691. Woodhouse says the cool U.S. response to their proposal led British officials temporarily to give up on the idea and even reduce their payments to the British agents who later played a key role in the coup. See Woodhouse, *Something Ventured,* 123. Roosevelt had been thinking about undertaking a coup against Mosaddeq since the summer of 1951.

See Roosevelt, *Countercoup,* 191–95. For a good account of Zahedi's background, see the *New York Times,* Aug. 20, 1953.

3. I interviewed four of the five CIA officers who carried out the coup in Iran; one other CIA officer, five U.S. Foreign Service officers, and a U.S. naval attaché who were stationed in Iran at the time; five CIA officers who worked on Iran at CIA headquarters during the coup; a British SIS officer and a Foreign Office official (George Middleton) who played important roles in these events; a U.S. army officer who played a key role; and one of the main Iranian participants. I agreed to keep the names of most of these people confidential. Except where noted, I have corroborated all of the details I report from these interviews with a second source. For my earlier account of the coup based mainly on these interviews, see Gasiorowski, "1953 Coup d'Etat," 261–86. The CIA history is Wilber, *Overthrow,* cited in note 1, above. The CIA produced at least two other histories of the coup, including Koch's *"Zendebad, Shah."* A heavily redacted version of this document was released to the National Security Archive recently under the Freedom of Information Act. It contains no significant revelations about the coup.

4. See Mark J. Gasiorowski, "Trying to Revisit the 1953 Coup in Iran: The CIA's Response to a Freedom of Information Act Request," *Society for Historians of American Foreign Relations Newsletter* 29, no. 3 (Sept. 1998): 11–14.

5. For more extensive analyses of the Tudeh Party and the considerations that motivated U.S. policy toward Iran in this period, see the chapters in this book by Behrooz and Byrne; and Gasiorowski, *U.S. Foreign Policy and the Shah,* 50–56. The biggest concern U.S. officials had about the Tudeh was that it had established a large network of officers in the Iranian army. In May 1952 they estimated that this network contained 280 officers, but they later learned that it was much larger. See "Political Trends Between March 1952 and the Fall of the First Mosaddeq Government," Sept. 15, 1952, RG 84, box 29, USNA; Behrooz, *Rebels with a Cause,* 12–13. The Tudeh also had heavily infiltrated the interior ministry. See Gurney to Henderson, Aug. 30, 1952, RG 84, box 32, USNA. Nevertheless, it is clear from Behrooz's chapter that U.S. officials overestimated the threat posed by the Tudeh. In an ominous development, Anatoly Lavrentiev, who had been the Soviet ambassador in Czechoslovakia during the 1948 coup there, became Soviet ambassador to Iran on Aug. 1, 1953. See Koch, *"Zendebad, Shah!"* 46.

6. Gasiorowski, *U.S. Foreign Policy and the Shah,* 67–71; Cable, *Intervention at Abadan,* 48–49; Henderson to Acheson, Aug. 3, 1952, RG 84, box 29, USNA; "Anglo-U.S. Discussions about the Persian Internal Situation and the Oil Question," July 29, 1952, PRO, FO 371/98691; "Anglo-U.S. Discussions on the Persian Situation," July 29, 1952, PRO, FO 371/98691; "Record of an Interview with Mr. Acheson on 31st July," July 31, 1952, PRO, FO 371/98691; "U.S. Proposals for a Joint Approach to Dr. Mussadiq," Aug. 12, 1952, PRO, FO 371/98693.

7. "Internal Situation," n.d., PRO, FO 248/1531; Henderson to Acheson, Aug. 11, 1952, RG 84, box 29, USNA; Henderson to Acheson, Sept. 28, 1952, RG 84, box 42, USNA; Henderson to Acheson, Oct. 8, 1952, RG 84, box 28, USNA; Henderson to Acheson, Sept. 26, 1952, RG 84, box 29, USNA. Kashani, Zahedi, and Nader Batmanqelich (see below) had worked together with German agents against the Allies during World War II. See "Index Guide to the Franz Meyer Documents," May 25, 1943, RG 59, box 5192, USNA. Ironically, Kashani even solicited U.S. support during this period. See Henderson to Acheson, Nov. 9, 1952, RG 59, box 2853, USNA. For an analysis of Kashani's prospects at this time, see Central Intelligence Agency, "Prospects for Survival of Mosaddeq Regime in Iran," SE-33, Oct. 14, 1952, Truman Library. Zahedi turned against Mosaddeq after the July uprising. See Henderson to Acheson,

Oct. 17, 1952, RG 84, box 29, USNA. For detailed overviews of these events, see the chapters in this book by Azimi and Katouzian.

8. Central Intelligence Agency, "Probable Developments in Iran Through 1953," NIE 75, Nov. 13, 1952, 1–2, Harry S. Truman Library; U.S. National Security Council, "United States Policy Regarding the Present Situation in Iran," NSC 136/1, Nov. 20, 1952, in *FRUS, 1952–1954* 10:529–34. Anthony Cuomo, who was the U.S. embassy's specialist on the Tudeh Party at the time, told me in an interview (Rome, Jan. 5, 1985) that the Tudeh really was not very powerful and that higher level U.S. officials routinely exaggerated its strength and Mosaddeq's reliance on it. Two CIA officers stationed in Iran at the time told me the same thing. Moreover, the CIA's anti-Tudeh "black" covert operations (described below) made the Tudeh appear more powerful and more active than it really was.

9. Central Intelligence Agency, "Probable Developments in Iran Through 1953," NIE 75/1, Jan. 9, 1953, 1–2, Truman Library; U.S. Department of State, Office of Intelligence Research, "Iran's Political and Economic Prospects Through 1953," Intelligence Report no. 6126, Jan. 9, 1953, Truman Library.

10. Acheson, *Present at the Creation*, 683–85; Roosevelt, *Countercoup*, 9, 16, 95, 126. Also see Gasiorowski interviews with Byroade; Gordon Mattison, Bethesda, Md., July 30, 1984; Roy Melbourne, Chapel Hill, N.C., Feb. 1, 1984; and Kermit Roosevelt, Washington, D.C., June 5, 1985. Henderson's biographer erroneously argues that Henderson was a driving force behind the coup. See Brands, *Inside the Cold War*, 279–80. For a very different view, see Roy M. Melbourne, *Conflict and Crises: A Foreign Service Story* (Lanham, Md.: Univ. Press of America, 1997), chap. 9. Roosevelt told me that Goiran and several CIA Iran desk officers opposed the coup. The Goiran quote was related to me by a CIA officer who worked closely with him in Iran at the time. The CIA history by Wilber says Goiran left Iran as part of the CIA's "war of nerves" against Mosaddeq. See Wilber, *Overthrow*, 30. This implausible statement may have been an attempt to downplay Goiran's departure at this auspicious time.

11. "The United States' Ideas of a Settlement of the Oil Dispute," Oct. 20, 1952, PRO, FO 371/98702; Gasiorowski interviews with Roosevelt and another CIA officer. For a good overview of the Eisenhower administration's foreign policy views, see Gaddis, *Strategies of Containment*, chaps. 5, 6. The main advocate of a coup in the Tehran embassy at this time was Roy Melbourne, the chief political officer.

12. Wilber, *Overthrow*, iv, 2–3; *FRUS, 1952–1954*, 10:696, 698, 702–3, 713. The meeting at which Dulles informally approved the operation is described in Roosevelt, *Countercoup*, 120–24. This is probably the meeting of February 18 described in Louis's chapter in this book. Ambrose states that Eisenhower approved the coup five weeks after the early February meeting, but he gives no source for this statement. Ambrose, *Ike's Spies*, 200. In March, Iranian general Nader Batmanqelich asked Henderson whether the United States would support a military coup against Mosaddeq. U.S. embassy personnel talked to Batmanqelich but concluded he was not capable of carrying out a coup. See Wilber, *Overthrow*, 2–3; and Roosevelt, *Countercoup*, 130. Batmanqelich later played an important role in the coup and was named army chief of staff by Zahedi. The "TP" prefix identified TPAJAX as a covert operation carried out in Iran. "TP" was also the initials of the Tudeh Party, and "Ajax" was the name of a common household cleanser, so "TPAJAX" implied an effort to "cleanse" Iran of the Tudeh.

13. Heiss, *Empire and Nationhood*, 169–75; "Political Summary," Feb. 11, 1953, PRO, FO 371/104574; "Dr. Musaddiq's Quarrel with the Shah," Feb. 23, 1953, PRO, FO 371/104563;

"An Assessment of the Internal Situation in Persia," Mar. 2, 1953, PRO, FO 371/104563; "Internal Situation," n.d., PRO, FO 371/104563; Azimi, *Crisis of Democracy*, 306–7, 320–21; "Internal Affairs," Feb. 24, 1964, PRO, FO 371/104562. See also the chapters in this book by Azimi and Katouzian on these events. Mosaddeq ended the oil negotiations on March 9 but did not publicly announce this until March 20. See *FRUS, 1952–1954*, 10:704, 717. Zahedi's son Ardeshir approached the U.S. embassy several times in February 1953 and explained his father's efforts to replace Mosaddeq. See Henderson to Dulles, Feb. 23, 1953, RG 59, box 4110, USNA. Homa Katouzian states that the CIA was involved in the kidnapping of Afshartus. Katouzian, *Struggle for Power*, 183. I know of no evidence to support this claim, and I think it is highly unlikely. It is widely rumored that the British were involved. See Azimi, *Crisis of Democracy*, 320; and *Iran Times*, May 31, 1985. After the Afshartus murder, Kashani helped Zahedi avoid arrest by giving him asylum in the parliament building. See "Summary for the Period April 30-May 13, 1953," June 23, 1953, PRO, FO 371/104568.

14. Roosevelt, *Countercoup*, 134; Gasiorowski interview with Byroade. For a good discussion of Mosaddeq's relations with the Tudeh in this period by a close observer, see Kennett Love, "The American Role in the Pahlavi Restoration on 19 August 1953," unpublished manuscript (1960), Allen Dulles Papers, Princeton Univ. Library, 20–27. Iran expert Richard Cottam still opposed the coup. See Mark J. Gasiorowski, "Obituary of Richard Cottam," *Iranian Studies* 30, nos. 3–4, (summer/fall 1997): 415–17.

15. Wilber, *Overthrow*, iv, 3, 5, E5; id., *Adventures in the Middle East*, chaps. 1–11. Ironically, Zahedi had told a British official in August 1952 that he opposed the growth of U.S. influence in Iran. See "Internal Situation," n.d., PRO, FO 248/1531.

16. Wilber, *Overthrow*, 5–10, A1; U.S. Department of State, "Memorandum of Conversation, Subject: Iran," May 16, 1952, RG 84, box 29, USNA; "Assesses the General State of Affairs in Persia," May 28, 1951, PRO, FO 371/91542. The British had arrested Zahedi during World War II for helping German agents plan "a concentrated move against allied troops," who were occupying Iran in conjunction with the war effort. See "Article by Brigadier Fitzroy Maclean, M.P.," 27 Aug. 1953, PRO, FO 371/104570; and Fitzroy Maclean, *Eastern Approaches* (London: Jonathan Cape, 1950), 266.

17. Wilber, *Overthrow*, 7; Woodhouse, *Something Ventured*, 111, 117–18; Stephen Dorril, *MI6: Inside the Covert World of Her Majesty's Secret Intelligence Service* (New York: Free Press, 1999), 571; interviews with Middleton, the SIS officer mentioned in note 3, and a retired CIA officer who later made a study of the Rashidian network; "Internal Situation," n.d., PRO, FO 248/1531; *New York Times*, Oct. 14, 1952. Ironically, the Rashidians were very anti-American. See Woodhouse, *Something Ventured*, 111. When told about the Rashidians, the Tehran CIA station stated that they were not nearly as powerful as Darbyshire claimed. See Wilber, *Overthrow*, 7. The "British" wing of the Tudeh Party was headed by the Lankerani brothers, according to the retired CIA officer cited here. Another retired CIA officer told me that a third of Iran's parliamentary deputies in 1951 were on the British payroll. The British also worked against Mosaddeq through a prominent labor leader named Amir Kaivan. See "Trade Unions in Persia," June 1, 1952, PRO, FO 371/98731.

18. Wilber, *Overthrow*, 7–8; confidential interviews with four retired CIA officers who worked on TPBEDAMN. One of my sources told me TPBEDAMN could place articles in over thirty Iranian newspapers in the late 1940s. The CIA also translated and published several pro-

Western or anticommunist books and disseminated them in Iran under TPBEDAMN, including *God's Green Acre: Moslems in the USSR,* a "black" book ostensibly written by the Tudeh that accused Iran's Shi'i clergy of practicing witchcraft, and a "black" fictionalized autobiography of the Iranian exile poet and Tudeh member Abol Ghassem Lahuti, which gave a very bleak view of life in the Soviet Union. A retired CIA officer told me that Wilber wrote the witchcraft and Lahuti books. For a reference to the latter, see Wilber, *Adventures in the Middle East,* 191. Another retired CIA officer described Wilber to me as a "master propagandist." Ja'fari apparently was called "the brainless" because he rammed a jeep through the gate of Mosaddeq's compound during the February 1953 crisis. See *New York Times,* Aug. 23, 1953.

19. Roosevelt, *Countercoup,* 78–81, 91–94, 98; interviews with Roosevelt and two other CIA officers who worked on TPBEDAMN; Wilber, *Overthrow,* 7–8; Gaddis, *Strategies of Containment,* 157. Roosevelt told me Jalali and Kayvani organized the anti-Harriman demonstration on their own, not on behalf of the CIA. The Tudeh apparently organized its own anti-Harriman demonstrations at this time as well.

20. Wilber, *Overthrow,* 8–11, A1-A8, B2. The U.S. embassy had learned in April that the Qashqa'i were making plans to march on Tehran in support of Mosaddeq if a coup attempt was made against him. See "Change of Government Tribal Administration," Apr. 10, 1953, PRO, FO 371/104565. This is probably why the coup planners were concerned about a Qashqa'i reaction.

21. Wilber, *Overthrow,* 11–13. See Katouzian's chapter in this book for an account of the Amini-Qashqa'i "plot." The CIA was working closely with the Qashqa'i *khan*s at this time. See Gasiorowski, *U.S. Foreign Policy and the Shah,* 54. Goiran therefore may have thought he could persuade them to turn against Mosaddeq, which U.S. officials apparently tried to do at some point. See Lois Beck, *The Qashqa'i of Iran* (New Haven, Conn.: Yale Univ. Press, 1986), 153. The Qashqa'i later sent threats to Roosevelt when the coup was underway. See Roosevelt, *Countercoup,* 152. The Amini brothers mentioned here were Minister of Court Abolqasem Amini and gendarmerie commander Gen. Mahmud Amini. Both were on good terms with Mosaddeq. The shah told Henderson that the two brothers wanted to establish "a stop-gap nationalist government to be followed by a strong government." See "Ambassador Henderson's Report," June 2, 1953, PRO FO 371/104659. A retired CIA officer who was close to the Qashqa'i *khan*s at this time told me they were plotting with one of the Amini brothers to overthrow the shah and destroy the Tudeh Party. He could not recall which brother was involved and what they intended to do with Mosaddeq if they succeeded. See also Brands, *Inside the Cold War,* 277–79. Abolqasem Amini was arrested during the coup by Mosaddeq loyalists, who apparently suspected he was involved. See Wilber, *Overthrow,* 49.

22. Wilber, *Overthrow,* B15-B17, B20-B24. On page B21, Wilber states that the CIA team planned to work through four prominent Islamic leaders and a "terrorist gang" associated with one of these leaders. Their names are blanked out in the version of the history published by the *New York Times* and are not given in the cryptome.org version (see n. 1). However, it is obvious from the *Times*'s version that the names of these leaders (in English transliteration) are nine, nine, seven, and six characters long and the name of the "terrorist gang" is seven characters long. These leaders therefore were probably Ayatollahs Behbahani, Borujerdi, and Kashani (or possibly Falsafi) and the clerical activist Navab Safavi; and the "terrorist gang" was probably the Feda'iyan-e Islam, which was led by Safavi and is often called "Fadayan" in English. Note that the history

states that the Islamic leaders who were to organize *bast* protests eventually refused to cooperate, and it gives no indication that they cooperated with the coup plot in any way (91). This is discussed further below. These Islamic leaders almost certainly were not told that the CIA was behind these protests. The Feda'iyan and many prominent clergymen strongly opposed Mosaddeq. See Katouzian, *Struggle for Power,* chap. 12. The history states (20) that the Pan-Iranist, SOMKA, and Toilers Parties would play only minor roles in these activities, presumably because they had split and become much weaker by this time, as discussed below.

23. Wilber, *Overthrow,* B2, B11–B12, B15, B17–B18. The history states that no military officers were bribed to participate in the coup (E22), but it is not clear what else the $135,000 given to Zahedi could have been used for.

24. Wilber, *Overthrow,* 18, B3–B10. Schwarzkopf's son, who had lived with his father in Iran during 1942–1948, commanded U.S. military forces during the 1991 Persian Gulf war.

25. Wilber, *Overthrow,* B13–15, B23–25.

26. Wilber, *Overthrow,* 18–19, B1.

27. Wilber, *Overthrow,* 16–18.

28. Roosevelt, *Countercoup,* 1–19; Wilber, *Overthrow,* 18.

29. Wilber, *Overthrow,* 4, 19–21, 30; Roosevelt, *Countercoup,* 139.

30. Wilber, *Overthrow,* D2–5; Gasiorowski interview with a CIA officer who worked with Farzanegan in TPBEDAMN. Riahi was a member both of the pro-Mosaddeq Iran Party and of a secret, pro-Mosaddeq faction in the armed forces called the Nationalist Officers, which had been led by General Afshartus until he was murdered in April 1953. Following suggestions made by the Nationalist Officers, Mosaddeq had dismissed many senior military officers because they were corrupt or disloyal to his government. See Katouzian, *Struggle for Power,* 130–32. Most of their successors were Mosaddeq loyalists, making it difficult for the CIA to organize an anti-Mosaddeq military network.

31. Wilber, *Overthrow,* D5–8, D10.

32. Wilber, *Overthrow,* D9–14, D17. The names of several members of the military network are given on D12.

33. Wilber, *Overthrow,* D15–17. Akhavi became "violently ill" during this period, apparently as a result of tension and fear, and was confined to his bed in the following days. Guilanshah had been plotting with Zahedi since July 1952 and was arrested with him in February 1953. See "Internal Situation," n.d., PRO, FO 248/1531; and "Musaddiq-Shah-Kashani Quarrel," Mar. 19, 1953, PRO, FO 371/104564.

34. Gasiorowski interviews with Roosevelt and four other CIA officers who worked on TPBEDAMN. These officers were not sure who authorized the use of TPBEDAMN against Mosaddeq, although most thought it was Roosevelt. I think Wisner and Smith may have approved it as well. Roosevelt was unable to recall to me who gave authorization. For a brief reference to these activities, see Roosevelt, *Countercoup,* 125–26. It seems very unlikely that Acheson or Truman approved this. Moreover, under the guidelines authorizing CIA activity, covert operations were to be used only "against hostile foreign states or groups or in support of friendly foreign states or groups." See William M. Leary, ed., *The Central Intelligence Agency: History and Documents* (Tuscaloosa: Univ. of Alabama Press, 1984), 132; and Ray S. Cline, *The CIA under Reagan, Bush, and Casey* (Washington, D.C.: Acropolis Books, 1981), 119–26. While the anti-Soviet and anti-Tudeh activities carried out under TPBEDAMN clearly fell within these guidelines, covert operations against Mosaddeq and the National Front clearly did not. The CIA

therefore appears to have been acting independently—as a "rogue elephant"—in carrying out these operations.

35. Interviews with the five CIA officers mentioned in n. 34. One told me that the CIA placed a cartoon in Iranian newspapers in the fall of 1952 suggesting that Mosaddeq was sexually molesting Kashani. Roosevelt told me about the CIA approaches to Kashani, Makki, and Behbahani. Middleton and the SIS officer mentioned in note 3 told me about the Rashidians' activities against Mosaddeq and the National Front but could not describe these activities in detail. One of Kashani's sons apparently approached the British embassy in the summer of 1952 seeking a subsidy for his father. The British refused to provide it. See "Oriental Counselor's Political and Economic Conversations," n.d., PRO, FO 248/1520. In May 1952 Robin Zaehner of the British embassy wrote of efforts to split Kashani, Baqa'i, and Makki away from Mosaddeq that were "created and directed by the brothers Rashidian." Baqa'i approached the Rashidians for help in August 1952. Falsafi strongly attacked both Mosaddeq and Kashani on at least one occasion, in February 1952. See "Internal Situation," n.d., PRO, FO 248/1531. After the coup, Falsafi made a speech attacking Mosaddeq and eulogizing those killed during the fighting. See "Tehran Situation Reports," n.d., PRO, FO 371/104570. On Falsafi, see also Katouzian, *Struggle for Power,* 172.

36. These are the views of two of the five CIA officers mentioned in note 34. The other three said it is simply impossible to judge the impact of these activities. On the splits in the National Front during this period, see the essays in this book by Azimi and Katouzian. On the splits in the Toilers and Pan-Iranist Parties, see "Internal Affairs," Apr. 24, 1953, PRO, FO 371/104567; and "The Friendly Relationship," Oct. 6, 1953, PRO, FO 371/104568.

37. "Prime Minister's Radio Address of July 27, 1953," July 28, 1953, RG 59, box 4116, USNA; Brands, *Inside the Cold War,* 285; Katouzian, "The CIA Documents," 56; *FRUS, 1952–1954,* 10:742. The CIA history by Wilber does not say whether the CIA team actually tried to "purchase" members of Parliament, although clearly this was a key element of the coup plan. See Wilber, *Overthrow,* 18–19. If this occurred, it was almost certainly carried out through the Rashidians, who had extensive contacts in Parliament. John Waller told me he was not aware of any effort by the CIA team to "purchase" members of Parliament, although he agreed that the Rashidians might have done this without his knowledge. Mark J. Gasiorowski interview with John Waller, Oxford, June 11, 2002. See also note 41, below. On parliamentary opposition to Mosaddeq in this period, see Azimi, *Crisis of Democracy,* 317–30.

38. Wilber, *Overthrow,* 20–37, 92; Wilber, *Adventures in the Middle East,* 188–89; Gasiorowski interview with a CIA officer involved in these activities; *FRUS, 1952–1954,* 10:739; *Newsweek,* Aug. 10, 1953, 36–38. Wilber's history states that this effort included giving a forty-five thousand dollar loan to a certain Iranian newspaper owner, who is identified in Azimi's chapter of this book as Abbas Mas'udi of *Ettela'at.* Wilber, *Overthrow,* 26. Wilber later says that the publisher of *Ettela'at* had promised to support the coup but then denounced the initial coup attempt after it failed (60). Six anti-Mosaddeq newspapers suddenly appeared in Tehran in June 1953, perhaps as part of this effort. See USARMA Tehran to DEPTAR, 3 Mar. 1953, RG 59, box 4113, USNA.

39. Wilber, *Overthrow,* 28–37; Gasiorowski interviews with four CIA officers who were involved in these activities. The "sham bombing" was probably a percussion device meant to scare people. Goodwin or some other U.S. official reportedly offered the Qashqa'i $5 million to oppose Mosaddeq, but they refused. See Beck, 153. The British tribal revolts presumably would

have involved Bakhtiari tribal groups, some of which had long-standing ties to the British and lived near the Qashqa'i.

40. Love, "The American Role" 15–17; Wilber, *Overthrow,* 28.

41. Wilber, *Overthrow,* 31. This passage in *Overthrow* describes an effort by the CIA team in late July 1953 to prevent Mosaddeq from closing Parliament by having his supporters resign. It does not say this was done by "purchasing" members of Parliament, but it does indicate that the CIA team had considerable influence in Parliament.

42. See Grady to Acheson, July 12, 1951, RG 84, box 32, USNA; Henderson to Acheson, July 7, 1952, RG 84, box 29, USNA; and Henderson to Dulles, Feb. 23, 1953, RG 59, box 4110, USNA. Henderson also initially opposed Zahedi. On February 23, soon after Dulles agreed to back Zahedi, he stated, "Zahedi is not (repeat not) [Mosaddeq's] ideal successor." See Henderson to Dulles, Feb. 23, 1953, RG 59, box 4110, USNA.

43. *FRUS, 1952–1954* 10:730–31.

44. Wilber, *Overthrow,* 22–24, 32; note 34 in Azimi's chapter in this book; Mark J. Gasiorowski interview with Stephen Meade, Southern Pines, NC, Mar. 28, 1984. For Ashraf's account of these events, see Princess Ashraf Pahlavi, *Faces in a Mirror* (Englewood Cliffs, N.J.: Prentice Hall, 1980), 134–40. Meade had previously carried out a number of daring covert missions for the CIA. See Miles Copeland, *The Game of Nations* (New York: Simon and Schuster, 1969), 50–53, 76–83. Meade told me he also played a minor role in developing the military aspects of the coup plan.

45. Wilber, *Overthrow,* 24–25.

46. Wilber, *Overthrow,* 25–30; "Visit of General Schwarzkopf to Persia," Aug. 6, 1953, PRO, FO/371/104569.

47. Wilber, *Overthrow,* 33–38. Nasiri claimed that the shah's wife, Queen Soraya, finally persuaded her husband to sign the decrees (38). For a very different account of these events, see Roosevelt, *Countercoup,* 155–57.

48. Wilber, *Overthrow,* 91. See also Roosevelt, who implies that the clerical leaders refused to cooperate because they were not offered enough money (Roosevelt, *Countercoup,* 71, 163).

49. Wilber, *Overthrow,* 39. For accounts of how the Mosaddeq government learned about the plot, see the chapters in this book by Azimi and Behrooz; and Katouzian, *Struggle for Power,* 189. The Tudeh had learned about the coup plot well before this time. Details of the coup plan were reported by Tass on July 15 and in Tudeh newspapers as early as August 13. See "Dr. Musaddiq's Move to Dissolve the Majles," July 21, 1953, PRO, FO 371/104569; and "Persian Army Officers Attempt to Overthrow Dr. Musaddiq," Aug. 16, 1953, PRO, FO 371/104569. However, the Tudeh could not have learned the key details of when and how Mosaddeq was to be arrested until at least the evening of August 13, since the final decisions about this were made only then or on the following day. Therefore, it was the inadvertent exposure of the plot during this period, rather than the Tudeh's previous knowledge of its general outline, that led to the failure of the initial coup attempt. One of the CIA officers involved in these events told me the CIA station believed the Tudeh had an agent in the embassy, presumably among the non-American staff members, who may have revealed the plot.

50. Wilber, *Overthrow,* 39–45; "Persian Army Officers Attempt to Overthrow Dr. Musaddiq," Aug. 16, 1953, PRO, FO 371/104569. The latter document says that when Zahedi's men arrested Mosaddeq's allies, they also robbed them. Wilber, *Adventures in the Middle East,* 189, strongly criticizes the "military cowards" who refused to act at this time.

51. Wilber, *Overthrow*, 45–60; *New York Times*, Aug. 17, 18, 19, 1953; Behrooz's chapter in this book. The shah claims he left the country in an effort to crystallize public opinion against Mosaddeq. See Mohammad Reza Shah Pahlavi, *Mission for My Country*, 104–5. By coincidence, when the shah was checking into a hotel in Rome, Allen Dulles checked into the same hotel for a vacation. See Koch, *"Zendebad, Shah!"* 60.

52. Wilber, *Overthrow*, 46, 50–51; Gasiorowski interview with one of the CIA participants. On McClure, see Alfred H. Paddock Jr., "MG Robert Alexis McClure: Forgotten Father of U.S. Army Special Warfare," *Perspectives*, reprinted at http://www.psyop.com/mcclure.

53. Wilber, *Overthrow*, 58, 61, 64; Gasiorowski interview with one of the CIA participants; *FRUS, 1952–1954*, 10:747; *New York Times*, Aug. 20, 1953.

54. Wilber, *Overthrow*, 45.

55. Wilber, *Overthrow*, 45–50, 59; Love, "The American Role" 31–32. The shah's decrees and the fabricated interview with Zahedi were published in the Tehran newspapers *Shahed, Setareh Islam, Asia Javanan, Aram, Mard-e Asia, Mellat-e Ma, Dad,* and *Journal de Tehran*. See Wilber, *Overthrow*, 65.

56. Wilber, *Overthrow*, 51–53, 58; "Approach by the Shah," Aug. 17, 1953, PRO, FO 371/104659; "United States Advice to the Shah," Aug. 18, 1953, PRO, FO 371/104659.

57. *New York Times*, Aug. 19, 1953; Roosevelt, *Countercoup*, 181; House Committee on Foreign Affairs, hearings, *The Mutual Security Act of 1954*, 83d Cong., 2d sess., May 3, 1954, 503.

58. Gasiorowski interviews with five of the CIA officers involved; *New York Times*, Aug. 19, 1953; "Summary of Political Events in Persia," July 31, 1953, PRO, FO 371/104569; Farmanfarmaian and Farmanfarmaian, *Blood and Oil*, 294; Behrooz's chapter in this book. These events are also mentioned briefly in Wilber, *Overthrow*, 59, 63; Lapping, *End of Empire*, 220; and Love, "The American Role" 33–34. This "black" Tudeh crowd was similar to the one Jalali and Kayvani had organized to protest the July 1951 Harriman mission. See note 19 and the accompanying text. U.S. embassy personnel noted that the crowds on August 17 contained "an unusual mixture of Pan-Iranists and Tudeh" members. See Mattison to Dulles, Aug. 17, 1953, RG 59, box 4110, USNA. Several of my sources believed Jalali and Kayvani may have worked partly through the Pan-Iranist Party to organize the black crowds. One of my CIA sources told me Jalali and Kayvani had active subagents in Tabriz, but it seems unlikely that they were responsible for the anti-shah activity that occurred in the other cities mentioned here.

59. Brands, *Inside the Cold War*, 284; Loy Henderson interview, Columbia University Oral History Research Office, 17–18; *New York Times*, Aug. 19, 1953; Wilber, *Overthrow*, 53, 61, 64; Behrooz's chapter in this book. Mosaddeq apparently had a tacit agreement with the Tudeh prior to this time that it would obtain permission from him before holding demonstrations. The sudden appearance of "Tudeh" mobs on August 17 may therefore have alarmed him and led him to have these mobs broken up. See Henderson to Dulles, Aug. 20, 1953, RG 59, box 4110, USNA. In his August 18 meeting with Mosaddeq, Henderson also denied rumors that the U.S. embassy was harboring Iranian participants in the coup. See *FRUS, 1952–1954*, 10:751.

60. Wilber, *Overthrow*, 56–58, 73; Roosevelt, *Countercoup*, 181. One of the CIA officers involved told me that the CIA team planned to launch this uprising on Friday, August 21—not on August 19—when the clergy could use Friday prayer sermons to mobilize crowds against Mosaddeq. A report of the plan to organize demonstrations on August 21 appeared several weeks later in the *Times of India*. See "Transmits a Further Series of Articles," June 16, 1953, PRO, FO 371/104568. The approach to Behbahani presumably was to be made by the Rashidians.

Ardeshir Zahedi, *Five Decisive Days,* 41–62, describes an elaborate plan allegedly formulated by his father after Nasiri's arrest to set up an independent state called Free Iran near Kermanshah. Local army and air force units would establish a base there and try to take over the whole country. The plan also involved sabotaging fuel, transportation, and communications facilities in Tehran. Although the CIA team discussed a number of contingency plans during this period, none of the CIA officers I interviewed could recall such a plan.

61. Two CIA officers involved in the coup told me they delivered ten thousand dollars to Aramesh on the morning of August 19. Neither could confirm that Kashani received this money and used it to organize demonstrations, but both believed he did. One of these officers told me about Ja'fari's role. Another CIA officer told me one of Kashani's sons visited him after the coup to remind him of the role his father had played. Roosevelt confirmed this in my interview with him. Kashani's supporters claim he opposed the coup and sent a letter to Mosaddeq on August 18 warning him about it, but this claim is problematic. See Katouzian, *Struggle for Power,* 173–74; and Azimi, *Crisis of Democracy,* 332. Aramesh later headed Iran's Plan and Budget Organization and apparently was killed in a shootout with the police in October 1973. See Hubert Otis Johnson III, *Recent Opposition Movements in Iran,* M.A. thesis, Univ. of Utah, 1975, 237–38. Love says a CIA officer who worked on the Iran desk at headquarters during the coup (but opposed the coup) told him Behbahani was the key figure behind these demonstrations (Love, "The American Role" 40). He also says that so much American currency found its way into Tehran's black market during the coup that the exchange rate fell from over one hundred rials to the dollar to under fifty (Love, "The American Role" 40). Lapping cites the same CIA officer as saying the Rashidians were involved (Lapping, *End of Empire,* 221). Richard Cottam says the expression "Behbahani dollars" was in common usage years later to refer to the money used to hire these crowds (Cottam, *Nationalism in Iran,* 226). On Behbahani's role, see also Shahrough Akhavi, "The Role of the Clergy in Iranian Politics, 1949–1954," in Bill and Louis, 113. The SIS officer mentioned in note 3 told me the Rashidians organized these demonstrations. Koch says the Rashidians were "almost certainly" involved (Koch, *"Zendebad, Shah!"* 63). Roosevelt claims the crowds were organized by the "Boscoe brothers," a pseudonym he uses to refer both to the Rashidians and to Jalali and Kayvani (Roosevelt, *Countercoup,* 186). On the roles of the SOMKA and Pan-Iranist Parties, see Henderson to Dulles, Aug. 19, 1953, RG 59, box 4110, USNA.

62. Wilber, *Overthrow,* 66–70; Love, "The American Role" 36–37.

63. Wilber, *Overthrow,* 67–69; Stephen Langlie, letter to author, Jan. 31, 2001. Langlie served in the U.S. military assistance mission in Tehran at the time of the coup and saw at least ten truckloads of Bakhtiari tribesmen arriving in Tehran on the morning of August 19. Since the Bakhtiari lived at least one day's drive from Tehran, their trip to Tehran must have been organized on August 17 or 18.

64. Wilber, *Overthrow,* 67–71; *New York Times,* Aug. 20, 1953. Wilber says one of Ayatollah Kashani's sons was among the speakers who began to broadcast on Radio Tehran and implies that the son had been assigned this task (perhaps unwittingly) by the CIA team. Wilber, *Overthrow,* 71.

65. Wilber, *Overthrow,* 72–73. One of the CIA officers involved in these events told me Mosaddeq's police had almost located Zahedi's hideout by this time and would have arrested him within an hour if Guilanshah had not arrived. Zahedi apparently was so nervous when Guilanshah arrived that a CIA officer had to button his uniform. See *Wall Street Journal,* Oct. 19, 1979.

66. Wilber, *Overthrow,* 70, 74; Love, "The American Role" 39; *New York Times,* Aug. 20, 21, 1953.

67. Wilber, *Overthrow,* 74.

68. Gasiorowski, *U.S. Foreign Policy and the Shah,* 86; *New York Times,* Aug. 20, 23, 1953; Henderson o Dulles, Aug. 22, 1953, RG 59, box 4110, USNA.

69. Gasiorowski, *U.S. Foreign Policy and the Shah,* 86–89. See Katouzian's chapter in this book for a broader discussion of the coup's long-term consequences.

70. Gasiorowski, *U.S. Foreign Policy and the Shah,* esp. 90–92, 101–2. Two CIA officers involved in these events told me Bozorgmehr worked in the TPBEDAMN network. He had been arrested in February 1953 for working with the British against Mosaddeq. See "The Arrest of Editors and Journalists under Martial Law," Feb. 1, 1953, PRO, FO 371/104561. On his subsequent activities and connections with the CIA, see Mark J. Gasiorowski, "The Qarani Affair and Iranian Politics," *International Journal of Middle East Studies* 25, no. 4 (Nov. 1993): 625–44. Meade became very close to Princess Ashraf during this period and was removed from his position as a result. See Roosevelt, *Countercoup,* 145. On SAVAK, see A. W. Samii, *The Role of SAVAK in the 1978–1979 Iranian Revolution,* Ph.D. diss., Univ. of Cambridge, 1994.

71. Roosevelt, *Countercoup,* 207; *Los Angeles Times,* Mar. 29, 1979. CIA officer and TPAJAX participant Howard Stone was deported from Syria in 1957 after trying to stage a coup there. He later received the CIA's highest medal. See *Wall Street Journal,* Oct. 19, 1979. I have never learned what became of Jalali and Kayvani. They apparently emigrated to the United States at some point after the coup and eventually died there. In any case, they never became prominent in Iran. Their roles in the coup were not widely known until their names were revealed in the www.cryptome.org version of Wilber's *Overthrow.* The CIA later leaked an account of the coup in the American press. See Richard Harkness and Gladys Harkness, "The Mysterious Doings of the CIA," *Saturday Evening Post,* Nov. 6, 1954, 66–68.

72. The CIA apparently destroyed almost all of its records on the coup many years ago. See Gasiorowski, "Trying to Revisit the 1953 Coup." Some useful documents may remain in the CIA's archives or in British government archives, although they are not likely to be released publicly any time soon. Most importantly, the two other CIA histories of the coup mentioned in note 3, above, might perhaps contain important new details. It is also possible that documents bearing on the coup exist in Iran or in private collections elsewhere, although Fakhreddin Azimi and other researchers have gone through the appropriate collectons exhaustively. Moreover, it seems unlikely that anyone made more of an effort to clarify these matters while the participants were still alive and memories were still fresh than Donald Wilber did in writing his CIA history. Any other documents on the coup that do exist therefore may not have much to add.

Selected Bibliography

Archives

Acheson, Dean. Papers. Harry S. Truman Library, Independence, Mo.
Chapman, Oscar L. Papers. Harry S. Truman Library, Independence, Mo.
Documentation Center, Islamic Revolution, Tehran.
Dulles, Allen. Papers. Princeton Univ. Library, Princeton, N.J.
Dwight D. Eisenhower Library, Abilene, Kans.
Iranian National Archives, Tehran.
Middle East Centre Archive, St. Antony's College, Oxford.
Mozakerat-e Majles, Tehran.
Muzakerat-e Sena, Tehran.
National Security Archive, George Washington University, Washington, D.C.
Public Record Office, London.
Spingarn, Stephen J. Papers. Harry S. Truman Library, Independence, Mo.
U.S. National Archives, College Park, Md.
U.S. National Archives Building, Washington, D.C.
Wright, Denis. Papers. Privately held.

U.S. Government Documents

Central Intelligence Agency. *Importance of Iranian and Middle East Oil to Western Europe under Peacetime Conditions, NIE 14.* Jan. 8, 1951.
——. *Prospects for Survival of Mosaddeq Regime in Iran, SE-33.* Oct. 14, 1952.
——. *Probable Developments in Iran Through 1953, NIE 75.* Nov. 13, 1952.
——. *Probable Developments in Iran Through 1953, NIE 75/1.* Jan. 9, 1953.
Department of State. *Foreign Relations of the United States.* Washington, D.C.: Government Printing Office, 1989.
Department of State, Office of Intelligence Research. *Iran's Political and Economic Prospects Through 1953, Intelligence Report no. 6126.* Jan. 9, 1953.
Koch, Scott A. *"Zendebad, Shah!": The Central Intelligence Agency and the Fall of Iranian Prime Minister Mohammad Mosaddeq, August 1953.* History Staff, Central Intelligence Agency, June 1998.

National Security Council. *The Position of the United States with Respect to Iran, NSC 107/2.* June 27, 1951.

————. *Report of the National Security Council on the Position of the United States with Respect to Iran, NSC 54.* July 21, 1949.

————. *United States Policy Regarding the Present Situation in Iran, NSC 136/1.* Nov. 20, 1952.

Wilber, Donald N. *Overthrow of Premier Mosaddeq of Iran: November 1952-August 1953.* Central Intelligence Agency, March 1954.

Other English Sources

Abrahamian, Ervand. *Iran Between Two Revolutions.* Princeton, N.J.: Princeton Univ. Press, 1982.

————. "The 1953 Coup in Iran." *Science and Society* 65, no. 2 (summer 2001).

Acheson, Dean. *Present at the Creation.* New York: Norton, 1969.

Afary, Janet. *The Iranian Constitutional Revolution, 1905–1911: Grassroots Democracy, Social Democracy, and the Origins of Feminism.* New York: Columbia Univ. Press, 1996.

Akhavi, Shahrough. "The Role of the Clergy in Iranian Politics, 1949–1954." In *Musaddiq, Iranian Nationalism, and Oil,* edited by James A. Bill and Wm. Roger Louis, 91–117. Austin: Univ. of Texas Press, 1988.

Alexander, Yonah, and Allan Nanes, eds. *The United States and Iran: A Documentary History.* Frederick, Md.: Univ. Press of America, 1980.

Ambrose, Stephen E. *Eisenhower: The President.* New York: Simon and Schuster, 1984.

————. *Eisenhower: Soldier, General of the Army, President-Elect, 1890–1952.* New York: Simon and Schuster, 1983.

————. *Ike's Spies: Eisenhower and the Espionage Establishment.* 1981; reprint, with an introduction by David Brinkley, Jackson: Univ. Press of Mississippi Banner Books, 1999.

Amuzegar, Jahangir, and M. Ali Fekrat. *Iran: Economic Development under Dualistic Conditions.* Chicago: Univ. of Chicago Press, 1971.

Anderson, Jack. *Fiasco.* New York: Times Books, 1983.

Andrew, Christopher. *Secret Service: The Making of the British Intelligence Community.* London: Heinemann, 1985.

Anglo-Iranian Oil Company. *The Anglo-Iranian Oil Company and Iran: A Description of the Company's Contributions to Iran's Revenue and National Economy and Its Welfare Activities for Employees in Iran.* London: AIOC, July 1951.

Arjomand, Said Amir. *The Turban for the Crown.* Oxford and New York: Oxford Univ. Press, 1988.

Azimi, Fakhreddin. "Fatemi, Hosyn." *Encyclopedia Iranica.*

————. *Iran: The Crisis of Democracy.* London and New York: I. B. Tauris and St. Martin's Press, 1989.

————. "On Shaky Ground: Concerning the Absence or Weakness of Political Parties in Iran." *Iranian Studies* 30, nos. 1–2 (winter-spring 1997–98): 53–75.

Bamberg, J. H. *The History of the British Petroleum Company.* Vol. 2, *The Anglo-Iranian Years, 1928–1954.* Cambridge: Cambridge Univ. Press, 1994.

Bayat, Mangol. *Iran's First Revolution: Shi'ism and the Constitutional Revolution of 1905–1909.* New York: Oxford Univ. Press, 1991.

Bayne, Edward Ashley. "Crisis of Confidence in Iran." *Foreign Affairs* 24 (July 1951): 578–90.

Beck, Lois. *The Qashqa'i of Iran*. New Haven, Conn.: Yale Univ. Press, 1986.

Behrooz, Maziar. *Rebels with a Cause: The Failure of the Left in Iran*. London: I. B. Tauris, 1999.

———. "Tudeh Factionalism and the 1953 Coup in Iran." *International Journal of Middle East Studies* 33, no. 3 (Aug. 2001): 363–82.

Bharier, Julian. *Economic Development in Iran, 1900–1970*. London: Oxford Univ. Press, 1971.

Bill, James A. *The Eagle and the Lion: The Tragedy of American-Iranian Relations*. New Haven, Conn.: Yale Univ. Press, 1988.

Bill, James A., and Wm. Roger Louis, eds. *Musaddiq, Iranian Nationalism, and Oil*. Austin: Univ. of Texas Press, 1988.

Blair, John. *The Control of Oil*. New York: Pantheon, 1976.

Bohlen, Charles E. *Witness to History, 1929–1969*. New York: W. W. Norton, 1973.

Bowie, Robert R., and Richard H. Immerman. *Waging Peace: How Eisenhower Shaped an Enduring Cold War Strategy*. New York: Oxford Univ. Press, 1998.

Brands, H. W. *Inside the Cold War: Loy Henderson and the Rise of the American Empire, 1918–1961*. New York: Oxford Univ. Press, 1991.

Brown, Bruce K. *Oil Men in Washington: An Informal Account of the Organization and Activities of the Petroleum Administration for Defense During the Korean War, 1950–1952*. N.p.: Evanil Press, 1965.

Bullock, Alan. *Ernest Bevin: Foreign Secretary*. London: Heinemann, 1983.

Byrne, Malcolm, and Thomas Blanton. "U.S. Perspectives on the Coup in Czechoslovakia: New Evidence from U.S. Intelligence Files." Paper presented at the conference "The Czechoslovak 'February,' 1948: Preconditions and Repercussions at Home and Abroad," Prague, Feb. 19–21 1998.

Cable, James. *Intervention at Abadan: Plan Buccaneer*. New York: St. Martin's Press, 1991.

Campbell, John C. *Defense of the Middle East: Problems of American Policy*. New York: Frederick A. Praeger, 1960.

Chehabi, H. E. *Iranian Politics and Islamic Modernism: The Liberation Movement of Iran under the Shah and Khomeini*. New York: Cornell Univ. Press, 1990.

Churchill, Winston S. *The World Crisis*. 2 vols. New York: Charles Scribner's Sons, 1923.

Clawson, Patrick, and Cyrus Sassanpour. "Adjustment to a Foreign Exchange Shock: Iran, 1951–1953." *International Journal of Middle East Studies* 19, no. 1 (Feb. 1987): 1–23.

Cline, Ray S. *The CIA under Reagan, Bush, and Casey*. Washington, D.C.: Acropolis Books, 1981.

Colville, John. *The Fringes of Power: 10 Downing Street Diaries, 1939–1955*. New York: Norton, 1986.

Committee for Defence and Promotion of Human Rights in Iran. Statement, Nov. 12, 1979. In League for the Defence of Human Rights in Iran, *Human Rights* 52 (spring 1981): 95–96.

Copeland, Miles. *The Game of Nations*. New York: Simon and Schuster, 1969.

Cottam, Richard. *Nationalism in Iran*. Pittsburgh, Pa.: Univ. of Pittsburgh Press, 1979.

Dadkhah, Kamran M. "Iran's Economic Policy During the Mosaddeq Era." *Journal of Iranian Research and Analysis* 16, no. 2 (Nov. 2000): 39–54.

———. "The Oil Nationalisation Movement, the British Boycott, and the Iranian Economy, 1951–1953." In *Essays on the Economic History of the Middle East*, edited by Elie Kedourie and Sylvia G. Haim. London: Frank Cass, 1988.

Diba, Farhad. *Mohammad Musaddiq: A Political Biography*. London: Croom Helm, 1986.

Donoughue, Bernard, and G. W. Jones. *Herbert Morrison: Portrait of a Politician*. London: Weidenfeld and Nicolson, 1973.

Dorril, Stephen. *MI6: Fifty Years of Special Operations*. London: Fourth Estate, 2000.

———. *MI6: Inside the Covert World of Her Majesty's Secret Intelligence Service*. New York: Free Press, 1999.

Eden, Anthony. *Full Circle: The Memoirs of Anthony Eden*. Boston Houghton Mifflin, 1960.

Elm, Mostafa. *Oil, Power, and Principle: Iran's Oil Nationalization and Its Aftermath*. Syracuse: Syracuse Univ. Press, 1992.

Elwell-Sutton, L. P. *Persian Oil: A Study in Power Politics*. London: Lawrence and Wishart, 1955.

Engler, Robert. *The Politics of Oil: Private Power and Democratic Directions*. Chicago: Macmillan, 1961.

Eveland, Wilbur Crane. *Ropes of Sand: America's Failure in the Middle East*. New York: W. W. Norton, 1980.

Falle, Sam. *My Lucky Life in War, Revolution, Peace, and Diplomacy*. Sussex: Book Guild, 1996.

Farmanfarmaian, Manucher, and Roxane Farmanfarmaian. *Blood and Oil*. New York: Random House, 1997.

Fatemi, Nasrollah Saifpour. *Oil Diplomacy: Powderkeg in Iran*. New York: Whittier Books, 1954.

Fawcett, Louise L'Estrange. *Iran and the Cold War: The Azerbaijan Crisis of 1946*. New York: Cambridge Univ. Press, 1992.

Ferrier, Ronald W. "The Anglo-Iranian Oil Dispute, a Triangular Relationship." In *Musaddiq, Iranian Nationalism, and Oil*, edited by James A. Bill and Wm. Roger Louis, 164–99. Austin: Univ. of Texas Press, 1988.

Foran, John, ed. *A Century of Revolution: Social Movements in Iran*. Minneapolis: Univ. of Minnesota Press, 1994.

———. *Theorizing Revolutions*. London and New York: Routledge, 1997.

Ford, Alan W. *The Anglo-Iranian Oil Dispute of 1951–1952: A Study of the Role of Law in the Relations of States*. Berkeley: Univ. of California Press, 1954.

Freeland, Richard M. *The Truman Doctrine and the Origins of McCarthyism: Foreign Policy, Domestic Politics, and Internal Security, 1946–1948*. New York: Knopf, 1972.

Gaddis, John Lewis. *Strategies of Containment*. New York: Oxford Univ. Press, 1982.

———. *The United States and the Origins of the Cold War, 1941–1947*. New York: Columbia Univ. Press, 1972.

———. *We Now Know: Rethinking Cold War History*. Oxford: Oxford Univ. Press, 1997.

Garthoff, Raymond L. *Détente and Confrontation: American-Soviet Relations from Nixon to Reagan*. Washington, D.C.: Brookings Institution, 1994.

Gasiorowski, Mark J. "The 1953 *Coup d'Etat* in Iran." *International Journal of Middle East Studies* 19, no. 3 (Aug. 1987): 261–86.

———. "The Qarani Affair and Iranian Politics." *International Journal of Middle East Studies* 25, no. 4 (Nov. 1993): 625–44.

———. "Trying to Revisit the 1953 Coup in Iran: The CIA's Response to a Freedom of Information Act Request." *Society for Historians of American Foreign Relations Newsletter* 29, no. 3 (Sept. 1998).

———. *U.S. Foreign Policy and the Shah: Building a Client State in Iran*. Ithaca, N.Y.: Cornell Univ. Press, 1991.

Gavin, Francis J. "Politics, Power, and U.S. Policy in Iran, 1950–1953." *Journal of Cold War Studies* 1, no. 1 (winter 1999): 56–89.

Goode, James F. *The United States and Iran: In the Shadow of Musaddiq.* New York: St. Martin's Press, 1997.

Grose, Peter. *Operation Rollback: America's Secret War Behind the Iron Curtain.* New York: Houghton Mifflin Company, 2000.

Harkness, Richard, and Gladys Harkness. "The Mysterious Doings of the CIA." *Saturday Evening Post,* Nov. 6, 1954.

Hasanli, Jamil. "The Creation of the Democratic Party and the Idea of Autonomy." Unpublished manuscript.

Heiss, Mary Ann. *Empire and Nationhood: The United States, Great Britain, and Iranian Oil, 1950–1954.* New York: Columbia Univ. Press, 1997.

Herz, Martin F. *A View from Tehran: A Diplomatist Looks at the Shah's Regime in June 1964.* Washington D.C.: Institute for the Study of Diplomacy, Georgetown Univ., 1979.

Hopkirk, Peter. *The Great Game: The Struggle for Empire in Central Asia.* New York: Kodansha International, 1994.

Jafari, Reza "Centre-Periphery Relations in Iran: The Case of the Southern Rebellion in 1946." D.Phil thesis, Faculty of Oriental Studies, Univ. of Oxford, 2000.

Johnson, Habert Otis, III. *Recent Opposition Movements in Iran* M.A. thesis, Univ. of Utah, 1975.

Katouzian, Homa. "The CIA Documents and the 1953 Coup in Iran." In *The CIA Documents on the 1953 Coup and the Overthrow of Dr. Musaddiq of Iran,* edited by Gholamreza Vatandoust. Tehran: Rasa, 2000.

———. "European Liberalisms and Modern Concepts of Liberty in Iran." *Journal of Iranian Research and Analysis* 16, no. 2 (Nov. 2000): 9–29.

———. *Iranian History and Politics: The Dialectic of State and Society in Iran.* London: Routledge Curzon, 2003.

———. "Land Reform in Iran, A Case Study in the Political Economy of Social Engineering." *Journal of Peasant Studies* 1, no. 2 (1974): 220–39.

———. "Liberty and Licence in the Constitutional Revolution of Iran." *Journal of the Royal Asiatic Society* 8, no. 2 (1998): 159–80.

———. *Musaddiq and the Struggle for Power in Iran.* 1990; 2d paperback ed., London and New York: I. B. Tauris, 1999.

———. "Oil Boycott and Political Economy: Musaddiq and the Strategy of Non-oil Economics." In *Musaddiq, Iranian Nationalism, and Oil,* edited by James A. Bill and Wm. Roger Louis, 203–7. Austin: Univ. of Texas Press, 1988.

———. "Oil Versus Agriculture: A Case of Dual Resource Depletion in Iran." *Journal of Peasant Studies* 5, no. 3 (1978): 348–68.

———. "The Pahlavi Regime in Iran." In *Sultanistic Regimes,* edited by H. E. Chehabi and J. Linz. Baltimore, Md.: Johns Hopkins Univ. Press, 199.

———. *The Political Economy of Modern Iran.* London and New York: Macmillan and New York Univ. Press, 1981.

———. "Problems of Democracy and the Public Sphere in Iran." *Comparative Studies of South Asia, Africa, and the Middle East* 18, no. 2 (1998): 31–37.

———. *State and Society in Iran: The Eclipse of the Qajars and the Rise of the Pahlavis.* London: I. B. Tauris, 2000.

————. "Towards a General Theory of Iranian Revolutions." *Journal of Iranian Research and Analysis* 15, no. 2 (Nov. 1999): 145–62.

Kaufman, Burton I. *The Oil Cartel Case: A Documentary Study of Antitrust Activity During the Cold War Era.* Westport, Conn.: Greenwood Press, 1978.

Keddie, Nikki. *Roots of Revolution.* New Haven, Conn., and London: Yale Univ. Press, 1981.

Kedourie, Elie. *Nationalism.* London: Hutchinson, 1960.

Kedourie, Elie, and Sylvia G. Haim, eds. *Essays on the Economic History of the Middle East.* London: Frank Cass, 1988.

Kennan, George F. *Memoirs, 1950–1963.* 2 vols. Boston: Little, Brown and Company, 1972.

————. "The Sources of Soviet Conduct." *Foreign Affairs* 25 (July 1947): 566–82.

Kennedy, Paul M. *The Rise and Fall of the Great Powers: Economic Change and Military Conflict from 1500 to 2000.* New York: Random House, 1987.

Krock, Arthur. *Memoirs: Sixty Years on the Firing Line.* New York: Funk and Wagnalls, 1968.

Kuhns, Woodrow J., ed. *Assessing the Soviet Threat: The Early Cold War Years* (Washington, D.C.: Center for the Study of Intelligence, CIA, 1997).

Kuniholm, Bruce R. *The Origins of the Cold War in the Near East: Great Power Conflict and Diplomacy in Iran, Turkey, and Greece.* Princeton, N.J.: Princeton Univ. Press, 1980.

————. "Perspectives." *American Historical Association Newsletter* 28, no. 5 (May/June 1990).

Kyle, Keith. *Suez.* New York: St. Martin's Press, 1991.

Lambton, Ann K. S. "The Impact of the West on Persia." *International Affairs* 33, no. 1 (Jan. 1957): 12–25.

————. *Landlord and Peasant in Persia.* London and New York: Oxford Univ. Press, 1953.

Lapping, Brian. *End of Empire.* New York: St. Martin's Press, 1985.

Leary, William M., ed. *The Central Intelligence Agency: History and Documents.* Tuscaloosa: Univ. of Alabama Press, 1984.

Leffler, Melvyn P. *A Preponderance of Power: National Security, the Truman Administration, and the Cold War.* Stanford, Calif.: Stanford Univ. Press, 1992.

Longhurst, Henry. *Adventures in Oil: The Story of British Petroleum.* London, 1959.

Louis, Wm. Roger. *The British Empire in the Middle East, 1945–1951.* Oxford: Oxford Univ. Press, 1984.

————. *Imperialism at Bay.* Oxford: Oxford Univ. Press, 1977.

————. "Musaddiq and the Dilemmas of British Imperialism." In *Musaddiq, Iranian Nationalism, and Oil,* edited by James A. Bill and Wm. Roger Louis, 228–60. Austin: Univ. of Texas Press, 1988.

Love, Kennett. "The American Role in the Pahlavi Restoration on 19 August 1953." Unpublished manuscript. Allen Dulles Papers, Princeton Univ. Library, 1960.

Lytle, Mark Hamilton. *The Origins of the Iranian-American Alliance, 1941–1953.* New York: Holmes and Meier, 1987.

Maclean, Fitzroy. *Eastern Approaches.* London: Jonathan Cape, 1949. Reprint, New York: Time-Life Books, 1964.

Majd, M. G. "The 1951–53 Oil Nationalization Dispute and the Iranian Economy, a Rejoinder." *Middle Eastern Studies* 31, no. 3 (July 1995): 449–59.

Mark, Eduard. "Revolution by Degrees: Stalin's National-Front Strategy for Europe, 1941–1947." Cold War International History Project, Working Paper no. 31. Woodrow Wilson International Center for Scholars, Washington, D.C., Feb. 2001.

————. "The War Scare of 1946 and Its Consequences." *Diplomatic History* 21, no. 3 (summer 1997): 383–415.

Martin, Kingsley. "Conversation with Dr. Mossadeq." *New Statesman,* Jan. 11, 1952.

Martin, Vanessa. *Islam and Modernism: The Iranian Revolution of 1906.* London and New York: I. B. Tauris, 1989.

Mastny, Vojtech. *The Cold War and Soviet Insecurity: The Stalin Years.* New York: Oxford Univ. Press, 1996.

May, Ernest R., ed. *American Cold War Strategy: Interpreting NSC 68.* Boston: Bedford Books of St. Martin's Press, 1993.

McCullough, David. *Truman.* New York: Simon and Schuster, 1992.

McGhee, George C. *Envoy to the Middle World: Adventures in Diplomacy.* New York: Harper and Row, 1983.

————. "Recollections of Dr. Musaddiq." In *Musaddiq, Iranian Nationalism, and Oil,* edited by James A. Bill and Wm. Roger Louis, 296–304. Austin: Univ. of Texas Press, 1988.

Meier, Daniela. "Between Court Jester and Spy: The Career of a Swiss Gardener at the Royal Court in Iran: A Footnote to Modern Iranian History." *Critique* 16 (spring 2000): 75–88.

Melbourne, Roy M. *Conflict and Crises: A Foreign Service Story.* Lanham, Md.: Univ. Press of America, 1997.

Mitrovich, Gregory. *Undermining the Kremlin: America's Strategy to Subvert the Soviet Bloc, 1947–1956.* Ithaca, N.Y.: Cornell Univ. Press, 2000.

Moaddel, Mansoor. *Class, Politics, and Ideology in the Iranian Revolution.* New York: Columbia Univ. Press, 1993.

Moghadam, Valentine. "Iran: Development, Revolution, and the Problem of Analysis." *Review of Radical Political Economics* 16, no. 3/4 (summer/fall 1984): 227–40.

————. "Populist Revolution and the Islamic State in Iran." In *Revolution in the World System,* edited by Terry Boswell. New York and London: Greenwood, 1989.

Morgan, Kenneth O. *Labour in Power, 1945–1951.* Oxford: Clarendon, 1984.

Morrison, Herbert. *An Autobiography.* London: Clarendon, 1960.

Musaddiq, Mohammad. *Musaddiq's Memoirs.* Edited and introduced by Homa Katouzian, translated by S.H. Amin and H. Katouzian. London: JEBHEH, 1988.

Nash, Gerald D. *United States Oil Policy, 1880–1964: Business and Government in Twentieth-Century America.* Pittsburgh: Univ. of Pittsburgh Press, 1968.

Offner, Arnold A. *Another Such Victory: President Truman and the Cold War, 1945–1953.* Stanford, Calif.: Stanford Univ. Press, 2002.

Ostermann, Christian F. *Uprising in East Germany, 1953: The Cold War, the German Question, and the First Major Upheaval Behind the Iron Curtain.* Budapest: Central European Univ. Press, 2001.

Paddock, Alfred H., Jr. "MG Robert Alexis McClure: Forgotten Father of U.S. Army Special Warfare," *Perspectives,* reprinted at http://www.psyop.com/mcclure.

Pahlavi, Ashraf, Princess. *Faces in a Mirror.* Englewood Cliffs, N.J.: Prentice-Hall, 1980.

Pahlavi, Mohammad Reza. *Mission for My Country.* New York: McGraw-Hill, 1961.

Painter, David S. *Oil and the American Century: The Political Economy of U.S. Foreign Oil Policy, 1941–1954.* Baltimore, Md.: Johns Hopkins Univ. Press, 1986.

Pechatnov, Vladimir O. " 'The Allies Are Pressing on You to Break Your Will': Foreign Policy Correspondence Between Stalin and Molotov and Other Politburo Members, September

1945–December 1946." Cold War International History Project, Working Paper no. 26. Woodrow Wilson International Center for Scholars, Washington, D.C., Sept. 1999.

————. "The Big Three after World War II: New Documents on Soviet Thinking about Post War Relations with the United States and Great Britain." Cold War International History Project, Working Paper no. 13. Woodrow Wilson International Center for Scholars, Washington, D.C., July 1995.

Powers, Thomas. "A Book Held Hostage." *Nation,* Apr. 12, 1980.

Resis, Albert. "The Churchill-Stalin 'Percentages' Agreement on the Balkans, Moscow, October 1944." *American Historical Review* 83, no. 2 (Apr. 1978): 368–87.

————, ed. *Molotov Remembers: Inside Kremlin Politics, Conversations with Felix Chuev.* Chicago: Ivan R. Dee, 1993.

Roosevelt, Kermit. *Countercoup: The Struggle for the Control of Iran.* New York: McGraw-Hill, 1979.

Royal Institute of International Affairs, *Documents on International Affairs, 1953.* London: Oxford Univ. Press, 1954.

Rubin, Barry. *Paved with Good Intentions.* New York: Oxford Univ. Press, 1980.

Samii, A. W. *The Role of SAVAK in the 1978–1979 Iranian Revolution.* Ph.D. diss., Univ. of Cambridge, 1994.

Sampson, Anthony. *The Seven Sisters: The Great Oil Companies and the World They Shaped.* 4th rev. ed. New York: Bantam Books, 1991.

Scheid, Fernande. Paper presented at a conference, "Iran and the Second World War," Tehran, Sept. 25–27, 1999.

Schwadran, Benjamin. "The Anglo-Iranian Oil Dispute, 1948–1953," *Middle Eastern Affairs* 5 (June/July 1954): 193–231.

————. *The Middle East, Oil, and the Great Powers.* New York: Council for Middle Eastern Affairs, 1959.

Sicker, Martin. *The Bear and the Lion: Soviet Imperialism and Iran.* New York: Praeger, 1988.

Sontag, Raymond James, and James Stuart Beddie, eds., *Nazi-Soviet Relations, 1939–1941: Documents from the Archives of the German Foreign Office.* Washington, D.C.: Department of State, 1948.

Stobaugh, Robert B. "The Evolution of Iranian Oil Policy, 1925–1975." In *Iran under the Pahlevis,* edited by George Lenczowski. Stanford: Hoover Institution Press, 1978.

Taubman, William. *Stalin's American Policy: From Entente to Détente to Cold War.* New York: W. W. Norton and Co., 1982.

Truman, Harry S. *Year of Decisions.* Garden City, N.Y.: Doubleday, 1955.

————. *Years of Trial and Hope.* Garden City, N.Y.: Doubleday, 1956.

U.S. House Committee on Foreign Affairs. *The Mutual Security Act of 1954.* Hearings, 83d Cong., 2d sess., May 3, 1954.

Walters, Vernon A. *Silent Missions.* Garden City, N.Y.: Doubleday, 1978.

Wilber, Donald N. *Adventures in the Middle East: Excursions and Incursions.* Princeton, N.J.: Darwin Press, 1986.

Woodhouse, C. M. *The New Concert of Nations.* London: Bodley Head, 1946.

————. *Something Ventured.* London: Granada Publishing, 1982.

Yegorova, Natalia I. "The 'Iran Crisis' of 1945–1946: A View from the Russian Archives." Cold

War International History Project, Working Paper no. 15. Woodrow Wilson International Center for Scholars, Washington, D.C., May 1996.

Yergin, Daniel. *The Prize: The Epic Quest for Oil, Money, and Power.* New York: Simon and Schuster, 1991.

———. *Shattered Peace: The Origins of the Cold War and the National Security State.* Boston: Houghton-Mifflin, 1977.

Young, George K. *Masters of Indecision.* London: Methuen, 1962.

Zaehner, Robin. *Zen, Drugs and Mysticism.* London: Collins, 1972; New York: Vintage Books, 1974.

Zahedi, Ardeshir. "Five Decisive Days, August 15–18, 1953." Mimeograph, n.d.

Zubok, Vladislav, and Constantine Pleshakov. *Inside the Kremlin's Cold War: From Stalin to Khrushchev.* Cambridge, Mass.: Harvard Univ. Press, 1996.

Persian Sources

Abadian, Hossein. *Zendeginameh-ye Siasi-y Doktor Mozaffar Baqa'i.* Tehran: Institute of Political Studies and Research, 1998/1337.

Abbasi, Mohammad Reza, and Behruz Tayarani. *Khaterat-e Nasrullah Entezam.* Tehran: Iranian National Archives, 1992/1371.

Abbasi, Ruhollah. *Khaterat-e Yek Afsar-e Tudeh'i 1330–1335.* Montreal: Farhang, 1989/1368.

Afrasiabi, Bahram. *Khaterat va Mobarezat-e Doktor Hossein Fatemi.* Tehran: Sokhan, 1987/1366.

———, ed. *Mosaddeq va Tarikh.* Tehran: Nilufar, 1981/1360.

Afshar, Iraj. *Namehha-ye Landan.* Tehran: Farzan, 1996/1375.

———, ed. *Zendegi-ye Tufani: Khaterat-e Sayyed Hasan Taqizadeh.* Tehran: Elmi, 1993/1372.

Ahmadzadeh, Taher. "Tahlili az Nehzat-e Melli-ye Iran." In *Mosaddeq va Tarikh,* ed. Bahram Afrasiabi. Tehran: Nilufar, 1981/1360.

Ala, Hossen. Daily Reports to the Shah. Text in *Tarikh-e Moaser-e Iran* 1, no. 2 (summer 1997/1376): 130–74.

———. Letter to Taqizadeh, Oct. 23, 1947/Aban 1 1326. Text in *Ayandeh* 16, nos. 9–12 (Nov. 1990-Mar. 1991/Azar-Esfand 1369): 796–97.

Al-e Ahmad, Jalal. *Dar Khedmat va Khiyanat-e Rowshanfekran.* 2 vols. Tehran: Kharazmi, 1978/1357.

Alikhani, Alinaqi. *Yaddashtha-ye 'Alam.* Bethesda, Md.: Iranbooks, 1995.

Amir-Khosravi, Babak. *Nazari az Darun beh Naqsh-e Hezb-e Tudeh-ye Iran.* Tehran: Ettela'at, 1996.

Amui, Mohammad Ali. *Dord-e Zamaneh.* Tehran: Anzan, 1998/1377.

Andarmanizadeh, Jalal, and Mokhtar Hadidi, eds. *Pahlaviha.* Tehran: Nazar, 1999/1378.

Atabaki, Mansur Ali, and Ahmad Bani-Ahmad. *Panj Ruz Rastakhiz-e Mellat.* Tehran, 1953/1332.

Azad Mard Shahid Tayyeb Haj Reza'i beh Revayat-e Asnad-e Savak. Tehran: Center for the Investigation of Historical Documents, Iranian Ministry of Information, 1999/1378.

Azimi, Fakhreddin. "Entekhabat Bedun-e Haqq-e Entekhab? Entekhabat-e Parlemani va Tadavom-e Farhang-e Siasi dar Iran." *Negah-e No,* no. 42 (fall 1999/1378): 13–47.

———. "Qavam va Soda-ye Chirehgar-e Qodrat." In *Haftad Maqaleh,* edited by Iraj Afshar and Yahya Mahdavi. Vol. 1. Tehran: Asatir, 1369/1990.

Baqa'i, Mozaffar. *Doktor Mozaffar Baqa'i Kermani dar Pishgah-e Tarikh.* Kerman: Param, 1979/1358.

Behzadi, Ali. *Shebh-e Khaterat.* Tehran: Zarrin, 1998/1375.

Borhan, Abdollah. "Aya Qatelan-e Afshartus Shekanjeh Shodand?" *Negah-e Nou,* no. 25 (Aug.-Sept. 1995/Mordad 1374).

————. *Karnameh-ye Hezb-e Tudeh va Raz-e Soqut-e Mosaddeq.* Tehran: Elm, 2000/1379.

————. *Nehzat-e Melli-ye Iran va Edalat-e Ejtema'i.* Tehran: Markaz, 1999/1377.

Bozorgmehr, Jalil. *Mosaddeq dar Dadgah-e Tajdid-e Nazar-e Nezami.* Tehran: Enteshar, 1986/1365.

————, ed. *Mosaddeq dar Mahkameh-ye Nezami.* 2 vols. Tehran: Tarikh-e Iran, 1984/1363.

Davani, Ali, et al., eds. *Khaterat va Mobarezat-e Hojjat al-Islam Falsafi.* Tehran: Documentation Center, Islamic Revolution, 1997/1376.

Dehbashi, Ali, ed. *Namehha-ye Jalal Al-e Ahmad.* Tehran: Bozorgmehr, 1988/1367.

Dehnovi, Mohammad. *Majmu'eh'i az Maktubat, Sokhanraniha va Payamha-ye Ayatollah Kashani.* 5 vols. Tehran: Ashna, 1982–85/1361–64.

Eraqi, Haj Mehdi. *Nagoftehha.* Tehran: Rasa, 1991/1371.

Esma'ili, Amir. *Jan Bar Sar-e Qalam.* Tehran: Esma'ili, 1987/1366.

Fateh, Mostafa. *Panjah Sal Naft-e Iran.* Tehran: Chehr, 1956/1335.

Fatemi, Hossein. "Khaterat." In *Mosaddeq va Tarikh,* by Bahram Afrasiabi. Tehran: Nilufar, 1981/1360.

Ghani, Cyrus, ed. *Yaddashtha-ye Doktor Qasem Ghani.* 12 vols. London: Ithaca, 1984.

Golsha'iyan, Abbasqoli. *Gozashtehha va Andisheha-ye Zendegi, ya Khaterat-e Man.* 2 vols. Tehran: Einstein, 1998/1377.

————. "Yaddashtha-ye Golsha'iyan." In *Yaddashtha-ye Doktor Qasem Ghani,* edited by Cyrus Ghani. London: Ithaca, 1984.

Gozashteh Cheragh-e Rah-e Ayandeh. N.p., n.d.

Haddadi, Nasrollah. *Salha-ye Bohran: Khaterat-e Ruzaneh-ye Muhammad Naser-e Solat-e Qashqa'i.* Tehran: Rasa, 1987/1366.

Jazani, Bizhan. *Tarh-e Jame'eh Shenasi va mabani-ye Esteratezhi-ye Jonbesh-e Enqelabi-ye Khalq-e Iran.* Tehran: Maziar, 1979/1358.

Katouzian, Homa. "Barkhi az Salha-ye Bohran dar Yeki az Qarnha-ye Bohran." In *Estebdad, Demokrasi, ve Nehzat-e Melli.* 3d ed. Tehran: Nashr-e Markaz, 2002/1381.

————. "Dalil-e Asli-ye Este'fa-ye Mosaddeq dar Vaqe'eh-ye Si-ye Tir." In *Estebdad, Demokrasi, Mosaddeq.* 3d ed. Tehran: Nashr-e Markaz, 2002.

————. "Kusheshha-ye Sefarat-e Inglis Bara-ye Ta'in-e Nakhost Vazir-e Iran az Melli Shodan-e Naft ta Khal'-e Yad." In *Estebdad, Demokrasi.* 3d ed. Tehran: Nashr-e Markaz, 2002.

————. "Mosaddeq va Pishnahad-e Bank-e Jahani." *Mehregan* (spring 1992), reprinted in *Estebdad, Demokrasi.* 3d ed. Tehran: Nashr-e Markaz, 2002.

Khoshniyat, Hossein. *Sayyed Mujtaba Navab Safavi.* Tehran: Manshur-e Baradari, 1981/1360.

Khosrow-panah, Muhammad Hossein. *Sazman-e Afsaran-e Hezb-e Tudeh-ye Iran 1323–1333.* Tehran: Shirazeh, 1999/1378.

————. "Tarikhcheh-ye Zohur va Soqut-e Sazman-e Afsaran-e Hezb-e Tudeh-ye Iran." *Negah-e No,* no. 33 (summer 1997/1376).

Kianuri, Nureddin. *Khaterat-e Nureddin Kianuri.* Tehran: Ettela'at, 1992/1371.

Ladjevardi, Habib, ed. *Khaterat-e Shapur Bakhtiar.* Cambridge, Mass.: Center for Middle Eastern Studies, Harvard University, 1996.

Makki, Hossein. Interview. *Tarikh-e Moaser-e Iran* 1, no. 1 (spring 1997/1376): 179–216.

———. *Ketab-e Siah.* 8 vols. Tehran: Bongah-e Tarjomeh va Nashr-e Ketab/Elmi, 1981–98/ 1360–77.

———. *Khaterat-e Siasi-ye Hossein Makki.* Tehran: Elmi, 1989/1368.

———. *Kudeta-ye 28 Mordad 1332.* Tehran: Elmi, 1999/1378.

———. *Tarikh-e Bist Saleh-ye Iran.* Tehran: Elmi, 1995.

———. *Vagaye'e Si-ye Tir 1331.* Tehran: Bongah-e Tarjomeh va Nashr-e Ketab, 1981/1360.

Maleki, Khalil. *Khaterat-e Siasi.* Tehran: Enteshar, 1989/1368.

———. "Mobarezeh ba Bozorgtarin Khatari Keh Nehzat-e Melli ra Tahdid Mikonad." *Elm-o-Zendegi* 2, no. 3 (May–June 1953/Khordad 1332).

———. "Sarnevesht-e Tarikhi-ye Liberalism dar Do Qarn-e Akhir." *Elm-o-Zendegi* 1, no. 7 (Aug.–Sept. 1952/Shahrivar, 1331).

———. "Tahlil-e Mokhtasari az Gozashteh." *Nabard-e Zendegi* 1, no. 10 (April–May 1956/Ordibehesht 1335): 27–59.

Mosaddeq, Gholam Hossein. *Dar Kenar-e Pedaram.* Tehran: Rasa, 1990/1369.

Mosaddeq, Mohammad. *Khaterat va Ta'allomat,* edited by Iraj Afshar. Tehran: Elmi, 1986/1365.

Mosavvar-Rahmani, Gholam Reza. *Khaterat-e Siasi: Bist-va-Panj Sal Dar Niru-ye Hava'i Iran.* Tehran: Ravaq, 1984/1363.

———. *Kohneh Sarbaz: Khaterat-e Siasi va Nezami.* Tehran: Rasa, 1988/1367.

Movahhed, Mohammad Ali. *Khab-e Ashofteh-ye Naft: Doktor Mosaddeq va Nehzat-e Melli-ye Iran.* 2 vols. Tehran: Karnameh, 1999/1378.

Nejati, Gholam Reza. *Mosaddeq: Salha-ye Mobarezeh va Moqavemat.* 2 vols. Tehran: Rasa, 1997/1376.

———, ed. *Shast Sal Khedmat va Moqavemat: Khaterat-e Mohandes Mehdi Bazargan.* 2 vols. Tehran: Rasa, 1998/1377.

Nouzari, Aryan. "Response." *Tarikh-e Moaser-e Iran* 1, no. 3 (fall 1997/1376): 313–25.

Nuri, Abdullah. *Shawkaran-e Eslah.* Tehran: Tarh-e No, 1999/1378.

[Puriya, Arsalan]. *Karnameh-ye Mosaddeq va Hezb-e Tudeh.* 2 vols. Florence: Mazdak, n.d.

Qanatabadi, Shams. *Sayri Dar Nehzat-e Melli Shodan-e Naft: Khaterat-e Shams Qanatabadi.* Tehran: Markaz-e Barrasi-ye Asnad-e Tarikhi, 1998/1377.

Reyman, Farhang. "Kashani va Mosaddeq." *Jebheh-ye Azadi,* May 1–27, 1953/16 Ordibehesht–6 Khordad, 1332.

Riahi, Manuchehr. *Sarab-e Zendegi.* Tehran: Tehran, 1992/1371.

Ruhani, Fo'ad. *Tarikh-e Melli Shodan-e San'at-e Naft-e Iran.* Tehran: Jibi, 1974/1353.

Sadiqi, Gholam Hossein. "Ruz-e Kudeta." *Donya-ye Sokhan* 13, no. 75 (Aug.–Sept. 1997/Mordad-Shahrivar 1376): 32–39.

Safari, Mohammad Ali. *Qalam va Siasat.* Vol. 1. Tehran: Namak, 1992/1371.

Sanjabi, Karim. *Omidha va Naomidiha.* London: JEBHEH, 1989/1368.

Sarreshteh, Hosseinqoli. *Khaterat-e Man.* Tehran, 1988/1367.

Sarshar, Homa, ed. *Sha'ban Ja'fari.* Los Angeles: Nab, 2002/1381.

Seyr-e komenizm dar Iran. Tehran: Kayhan, 1957.

Shaikh al-Islami, Javad. *Sima-ye Ahmad Shah Qajar.* Tehran: Goftar, 1989/1368.

Shakeri, Khosrow. *Asnad-e Tarikhi-ye Jonbesh-e Kargari, Sosyal Demokrasi va Komonisti-ye Iran.* Florence: Mazdak, 1977.

———. *Asnad va Didgahha.* Tehran: Tudeh, 1979.

————. *Tarikh-e Moaser-e Iran.* Tehran 1992/1371.

Torbati Sanjabi, Mahmud. *Kudetasazan.* Tehran: Farhang-e Kavosh, 1997/1376.

Torkaman, Mohammad. *Beh Yad-e Shahid Doktor Hossein Fatemi.* Tehran: Hazaran, 1995/1374.

————. *Namehha-ye Doktor Mosaddeq.* 2 vols. Tehran: Hazaran, 1995–1998/1374–7.

————. *Tashannojat, Dargiriha-ye Khiabani va Tote'ehha dar Doran-e Hokumat-e Doktor Mohammad Mosaddeq.* Tehran: Rasa, 1980/1359.

————. *Tote'eh-ye Robudan va Qatl-e Afshartus.* Tehran: Rasa, 1984/1363.

Vosuq, Sepahbod Ahmad. *Dastan-e Zendegi.* Tehran, n.d.

Zirakzadeh, Ahmad. *Porseshha-ye bi Pasokh dar Salha-ye Estesna'i: Khaterat Mohandess Ahmad Zirakzadeh.* Tehran: Nilufar, 1998/1376.

Interviews

Afshar, Iraj. Interview by Fakhreddin Azimi. July 2000.

Alavi, Bozorg. Interview by Fakhreddin Azimi. Spring 1983.

Baqa'i, Mozaffar. Interview by Fakhreddin Azimi. Summer 1979.

Behrouz, Jahangir. Interview by Maziar Behrooz. London, June 2001.

Bowie, Robert R. Interview by Malcolm Byrne. Feb. 24, 2000.

Byroade, Henry. Interview by Mark J. Gasiorowski. Potomac, Md., Aug. 7, 1984.

Cuomo, Anthony. Interview by Mark J. Gasiorowski. Rome, Jan. 5, 1985.

Darbyshire, Norman. Interview by Fakhreddin Azimi. April 1984.

Kalantari-nazari, Mansur. Interview by Maziar Behrooz. London, June 2001.

Khazeni, Nosratullah. Interview by Fakhreddin Azimi. June 1997, July 1999, July 2000.

Mattison, Gordon. Interview by Mark J. Gasiorowski. Bethesda, Md., July 30, 1984.

Meade, Stephen. Interview by Mark J. Gasiorowski. Southern Pines, N.C., Mar. 28, 1984.

Melbourne, Roy. Interview by Mark J. Gasiorowski. Chapel Hill, N.C., Feb. 1, 1984.

Middleton, George. Interview by Mark J. Gasiorowski. London, Jan. 16, 1985.

Nasr, Abdollah. Interview by Maziar Behrooz. Tehran, June 2001.

Roosevelt, Kermit. Interview by Mark J. Gasiorowski. Washington, D.C., June 5, 1985.

Shahabi, Akbar. Telephone interview by Maziar Behrooz. Tehran, July 2001.

Waller, John W. Interview by Maziar Behrooz. London, June 10, 2001.

————. Interview by Homa Katouzian. Oxford, June 11, 2002.

————. Interview by Mark J. Gasiorowski. Oxford, June 11, 2002.

Yazdi, Mehdi Ha'eri. Interview by Fakhreddin Azimi. Sept. 1985.

Index